rethinking the holocaust

rethinking the holocaust

Yehuda Bauer

Yale University Press · New Haven and London

First published as a Yale Nota Bene book in 2002.
Hardcover edition first published by Yale University Press in 2001.

Published with assistance from the foundation established in memory
of Amasa Stone Mather of the Class of 1907, Yale College.

For information about this and other Yale University Press
publications, please contact:

U.S. office   sales.press@yale.edu
Europe office   sales@yaleup.co.uk

Printed in the United States of America

The Library of Congress has catalogued the hardcover edition as
follows:
Bauer, Yehuda.
Rethinking the Holocaust / Yehuda Bauer.
p. cm.
Includes bibliographical references (p.   ) and index.
ISBN 0-300-08256-8 (cloth: alk. paper)
1. Holocaust, Jewish (1939–1945)—Historiography. 2. Holocaust,
Jewish (1939–1945)—Influence. I. Title.
D804.348.B39 2001
940.53′18′072—dc21
00-043308

ISBN 0-300-09300-4 (pbk.)

A catalogue record for this book is available from the British Library.

10   9   8   7   6   5   4   3   2

contents

preface

Historians, when they present their books, normally start by thanking the institutions, archives, and colleagues who helped them and aided their work. This is what I did, too, in my previous books. But this time, only my wife, Elana, knew what I was working on. Yad Vashem, where I work almost daily as director of the International Research Institute, and the director of Yad Vashem, Avner Shalev, who, with my colleagues, was and is supportive and helpful in everything I do, knew I was doing something, but all were blissfully unaware of exactly what. They deserve my sincerest thanks. That goes for the Yad Vashem archive as well, which I used to find material for some of the case studies presented in this book, even though my book is mostly based on secondary sources.

Many colleagues influenced my thinking, although I did not consult with them explicitly. First and foremost is my closest friend and associate, Yisrael Gutman, with whom I share the basic conviction that it is best to look at the Holocaust from a Jewish perspective, which both of us do, without in any way disregarding the history of the perpetrators and the "bystanders," as will be clear from reading this work. I have learned a great deal from David Bankier, Christopher R. Browning, Ian Kershaw, Dov Kulka, Franklin H. Littell, Michael R. Marrus, Dalia Ofer, and many others, all of whom were innocent of any knowledge of what I was going to write. Especially fruitful is my friendship with Raul Hilberg, whose integrity, straightforwardness, commitment to truth ("we are in the truth business," he is wont to say), and vast knowledge have always been an inspiration, despite our disagreements on a considerable number of issues.

The people who are really behind this book are my students at the Institute of Contemporary Jewry at the Hebrew University. I am supposed to be a retired professor, but I continue to teach, and they have forced me to think and rethink, to go back to the sources, to argue and defend, or to retreat from positions on a large number of problems.

Finally, as with every writer, there is the family—my two daughters, Danit and Anat, and their children, who gave me peace of mind, and Elana ("Ilaniki"), who pushed and sustained me.

Introduction

          This is not another history of the Holocaust. Rather, it is an attempt to rethink categories and issues that arise out of the contemplation of that watershed event in human history. True, I make the occasional regression into a historian's professional deformation and camouflage my research in case studies that illustrate some of the more general points I am trying to make. But my case studies have another rationalization. A historian, in my estimation, has to do two things, especially when dealing with a subject such as this: one, research and analyze; and two, remember that there is a story to be told, a story that relates to people's lives. So a real historian is also a person who tells (true) stories. This does not mean that the main task lies outside documents and their interpretation—anyone who has ever heard my friend and colleague Raul Hilberg pronounce the word *d-o-c-u-m-e-n-t* will know what I am talking about—but a historian must also be a teacher, and teachers have to remember that their pupils, and indeed themselves, are just like the people they talk about in their telling of history. Hence the case studies; hence the occasional testimony; hence the stories in the Conclusion.

Has the time come for a historian to present the Holocaust as a whole, or at least from one of many possible wide angles? I believe so. These lines are written in early 1999, after a few years of radical progress in understanding the events of the Holocaust on the part of historians and sociologists, especially those in the younger generation. We the historians and storytellers have been down in the cellars digging for facts, developments, connections, contexts. We still are, and we will be there for a very long time. We tremble with excitement, and very often with horror, at what we discover in archives or hear in testimonies. We would frequently like to run away from the abyss that opens in front of us time and time again. But we must overcome that temptation; we must tell the story. Occasionally, too, we have to view the Holocaust from an angle that may give a broader view. The trees are vitally important. The forest is no less so.

The idea came from Elana, as most good things in my life do nowadays. "Why don't you reprint some of the articles and chapters you wrote over the past fifteen years or so?" she said. Marvelous idea, I thought, and I sat down to make selections. Out of the question, I found. I had to rethink all I had ever written; then I had to rewrite everything—no, I had to write anew. I had to ask the big questions and hope that I would come up with answers that would not be too small. I sometimes disagreed with what I had written in the past; new findings had opened up new, not necessarily more comfortable, vistas. The more I knew, it seemed, the more I felt the compulsion to be as humble about it as I could.

The Holocaust was a genocide, but of a special and unprecedented type. In the past two decades or so, an amazing phenomenon happened: The Holocaust has become a symbol of evil in what is inaccurately known as Western civilization, and the awareness of that symbol seems to be spreading all over the world. A museum near Hiroshima commemorates Auschwitz; a Chinese university has translated a summary of Holocaust literature into Chinese. When people want to liken "ethnic cleansing" in the Balkans or other mass murders to a similar event, they often compare it not with another mass murder somewhere else but with the Holocaust, whether such an analogy stands up to analysis or not (it doesn't). Not a month passes without the appearance of Holocaust-related books, films, musical works, theatrical productions, and so on. The press, the serious and the less serious alike, is full of debates on Holocaust-related topics. Politicians mention it constantly. The television industry presents shows, documentaries, and conversations about it again and again. Why?

Because, it seems to me, the realization is sinking in that the Holocaust says something terribly important about humanity. It is, on the one hand, a genocide and must be compared with other genocides; that universal dimension of comparability should concern everyone, from Kamchatka to Tasmania and from Patagonia to the Hudson Bay. On the other hand, it is a unique genocide, with unprecedented—and, so far, unrepeated—characteristics. There is a third element: the Holocaust concerns one of the core groups in what used to be the Christian-Muslim area of civilization, namely the Jews, whose culture, influenced by the context of their original Middle Eastern habitat, was, in turn, crucial in the development of Western civilization. The Holocaust has, therefore, become the symbol for genocide, for racism, for hatred of foreigners, and, of course, for antisemitism; yet the existence of rescuers on the margins provides a hope that these evils are not inevitable, that they can be fought. The result is the beginning of international cooperation to educate as many people as possible—to warn them and at the same time provide a realistic hope for a possible change of direction in human affairs. That the impact of the Holocaust is growing, not diminishing, is a major motive for the writing of this book.

I am a Jewish historian, living among Jews in a Jewish state; I have to take such preconditioning into account. Israeli Jewish society and

Jewish society generally are traumatized societies. Generations after the
catastrophe, the realization that one third of the Jewish people were
murdered for no political, economic, or military reason is sinking in; the
consciousness of the loss has permeated those societies, but the reasons
for it are unclear, and the fear that it might recur is pervasive. Beneath
the simple fact of that consciousness is the usually unconscious rebellion
against that realization, the attempt to compensate, to "learn lessons,"
usually wild ones. Israeli politicians instrumentalize the Holocaust for
political purposes, often without realizing that they are doing so. Right-
wingers see all Arabs as Nazis (Arafat in Beirut in 1982 was compared
to Hitler in his Berlin bunker). Left-wingers accuse the Israeli Army on
the West Bank of being a kind of German *Wehrmacht* in an occupied
land. Government ministers dream of Jews immigrating to Israel by the
millions—the millions who were killed in the Holocaust. Jewish politicians accuse each other of antisemitism and compare opposing political
parties to the Nazi party.

But elsewhere, too, the horror has penetrated: a person stopped by a
traffic policeman objects to "Gestapo" tactics. A Chief Rabbi calls what
the Reform Movement in Judaism is supposedly doing to the Jewish
people worse than the Holocaust. Literature, theater, music, television
and, of course, the press—there is hardly a day that an Israeli newspaper
(*any* Israeli newspaper) does not have an article or a news item touching
the Holocaust, and this is more than fifty years after the event. There
are calls, sometimes even from Holocaust survivors, to cease the cover-
age, speculation, extrapolation, comparison, but to no avail—the trauma
is stronger than all such pathetic exhortations.

The only way we can deal with a trauma is to face it, to confront the
facts, to ponder them, to do what the Jewish people could not do at the
time: weave the Holocaust into their historic memory. First we must
work through the mourning, the loss. Millions from among the victims
vanished in the smoke of crematoria, and there are no cemeteries where
we can conduct mourning ceremonies. Ways have to be found to mourn;
otherwise the survivors and descendants will never have peace. The

Holocaust has to be incorporated into life, into the present and the future, to give it a meaning that it did not have when it occurred.

In doing all this, Jewish society has to open up to the world, especially to Christianity, because the murderers and the societies from which they and the so-called bystanders sprang were baptized in churches to worship a loving God who had been a Jew. The Holocaust poses a basic problem for Christianity as well as for Judaism, hence the convoluted and often unfortunate, but genuine, efforts of the Catholic Church and of other churches to confront the Holocaust. As the awareness of the universal implications of the Holocaust spreads, the Holocaust becomes—again—two things: a specifically Jewish tragedy and *therefore* a universal problem of the first magnitude. Human beings who were Jews were murdered for one reason only: because they were Jews. The murderers also tried to dehumanize their victims—a matter for all humans to ponder. It is we today who have to deal with the Jewish tragedy as a general human tragedy. People of all persuasions, but especially Jews and those who call themselves Christians, need to find a language that will enable all of them to deal with this universal issue. The warning to humankind is written on the wall: beware and learn.

Learning is crucial here, not only for Jews but for everyone, children as well as adults. We need the politicians for the education effort to succeed—people who, in democratic countries, are elected not because they know something about the Holocaust and genocide but because they promise to lower taxes. The politicians have to be taught first, and that will be a long process—not a hopeless one, but a very difficult one, the accomplishment of which is not guaranteed. The United Nations does have a Convention Against Genocide, but genocide is with us. We need more than a convention. Life on the planet is growing uncomfortably close; we are increasing in numbers, and we don't have the space around us to feel at ease and friendly. We need political tools, international tools, to at least limit and then perhaps, in a more distant future, eliminate the threat of massive mutual slaughter.

This book consequently has a political aim in the sense that I wish to contribute to the work of those who would stop, even reverse, a murderous trend. Too many humans have been murdered, and the time has come to try and stop these waves that threaten to engulf us.

All of the above is implied, though not spelled out, in in the chapters of this book. Obviously, I have to define the subject, deal with alternative interpretations, and then address some—by no means all—of the issues. I therefore start with definitions, then continue with historiosophy ("Is the Holocaust explicable?"), in order to confront the central issue of comparisons with other genocides. In recent years, important historians and sociologists have tried to provide overall explanations of the Holocaust, and I try to analyze such attempts, by Zygmunt Bauman, Jeffrey Herf, Goetz Aly, Daniel Goldhagen, John Weiss, and Saul Friedländer, so that my own interpretation will become more precise. I do not claim that what I have to say is more correct than what they say; we live in a world in which competing interpretations vie for the support of readers and listeners. Nor do I claim that the last word will ever be said on this subject. Mine is one such interpretation. Naturally, I find it convincing; others may not.

To show how such interpretations may work, I present issues that I have found interesting or important or crucial. The core of my interpretation appears in Chapters 6 and 7, where I deal with Jewish reactions during the Holocaust. I do not contribute to the discussion so dear to my German and American colleagues, about the decisionmaking process in Nazi Germany: Who, if anyone, gave the order to murder the Jews, and when? Not that I do not appreciate the importance of this intensive and productive research effort—I participate in it myself, attend meetings, and read the material. But, when all is said and done, what is the essential importance of this quest? If we, at some future date, know the exact way the murder was implemented, what will that knowledge give us? We will know who, what, and when, but we will not have asked the really important question: Why? Once my colleagues address that question, and some of them have already done so, the next question will be, What role do the victims play in that story?

In my opinion, there will always be more victims than perpetrators. In fact, all of humanity is likely to be a victim, given the current state of possibilities of destruction and unrest. Victims are not passive, except in their last moments. We must know how the Nazis' victims behaved, what cultural baggage they had to start with, and whether their behavior or their baggage was useful in any way. We must know what they thought, how they reacted, what they did. Therein lies a lesson, possibly, or a warning, possibly, or an encouragement, possibly. Therefore my predilection is to deal with the Jewish victims of the Holocaust—they are of tremendous universal import, as well as important for the Jewish societies of today. Two chapters in this book are devoted to the reactions of Jews in Nazi Europe to persecution.

Are contemporary gender studies pertinent to the Holocaust? I analyze one case study that may have implications for the whole field, from both the Jewish and the universal angle. Does theology have any answers? Again, I deal with Jewish theology—Christian theology is undoubtedly equally important, but its contributions have to be considered by those more knowledgeable in the field. Then comes the question of rescue attempts, with a case study to illustrate my approach. Finally comes the vexed issue of the impact of the Holocaust on the establishment of Israel—seemingly a local, or perhaps a Jewish, question but in fact a universal one: I examine the immediate impact of a tragedy on the world immediately after it occurred.

After some hesitation, I decided to include in an appendix my speech to the German Bundestag on January 27, 1998. I hope I will not be accused of an ego trip; I included it because it says in a nutshell all I have to say on the subject. The stories told there have a subtext: I myself, the storyteller, was not in Europe during the Holocaust; my parents had the good sense to escape in 1939, and I grew up in Mandatory Palestine, where I went to school and played soccer while my relatives and everyone else in my former home were being murdered. I studied in Britain, participated in the Israeli War of Independence (and a few other Israeli wars, as all my friends did), and came to the study of the Holocaust because I wanted to be a historian of Jews. The Holocaust was unfortunately, I soon realized, the central event in modern or perhaps all Jewish history. And when I said to my friend and mentor Abba Kovner, survivor, poet, and fighter, that that realization scared me, he answered that being scared was an excellent basis for studying the Holocaust. The Bundestag speech, then, is a summary and a conclusion to this attempt at rethinking the Holocaust. And I am still scared.

chapter one
What Was the Holocaust?

           The objectivity of the historian be-
comes an issue with subjects besides the Holocaust, but a historian
dealing with the Holocaust cannot avoid the issue.

Following upon some ideas put forward by Karlheinz Deschner,
among others, it is important to start by denying the possibility of an
"objective" stance.[1] Many have said this before: we are the product of
our environment, tradition, education, prejudices, and so on. The influence of our environment can be disastrous, for we may be swayed by a
regime and its consensual impact, or even by a consensus created by our
fellow-historians, and hence write what is "politically correct," even
knowingly suppress what we feel should be said. Worse, we sometimes
really believe that what we say is our own view, even when it is nothing
but a reflection of the views of a majority, or a group, or a charismatic
individual, or some other outside source. We need to be aware of our
biases, our subjective approach, in order to formulate an interpretation of facts that will be legitimately rooted in the atmosphere and the

context of whatever period we describe. We must be aware of the obvious truth that the very decision to deal with some facts, some aspects of
reality, rather than with others, is a subjective choice. Goethe said,
"Every fact is already a theory." Johann G. Droysen, the nineteenth-
century German historian, said, "Only a mindless person is objective"—
and indeed, objectivism is basically uninteresting, because it reflects the
chaos of an infinite chain of events, a chaos that in itself has no meaning.[2]

Do we then conform to a subjectivism that dictates the rewriting of
history in every generation? In a sense, we do, partially. After all, people
in every period look at past events from a different perspective: the historians of 2089 will look at the French Revolution differently from the
way the historians of 1789, 1889, or 1989 looked at it. Yet the knowledge and self-perception that accompany an approach whose biases are
articulated can neutralize those biases to a considerable degree—never
completely, but sufficiently to enable the historian to draw what may be
termed "legitimate" conclusions from his or her study. Such conclusions
would avoid the traps of a mindless objectivism, a solipsistic subjectivism, and an endless relativization of facts. A legitimate conclusion is
one that not only avoids identification with known outside pressures
or interferences but also reflects an attempt to understand the period
under discussion from its own perspective and in its own terms. We
realize that another age will reinterpret the same events in its own
distinct way; hopefully, our own findings will become part of any future
analysis, if we state, to ourselves as well as to our public, what our biases
may be.

Let me state my biases. I think that the planned total murder of a
people was an unprecedented catastrophe in human civilization. It happened because it could happen; if it could not have happened, it would
not have done so. And because it happened once, it can happen again.
Any historical event is a possibility before it becomes a fact, but when it
becomes a fact, it also serves as a possible precedent. And although no
event will ever be repeated exactly, it will, if it is followed by similar
events, become the first in a line of analogous happenings. The Holo-

caust can be a precedent, or it can become a warning. My bias is, in a sense, political: I believe we ought to do everything in our power to make sure it is a warning, not a precedent.

My second bias is that I am not neutral as between Nazism and anti-Nazism. I detest Nazism. I am against antisemitism and racism of any sort. I am not neutral there, either. I believe, on the strength of the historical evidence, that the Nazi regime was just about the worst regime that ever disfigured the face of this earth. Worst from what point of view? From a basically liberal point of view that, in line with Jewish and other traditions, sees human life as a supreme value. In all this I am not being "objective"; but an objectivity that would reject these starting points would be nonobjective, besides being totally unacceptable to me because it would run counter to what I assume—another clear bias—to be the understanding that most people have of morality. Morality, in this context, is based on the idea that acts or intentions that run counter to the right of individuals and groups to exist, to live fully, also run counter to the existence of human life altogether, hence their unacceptability. Morality as here presented is an absolute value, then—absolute, that is, as long as one posits the continuation of the human race as a desired condition.

Now that I have stated my biases, and before we deal with the definition of *Holocaust*, we have to sidestep what appears to be another pitfall, namely, our propensity to say that because something happened, it had to happen. The American Revolution happened, but it did not have to happen. If British politicians had understood the importance of the tax issue to the American colonists and the danger of a successful rebellion, they might well have turned events toward a Canada-like resolution. Likewise, it was the obstinacy of the French royalist regime that led to the storming of the Bastille. World War II might well have been averted, in their own best interest as it turned out, by Britain, France, and the USSR, as late as June 1939 (when military delegations of the three Powers were discussing a possible alliance against Germany), had they overcome their mutual suspicions.

The scourge of determinism, Marxist or otherwise, is very much in evidence in discussions of the Holocaust, and I must say clearly that the Holocaust happened but that it did not have to. It was, to be sure, one of the possibilities inherent in the European situation, but not the only one. True, from a certain point onward—and one could perhaps, with some effort, establish that point—the annihilation of the Jews became inevitable, given Nazi ideology, the development of German society and bureaucracy, and German political and military superiority in Europe. Or perhaps it became inevitable that annihilation should be attempted. But if we retreat in time from early 1941 to the beginning of the war in 1939, or before that, then the Holocaust was not inevitable. Anglo-French-Soviet talks in the late spring of 1939 might have prevented German expansion, at least in the form that it ultimately took. Equally, a different coalition of Powers around the Sudeten issue in 1938, coupled with the disaffection of the German military group led by Ludwig Beck, might have prevented the development toward war and thus the opportunity for the Nazis to act upon their murderous ideology.[3]

Intentionalist historians, such as Eberhard Jäckel, Helmut Krausnick, Gerald Fleming, and Lucy Dawidowicz, have argued that Hitler's intentions, and therefore his role, in the process leading up to the Holocaust are central because of the godlike position he occupied in the regime; the other Nazis were an indispensable supporting cast. The entourage of Hitler, according to Jäckel, was rather uncomfortable about the developing decisions to mass-murder the Jews.[4] Heinrich Himmler, for instance, did not envisage mass murder before 1941, as his memorandum of May 25, 1940, on the treatment of aliens in Poland, shows; he says there that the idea of physically destroying a nation was a Bolshevik concept unacceptable to Germans.[5] Structuralists or functionalists, such as Hans Mommsen and Goetz Aly, have explained the factors bringing about the Holocaust by concentrating on the development of social and economic structures that led to impasses that more or less forced the Germans to take the most radical solutions. They do not believe that ideology or decisions by central authorities were at all crucial, but even they would agree that without approval by Hitler and his closest circle the murder would have been impossible.[6]

A new finding in the Moscow archive, published in Germany in 1999, puts this discussion—which in any case has been superseded by analyses that combine the two perspectives—in a new light. A part of Heinrich Himmler's appointment notebook has come to light, for December 1941. On the 18th he notes that he discussed the "Jewish question" (*Judenfrage*) with Hitler and that the result was "*als Partisanen auszurotten*"—"to exterminate [them] as partisans," which probably means to exterminate them on the pretext that they are partisans. It cannot refer to the countries outside the occupied areas of the USSR, because in 1941 it would not have made any sense to accuse German or Czech or Italian Jews of being partisans. In the occupied Soviet areas extermination had been going on for months already, and Hitler had been receiving the detailed reports of the *Einsatzgruppen* (murder squads). The Himmler note may indicate approval by Hitler of a propaganda line that had been pursued in the East vis-à-vis the German soldiers and that could be used for Germans generally. This alone already indicates that Hitler was involved as the central decisionmaker. It also, and incidentally, indicates that Reinhard Heydrich occupied a subordinate position; the person who discussed these things with the dictator and received his instructions was Himmler. Six days before that, on December 12, as Joseph Goebbels's diary shows, Hitler spoke in front of some fifty top Nazi officials, Gauleiters and others, and reminded them that he had warned of the coming annihilation of the Jews if a world war broke out (initiated by the Jews, as he put it on January 30, 1939). On December 11, 1941, Germany had declared war on the United States in the wake of Pearl Harbor and the American declaration of war on Japan. The situation that he had "predicted" in 1939 had come about, and the time had come to do what he had told the Jews he would do: *Vernichtung* (annihilation).[7]

We probably do not have before us a Hitler "decision," because Hitler rarely operated that way. But we may well have here a statement that Hitler intended as a general guide to action, in effect a call to his minions to get to work and to show initiative in implementing the guideline. Most historians do not think that such a guideline had ever been uttered in any formal way, perhaps only in private discussions. But on December 12, 1941, there was a clear expression of what was known in the Third Reich as "the Führer's wish"—a euphemism for the way he ordered things to happen. On the face of it, the intentionalists have it; on closer examination, however, we see that without the readiness of the party and state structures to accept and execute this "wish," Hitler would not have formally expressed it. Plainly, *some* of the historians' debates are now out of date: Hitler *was* the decisive factor, though by no means the only one, and he was not the weak dictator that some historians have posited. He was directly involved. He pointed out the direction in which he wanted things to develop. German society was involved, too, both at the top and at the middle, and the lower ranges became part of the consensus.

Another recent and important correction to our understanding is that added by a group of young German historians working with Ulrich Herbert, of the University of Freiburg.[8] Herbert and his coauthors present examples from eastern Galicia, Lithuania, Belorussia (Belarus), the "Generalgouvernement" (Poland), and France that show how local initiatives led to the mass execution of Jews in late 1941 and early 1942. The perpetrators rationalized these murder campaigns by practical considerations, such as the "need" to find lodgings for Germans, or to carry out resettlements of Germans and Poles, or to do away with superfluous mouths to feed, or to avenge the killings of German soldiers by the French underground movement in Paris. In fact, behind all these rationalizations lay an ideological motivation in the form of a consensus developed prior to the war by a radicalized, antisemitic intelligentsia, who found it natural to adopt the ever more radical solutions that the Nazi core elite expected them to. Neither the Berlin center nor the local groups could have acted without the other. Herbert talks of mutual understanding and of constant communication between central authorities and the periphery. The Berlin leaders, he says, were motivated by racist political ideology when they insisted on large-scale "solutions" involving population transfers. These transfers were planned around the "green table" at the Berlin center. There the strategic decisions were made, so Hitler was undoubtedly present.[9] I shall return to the Nazi decisionmaking process later, but it is clear that the explanation has to be multicausal, that the old rift between intentionalists and functionalists is outdated, and that ideology is the central determinant of the Holocaust.

Just as the murder of the Jews was not inevitable, it was not inexplicable, as I will argue in the next chapter. An aspect of that discussion belongs here: the inclination of people who take refuge in mysticism to argue that an event of such magnitude—a "tremendum," as they sometimes call it—cannot ultimately be explained.[10] This retreat into mysticism is usually reserved for the Holocaust, whereas all other events are deemed liable to rational explanation. I am afraid I cannot accept that exception to the rule. The murder was committed by humans for reasons whose sources are found in history and which can therefore be rationally analyzed. The mystifiers, with the best of intentions, achieve the opposite of their presumed aim, which is to achieve identification and empathy with the victims. You cannot identify with what is inexplicable. True, the depth of pain and suffering of Holocaust victims is difficult to describe, and writers, artists, poets, dramatists, and philosophers will forever grapple with the problem of articulating it—and as far as this is concerned, the Holocaust is certainly not unique, because "indescribable" human suffering is forever there and is forever being described. In principle, then, the Holocaust is a human event, so it can be explained, because it was perpetrated for what were unfortunately human reasons. This does not mean that the explanation is easy. On the contrary.

In a brilliant statement (in Jerusalem, on December 24, 1997), in the course of a discussion of his latest book, Saul Friedländer explained that the Holocaust presents problems that have so far not been solved.[11] In the past he himself had used the expression "the unease of the historian."[12] He did not mean that these problems cannot ultimately be understood, but that tremendous difficulties stand in the way of understanding them. He did not want to imply a mystical interpretation of the Holocaust events; but because convincing explanations are still unavailable or are being argued about, he wanted to avoid what he called "closure" of the argument, as though we historians had found satisfactory answers to our questions. He advocated a certain open-endedness whenever we put forward our views: we might, he implied, be wrong—there is nothing terrible about that—and, in any case, others will come along and present new findings and insights.

On the face of it, this argument is almost self-evident and would hold true for any historical (and many other) investigations, but it is especially apposite regarding the Holocaust. Because I basically agree with Friedländer's approach, all I am trying to say in these chapters should therefore be taken as obviously subject to discussion and change.

We now come to the problem of definitions. Is the Holocaust definable? Is it desirable to define it? After all, definitions are abstractions from reality and are useful only insofar as they help us to better understand the world around us. Any historiographical definition is designed to help us understand the event or events being defined. Because life is infinitely more complex than any definition, definitions, *by definition*, can never be fully adequate to the events they are supposed to define. We can but hope that they approximate descriptions of reality. Inevitably, our definitions are selective—they deal with parts of a phenomenon. That makes it even more important for our definitions to be as precise as possible in defining at least those parts of the phenomenon that they claim to define. And if experience shows that the definition does not fit reality, then the definition has to be changed, not the other way around. In order to define the Holocaust, it *must* be compared to other events if it is, as I have just argued, a human event. It is only by comparison that we can answer the question of whether it is unprecedented and has features not found in similar events.

The term *genocide* was coined by Raphael Lemkin, a refugee Polish-

Jewish lawyer in the United States, in late 1942 or early 1943. Lemkin's definition is contradictory. On the one hand, he defines *genocide* as the "destruction of a nation or of an ethnic group. . . . Generally speaking, genocide does not necessarily mean the immediate destruction of a nation. It is intended rather to signify a coordinated plan of different actions aiming at the destruction of essential foundations of the life of national groups, with the aim of annihilating the groups themselves."[13] (It seems that he intends to say "the groups as such," not necessarily all the individuals in them.) Yet in the preface of the same book he says that "the practice of extermination of nations and ethnic groups . . . is called by the author 'genocide.'" The destruction of the essential foundations of national life includes, according to Lemkin, the destruction of the national economic structure, its religious institutions, its moral fiber, its education system, and, always, selective mass killings of parts of the targeted population.[14] What he describes are two distinct alternatives: one, a radical and murderous denationalization accompanied by mass murder, which destroys the group as an entity but leaves many or most of the individuals composing it alive; the other, murder of every single individual of the targeted group. It may perhaps be argued that partial mass annihilation leads to total extermination. But this is not what Lemkin says, though such a possibility certainly cannot be discounted.

The discussion here is not just academic. Lemkin's definitions were adopted, in large part, by the United Nations. In the Genocide Convention, approved on December 9, 1948, *genocide* is defined as "any of the following acts committed with the intent to destroy, in whole or in part, a national, ethnical or religious group, as such." Again, both meanings are included, and the phrase "in whole or in part" indicates that what is meant is not the development of partial destruction into total murder but two variations that do not necessarily follow one upon the other.

The historical context for Lemkin's work in early 1943 consisted of the information he possessed as to what was happening to Poles, Czechs, Serbs, Russians, and others. Horrifying information had been received concerning the fate of the Jews, but decent human beings evinced an understandable reluctance to believe that the accounts were literally and completely true. What was happening to some of these people, mainly perhaps the Poles, fitted Lemkin's description of denationalization accompanied by selective mass murder. It seems that he made his definition fit real historical developments as he saw them; the vagueness with which he contemplates the possibility of murdering all Jews reflects the state of consciousness in America of the Jewish fate.

We then come to 1948. The United Nations is not a symposium of scholars—far from it. Documents emerging from that quarter are less than perfect, because they reflect political pressures and horse trading between states. Thus, unsuccessful pressure was exercised in 1948 to include, for instance, the destruction of political groups within the definition of genocide. The inclusion of religious groups—not a part of Lemkin's definition—was accepted after a long struggle. The lack of consistency in the U.N. convention is apparent the moment we continue the quotation: Genocide, it says, means any of the following acts: "(a) Killing members of the group; (b) Causing serious bodily or mental harm to members of the group; (c) Deliberately inflicting on the group conditions of life calculated to bring about its physical destruction in whole or in part; (d) Imposing measures intended to prevent births within the group; (e) Forcibly transferring children of the group to another group."[15] We again see inclusion of both partial and total destruction.

The conclusion to draw is that one ought to differentiate between the intent to destroy a group in a context of selective mass murder and the intent to annihilate every person of that group. To make this as simple as possible, I would suggest retaining the term *genocide* for "partial" murder and the term *Holocaust* for total destruction. I will argue that *Holocaust* can be used in two ways: to describe what happened to the Jews at Nazi hands and to describe what might happen to others if the Holocaust of the Jewish people becomes a precedent for similar actions. Whichever way *Holocaust* is used, it and *genocide* are clearly connected; they belong to the same species of human action, and the differences between them remain to be seen, beyond the obvious one of partial versus total destruction.

The next point to consider is crucial: which groups to describe when we talk about genocide. Lemkin talked only about national or ethnic groups, and he would probably have agreed to extend his category to include so-called racial groups. The U.N. convention adds religious groups. A number of scholars have added political groups as well.[16] Neither of these last two additions makes much sense. People persecuted because of their religious beliefs can, in principle if not always in practice, go over to the persecutors' religious faith and save themselves. The persecution of the Jews in the Middle Ages is an excellent example: accepting baptism usually—not always—meant rescue. During the Nazi regime, Jehovah's Witnesses were persecuted in Germany because they refused to recognize the supreme authority of the state and objected to being recruited into the army. But those few members of the group who yielded and joined the army or who acknowledged the Nazi state as having authority over them were no longer persecuted, and if they were in concentration camps, they were usually released.

The same applies to political persecutees. Even in Soviet Russia, joining the Communist Party was often—not always—a way of avoiding stigmatization as "bourgeois." Alexandra Kollontai, a member of the Russian aristocracy, became a leading Bolshevik and served as Soviet ambassador to Sweden. Most of the leading Bolsheviks were originally "bourgeois" intellectuals and sometimes former aristocrats. In Nazi Germany, millions of Communists became loyal Nazis.

For both religious and political groups, membership is a matter of choice—again, in principle, if not always in practice. One can change one's religion or one's political color. One cannot change one's ethnicity or nationality or "race"—only the persecutor can do that, as the Germans did when they "Germanized" Polish adults and children. Without such action, there is absolutely no way out for the member of a targeted ethnic or national group: that person is a Pole, or a Rom ("Gypsy"), or a

Jew, or a Serb. Hence my conclusion that the term *genocide* should be used only for attacks on the groups specified by Lemkin.

Genocide, then, is the planned attempt to destroy a national, ethnic, or racial group using measures like those outlined by Lemkin and the U.N. convention, measures that accompany the selective mass murder of members of the targeted group. Holocaust is a radicalization of geno-cide: a planned attempt to physically annihilate every single member of a targeted ethnic, national, or racial group.

How important is such a definition? It may help us differentiate between different crimes against humanity, the ultimate purpose of such analyses being to help lessen, and in some future perhaps do away with, such horrors. In the end, as I have pointed out, reality is more compli-cated by far than our attempts to describe it. I would therefore suggest that these definitions be used to describe a continuum of human mass destruction. One could even use the term *self-destruction*, because by destroying other humans, the perpetrators very radically diminish their own humanity. Such an approach may well use the paradigms proposed by Rudolph J. Rummel in his books *Democide* and *Death by Government*.[17]

According to Rummel, between 1900 and 1987 close to 170 million civilians (and disarmed POWs) were killed by governments and quasi-governmental organizations (political parties, etc.), the overwhelming majority of them by nondemocratic regimes. He calls this phenomenon "democide" (killing of people). He says that 38 million of the people killed were victims of genocide (he uses the definition of the U.N. con-vention), and close to 6 million of those were killed in the Holocaust. There is no reason not to expand Rummel's paradigm to include wars, which are reciprocal mass murders committed by opposing groups of people, usually males, distinguished from one another by funny clothes called uniforms; such mass murders, too, are committed at the instiga-tion of governments and quasi-governmental organizations. Adding wars gives us a continuum of human actions of deadly violence ranging from wars, via the murder of civilians for a vast variety of reasons, to genocide and Holocaust. This does not mean that wars are "better" than genocides, nor that the mass murder of civilians is less reprehensible than genocide; it does mean that there are obvious connections between all these, and that occasionally one form merges into another.

No gradation of human suffering is possible. A soldier who lost a leg and a lung at Verdun suffered. How can one measure his suffering against the horrors that Japanese civilians endured at Hiroshima? How can one measure the suffering of a Rom woman at Auschwitz, who saw her husband and children die in front of her eyes, against the suffering of a Jewish woman at the same camp who underwent the same experience? Extreme forms of human suffering are not comparable, and one should never say that one form of mass murder is "less terrible," or even "better," than another. The difference between the Holocaust and less radical genocides lies not in the amount of sadism or the depth of hellish suffering, but elsewhere. It is now time to turn to comparisons that will clarify the difference.

chapter two

Is the Holocaust Explicable?

It has often been said that if the Holo-
caust is totally inexplicable, utterly mysterious, or "uniquely unique"—
in a sense that the author of the phrase, A. Roy Eckardt, did *not* mean—
then it is also outside history and therefore irrelevant to rational
discourse.[1] Absolute uniqueness thus leads to its opposite, total trivial-
ization: if the Holocaust is a onetime, inexplicable occurrence, then it is a
waste of time to deal with it. Some authors take good care to state that
when they talk about its inexplicability, they do not mean the processes
that led to the establishment of the Nazi state, or the irrational rationale
of establishing ghettos or concentration camps, but some inner quality,
expressed by the senseless brutality of the perpetrators, the silence of
the bystanders, the stunned reaction of the unsuspecting victims, the
vastness of the crime, and the allegedly inexplicable involvement of very
large numbers of civilized people.[2] How do cold bureaucratic decisions
become machine-gun bullets and crystals of poison gas? The reply
offered is, not infrequently, that we will never know.

I have written on this topic before, more than twenty years ago, in a statement against mystification.[3] Then, as now, I disagreed with some good friends, chief among whom was, and is, Elie Wiesel, whose work and words I greatly admire. Wiesel's stand is contradictory, but I think he sees no harm in paradoxes. On the one hand, he says that there are aspects of the Holocaust, mainly the suffering of the victims and the brutality of the perpetrators, that can never be fully grasped or understood, and that therefore the Holocaust is ultimately inexplicable. On the other hand, he does everything in his power to transmit those experiences and make people understand them. His readers see the Holocaust shrouded in irrationality and mystification and consigned to an impenetrable mist—from which they inevitably run away. He often expresses his fear that in future generations no one will remember the Holocaust—a prophecy that might be fulfilled if the mystification spread by him and many, many others wins out. Yet by his great literary work, he actually does the opposite of mystifying: he explains. The mystifiers, fortunately, act against their own predilections.

My own response is that of a historian. From the historical point of view—and history, after all, is not a science but a post facto reconstruction of the course of human events in accordance with certain rules for sifting facts and analyzing sources—several aspects should, I think, be considered. First, is the Holocaust comparable to other historical events? Second, if it is comparable, what are the differences from, as well as the similarities with, such events? Third, are there possible models of explanation to apply to the baffling problems that the Holocaust presents? Lastly, are such models convincing enough to make the Holocaust explicable in principle, even though we may have to grapple with alternative explanations for a very long time to come?

If the answers to these questions were that certain "internal" aspects of the Holocaust are ultimately beyond the reach of human explanation, we would still have to contend with the argument that, in that case, the Holocaust is beyond human history and can be explained only by the intrusion of forces beyond human comprehension and hence external to human experience. Terms such as *devilish* for the Nazi mind and *holy* for the victims might point to such conclusions, although they may also be a *façon de parler* to indicate the moral quality of perpetrator and victim. If some God or some Devil, or a combination of both, or some mysterious force that is neither, were drawn in to explain the inexplicable, or if the event were simply left unexplained, then again we would be removing the Holocaust to an ahistoric sphere where it could not be reached by rational thinking, not even by rational explanations of the irrational.[4] The inevitable conclusion must again be that if we label the Holocaust as inexplicable, it becomes relevant to lamentations and liturgy, but not to historical analysis.

Some historians (including myself), social scientists, theologians, and other specialists have come to the conclusion that the Holocaust can be repeated, even though it is in some ways the most extreme form of genocide known to us to date and the first known occasion for certain types of murderous crimes or criminal thinking, as I will try to show later. We live in an age in which Holocaust-like events are possible. Obviously, the Holocaust could have been avoided by forces that had little to do with the Jews. I have already mentioned the abandonment by France, Britain, and the Soviet Union of their military discussions in the summer of 1939, which were to have led to a military alliance against Nazi Germany. This outcome was in their own worst interest, for they could well have avoided many millions of casualties. Other examples could be cited to show the lack of determinism in the development of a situation that made the Holocaust possible. Had there been no such event as the Holocaust, would we have been able to say that a Holocaust was avoided? Surely this is absurd, because we would not have known what a Holocaust was. Once it has occurred, however, we can say that we live at a time when the elements that produced the Holocaust are with us. Because historical events never repeat themselves exactly, that is, they are not clonelike in all their details, we should say that Holocaust-like events are possible if conditions similar or equivalent to those that produced the Holocaust in World War II were to arise.

The difficulty could be expanded but, paradoxically, eased as well by arguing that all of human history is in a sense inexplicable and must be guided by some extra-historical forces, good or bad or both, or by forces lacking in values we call human. The Holocaust would then be only an extreme form of this essential inexplicability of human destiny. It is very hard to argue with such a metaphysical explication of inexplicability, but one might put forward the argument that we are dealing, in all cases, with human actions, performed toward or against or in favor of humans. The assumption is that humans are related in makeup, and actions performed by any one individual could in principle be performed by others as well, so the explicability of such actions is a prerequisite for human relations. Human attitudes in any society at any period are distinct and recognizable; and given their interrelatedness, they must be understood in order to have meaning for anyone—hence the accessibility, in principle at least, of the actions of one individual or a group of individuals by others.

Of course, no individual can feel the pain of another. When your child scratches its finger, the pain is the child's, and however much you empathize, the pain is not yours to feel. But you know how it feels because of your own similar experiences. This trivial example becomes less trivial when we consider criminal actions. We can understand the motivations for criminal actions because we have experienced similar or equivalent motivations ("temptations"), although we may reject the conclusions that bring the thieves or murderers to their crimes. Occasionally, as in the Holocaust, the capabilities of humans to act in a certain fashion expand, capabilities that were not suspected before. The very fact, however, that a certain action occurred means that human beings, in their souls, instincts, drives, whatever, contain the seed of such possible actions. This holds true for all types of actions—whether we define them as evil, good, or neither.

Indeed, the basis of intelligible historical writing is this comparability of human experience. If there are recognizable patterns in the unrolling of human history, then there is a point in examining them. They may explain how we got to where we are, and may indicate what might happen if other things remain equal, which of course they never do. But even that knowledge is a guide to action, intelligent or otherwise. If, on the other hand, humans and their actions are unintelligible to other humans, then we are in a chaotic situation where neither history or anything else is explicable.

Is there not, nevertheless, a mysterious something that is part of our individual and collective lives and that contains elements of transcendence? If such transcendence is common to all humans, at least potentially, then it is a human characteristic and explicable in general terms. If it is a metaphysical transcendence that acts as a possible, but imponderable, factor in human history, then again all history becomes in principle an inexplicable series of events affected by an outside, nonhuman source. In that case, the development of British history between the two world wars is no more accessible than the Holocaust or any other event in history. The upshot seems to be that either the Holocaust is part of human history, in which case its explicability is, in principle, the same as that of other events, or it is not, in which case it becomes relevant only as an instance of nonhuman intervention in human history.

The history of the Holocaust tells us of horrors and brutalities that are "indescribable," by which we mean that we view them with total revulsion—but they have of course been described, which is how we know about them. They are extreme in that they present the depths of human depravity and human suffering. The extreme humiliation of individuals in huge numbers, the brutal murder by club, bullet, and gas, mass death by starvation and induced diseases, and, beyond everything else perhaps, the murder of children, are part of the historical record. The burning or burying alive of children are among the most horrible scenes described. Such events are so far beyond the trivialities of everyday life, even beyond the tragedies of everyday life, that we tend to say to ourselves that we can never fully understand them because we cannot imagine ourselves experiencing them. Yet these atrocities were committed by human beings, and we all have within us instincts that under certain circumstances of birth, education, society, social history, and the like might lead us to actually understand them. German historical theorists of the nineteenth century argued that "understanding" lies beyond "explanation"; and we can "understand" only when we can place ourselves, instinctively or existentially, in the shoes, so to speak, of the historical actors. What do we mean when we say that we can place ourselves in the shoes of Heinrich Himmler? Naturally, most of us will reject such placement with disgust: we could *never* act like that. But we protest too loudly. He was human, and so are we. The warning contained in the Holocaust is surely that the acts of the perpetrators might be repeated, under certain conditions, by anyone.

We can check this in the laboratory of history. Have people been brutally killed before, after being humiliated and dehumanized?

By *dehumanization* I do not mean that perpetrators or victims ceased to be human. I do mean to describe acts of humiliation and oppression so extreme that the victims were deprived of all privacy and personal feelings of shame, of any kind of individuation in their surroundings, of their names, personalities, and family connections, of control over their bodily functions, and that many were reduced to walking automatons on the verge of death (called *Musselmänner* in camp language). The term also describes people capable of carrying out such acts, who thereby proved that they had lost their connection to ordinary moral precepts as they were understood in most European and other societies prior to 1933.

Were the Midianites in the Jewish Bible humiliated, dehumanized, and brutally murdered? The story as related in Numbers 31 may or may not be a historical account, but clearly, the massacre was perceived as something that could have happened, even as desirable. All Midianite men are killed by the Israelites in accordance with God's command, but his order, transmitted by Moses, to kill all the women as well is not carried out, and God is angry. Moses berates the Israelites, whereupon they go out and kill all the women and all the male children; only virgin girls are left alive, for obvious reasons. Other biblical examples are too well known to be dwelt upon. Similar stories abound in all religious traditions.

What about the French town of Beziers, where Cathars and other "heretics," and Catholics who happened to live there, including women and children, were brutally murdered in 1209?[5] What about the Spaniards in the New World? Did they not, in the name of a loving God, burn Indian men, women, and, yes, children, alive? What about the fate of the Nez Percé in the northwestern and western United States? What about the black men, women, and children transported to the Americas who were enslaved or killed?

The histories of many peoples around the globe abound with descriptions that parallel the horrors already referred to. Timur Lenk's treatment of Persian towns, coming after Genghis Khan's incursions into Russia and Europe, the burning and murder of the Christians in Japan in the early seventeenth century, the mutual slaughter and enslavement of African nations—they all are evidence of the capability of humans to engage in mutual brutalities. The twentieth century started with the destruction of the Herrero people in what is now Namibia at the hands of the German military; there followed the genocide of the Armenians, the mass murder of Chinese civilians by their own government and then by the Japanese invaders, the mass murder of the Roma (Gypsies) at Nazi hands, the cruelties of the Gulag, the ravages of the Pol Pot regime in Kampuchea, the mutual genocidal massacres of Hutu and Tutsi in Rwanda and Zaire. All these and many others show that we are capable, under certain circumstances, of all the brutalities committed by the Nazis—each brutality separately and all of them together. Every nation can tell of comparable instances in its own history, whether it was on the perpetrating or the victimized side.

The uniqueness—I shall henceforth use the term *unprecedentedness* despite its awkwardness—of the Holocaust does not lie, therefore, in the level of brutality reached by the Nazis and their helpers, although that was undoubtedly a peak.[6] The genocide of the Jews was neither better nor worse than any other. Using terms such as *beastly* and *bestiality* to describe the Nazis is an insult to the animal kingdom and should not be used, because animals do not do things like that. The behavior of the Nazis was not "inhuman." It was only too human. It was evil, not inhuman, and was probably, in its concentrated but not entirely unprecedented form, the closest approximation to what could be termed "absolute" evil that human history has seen.

The case of Himmler is instructive. In his famous Poznań speech of October 4, 1943 (which is even recorded on a Nazi gramophone record), he talks openly about the murder of the Jews and adds that this murder should never and will never become known.[7] Does he imply that no one will ever be able to understand him? I do not think so. Himmler was, after all, not unique in his murderous intentions, as we have seen. Not to understand him would mean that we cannot understand any parallel or similar event in history. If we cannot understand this aspect of human history, we cannot explain anything at all, because half of history is murder and brutality. In that case, history—again—becomes irrelevant.

But if Himmler was human—and he was—then his motives were human. Can we find in ourselves elements of Himmler's motivations that would build enough of a bridge between ourselves and him to enable us to understand him? I would claim that we can. The life-preserving instincts discussed by Freud and his followers and the death urge or destructive instincts discussed by Erich Fromm and others might serve as examples of explanatory models. If all humans contain in themselves the seeds of attitudes that we term positive and negative, we can explain Himmler as a person in whom the negative elements manifested themselves in extreme form, undoubtedly as a result of the confluence of social and personal-individual factors. If Himmler can be thus explained, then his statement that the murder should never become known is simply the expression of his fear, pointed out in a previous passage of the same speech, that the German people would not understand the Nazi motivation if the murder was acknowledged and might reject the murder. In addition, he foresaw a world without Jews, and he thought that future generations of Germans would not understand why total mass murder had been necessary, because they would have had no experience of who and what the Jews had been.

Himmler's statement is therefore explainable and his actions can be understood. Indeed, as far as brutality, the will to murder, and sadism are concerned, little is unique about the Nazis except that they went further than any of their predecessors.

If not brutality, what was extraordinary about the Nazi attitude toward the Jews? It is important to note that for the Nazis, the "Jewish problem" was not a German or even a European issue but a global problem of the greatest magnitude. The delivery of humankind from the Jews was conceived in pseudo-religious, messianic terms. On the "solution" of the problem depended the future of humankind. The Holocaust is unprecedented, then, basically because of the motivation of the murderers. The elements of this unprecedentedness will be discussed in the next chapter. They are perfectly explicable.

Arguing for the explicability of the Holocaust does not mean that we are today at a stage where we can actually explain it, nor is it likely that we shall be able to do so in the foreseeable future, if at all. That something is in principle explicable does not mean that it has been explained or that it can readily be explained. Furthermore, explaining something horrific is extremely difficult when the presumably civilized historian is not among those who were victimized or who victimized others. That means that although the events described are not in themselves inaccessible—because of their quality as human events—the historian will face great obstacles in the effort to feel the situation, and even greater ones when trying to overcome a natural rejection of the (correct) assumption that the perpetrators were in any way like himself or herself. The historian *can* overcome the difficulties and reach an understanding, but may well fail when trying to reconstruct the terror, the fear, the suffering of the victims or "the sadistic enjoyment and brutality of some of the perpetrators."[8] The historian's art is, after all, limited, and the writer, the poet, the artist, the dramatist, the musician, the psychologist, and, for the religious among us, the theologian have to be asked to add their insights to enable the historian to probe deeper into that darkness. Above all, we need the witness. There is no Holocaust history without witnesses.

The direct testimony of the survivors and the authentic surviving descriptions (diaries, letters) by Jews who did not survive themselves ease our understanding. Because most of us will identify with the victims, and because suffering lies within the range of our psychological makeup, we can get nearer to understanding them than we can to understanding the perpetrators. Essays, dramas, music, sculptures, films, and so on, help us in this. Again, we do not experience what the witnesses went through, nor do we—or they—wish to do so. But we can approach as close to understanding the Holocaust as to understanding other historical events.

This touches upon an important methodological debate: What is the value, for the historian's craft, of testimonies, especially those taken many years after the event? Some colleagues will argue that memory is a weak reed to rely on, that many testimonies are warped by the games that memory plays, by the desire to appear in as good a light as possible and to hide actions that were or may appear in hindsight to have been reprehensible. More than that, sometimes testimony is intended to mislead. The only reliable testimony is, so it is claimed, a document created at the time an event happened. This, especially, is the argument presented by such first-rate historians as Raul Hilberg.

In themselves, the arguments are weighty enough. They do not present the whole story, however. When we take written documents of the time, they are predominantly German documents. It is at least as dangerous to rely on these as it is to rely on oral testimonies. Documents of the perpetrators were very often designed to mislead rather than to inform, to hide rather than to reveal. An obvious example is the minutes of the Wannsee meeting of Nazi bureaucrats on January 20, 1942. The minutes, edited and doctored by Adolf Eichmann, according to his statement in Jerusalem in 1961, present the way the meeting was supposed to be remembered by the S.S. authorities who called it. Explicit discus-

sion of the murder program was translated into the veiled language of
the minutes.[9] Or, if we take Jürgen Stroop's report on the Warsaw
ghetto rebellion, we find an overt attempt to curry favor with Himmler
by beautifying—if that is the right word—German actions.[10] I would
not rely on the report to describe events or even to enumerate German
casualties. In other words, one has to approach a written document with
as much care as a testimony.

Generally speaking, testimonies are one of the most important
sources for our knowledge of the Holocaust, because the Germans tried
to murder the murder: they tried to prevent Jews from documenting
what happened. They were not completely successful, however, and the
Ringelblum Archive in Warsaw, the Mersik Archive in Bialystok, and a
large number of diaries and many letters remain to document Jewish life
and death in eastern Europe. For western Europe, much more remains.
Some of this Jewish documentation is also suspect: discussions of the
Bialystok or Lublin Judenräte (Jewish Councils) were recorded with the
knowledge that Germans might read them and that certain topics discussed should not be written down for a number of reasons. Testimonies, with all their disadvantages, do not suffer from problems such
as these. There are still "documents" walking among us on two legs—
namely, the testimonies that we have not yet taken down. But we should,
of course.

Testimonies taken down after decades are not necessarily less reliable
than those taken immediately after the war. Old people remember their
youth better than the immediate past, and although memory often fades,
in other cases it becomes sharper. In the past, the witness may have had
reasons to hide or misrepresent things, reasons that have in the meantime disappeared. In the immediate postwar period many people still
suffered from the shock of their experiences, whereas now some can
view them with greater detachment. Thus, the present testimony may
be more truthful than the former.

To sum up: a historian's tools include the analysis of written documents of the period, of diaries, of letters, and of testimonies of survivors,

not to mention remnants of sites. Because the documentation is largely one-sided, that is, German, survivors' testimonies are crucial to understand the events of the period. They become extremely useful and reliable when cross-checked with and borne out by many other testimonies. They are then, I would argue, at least as reliable as a written document of the time.

All of this has to be stated explicitly because it strengthens the argument for the explicability of the Holocaust: the more testimonies we have, as well as documentation, the greater our chances of explaining and understanding what happened.

Explicability is not equivalent to a one-dimensional, dry historical narrative or analysis. A cognitive analysis may help us to understand; an analysis combined with the telling of the story as it happened to individuals, families, villages, and towns is much better. To show how even a dry historical analysis can contribute to understanding, let me ask a perplexing question: Why did the Jews of Poland behave the way they did, why that mixture of cowed or dignified despair, on the one hand, and stiff-necked, even violent, resistance, on the other?

Polish Jews had been living in an extreme economic crisis for quite some time before the Nazis occupied Poland. In 1935–1939, about one-third of them had been on the verge of poverty or below the poverty level, many of them close to starvation. Their ability to offer effective physical or economic resistance was therefore limited from the very start. The non-Jewish people of Poland, themselves in harsh economic distress in the thirties, were by and large indifferent to their Jewish compatriots' fate; a large minority were actively hostile, and a small minority could be counted upon to help the Jews, although there would be no physical opposition to the Germans. The German army had overrun Poland in three weeks, and Polish resistance took the line that it would act only when the Germans were on the point of defeat.[11] The Germans were the masters of the country.

The Germans did not know, until sometime in 1941, what they would do with the Jews: the decision to murder them was not taken until then.

If the Germans did not know, the Jews cannot be expected to have known either. Their problem, as they saw it, was how to survive an occupation that would end one day. The efforts made by the Judenräte, whose members in most cases had been among the legitimate prewar representatives of the Jewish communities, were directed toward that goal. That meant, to use Isaiah Trunk's terminology, not "collaboration," but "cooperation"—that is, yielding to the demands of the conqueror while trying to evade the worst excesses; cooperation did not mean agreement with the conqueror's policies or war aims, and it was based on the assumption that the Germans would ultimately be defeated.[12] Most Judenräte were liquidated at some stage, and more pliant groups were nominated in their stead. At first, most Judenräte refused to hand over Jews for murder, as Aharon Weiss has found.[13] Most Jews supported the policies of the Judenräte as the lesser evil, compared with direct rule by the Germans. There was the constant hope that the Germans would be defeated and the Jews would be liberated. Until then, heads had to be temporarily bowed. While submitting, many (but by no means all) Jewish communities maintained morale-building activities, often in contravention of German orders. Education, social aid, cultural activities, maintenance of religious life, underground newspapers, underground collection of materials documenting Nazi atrocities were expressions of this popular spirit of unarmed resistance, which went hand in hand with yielding to superior force.

Once it began to dawn upon the Jewish populations of Europe that the Germans had decided to murder them, the reaction was flight, hiding, armed resistance on the part of a small minority who were able to obtain weapons, attempts to seek employment that would be essential to the Germans, and a despairing but often dignified acceptance of inevitable death. Psychologically, Jewish responses to knowledge of impending destruction were no different from similar responses of other groups. Russian or Polish peasants on the point of execution by German troops, French resistance fighters caught and sentenced to death, Serb villagers confronting Croat or German murderers—people facing in-

escapable destruction behave in much the same way. The range of reactions extends from numbed fear and hysterical crying to heroic de-
fiance. We value the latter, which was indeed quite widespread. But the
other kinds of response are no less human, no less understandable or
worthy of empathy. In all cases, they are perfectly explicable.

A certain religious type of explicability is often used in Jewish
theological-historiosophical discourse. The claim is made that the Holocaust ought to be viewed as just one, though perhaps the most destructive, of a series of calamities that have befallen the Jews, starting
with the destruction of the First Temple, in 586 B.C.E., followed by the
destruction of the Second Temple, in 70 C.E.[14] In principle, therefore,
there is nothing extraordinary in the Holocaust. The idea (analyzed
later in this volume) that it is a sign of God's wrath is then adduced to
make the Holocaust explicable in terms of the Jewish religious tradition.
The argument is, however, flawed.

The Holocaust is different in principle, not just quantitatively, from
other Jewish disasters, first, because the threat in the repeated destructions of the temple was political, spiritual, and cultural, not physical
and existential. True, selective mass murder was practiced by both the
Babylonians and the Romans, but in both cases the vast majority of the
Jews were left alive. Some of them were enslaved or deported, but most
of them were not uprooted. For several centuries, after the second destruction, the Jews remained a majority in Palestine, contrary to per-
sistent historical myth. In the Holocaust, by contrast, Jews were threatened with total physical extinction; the Nazi design to conquer the
world by their own might and through firm alliances with like-minded
states under German leadership threatened, for the first time, the very
existence and physical survival of all Jewish individuals.

Second, Nazi ideology saw in the Jews a universal devilish element,
so the pursuit of Jews was to have been a global, quasi-religious affair,
the translation into practice of a murderous ideology. The temple destructions, by contrast, were political acts directed against an independent or semi-independent people. The persecutions during the Middle

Ages and the modern period (in Russia in the 1880s, for instance) were
due to a mixture of religious, economic, and political factors. In the Nazi
case, by contrast, the persecution of the Jews was pure, abstract antisemitic ideology in the context of biological racism, and it became a
central factor in Hitler's war against the world. In the minds of the Nazi
elite, the main enemies of Germany—the Soviet Union, France, the
United States, Britain—were controlled by the Jews. The proof of Jewish control of a country lay in the very fact that it turned against
Germany. After all, World War II was started by Germany not for any
economic or military reasons—nobody threatened Germany in 1939,
and the economy had risen from the depth of the world economic crisis
to almost full employment and prosperity. The desire to expand to the
east and control Europe was motivated by a phantasmagoric racial-
biological ideology in which the enemy was controlled by Jews; therefore, the Jews were, from the Nazi point of view, the main enemy. The
war was indeed a "war against the Jews," and Lucy Dawidowicz's well-
known book does have the correct title (although she meant something
different by the term).[15]

All this was novel, a new type of threat: genocide turning into Holocaust. Christian antisemitism, with all its anti-Jewish ideology and
bloody persecutions, never produced a genocidal policy, as Steven T.
Katz has argued convincingly, so there is a vast difference between
persecutions of Jews in Christendom (and under Islam, where the attitude toward Jews was less murderous) and the genocidal program of the
Nazis.[16] Those religious commentators who wish to reduce the frightening dimensions of the Holocaust into the familiar context of persecutions of Jews through the ages are in error—their aim is not achievable;
the Holocaust refuses to merge into that background. The explicability
of the Holocaust does not mean that it lends itself to easy exercises of
this kind.

Another central issue of explicability arises when one ponders the
following, much discussed question: "How did the German people become a band of murderers and murderers' accomplices?"[17] How could a

people who had created, in Central Europe, one of the greatest civilizations in history commit itself to such an ideology as the Nazi one and stick to it through the most destructive war in human annals (so far), to the bitter end?

The many historians who have tried to answer the question offer a number of explanations. The functionalist school traced the development toward murder through the history of the social and economic structures of German society, sometimes from the late nineteenth century, sometimes from the early twentieth, and often from the Weimar Republic. Basically, the argument runs, the economic, political, and social crises in Germany, together with preexisting social, especially bureaucratic traditions, pushed German society toward an authoritarian regime. That regime was characterized by deep internal contradictions: a dictator who served as an arbiter of last resort between warring administrative fiefdoms; a tendency toward uniformization, on the one hand, and the disorder of competing authorities and individuals seeking power, on the other hand. It was this disorder that led to impasses, apparently resolvable only by the exercise of brutal, murderous force. Racism and antisemitism were in the background, but by themselves would not have led to the so-called Final Solution—the extermination of all the Jews.

The intentionalist school put the primary emphasis on the ideology-ridden dictatorship, which intended to establish a racist utopia and which saw in the Jews a prime target for physical elimination. Hitler, it was said, had intended the destruction of the Jews well before the outbreak of war in 1939 and grasped at the opportunity once it developed with the prospect of complete control of Europe in 1941.

Both these approaches are, I think, lacking in many respects and, as already pointed out, are fading away. As Raul Hilberg has pointed out, German railway officials used the same administrative techniques to send German children to summer vacation camps and Jews to death camps. The question is why they did the latter, not why they did the former. To explain their techniques for transporting Jews by analyzing the structure of the bureaucracy and the conflicts between different authorities is begging the question. Structures do not explain why bureaucrats sent people to their deaths; they may explain *how* they did it and how it fit into the context of their social traditions. But many societies have been ruled by inefficient and contradiction-ridden autocratic regimes that did not produce genocides. Why, then, did this particular dictatorship produce mass murder on an unprecedented scale, of Jews and many others? What made the bureaucrats do it?

The intentionalist school of thought has a hard time proving Hitler's intentions toward the Jews in the 1920s and early 1930s, because he never really said what he would do with the Jews, except for uttering endless streams of gutter invectives. Nowhere in his book *Mein Kampf*, or in his second book, which was not then known and which was published only after his death, or in his speeches after 1922 or so (before that he did talk in general terms about doing away with the Jews) is there a clear indication of his intent, and there certainly was no actual planning of the genocide before 1941.[18] Even if intent to murder was proved, there is still no explanation of why German society lent itself to collaboration with such an intent. I will deal with this in greater detail when I discuss the Goldhagen thesis later in this volume. Here let me state that although both functionalist and intentionalist approaches have been productive for historical investigation, they do not provide a model of explanation for the basic question posed above.

There is, as I just said, a growing tendency in the historiography of the Holocaust to consider the functionalist-intentionalist dispute outdated, and I have already mentioned the attempt by Ulrich Herbert and others, in the previous chapter, as a more persuasive attempt to explain the development. Other historians, such as Otto Dov Kulka and Ian Kershaw, have pioneered different explanatory models, which are, I believe, even more convincing.[19] Kershaw's analysis in particular appears to be an excellent starting point. It seems that most ordinary members of the Nazi Party were not quite certain of the centrality of antisemitism to their ideology. The sociologist Peter Merkl has suggested that a high proportion of Party members were not extreme antisemites; rather, they shared an antisemitism that one could define as pervasive, yet not necessarily murderous, perhaps even "moderate."[20] But it was not only the membership of the Nazi Party that may have been "only moderately" antisemitic. This kind of moderate antisemitism was shared by a considerable part of the German population, although its pervasiveness is difficult to estimate. The Jews were a rather unpopular minority, well known yet strange, certainly not considered to be Germans (contrary to the self-perception of the Jews themselves), and people generally would hardly object if they were removed from the German economy, culture, and government administration. In fact, it was fairly widely believed that Germany might gain from their removal. Another very considerable, largely non-antisemitic, or only latently antisemitic, part of the populace was represented by the Social Democrats, the Communists, and the Catholic Center Party (Zentrum), but even there one could discern anti-Jewish feelings. These moderate, even hardly noticeable feelings of unease toward the Jews would not have led to the gas chambers of Auschwitz. In fact, the situation in Germany was not much different from the situations in other western European countries. In eastern Europe, anti-Jewish feelings were very much stronger.

It was the elite of the Nazi Party, possibly a couple of hundred persons (whom Christopher R. Browning has called, in some of his lectures, "true believers"), who saw in the Jews the major threat to German, Nordic, Aryan humankind. It was within that group that the murderous inclinations developed. Hitler himself, Joseph Goebbels, Richard Walter Darré, Heinrich Himmler, Martin Bormann, Alfred Rosenberg, Julius Streicher, Wilhelm Frick, Otto Thierack, Hans Frank, Reinhard Heydrich are some of the more prominent names that come to mind. The leadership of Hitler was crucial, because he was undoubtedly the radicalizing factor. People like Himmler or even Göring were moved into their murderous stance by Hitler; it is unlikely that they would have reached that point without him. Hitler influenced a group of what might be called pseudo-intellectuals who were prepared, socially, psychologically, and politically, to accept radical, murderous programs. Karl Marx called the displaced, unorganized, unemployed, declassed part of the working class *Lumpenproletariat* (proletariat of rags); the Nazi elite might be called Lumpenintellectuals—largely unemployed, exceedingly bitter regarding the bourgeois society that rejected them for a variety of reasons, searching for explanations for their disappointment in a society that had lost a war but did not understand why, a society that appeared to be disintegrating.

These Lumpenintellectuals did not come to power as a result of the ballot. The Nazis suffered a defeat in the last free election in pre-Nazi Germany, in November 1932. They lost thirty-four mandates in the Reichstag and two million votes. They remained the largest party, yet the combined (but bitterly split) Left had 221 mandates compared to their 196. Apparently, it was precisely because they lost the elections in which the Communists actually gained votes that they were no longer considered to be a real threat to the right-wing politicians who wanted to use them against the Center and the Left—hence the nomination of Hitler as chancellor at the end of January 1933. Those who voted for the Nazis knew they were voting for an antisemitic party, but clearly, antisemitism was not foremost in the minds of the voters. Nor did the Nazis put antisemitism first among the topics that their propaganda dealt with, although it was always present. Their campaign dealt with mass unemployment, the economic and social crisis generally, and the defeat of Germany in World War I and the consequent military and political humiliation from which Germany should rise. The voters were not repelled by the antisemitism of the Party, because what the Party demanded was in line with the moderate antisemitism just described: removal of the Jews from their prominent economic, political, and cultural positions in German society. Undoubtedly, many of the Nazi supporters were also moved by envy and hoped to gain personally by replacing Jews in different social and economic roles. The Nazis said very little in their program about what should be done with the Jews, and voters appear to have identified with what they read or heard from

Nazi propagandists. But all this was very much secondary to the primacy of concerns regarding the economic and social crisis of Germany. No one thought in terms of an Auschwitz: not the Nazis, not the general German population, and not the Jews.

Long before the Nazis came to power, in the nineteenth century, the universities had become centers of an integralist, exclusive, and radical German nationalism, with growing racist-biological overtones. Jews were unwelcome as students, and student societies (*Burschenschaften*) increasingly excluded them. Few Jews became professors. Radical antisemitism spread. If there was a uniquely German phenomenon that prepared the ground for Nazism, it was not the spread of antisemitism among the population in general but its spread among the intellectual elites. I shall return to this point later, in the discussion of contemporary attempts to explain the Holocaust. In the 1920s the Nazis attracted an important section of the intellectual classes—the teachers and students especially, because the universities had become a hotbed of extremist right-wing ideas decades before. Students' and teachers' associations were indeed among the first to join the Party. Some lower-ranking bureaucrats, lawyers, doctors, engineers, Protestant pastors, even elements in the army and the aristocracy, joined as well.[21] Once in power, the Nazis quickly gained the overwhelming support of the people. The economic depression had reached its lowest point just before the Nazis came to power, and the new regime latched on to the beginning of the economic revival; to the masses, the regime seemed the cause of the upswing—most importantly, of the progressive reduction of the unemployment rate. But without the enthusiastic support of the intelligentsia, neither war nor Holocaust would have ensued.

One can follow the swift increase of the intelligentsia's support for the regime in the diary of Victor Klemperer, a professor of Romance languages and literature at the University of Dresden, a converted Jew, a war veteran, supporter of German nationalism, husband of a non-Jewish wife.[22] The intelligentsia, like the working class, the peasantry, and the middle classes, supported the regime not because of its antisemitism but because of its success. What attracted them, beyond the immediate economic programs and concerns for their social status, was the utopia that the regime promised all Germans: the humiliated German people would become the center of a European and perhaps global empire based on their racial qualities, which made them superior to all Aryans of a lower status (such as Latins) and certainly to mixed races (such as the Slavs, who in Nazi eyes were a mix of Aryans and Mongols) and to non-Aryans and "colored" peoples. Implied in this racist ideology, which penetrated the minds of academically trained people, was the notion that pure Aryans had not only the right but the duty to rule the others and to destroy those who were harmful.

Germans were themselves judged for harmfulness. The German Ministry of the Interior circulated guidelines, on July 18, 1940, which divided the German population into four categories in accordance with their social and economic performance. The lowest category consisted of "asocial persons," who would be excluded from all social aid. The category above it was composed of people whose behavior was just about "bearable," and the possibility of their sterilization was considered. There was no such provision for the lowest category; instead, "measures of negative population policy"—deportation, forced labor, and annihilation—were to be considered. This document, published by Goetz Aly and Heinz Roth in 1984, shows that the Nazis were planning to mass-murder healthy Germans, never mind the handicapped, in the name of racial purity.[23] The German intelligentsia, which was captivated by the racist utopia of the regime, would no doubt have collaborated in the murder of German people as well.

For the intelligentsia, the crucial element of any murder plan was that the regime had to declare it an essential part of the utopian program, a part vital to the interests of Germany. Thus, Dr. Josef Mengele (he was a doctor doubled: he had an M.D. and a Ph.D.), the main figure among the twenty-three Auschwitz doctors who selected many hundreds of thousands of Jews to die, had no previous record of antisemitism. He had, however, acquired, as a typical intellectual, total identification with the Führer and the Party. He and his peers were the product of a network of the best universities in Europe, which had turned out what Franklin H. Littell has termed "technically competent barbarians."[24]

In a society that had willingly accepted the absolute leadership of a ruling elite and especially of its head, the intellectuals became the chief transmitters of murderous orders. And if the people with social and intellectual status led the way in executing such orders more efficiently, recruiting ordinary murderers from the lower ranks of society became very easy—insofar as the intelligentsia did not do the murdering themselves.

It may now be possible to provide an answer to a supplementary question: How did "dehumanizing" the victim—which actually meant that a "dehumanized" perpetrator—that is, a person devoid of any moral scruples—tried to reduce the victim to his or her own level—occur? How was the victim removed from the "universe of human obligation," as Helen Fein has put it?[25] Some psychologists suggest that there exists a process of transferring one's moral responsibility to an outside factor—Hitler, in this case—a process that would rid the perpetrator of further problems of conscience. Transference would be the result of the total identification of the perpetrator with the regime. If we go back to our explanation, we arrive at the point where the frustrated, partly unemployed intelligentsia of a defeated nation, faced with the disintegration of that nation's social fabric, looked for and found a pseudo-messianic regime and a leader who absolved them from moral responsibility, explicitly taking that burden on himself.

Two of the four Einsatzgruppen, the murder groups detailed in 1941 to kill targeted groups, mainly Jews, in the newly occupied Soviet territories, were commanded by Dr. Walther Stahlecker, and Dr. Otto Rasch (another intellectual with two Ph.D.s). A third was commanded by Otto Ohlendorf, an outstanding economist and lawyer. I have already mentioned the doctors at Auschwitz. Some of the concentration camp commanders boasted university degrees. The doctors, biologists, chemists, engineers, bureaucrats, and so on, who were involved in everything from deportations to death camps to medical "experiments," were central, not incidental, parts of the murder machine. The same must be said about the scientists, philosophers, historians, and theologians at universities, who supplied the rationalizations for the murder machine with verve and a great deal of individual initiative. On the other hand, local sadists in charge of the liquidation of ghettos in the East mostly came from lower-middle-class or peasant backgrounds or from the déclassé produced by the crisis-ridden German society of the 1920s. Neither they nor the intelligentsia had, in most cases, undergone training in the special schools set up by the S.S. But once the Führer expressed a desire and once an enthusiastic class of educated people backed it, the simpler folk who did the shooting and beating and child-murdering were easily found.

The moderate antisemitism of a large part of the German population, or even the queasiness that many, if not most, Germans felt in connection with the Jews, was absolutely crucial. It prevented any effective opposition to the murder of an unpopular minority.

Let me make two further points. It is essential to mention the brutalization of European society in the wake of World War I. The death of millions of soldiers, as well as the harsh treatment of civilian populations, including women and children, during and especially after the war, established a precedent, which was followed by the Nazi murderers and their helpers of various nationalities.

In addition, one should not forget, in this overall analysis, that the Nazi regime was not as totalitarian as most people seem to think. Of the many proofs of this let me mention the well-known fact that the murder of handicapped Germans, the so-called euthanasia, was stopped, at least officially (although in fact it was continued on a smaller scale), by protests from the German churches, segments of the public, and even Party members. When the authorities wanted to remove crucifixes from schools in Bavaria, there was something of a rebellion, and the government desisted. But more apposite to our topic is the fact that at the end of February and during the first days of March 1943, hundreds, maybe more, German women demonstrated—successfully—in the Berlin Rosenstrasse in front of a police building to demand that the Gestapo return their Jewish husbands to them.[26] Resistance to Nazi policies was possible, and not one case is known of a German who refused to participate in the murder (and there were such individuals, including the occasional intellectual) who was punished by incarceration or execution.

In summary: it seems that a political elite of Lumpenintellectuals who had achieved power for reasons that had little to do with their racism, who were obsessed with pseudo-messianic concepts of saving humanity from the Jews, had used a broad stratum of the intelligentsia, people who totally supported Nazi utopianism, to execute a genocidal program. That program went unopposed largely because anti-Jewish tendencies in the general population, ranging from mild discomfort about Jews to open but nonlethal antisemitism, both prepared the way for the extreme, murderous variety of antisemitism and prevented effective resistance to the genocide. I might venture the conclusion that this German-Nazi example might be part of a more generalized analysis of any "warning system": "Moderate" social ostracism of a targeted group or "moderate" dislike of a minority may well lead to mass murder when a political elite that gains power wants to eliminate the targeted group, provided the intelligentsia identifies with the political elite and the regime established by the elite, even without being ideologically persuaded that the murder is justified.

In other cases of genocide, such as those of the Armenians, the Cambodian Khmer and Cham, and the Tutsi, one can distinguish certain parallels. Medical doctors were prominent in planning the Armenian genocide, and bureaucrats and army officers, all of whom had had a fairly good education, participated. The murder of the Tutsi and some Hutus was planned by a group of Hutu intellectuals, and the horrors of the Pol Pot regime were guided by former students of French universities. As far as the Holocaust itself is concerned, one might add that for the murder of some 260,000 Jews by the Romanian army, gendarmerie,

and "ordinary" Romanians, the groundwork was laid by two generations of the best Romanian intellectuals and executed with the guidance
of other intellectuals.

I do not claim that this explanatory model is final; it is intended more
as a stimulant for discussion. The fact that the Holocaust is explicable
does not imply any kind of closure. More than one satisfactory explanation can be offered. What is totally unsatisfactory is an attempt to escape
historical responsibility by arguing that this tragedy is something mysterious that cannot be explained. If this were true, then the criminals
would become tragic victims of forces beyond human control. To say
that the Holocaust is inexplicable, in the last resort, is to justify it.

chapter three

Comparisons with Other Genocides

I have said already that the only way to clarify the applicability of definitions and generalizations is with comparisons. The question of whether the Holocaust had elements that have not existed with any other form of genocide (whereas there are no major elements of other genocides that cannot be found in yet other genocides) is extremely important if we want to find out more about social pathology in general.[1] When one discusses unprecedented elements in a social phenomenon, the immediate question is, Unprecedented in comparison with what? The very claim that a historical event is unprecedented can be made only when that event is compared with other events of a presumably similar nature with which it shares at least some qualities. Unless one finds a measure of comparability, unprecedentedness can mean only that the event is not human—in other words, is not historical—in which case it is useless to talk about it except in putative theological or mystical contexts.

There are rather obvious psychological barriers to understanding mass murders and genocidal events such as those described by Rudolph Rummel, whose work was mentioned in the first chapter and will be the basis of much of what is said here as well. We all know that humans evince a tendency to deny the existence of life-threatening events. In school textbooks, wars are described in terms of political or other motivations and in terms of military strategies and tactics. Napoleon, for instance, won the battle of Austerlitz—but was he there alone? Was he not helped a little bit by a few tens of thousands of soldiers whom he (and others) led into battle? How many soldiers were killed on both sides? We do not usually find these figures in history textbooks. The meaning of such statistics is discussed even less. We rarely find accounts of medical practices, including the cutting-off of limbs and the like, or descriptions of what happened to those mutilated. According to the English ballad of the late sixteenth century about the great Lord Willoughby's exploits in Flanders, "To soldiers that were maimed, and wounded in the fray, the Queen allowed a pension of eighteen pence a day." Well, that's something. The rest—medical treatment, wives and children, and so on, is not mentioned. Other soldiers in other wars were not lucky enough to have the great Lord Willoughby put in a word with Queen Bess—were such songs written about Napoleon, or von Moltke, or the Duke of Marlborough? And what about the civilians near the roads that the armies traveled on? What about the dead, the wounded, the raped, and the dispossessed? We teach our children about the greatness of the various Napoleons, Palmerstons, and Bismarcks as political or military leaders and thus sanitize history.

We all know that human history is colored with blood. We try to minimize, ignore, not teach about, this dark side of history, because it is a constant threat to our feeling of security, and we want to avoid danger by looking the other way. Erich Fromm used the concept of Thanatos, the destructive instinct, to explain our behavior.[2] It appears that humans veer between the urge for life, the "libido" described by Freud (in much too sexual terms), and the life-destroying urge. I would argue that the idea of "good" gods, or a just, omnipresent, and all-powerful

God, or transcendental nonhuman beings generally who are supposed to be the repositories of morality, and their opposite—devil figures, or evil gods, or a monotheistic God who hides his face—stem from that immanent inner conflict. We have these opposites within us, genetically fixed by a long history of human development; we can be either "good" and "just" and "humane," or the opposite. We transfer these qualities outside ourselves and create images of transcendental beings who will personalize these qualities for us. We make these gods, or a God, whom we invented for the purpose, to come back to us and impose a "good" morality upon us, in order to have an authority that will prevent us from becoming what we know we can become and fear to become—namely, "bad," "devilish" creatures. When we stray from the straight and narrow, some of us will call our straying a sin. When we *want* to sin, we have our G(g)od(s) instruct us to do so. The result, for the twentieth century, is Rummel's statistics.

Genocide and mass murder are described in all so-called sacred books, whether the Indian Vedas, or the Bible, or the Quran. As a Jew, I must live with the fact that the civilization that I inherited also encompasses the call for genocide in its canon. In the previous chapter I mentioned the story about the murder of the Midianites (Numbers 31). If that story is not a "divine" justification for genocide, I don't know what is. Later generations of sages had the unenviable task of explaining it away—but let it be said that they felt uncomfortable about the murder and did *not* want it to become a precedent for the Jews' behavior, so they did their pathetic best to eradicate it by "interpretation." This strategy of changing texts by (re)interpreting them is, on the whole, one must admit, the mark of a reasonably advanced civilization.

Theological justifications for mass murder and genocide exist outside the monotheistic religions, of course; it would be worthwhile, however, to examine the question of whether monotheism is not more murderous than other forms of religion. After all, millions of Christians and non-Christians have been killed by other Christians in the name of a loving God. The point is that the monotheistic God of the Middle East was created in the unfortunately very accurate image of (wo)man, who alternates between bloodthirsty murderousness and wonderful, justice-seeking morality.

On the other hand, human beings do not need theological justifications to commit mass murders and genocides. The Romans at Carthage, the Mongols at Isfahan, the Danes in post-Roman England, the Indians and the Chinese in various historical periods are just random examples. Marxism-Leninism is (was) a form of a nontheistic religion, and one can put the atrocities committed by the various communist regimes in the twentieth century toward the top of our list.

It is with this in mind that one ought to look at genocide, defined in the first chapter as a "natural" "human" activity, as the result of a tendency that can be fought and perhaps avoided by strengthening the opposite inclinations of humans. That these antimurderous inclinations exist and that their importance may be no less than that of the murderous ones will be discussed later.

In this analysis I choose to start with National Socialism and then go backward and forward in history because my central concern and starting point is the Holocaust. The following, however, must be stated and emphasized: *The horror of the Holocaust is not that it deviated from human norms; the horror is that it didn't.*

As I try to show in other parts of this book, I believe, contrary to many of my colleagues, that Nazi racial antisemitic ideology was the central factor in the development toward the Holocaust. It is a well-worn truth to say that Nazi ideology owes its image of the Jew to Christian antisemitism.[3] The main Nazi accusations against the Jews were that there was a Jewish conspiracy to rule the world; that Jewish influence is satanic, and Jews are out to corrupt the civilizations of their host peoples and countries; that the Jews are parasites and bloodsuckers; that they kidnap or kill Christian children, and so on. All these fantasies were developed by Christian antisemites over many centuries. They are based on the satanization of the Jews by their Christian opponents.

The origins of the satanization are to be found in the Christian-Jewish confrontation that started off as a family quarrel of Jewish sects. As the Gentile-Christian group split off from the original Jewish church, the need arose to show the differences between the two theologies. In the first centuries of the Christian era these differences crystallized into enmity and mutual satanization.[*] Each side thought only one interpretation of God's will was legitimate, and Christian ideology, which by the fourth century had become sanctioned by state power, had to show that the Jews were driven by a pact with the devil; otherwise, a pagan who wanted to accept monotheism would go to the Jewish source rather than to the Christian imitation. What did Satan want, if not to conquer the world and make it rebel against God? Who if not the Jews were possessed by Satan, because who would kill God—as the false accusation of Jewish responsibility for the crucifixion went—but a people possessed by Satan? The logical conclusion was that the Jews wanted to control the world for Satan. Nazi antisemitism adopted the antisemitic images while rejecting the Christian theology; in effect, it adopted Christian antisemitism without Christianity, which it saw, quite rightly, as a Jewish invention. In this, as in some other aspects of its ideology, National Socialism's source was the Enlightenment and the French Revolution. François Marie Voltaire, after all, was one who rejected Christianity and saw in it a destructive force introduced into Europe by Judaism and the Jews, whom he despised.

Another aspect of Nazi ideology was, as we know, Social Darwinism—namely, that perversion of Darwin's ideas in which human "races" are considered to be locked in a constant struggle with one another. Accordingly, stronger is better and more beautiful, and whoever is better has the moral right—even the duty—to rule over and, if necessary, destroy the others. This variety of racism is usually viewed as the general type of which antisemitism is a special case. However, upon close examination of Nazi writings and speeches, we see that the Nazis' racism was intimately connected with a thoroughgoing antisemitism. It might well be that their explanation of the way societies behaved, which was based on antisemitism, used racism as a kind of "superstructure," to use a Marxist term; that is, we might consider Nazi antisemitism as the primary motivation, and the adoption of a racist ideology as a logical follow-up. To put the same idea differently and more pointedly: racial ideology, which was the overarching element in Nazi ideology, was antisemitic at its very core, which means that antisemitism may have been the basic motivation for adopting a Social Darwinistic approach, which had been developed in the second half of the nineteenth century in France, Britain, America, Austria, and Germany.

When one reads Nazi sources, it is almost impossible to avoid a centrally important conclusion: the Jews were, in Nazi eyes, *the* central enemy, the incarnation of the Devil. I would argue that the Nazis externalized their concepts of absolute good and absolute evil into their notion of the Germanic, or Nordic, peoples of the Aryan race and the nonhuman Jewish anti-race, respectively. God and Satan became real.[5] That they identified the negative pole with the Jews was conditioned by Christian tradition. Their hierarchy of races was also, in a real sense, based on Christian precedents: after the expulsion of the Jews and the Moors from Spain in 1492, individuals aspiring to certain important positions in the Spanish kingdom had to prove their *limpieza de sangre*, their purity of blood—that they had no Jewish or Moorish "blood."[6] Ideas that we would today call racist were certainly not foreign to European colonists in the New World, or the Far East, or Africa. True, the Nazis developed these notions in novel ways, but they did have something to build on. This is not to say that there was, necessarily, a direct line of development from pre-nineteenth-century racism to the modern kind. The jury is still out on this very important issue.

I discuss interpretations of Nazism in other chapters of this book, but let me say here that for the Holocaust, the importance of the bureaucracy and other such factors as part of modernity and the importance of the impact of economic, social, and political crises are generally accepted, but without a guiding ideological motivation and justification, mass murder generally, and the intent to annihilate the Jewish people in particular, would have been unthinkable. Ideology is central.[7]

But not just any ideology. The *kind* of ideology crucial here is an ideology, shaped around an antisemitic core, that sought to establish a new form of society, one built on a hierarchy of races; a utopia whose flip side was the murder of a people who occupy a unique position in Christian-Muslim society. The Nazi motivations for killing the Jews consisted of, first, their view of them as Satan incarnate, out to control the world; second, their view of them as corrupting parasites and viruses whose elimination was a problem of world racial hygiene, in other words, a medical problem; third, the utopian dream of a new kind of humanity that would arise once the Jews were eliminated. Saul Friedländer, in his recent *Nazi Germany and the Jews*, aptly calls this set of motivations "redemptive antisemitism," because an important element was the dream of universal redemption, here a kind of (false) messianism that one normally finds in Christianity and Judaism.[8] This kind of pseudo-religious utopianism, which one also finds in Marxist-Leninist thought, contains the seed of mass murder. I know of no such redemptive ideology that is not murderous—from crusading Christianity, to contemporary Jewish, Muslim, or Hindi fundamentalism, to Chinese communist dreams of a leap forward. Utopias with a universal message are a sure way to mass murder.

In the case of National Socialism "redemptive antisemitism" led to an unprecedented form of genocide. The motivating ideology was purely nonpragmatic and irrational. In the Armenian genocide, arguably the closest parallel to the Holocaust, the motivation was political and chauvinistic, that is, it had a pragmatic basis. The Jemiyet (Committee for Union and Progress) of Talaat and Enver and their clique, the so-called Young Turks, wanted to establish a Pan-Turkic empire stretching from Edirne, in European Turkey, to Kazakhstan, an empire dominated by Turkic-speaking peoples. The Armenians, an "alien" nation, occupied stretches of Anatolia, the heartland of Turkey. They had to be done away with. Apart from Armenian peasants, there was the Armenian middle class in the Turkish towns and cities, which had an important commercial, cultural, and intellectual influence. Armenian Christian civilization competed with Turkish civilization, which it had preceded on what later became Turkish territory by many centuries.

Persecuted by the Turks, the Armenians naturally tended to seek support from the Russians, the bitter enemies of the Ottoman Empire. Autonomist and, by implication, independence-seeking Armenian political parties increased Turkish suspicions and were, in Turkish eyes, a threat at the very heart of Turkish ethnic territory. The Western Powers used Armenian aspirations to press the Ottoman authorities to give up important elements of Ottoman sovereignty; they seemingly supported Armenian aspirations, but dropped them when it was no longer in their interest to do so. The Armenians were abandoned and before, during, and after World War I were killed in huge numbers. Their genocide served the pragmatic purposes of political expansion, acquisition of land, confiscation of riches, elimination of economic competition, and the satisfaction of chauvinistic impulses of the revolutionary core of the dominant ethnic group, impulses exacerbated by feelings of utter frustration and humiliation in a crisis-ridden and disintegrating empire.[9]

In the case of the Tutsis in Rwanda, the dominant clique of Hutus, led by a French-educated intelligentsia, was after the land that the Tutsis occupied—in an agricultural economy where land is scarce—and after the base of power of the Tutsi Rwandan class cum ethnic group, a minority that had comprised the traditional ruling class for centuries and had a record of oppressing the Hutu majority. This, again, was a pragmatically motivated genocide.[10]

The definition of the Cambodian disaster as genocide presents problems, because the aim of the Khmer perpetrators was obviously not the disappearance of the Khmer people. Yet it certainly has elements of a genocide. According to Ben Kiernan's findings, there were three groups of victims: ethnic Khmer who were city dwellers or who in some other way were deemed potential or real enemies; Chams, Muslims who were massacred in large numbers; and Vietnamese living in Cambodia, many of whom managed to escape to Vietnamese territory. What concerns us here is that the motivation for the murder of Khmer by Khmer was the achievement of a class-based utopia, according to which the putative real interests of potentially oppositional city dwellers were to be eliminated by annihilating the city dwellers themselves. Agricultural communism of an extreme sort could be assured only by removing all possible centers of dissent—a clear political motivation, which showed a kind of distorted rationality despite the irrationally extreme sadism and brutality with which it was executed.[11]

It would be superfluous to analyze the motivation for the annihilation of the Caribs at the hands of the Spaniards, or the genocide of Mexican and Peruvian Indian peoples that followed—clearly, the quest for gold, commerce, and natural riches was the central motive, and the conversion to Christianity an ideological "superstructure."

Even in the case of the Roma (Gypsies) the pragmatic aspect stands out. In the territory of the German Reich, a racist ideology demanding their complete removal, in large part by their annihilation, predominated, but outside the Reich, matters were different. Nazi policy toward the Roma was hazy. Recent research has shown that from early 1942 on, the Wehrmacht, probably following a consensus emanating from the Party, distinguished between sedentary and wandering Roma. The latter were to be murdered, because they were in the way and could not be integrated in a future German-dominated political order. The Nazis did not usually bother about the former, although there were some exceptions. The settled Roma (the definition of who was "settled" was vague) were largely treated like other local inhabitants.[12] I will deal with this issue below.

One major difference between the Holocaust and other forms of genocide is, then, that pragmatic considerations were central with all other genocides, abstract ideological motivations less so. With the Holocaust, pragmatic considerations were marginal. Yes, a tremendous effort was exerted to rob the Jews of their property or to take it after they were murdered. But no serious historian has ever claimed that robbery was the basic reason for the murder. Robbery was the outcome of the Holocaust, not its cause. The Jews had no territory to be coveted. Contrary to legend, German Jews did not control the German economy, although they were prominent in some of its branches—and they did not act as a group but as competing individuals. Further, they had no military power, and in Germany itself their political power was marginal at best. Politically, the only prominent Jew in the Weimar Republic after 1920 was Walther Rathenau, the minister of foreign affairs, and he was murdered in 1922 by right-wing extremists. No, the basic motivation was purely ideological, rooted in an illusionary world of Nazi imagination, where an international Jewish conspiracy to control the world was opposed to a parallel Aryan quest. No genocide to date had been based so completely on myths, on hallucinations, on abstract, nonpragmatic, ideology—which then was executed by very rational, pragmatic means. Just as Christian antisemitism was based on theological speculations that fulfilled important practical functions, so Nazi antisemitism, which originated in the same Christian delusions but which abandoned the moral principles of Christianity along with its religious beliefs, translated its murderous abstractions into gradually developing policies of segregation, starvation, humiliation, and, finally, planned total murder. The murder of the Jews took place because a murderous ideology motivated it, but first the ideology overcame contrary ideas and notions in German society in the concrete historical context of converging crises.[13]

A second reason why the Holocaust is unprecedented is its global, indeed, universal character. All other genocides were limited geographically; in most cases, the targeted group lived in a reasonably well defined geographic locale (Indian peoples in the Americas, Khmer and Cham in Cambodia [Kampuchea], Tutsi mainly in Rwanda, Uganda, Burundi, and Zaire; and so on). The Turks targeted Armenians in ethnically Turkish areas; they did not care about Armenians elsewhere; even the Armenians in Jerusalem, which was considered to be ethnically Arab and which was controlled by the Ottomans, were not targeted.

Wandering and settled groups of Roma were murdered in Germany, but outside Germany, settled Roma were of no special concern; the Nazis did not attempt to register Roma outside the Reich. In the case of the Jews, persecution started in Germany but spread all over what the Germans called the German sphere of influence in Europe and then became a policy of total murder.[14] Because the Germans fully intended to control not just Europe but the world, whether directly or through allies, this meant that Jews would ultimately be hunted down all over the world. Hitler's well-known expression, that in fighting the Jew he was doing the work of the Lord, had a clear universalist implication. Indeed, it was antisemitism that was exported from Nazi Germany, everywhere. This global character of the intended murder of all Jews is unprecedented in human history.

A third element sets the Holocaust apart from other genocides: its intended totality. The Nazis were looking for Jews, for all Jews. According to Nazi policy, all persons with three or four Jewish grandparents were sentenced to death for the crime of having been born. Such a policy has never been applied in human history before and would have undoubtedly been applied universally if Germany had won the war. If we compare this to other genocides—for instance, the case of the Caribs, who were indeed totally exterminated by Spanish policies—we find that there were never plans to achieve that aim, nor was it express state policy to do so, although that was the practical outcome. In Ottoman Turkey, some Armenian women and small children were spared to be sexually used or to be educated as Turks. Further, as I pointed out above, Armenians were intended to be eradicated in mainly ethnic Turkish areas, not necessarily elsewhere. North American Indian tribes were victims of genocide for reasons of greed and exploitation, and murder was the outcome of national policies, but again, there was no governmental plan for total extermination. In genocidal attacks on peoples before the twentieth century, the technology, on the one hand, and the complicated bureaucratic structures guided by universalistic utopian ideologies, on the other hand, had not yet developed. One could argue that had the murder of the Caribs and the North American Indians taken place at a time when state-directed annihilation was possible, that policy would have been followed. This may well be so, which shows not only that the Holocaust was unprecedented but that human civilization is prone to make Holocausts possible when conditions are ripe—which is another central point in our argument. In other words, the Holocaust can be repeated, not to be sure in exactly the same way, not by Germans, not toward Jews, but by anyone toward anyone. It was the Jews the last time round; we do not know who the Jews may be if there is a next time.

If this analysis is correct, then the Holocaust is an extreme form of genocide. It is important to restate what is meant here by "extreme." The suffering of the victims of this genocide was in no sense greater than the suffering of victims of other genocides—there is no gradation of suffering. Thus, the fate of Roma victims at Auschwitz was exactly parallel to that of the Jewish victims.[15] What is meant by "extreme" is expressed by the three elements described above: the ideological, global, and total character of the genocide of the Jews. The extremeness of the Holocaust is what makes it unprecedented.

Various commentators have labeled as unprecedented a number of other aspects of the Holocaust. One is the supposed *furor teutonicus*, some quasi-genetic, peculiarly German expression of extreme violence or sadism.[16] This explanation is less than convincing, quite apart from smacking of reverse racism. Collaborators with the Nazis from among other European nations were certainly no less brutal than the Germans were. The Croatian concentration camp of Jasenovac was, if anything, more horrible than its Nazi counterparts. Romanian troops and police showed their mettle at such death traps in Transnistria as Bogdanovca and during the death marches of Bessarabian Jews into the Transnistrian territory: some 260,000 Romanian and 100,000 Ukrainian Jews were murdered by Romanian perpetrators.[17] Most Lithuanian Jews were murdered by Lithuanian collaborators, although with German encouragement and in large part under German supervision. And in all other genocides known to us, the perpetrators acted similarly, as anyone who has researched the Spaniards in the New World, European settlers in North America, Cambodian communists or Hutu perpetrators, to name but a few, will readily acknowledge.

Is modern efficiency a special hallmark of the Holocaust? That may seem to be the case, but in some other genocides, too, the contemporary state of technology was fully utilized. Probably the best example is the Armenian case: the Turkish perpetrators used the telegraph to inform their people of the steps to be taken against the targeted victims, they used railways to transport troops, and they established an armed force directed from the center to serve as the chief agency for perpetrating the murder.[18] One might make a similar argument regarding the destruction of the North American Indians at the hands of white Americans.

On the other hand, although the Nazis did not invent the concentration camp, they developed it in new ways. Especially novel was the intricate procedure by which they deprived inmates of their "normal" human attributes by systematic humiliation, which reached its peak in their use of what may be called excretionary control—total humiliation by controlling human excretions. Perhaps the most frightening aspect of this development is that, to date, no Nazi document has been found that points to a discussion of how to humiliate victims. The conclusion is inevitable: humiliation was not the result of planning but of a consensus that did not require orders or bureaucratic arrangements. In other words, probably the most extreme form of humiliation known to us was the natural result of the Nazi system.

Also novel in its extremity, though not in its essence, was the Nazi use of camp inmates against other camp inmates. The same basic policy was followed in the East European ghettos.

I believe one should as far as possible avoid the term *dehumanization* to describe what happened to the inmates of camps and ghettos, because, if anything, the term fits the Nazis: they "dehumanized" themselves. What they did to their hapless victims was to transfer their own abandonment of all previous norms accepted as "civilized" onto *really* civilized beings, Jews and others. The common use of the term *dehuman-ization* would leave the perpetrator as the "human" and the victim as less than human. That, indeed, was the intended outcome, but in fact the Nazi treatment of those interned in camps and ghettos showed the opposite, because it was the Nazis who lost the characteristics of civilized human beings. When that minority of inmates who survived were liberated, they returned to their civilized ways of life; it is highly doubtful whether their torturers did, unless they repented, which apparently very few of them did. In other words, the Nazis remained dehumanized even after the nightmare ended; those of their victims who survived did not.

Arguably, therefore, one may add a fourth element of unprecedentedness to the three mentioned above: because the Jews were at the bottom of the hell that was the Nazi concentration camp, they were the victims of an unprecedented crime of total humiliation and fared worse than others who were victims of the same crime.

Yet a fifth element might be added. It refers to the regime from which the Holocaust sprang, and may provide some of its context: all the revolutions before National Socialism that aimed at organizing humanity were made in the name of class, nation, or religion. They were attempts to reshuffle society and make one real or imagined class, or ethnic or national group, or religious belief dominant while abolishing or subordinating others. The list of revolutionaries includes communists, for instance, who, originally at least, tried to define a new class structure of society. Today, the fundamentalist regimes of Iran, Libya, and Sudan try to make their version of Islam the defining element of society.

Attempts like these have been made before the twentieth century. Catholicism, in the past, claimed preeminence and absolute authority. Tsarist Russia claimed absolute power for the monarchy and aristocracy and the Orthodox Church. The Incas ruled over an empire in which only a certain class of people had a say in running society; the same applied, even more forcefully, in the caste system in India. But the Nazis tried to rule not just Germany but Europe, and ultimately the world, in the name of a new principle, the principle of "race." True, they started from nationalism and acted in the name of the German people. But, moved by their interpretation of the racial doctrine, they distanced themselves progressively from a purely German ideology. The fascinating document of July 1940 shows that the murder campaign was intended to decimate the German people as well—the monster was about to devour its own children.[19] The world was to be ruled by the stronger, better races, with the Germanic peoples of the Aryan race at the top of the new hierarchy.

To reach such a utopian situation, they had to oppose, I would argue, the major achievements of the European culture that preceded them, especially the legacy of the French Revolution and the Emancipation. If one is to believe Hermann Rauschning's record of his talks with Hitler—and that may be problematic, because he wrote them down from memory and published them years after they took place—then Hitler appears to have been aware of the tremendous import of his rebellion against humanity.[20] I would go further than that and claim that the National Socialist rebellion against humanism, liberalism, democracy, socialism, conservatism, pacifism, and so on, was the most radical attempt at changing the world that history has recorded to date: the most novel and the most revolutionary. The Nazi regime was unprecedented, to use the term I have suggested as a description of the Holocaust. It is the unprecedented quality of the Nazi regime that goes very far in explaining the unprecedented nature of the Holocaust. In attacking everything that had been defined as humane and moral before it, that Nazism saw the Jews as its main enemy was logical in a way. Why should this be so?

The Jews are a very peculiar group of people. They most certainly cannot be defined in racial-genetic terms, despite the better representation of certain illnesses among Jews than among others and despite the recent claim that certain genetic qualities set the priestly or quasi-priestly part of the Jewish population apart from others (many people whose name, Cohen, means "priest" share certain genetic characteristics). Clearly, Ethiopian, Indian, Moroccan, and Russian Jews show the result of intermingling with other groups. In the first century of the Common Era (the century that saw the destruction of the Jerusalem Temple) the Jewish population multiplied by at least 100 percent, if not more, and that was the result not of natural increase but of the addition to the Jewish people of large numbers of gentiles by a process whose details are still not quite clarified. In Jewish sources of the period they are called "the God-fearing ones" and appear to have joined Jewish communities without full membership; however, their children were converted at birth, so the next generation was fully Jewish.

If the Jews are not a "race," they certainly inherited a culture and a civilization in which their unique religion played a dominant part. That civilization created a vast oral tradition, which became a written tradition and decisively influenced modern civilization. Christianity and Islam are offshoots of this tradition. If, say, in the eighteenth century an ordinary European possessed a book at all, it would have been the Christian Bible, which was composed of two parts, the Old and the New Testaments. Both were largely written by Jews. The impact of the Jewish tradition can be seen in all of "Western" or "Northern" culture, from Chaucer, Shakespeare, and Dante to Polish and Russian literature, from the impact of the moral teachings of the prophets to legal concepts and the Rights of Man. The Jews themselves do not follow their moral precepts any more than anyone else does, and they are neither better nor worse than any other group. But they are different insofar as they are the bearers of this special tradition, although most of them desperately want not to be different at all. Others emphasize the difference to the extent of creating an impassable barrier between themselves and others.

Western or Northern civilization (if one can call it a civilization, after Auschwitz) is built on two pillars: Athens and Rome, and Jerusalem. But Athens and Rome, which are the source of modern aesthetics, much of modern literature, modern law, and much else, are no more. Contemporary Greeks and Romans speak different languages, derived though they are from the ancient ones; they no longer worship the same gods; they no longer write continuations of the same literature, nor do they follow similar customs. But the Jews are still here, and their culture is, if not the oldest, one of the oldest continuing civilizations we know. Anyone reading modern Hebrew can read texts that were written three thousand years ago without a dictionary. Let a modern reader of English try that with Chaucer, or a modern reader of Indian languages with Sanskrit.

I would argue that there was an internal logic to the Nazi attack on the Jews, who were the symbolic surviving remnant of the values and the heritage the Nazis wanted to destroy. This may be a contributing factor to the definition of the Holocaust.

Raul Hilberg, in his monumental, brilliant, and, in my view, unsurpassed analysis of the Nazi bureaucracy may not have intended to present us with the picture of a stereotypically efficient "teutonic" bureaucracy, but that is what many observers have seen. In actual fact, Nazi bureaucracy was riddled with inefficiency, and much leeway was given to individual initiatives, which sometimes clashed with planned action. From existing descriptions, one might perhaps dare to suggest that as long as experienced pre-Nazi bureaucrats filled responsible positions, the system worked more or less smoothly qua bureaucracy; as time went on, however, and the Nazi regime impacted more and more on the routines and policies of government, efficiency slackened considerably.[21] There was competition between quasi-feudal Nazi lords responsible for one or another bureaucratic structure, and there were the inherent inadequacies of a dictatorship that worked, in a period of crisis and war, according to a leadership principle that encouraged self-aggrandizement and escape from responsibility—more so than in a non-authoritarian regime.

Cost-efficiency was not, as some have argued, in evidence in Nazi genocidal policies. Quite apart from the fact that the death camps

(Auschwitz-Birkenau, Chelmno, Sobibor, Treblinka, Belzec, Maly Trostinetz)[22] were designed to kill Jews (several thousand Roma, and some hundreds Poles and Soviet POWs were also gassed in them),[23] the murder of these multitudes, people who could have been used, at the very least, to produce armaments, build airfields or roads, work in fields and factories, was opposed to modern economic principles.

Another aspect of unprecedentedness is perhaps more elusive. The way a modern society that had given the world some of the most important achievements of a humanistic culture became, in a horrifyingly short time, a recruiting ground for brutal murderers is a fact with which we have to grapple constantly.[24] What is so stunning is the participation of a vast majority of the Germans in genocidal projects, first and foremost against Jews, but also against others. What is frightening is the thought that if it could happen in Germany, it can happen elsewhere. The stereotypical genetic accusation against Germans as such, so dear to many Jews and non-Jews, is a way of saying that it could happen only in Germany, with Germans, and because "we" are not Germans, we need not be troubled too much.[25] It is an obvious case of anxiety repression.

The discussion about the unprecedented features of the Holocaust leads us into the question of the relation and comparison of the Holocaust, as an extreme case of genocide, to other genocides. In order to do so, let us return for the moment to the vexed question of existing definitions. I would argue that genocide is the proper name for the brutal process of group elimination accompanied by mass murder resulting in the partial annihilation of the victim population as described by Lemkin and the U.N. Convention. Total annihilation can be labeled *Holocaust* for want of a more acceptable word. Defined in this way, the term *genocide* would be applicable, for instance, to what the Nazis attempted to do to the Polish people. There was no intent to annihilate every Pole; there was an intent to eliminate the Polish people qua people, qua community, by the destruction of autonomous Polish economic structures, by the decimation of their religious leadership, by the destruction of all educational institutions, and by the prevention of any kind of Polish political structures. All this was accompanied by enslavement, kidnapping of children, forceful Germanization, and mass murder.

The parallels between the genocide of the Jews and the genocide of the Poles are obvious. What are the differences? For the Poles, there were no plans for total annihilation. A first draft of the so-called *Generalplan Ost*, which was submitted to Himmler at the end of 1941 by Dr. Konrad Meyer-Hetling, foresaw the expulsion of 31 million people in the Polish and Soviet areas and the Germanization of the rest, presumably by methods that would include the liquidation of the intelligentsia and any potential leaders, a policy that had in any case been pursued vis-à-vis the Poles from September 1939. The plan did not go into any details; these were later considered by Dr. Erhard Wetzel, an important S.S. official and racial expert. The Baltic peoples were to be eliminated as separate groups, the Germanizable elements were to be absorbed, and those who were not Germanizable (*eindeutschungsfähig*) were to be invited to become the ruling class of the Slavic expellees in the East. Wetzel found it "obvious that the Polish question cannot be solved in such a way that one would liquidate the Poles in the same manner as the Jews. Such a solution . . . would be a standing accusation against the German people into the far distant future."[26] He proposed to Germanize some and deport the rest to western Siberia, where their antagonism to the Russians would ensure that no united anti-German front would ever be formed. The anti-German elements would be annihilated. Ukrainians who could not be Germanized would also be used against the Russians, and the Belorussians would form a helot population reserve, to be used for labor.

Wetzel likewise opposed the total mass murder of the Russians, which had been proposed by Dr. Wolfgang Abel of the Kaiser Wilhelm Institute, the same illustrious institution of academic learning that had supported that other famous medical doctor with a Ph.D., Josef Mengele of Auschwitz notoriety. Wetzel thought that Russians would be needed for labor but had to be kept on a very short leash. Himmler's reaction to these proposals was positive. The Nazis might well have tried to translate these plans into practice had the defeat at Stalingrad not put an end to them. No less important was the plan—which did not work in practice—to starve about 30 million of the conquered Soviet population to death in order to make food available for Germany.[27] So: slavery, deportation, destruction of nationalities as identifiable groups, mass murder by hunger and by active killing—in other words, genocide. But not Holocaust.

The term *genocide* applies to the Armenian case even more aptly. There, too, the elimination of Armenian identity was aspired to, and all Armenians in what was considered to be Turkish ethnic territory were extinguished by mass murder, although the death of every single Armenian everywhere was not postulated as an aim. Persecution was ethnic, not racial, as in the Jewish case. The fate of the Ottoman Armenians was decisively affected by a development already alluded to: the Great Powers intervened in favor of the Armenian desire to develop cultural and political autonomy within the framework of the Ottoman Empire in order to influence and weaken the empire, but were not prepared to follow through. The Armenians, encouraged by the stand of the Powers, demanded autonomy, incensing Turkish nationalists, but were left in the lurch by those who had seemingly supported them. Nobody cared about the Armenians, and their tragedy was forgotten, as Hitler is supposed to have said in regard to them when discussing the fate of the Poles before his armies attacked Poland.[28] The Jews were equally abandoned by the Western Powers, who kept expressing their sympathy for their fate, but Jews, contrary to the Armenians vis-à-vis the Turks, never actually demanded anything from the Germans. The parallels and differences are again apparent, the differences being that the Armenians were a recognized ethnic group within the Ottoman Empire, whereas the Jews were sometimes considered an ethnic group, sometimes a purely religious group, and sometimes a combination of both; nor was there an international legal precedent that would have obligated the Powers to intervene in their favor, contrary to the Armenian case. In the Armenian case, again, the number of victims compared to the total number of the targeted population (probably at least one-half) is most likely higher than in the Jewish case (one-third of the Jews of the world were killed—which may be comparable to the Tutsi case as well).

One striking feature of the Armenian genocide is its denial by the heirs of the perpetrators. Nazi Germany was defeated, and its heirs, by contrast, acknowledged the murder of the Jews, the Holocaust, as well as the murder of other victims. The United States has accepted that nineteenth-century Americans were responsible for the murder of North American Indians, and Spain has recognized what Spaniards did in the Americas. This is true of some other genocides as well, though not all. Modern Turkey, however, adamantly refuses to acknowledge the mass destruction of the Armenian people, although the Turkish republican regime established by Mustafa Kemal Pasha Atatürk at one point not only, in his own words, acknowledged the facts but explicitly condemned the government of "Young Turks" that had been responsible.[29] Republican Turkey reversed the defeat of the Turkish armies at Allied hands, forced an exchange of populations with Greece, thereby establishing a homogeneous nation (with the exception of the Kurds in eastern Turkey), and became determined to suppress the memory of the genocide. It could do that because it became, thanks to the efforts of the Kemalist government, in a very real sense a victorious power. Victorious powers need not search for skeletons in their cupboards. What this denial does to Turkish national identity is another matter. One could argue that Turkey will never achieve a balanced identity unless it acknowledges that the predecessors of the present regime presided over the murder of another people.

A similar conclusion might be drawn from the murder of Roma. Two American (Jewish) historians, Sybil Milton and Henry Friedlander, have argued, in a series of publications, that what they call the Holocaust is what the Nazis did to Jews, "Gypsies," and the German handicapped (about 70,000 of whom were murdered in the first stage of what was euphemistically known as the "euthanasia" program, until August 1941, and many thousands more half-secretly afterward).[30] The argument is that the Nazis' policies regarding the Roma and the handicapped were motivated by the same kind of racist ideology as was their policy on the Jews.

Nazi policies toward the Roma and the handicapped were, it is true, formulated in racist terms and based on a biological-racist ideology. Quotations by these and other authors from orders by Himmler and opinions and policy directives by other Nazis are adequate proof of that. The fact, however, is that *all* Nazi policies toward other peoples were governed by their racist approach. Thus, for instance, S.S. officers were not allowed to marry Italian women without receiving special permissions, because Italians were not considered to be equal to the master race, even while Italy was an ally of Germany. Of course, it was impossible to maintain these racist principles in the real world. Slavs were considered to be inferior Aryans, but Slovaks, Croats, and Bulgarians— all Slavs—were allies, so there was no general anti-Slav policy. Instead, some Slavs were treated as subhuman Aryans; others were not. Latins were considered to be better than Slavs, but the poor performance of Italian soldiers on the battlefields apparently caused some doubts about that in the minds of good Nazis. Nazi attitudes toward Roma were complicated by their place of origin, northwestern India, which made them Aryans. The solution was to label them low-type Aryans who had mingled with the lowest of the European Aryans (including the lowest of the German population itself). They had become, in Nazi eyes, hereditary asocial criminals. This stereotyping can be documented from a large number of Nazi sources. The Nazis set up a special organization, the Rassenhygienische und Bevölkerungsbiologische Forschungsstelle des Reichsgesundheitsamtes (Research Institute for Racial Hygiene and Population Biology at the Reich Health Office), implying that the "Gypsy" problem (like the Jewish one) was basically a problem of social (preventive) medicine. The institute was run by a young doctor, Robert

Ritter, and a medical practitioner-nurse, Eva Justin (who received her M.D. later). They managed to divide 18,922 of the 28,607 "Gypsies" in Germany according to "race": 1,079 were classified as "pure" Gypsies, 6,992 as "more Gypsy than German," 2,976 as "half-breeds," 2,992 as "more German than Gypsy," 2,231 as uncertain, and 2,652 as "Germans who behaved as Gypsies."[31]

In 1938, Himmler declared that the "solution" of the Gypsy problem should be in accordance with racial principles. In the wake of the arrest of many German Roma (of the Sinti clans in the main)—many were put in special camps, and quite a number were sent to concentration camps—a problem arose for Himmler: after all, Sinti Gypsies were not Jews, and in principle Nazi ideology was supposed to respect the unique qualities of every race (except Jews and, presumably, blacks), especially when Gypsies were, after all, at least part Aryan, and some of them, the "pure" Gypsies, had to be treated even better than the part Aryans. Himmler therefore decided to separate German Gypsies in accordance with Ritter's findings. The pure Gypsies, and those who were more Gypsy than German would be protected from destruction under an arrangement reminiscent of the Jewish Councils: nine Sinti chiefs would run these groups. He even considered giving them permission to maintain their life of wandering. Hitler's powerful secretary, Martin Bormann, demurred (December 3, 1942). The American historians mentioned above quote this objection to show that nothing came of Himmler's idea to segregate pure Gypsies in order to keep them alive. However, there now are new findings: Himmler met with Hitler on December 6, 1942, and as a result, on February 27, 1943, Himmler informed the minister of justice, Otto Thierack, that "the Gypsy question" should be discussed further in accordance with information received from the party secretariat (Bormann). "Recent research" had made it clear "that there are positive racial elements also among the Gypsies."[32] Bormann was assured that there was no plan to let the Gypsies wander about in Reich territory; they were to be permitted to travel in a circumscribed area outside the Reich's boundaries, in groups controlled, presumably, by German police. It seems clear that Himmler had decided, in principle at least, to let these Roma live.

It also appears that, as a result of these discussions with Hitler, the rest of the German Roma were to be murdered after being used as a working force: on December 16, 1942, Himmler ordered all the Roma in the Reich not included in the pure category (and some others) to be sent to concentration camps. Those who were not to be sent there would be sterilized (discussions held early in January 1943 between various branches of the S.S.). Thus, with the possible exception of the pure Roma, who would in any case not be permitted to stay in Germany, all the other Roma in the Reich would be "removed," whether by murder or by sterilization.

Here I must point to two major differences between the treatment of Jews and the treatment of Roma. In the Jewish case, the main murderous attack was on Jews who had three or four Jewish grandparents. "Half-Jews" (*Mischlinge*) had a chance of survival because the Nazis were unsure how to deal with them.[33] By contrast, the main assault on the Roma was on the "half-breeds," because the danger, from a Nazi point of view, was one of penetration of Gypsy blood into the Aryan race. In principle, such mixing was possible because Roma were not Jews; but because mixing was undesirable, it had to be prevented. Hence, pure Roma in the Reich had a chance of survival; pure Jews did not.

A second point is much more important: the whole Gypsy problem was of marginal importance to the Nazi regime. Hitler himself appears to have mentioned the Gypsies twice only, both times during rambling afterdinner conversations. Once, on May 2, 1940, Hitler objected to the presence of Gypsies in the Wehrmacht and said that he would talk to Wilhelm Keitel about that, but the order to remove Gypsies from the army was not issued until February 1941. And on October 2, 1941, Hitler complained about the suffering of German peasants at the hands of Gypsies and opined that Hungarians were like Gypsies.[34] I have stated repeatedly that the Nazis saw in the Roma a marginal problem, and was attacked for having said that *I* thought they were a marginal problem; this, of course, is nonsense. It is simply a fact that the Jews were, *for the Nazis*, the central enemy, a metahistorical satan who had to be destroyed. Roma, *for the Nazis*, were a minor irritant, and, as with other social problems, the tendency for the Nazi regime was to solve it by murder.

Roma living in the Reich were but a very small minority of the European Roma. Michael Zimmermann has examined a great amount of material on the Roma living in other European countries. Although new findings may change the conclusions he reached, his conclusions are well worth repeating. In Serbia, which was the first country where *all* Jews were murdered, massacres of Roma and Jewish men occurred. The first massacre was a reprisal for the killing of German soldiers by partisans. Then all Jewish men and, later, women and children as well were murdered, and also some Roma, using the same location for both Jews and Roma. On December 8, 1941, a camp was established at Semlin, next to the Roma settlement near Belgrade, and between 6,280 and 7,500 Jews, including women and children, were incarcerated there, along with 292 Roma women and children. The Jews were murdered; the Roma families were released.[35] There were 115,000 Roma in Serbia in 1943. By the end of the war, about 1,000, mainly men, had been killed by the Germans. Although many of the others suffered and died in the course of the war, including some as victims of anti-partisan German atrocities and some as partisans and soldiers, the vast majority survived.

The real test of Roma-related policies comes in the occupied Soviet territories. Orders given to the Einsatzgruppen in August 1941 apparently extended the murder from Jews and Communists to Roma. But three Einsatzgruppen, A, B, and C, did not look for Roma, so relatively few Roma were victimized. By contrast, Otto Ohlendorf's group D murdered "all" Gypsies "because they were not settled," which would indicate that he targeted wandering Roma, not settled ones, although there is no clear corroborating evidence.[36] In the Crimea, settled Roma were murdered as well as wanderers (by Ohlendorf's men, mainly): 824 Roma, plus 17,645 Jews in late 1941, and an additional 1,583 Roma, some of whom were probably settled, and about 10,000 Jews in early 1942, for a total of 31,000.[37]

Yet, slowly, a different policy evolved. On November 21, 1941, the general commanding the rear areas on the Northern Front decreed that "settled Gypsies, who have been living in the same place for two years, and are under no political or criminal suspicion, should be left alone."[38] There were exceptions, such as the commander of the 339th Infantry Division, who wanted to kill all Gypsies. But from early 1942 on, the general policy, as Zimmermann shows for the Baltic region, was to differentiate between settled and wandering Roma, though in practice, in Latvia for instance, this distinction was not necessarily made until April 1942, when the commander of the Order Police (Ordnungspolizei, or ORPO), Karl Friedrich Knecht, decided that "only vagabond Gypsies" should be exterminated. As a result, almost one-half of Latvia's 3,800 Roma died. Especially in Estonia, the new policy came too late to save the small local Roma population.[39] The Ostministerium (responsible for civilian administration in the Baltic areas and parts of Belarus) run by Alfred Rosenberg provides a good example of this wavering policy. In 1942 it was decided not to differentiate between settled and wandering Roma. Then on May 11, 1943, when an order suggested by the local administration was sent to Berlin for review, Himmler made it clear that "settled Gypsies should be treated like the local population."[40] For occupied Poland, Himmler, through the commander of the Order Police there, on August 13, 1942, ordered that there should in principle be no police intervention against settled Gypsies.[41] That such decisions left a great deal of room for murderous initiatives is obvious. A Polish historian, Jerzy Ficowski, quoted by Zimmermann, claims that out of 28,000 Roma in Poland, 8,000 were murdered.[42] If now, fifty years later, according to incomplete information, there are considerably more than

100,000 Roma in Poland, the figure of 28,000 prewar Roma is problematic; it would appear that more research is needed.

Probably the only area where no distinction between settled and wandering Roma was made was Croatia, where between 25,000 and 50,000 Roma were murdered. There, however, the initiative most certainly was not German but local. The Croat fascist regime under Ante Pavelic murdered hundreds of thousands of Serbs, tens of thousands of Roma, and some 35,000 Jews, with the Germans looking on benignly—there was no need for them to intervene or guide. Only with the Jews did the Germans "help": the remnants of Croat Jews were deported to death camps in Poland.[43] In Romania, the local fascist regime deported some 20,000–26,000 Roma (out of 300,000), not soldiers or craftsmen, to Transnistria, the Romanian-administered area between the Dniester and the Bug in occupied Ukraine, along with 170,000 Jews. Of the deported Roma, 8,000–9,000 are estimated to have died, although one, not very reliable Romanian source says a total of 36,000 Roma died in Romania during the war.[44] The losses in Slovakia and Hungary were small by comparison and took place in the final stages of the war, with their attendant confusion and the increased brutality of the withdrawing German armies.

In accordance with Himmler's orders, 22,600 Roma were deported to Auschwitz, some 81 percent of whom came from the Reich and the "Protectorate" (the Czech lands) and 6 percent from Poland. The Auschwitz records show that more than 5,600 were gassed, and more than 13,600 died of hunger, disease, and exhaustion. Of the German and Austrian Roma, 2,500 were sterilized, which was an indescribable disaster, in a sense worse than death, in terms of the Roma culture. In addition, 5,007 Austrian Roma who were deported to the Jewish ghetto of Łódź died at Chelmno, and of the 2,330 deported to Poland from Germany in the early stages, over 50 percent died, as did half of the about 1,000 Roma from the Reich detained in various concentration camps. In all, about 15,000 German and 8,250 Austrian Roma died (out of a total of 37,000, excluding for our purposes those defined by Ritter as Germans behaving like Gypsies). Whether those who were not killed were pure Gypsies or more Gypsy than German is not clear.

Zimmermann provides no overall figure of Roma losses, but if we add up the figures for individual European countries contained in his research, we arrive at a grand total of about 150,000. Because we do not know how many Roma there were in 1939, we cannot estimate the losses in percentages.[45]

I wish to repeat that there is no gradation of suffering and that the number of victims does not determine the cruelty of the onslaught. Clearly, the Nazis wanted to eliminate the Roma as an identifiable group of people, the bearers of a culture. They carried out this policy by mass murder, humiliation, and the utmost brutality and sadism. Within the Reich, this meant total elimination, by murder, sterilization, or deportation. Outside the Reich, after a period of hesitation and mixed signals, wandering Roma were murdered, whereas settled Roma were, by and large, left alone.

What we have here is a genocide, not a Holocaust, that is, not an intent, nor its implementation (as far as the perpetrator managed to complete it), to murder every single individual of the targeted population on a global scale. The Nazis did not intend to murder all the Roma. In fact, Himmler writes in his appointment diary, on April 20, 1942, after a meeting with Hitler, *"Keine Vernichtung der Zigeuner"* (No extermination of the Gypsies).[46] The view expressed so often by various historians that the Germans planned to annihilate all Roma is wrong.

I have devoted some attention to the comparison of the Holocaust with the genocide of the Roma because of what I believe to be an erroneous interpretation that is gaining ground in the literature about genocide. The root of the error might be expressed in the very legitimate question What is the point in emphasizing differences when the parallels, especially the basic fact of the mass murder, are so obvious? There are a couple of answers. One is that if we consider all brutality and murder to be the same, there is no point in making any difference between mass murder, genocide, and, say, the amok killing of children in a Scottish village by a disturbed individual: all victims of murder would be classified alike. We differentiate for a pragmatic reason: to facilitate the struggle against all these kinds of murder. Just as we cannot fight cholera, typhoid, and cancer with the same medicine, mass murder for political reasons has to be fought differently than genocides and Holocausts.

That leads us to a second reason why the differences should be analyzed: by learning what has happened last time, we learn not only about the perpetrators but also about the so-called bystanders and about the behavior of the victim populations and their leadership groups under this kind of ultimate threat. Acquiring knowledge makes clear the dialectic relationship between the particularism and the universalism of the horror. The Holocaust happened to a particular people for particular reasons at a particular time. All historical events are concrete in this manner: they happen with particular people for particular reasons at particular times. They are not repeated exactly but approximately and with the same characteristics of particularity. And that is exactly what makes them of universal significance. What happened before can happen again. We all are possible victims, possible perpetrators, possible bystanders. With Rwanda, Cambodia, former Yugoslavia, and other places, most of us *are* bystanders, who have so far learned very little from the past. The Holocaust is a warning. It adds three commandments to the ten of the Jewish-Christian tradition: *Thou shalt not be a perpetrator; Thou shalt not be a passive victim;* and *Thou most certainly shalt not be a bystander.* We do not know whether we will succeed in spreading this knowledge. But if there is even a chance in a million that sense should prevail, we have a moral obligation, in the spirit of Kantian moral philosophy, to try.

chapter four
Overall Interpretations: Zygmunt Bauman,
Jeffrey Herf, Goetz Aly

The beginning of Holocaust histori-
ography is marked by attempts to deal with the destruction of the Jews
of Europe in an overall, general manner. This is true mainly of the first
great pioneers of Holocaust research: Gerald Reitlinger, Joseph Tennenbaum, Raul Hilberg, Karl Schleunes, Dietrich Uwe Adam, and some
others.[1] Basically, all their attempts concentrated on explaining how the
German National Socialist state organized the murder of the Jews. In
other words, they dealt mainly with the perpetrators, and the research
was based largely on German documentary materials. Later the first
attempts were made to describe the way Jews reacted. The initial publication was probably Philip Friedman's *Their Brothers' Keepers*,[2] but
he was not followed until very much later, when Isaiah Trunk published his *Judenrat*.[3] Important breakthroughs were made with books
by Yisrael Gutman on the Jews of Warsaw, Michael Marrus and Robert
Paxton on the Jews of France, and Louis de Jong and Jacob Presser on
Holland, among others.[4] In the United States a number of books dealing

with the American attitude toward the destruction of Europe's Jews were published, from Arthur Morse's *While Six Million Died* to the two volumes by David S. Wyman describing and analyzing American policies from 1933 to 1941 and beyond.[5] A pioneering attempt by Joshua A. Sherman in Britain to deal with British policies was followed by Bernard Wasserstein's authoritative *Britain and the Jews of Europe*.[6] Other books dealt with Switzerland, Palestinian Jewry and its relation to the catastrophe—Dina Porat's English translation, *The Blue and Yellow Star of David*, of her Hebrew volume comes to mind—and with other crucial but specific issues.[7]

The books dealing with the German attack on the Jews were considered by many to be general descriptions of the Holocaust, which they were not. The total picture should have included the Jews themselves (and their life both before and during the Holocaust), the host nations in Europe and their relations with the Jews, the churches, the Allies, the Jews in the free world, and the neutrals, to mention just some of the main issues.

After the early 1960s, after Reitlinger's and Hilberg's publications appeared, a hiatus occurred, and emphasis moved to exploration of specific themes, countries, populations, organizations, and so on. In the last couple of decades, this has changed somewhat, and again a number of books have been written that try to analyze and explain the Holocaust as a whole.[8]

In this context it is important to comment on some of the salient ideas in two important books: Zygmunt Bauman's *Modernity and the Holocaust* and Jeffrey Herf's *Reactionary Modernism*.[9]

Bauman's contribution is especially significant. He is a sociologist, a Polish Jewish academic who fled his country of birth in the wake of anti-Jewish persecutions by the communist government of Poland and who now teaches in Britain, where he has become a respected writer and commentator on sociological theories and analyses. In the book discussed here, Bauman submits contemporary sociology to a devastating critique, arguing that by not dealing with the Holocaust in a systematic way it has missed a centrally important aspect of the social structures of modern society. Although he does not define what he means by modernity, he clearly sees it as being characterized by a rational allocation of resources, by a constantly developing technology that becomes a central hub of civilization, and, most importantly perhaps, by a bureaucratic culture, almost a way of life, of which the *Endlösung* (Final Solution) was an outcome. Bureaucratic culture means the hierarchically controlled rational way piecemeal decisions are taken, decisions that together create the *Gestalt* of state policy. The Holocaust was, he says, indicative of the negative face of modernity, not the one presented by an optimistic, positivist sociology that saw in modern, civilized society a barrier to mass murder. Bauman emphasizes—as does Hilberg—the assumption that the Holocaust was caused by a modern bureaucracy. Not all modern bureaucracies are like the one that produced the Holocaust, but no aspect of modernity would prevent a bureaucracy from bringing it about. Modern civilization, says Bauman, was not the sufficient condition for the Holocaust; it was, however, its necessary condition.[10] And he quotes Richard Rubenstein: "It bears witness to the advance of civilization."[11]

Relying on the functionalist school of thought, and mainly on *The Twisted Road to Auschwitz* by Karl Schleunes, whose name he consistently misspells, he argues that the choice of physical extermination as the right means to the task of "removing" (*entfernen*) the Jews was a product of routine, rational, bureaucratic procedures. It was untrue that bureaucracy *must* result in Holocaust-style phenomena; however, the fact that the rules of instrumental rationality were singularly incapable of preventing them is explained by the statement, to which there can hardly be any exception, that bureaucratic decisions have no intrinsic moral values and are indeed totally removed from any moral calculus.

Bauman repeats what others have said before him, namely, that the bureaucrat does not develop guilt feelings because he is usually not immediately responsible for the results of his actions (the fact, by the way, that he exclusively uses the masculine gender to describe bureaucracy reflects the real situation of a patriarchal society in which women were not employed as bureaucrats, but of course large numbers of German women are found among the perpetrators). Such actions cover only a small portion of the largely anonymous procedure that ultimately leads to murder; consequently, the bureaucrat rarely grasps the whole picture of which he is but a small part.[12]

It is difficult to see in these statements anything but a further, admittedly forceful and well-argued repetition of theses presented in Raul Hilberg's monumental *Destruction of the European Jews* some thirty years earlier. The difference would seem to lie in Bauman's attempt to do what Hilberg was very careful not to do: to answer the question of what motivated the bureaucracy to do what it did.

Antisemitism, says Bauman, is no answer. Being perpetual and ubiquitous, antisemitism cannot by itself account for the Holocaust's uniqueness, just as resentment generally is not in itself a satisfactory explanation of any (other) genocide. The Holocaust was something new, he avers, whereas antisemitism is old, so the latter cannot explain the former. In Germany, antisemitism was a poor second to the antisemitism prevalent in many other European nations. And yet, Bauman says, that antisemitism, too, was an "admittedly necessary," though not a sufficient, condition for the Holocaust. He quotes Norman Cohn, who says that the presence of "professional Jew-killers" was "not unconnected" to antisemitism.[13] In other words, when people murder Jews, this may indeed have something to do with their not particularly liking them.

Antisemitism is, in Bauman's view, a matter of drawing social boundaries based on feelings of fear and revulsion for the Jews' "homelessness" and the additional fear of the foreigner in society's midst. In premodern society, he claims, there was a measure of accommodation to the existence of the Jews; they had a place, however lowly, in Christian society, as a people who were coextensive with Christians. In fact, he argues, the self-identity of Christianity was based on the estrangement of the Jews. His historical analysis of antisemitism centers on the

illogicality and mythicality of Christian antisemitism, and it is not at all
clear where the fear and the boundary drawing come in, nor which is
primary: Christian theology (explained in historical or psychological
terms, or both) or social, sociopsychological, or economic factors. The
Jews, he says, served to define and unify Christianity; they were a potent
demonic force that was, above all, frightening. "[Christianity] endowed
the Jews with a powerful and sinister fascination they would otherwise
hardly possess."[14] This fascination persisted into modern times, when
Jews were (are?) perceived as embodiments of inner demons whose
exorcisms were officially disallowed and forced underground. There
emerged the "conceptual Jew," the stereotype, which was firmly removed from the real Jewish individuals who inhabited the spaces of
Christian Europe.[15]

Bauman picks up well-established analyses of antisemitism in his
argument. The Jewish stereotype and its historical development was
analyzed in depth by such historians as Shmuel Ettinger, Chaim Hillel
Ben-Sasson, and Jacob Katz, none of whom Bauman mentions. His lack
of clarity regarding the place occupied by ideology, specifically Christian theology, makes his analysis more rather than less problematic.

In an odd passage, he notes the fatal social role of the Jewish middle-
men in Eastern Europe, presumably in the early modern period. The
peasants saw them as exploiters and attacked them, while the nobles
saw them as servants, whom they despised (this actually was the situation in Polish-occupied Ukrainian areas in the seventeenth and eighteenth centuries and to some extent in Poland itself). Bauman ascribes
this discovery of role and consequences to a contemporary Polish
scholar in Lublin by the name of Anna Zuk.[16] He was apparently unaware that such analyses are very old indeed, going back to such historians as Meier Balaban, Emmanuel Ringelblum, Raphael Mahler,
Shmuel Ettinger, Israel Halperin, and a host of others who flourished
between the thirties and the sixties of the twentieth century. What role
this socioeconomic analysis plays in the overall history of antisemitism
is unclear. According to Bauman, that history, at least in Christian

Europe, seems to have been based on irrational and unexplained mythic elements (but he never so much as mentions theological developments). He says that the fate of the Jews epitomized the awesome scope of social upheaval. Although this may well be true for both the premodern and the modern ages, the link between that statement and the ones about Christian antisemitism remains wobbly indeed. And if antisemitism is no explanation for the Holocaust, why does he expend so much effort on explaining it? Bauman is hardly an expert on the subject, so why does he expose himself to justified criticism for doing a superficial job at best?

Beginning with Marx and the identification of Jews with capitalism, antisemitism became, in Bauman's view, a modern ideology. But, he then argues, with a great deal of justice, it seems, that premodern anti-semitism was a "phobia" and that only the irony of history "would allow the anti-modernist phobias to be unloaded through channels and forms only modernity could develop."[17] Modernity gave antisemitism an outlet.

Bauman appears to link the interpretation of the Holocaust as a result of antisemitism, which he rejects, with what he sees as the proprietary attitude of mainly Jewish historians who see the Holocaust as the Jews' private property and who deny, in his view, the Holocaust's universal meaning. Who he means is not clear, because his admiration of Hilberg, Arendt, and Rubenstein, who are Jews, is obvious, but I have a sneaking suspicion that he means people like Yisrael Gutman and myself—in other words, Israeli historians. Certainly, the attitude of some Jewish historians is little more than sectarian, but that does not disqualify the argument about the unprecedented quality of the Holocaust by others, Jews or non-Jews. Bauman himself repeatedly and pointedly talks of the Holocaust as a unique phenomenon, as do non-Jewish historians, such as Christopher R. Browning, although they may be using different terms. There is something rather repellent in identifying a historian's ethnicity a priori with his or her views. Some historians, including myself in these chapters, have made the point that "uniqueness" (that is, unprecedentedness) and universality are intimately and dialectically connected; the very unprecedentedness of the Holocaust—that is, its specificity regarding the character of both the perpetrator and the victim—makes it of universal importance, because the ethnic or national or racial groups that could be future victims are as specific as the German Nazis and the Jews. Although the Holocaust has no precedent, it could become one.

As has been shown in these chapters, and Bauman appears to agree, the relatively mild anti-Jewishness of many Germans was a formidable obstacle to opposition to the genocidal attack on the Jews, but that moderate anti-Jewishness is no explanation for the Holocaust. Bauman here repeats findings of colleagues such as Sarah Gordon, Ian Kershaw, Otto Dov Kulka, and myself; he could have enlarged on this point, for most of the actual murderers had no specific background of antisemitic indoctrination or behavior, as Browning has shown.[18] But if, for Bauman, antisemitism does not provide a central explanation for the Holocaust, what does?

According to Bauman, no answer is to be found in ideology generally. He defines the role of ideology in modernity: "Modernity meant . . . a new role for ideas—because of the state relying for its functional efficiency on ideological mobilization."[19] In other words, ideology fulfills a purely instrumental function, which means either that the people who preach it don't believe in it and use it in a cynical fashion, or that they believe in what they say and use it as a tool for the mobilization of the masses. Bauman implies, although he does not say it, that the hidden mechanism that makes them believe something and that makes them use their belief as a tool is modernity. He says that modernity is a kind of monster independent of human willpower but that it has ideational direction. Bureaucracy "has a logic and a momentum of its own. Given an initial push (being confronted with a purpose)," it will act. Who provides that push and why remains unclear. In another passage he talks about "ideational processes" that, together with technical resources, have been conditioned, created, and supplied by modernity. Again, modernity is acting like a monster with a will of its own. On the one hand, it is directed by ideational processes, or ideologies; on the other hand, these processes, or ideologies, have at best a very secondary impact on reality. The question becomes, Who or what made the German bureaucracy commit the Holocaust? Were the processes entirely internal to the bureaucracy?

"It so happened in Germany half a century ago," Bauman says, "that bureaucracy was given the task of making Germany *judenrein* ["pure of Jews"]."[20] What does he mean by "it so happened"? Who gave bureaucracy the task? And why did nobody give that task to British or American bureaucracies? Why did they not cause a Holocaust—were they unaffected by modernity?

In the final analysis, how does Bauman explain the Holocaust? How do the necessary conditions add up to a sufficient combination? Bauman says that it was caused by "the short circuit"—does he mean a chance encounter?—"between an ideologically obsessed power elite and the tremendous facilities of rational, systemic action developed by modern society," and such a short circuit "may happen relatively seldom."[21] So the Holocaust was a rare case in which ideology and modernity, in the form of a power elite—in other words, a dictatorship—worked toward destruction. Would it be unkind to ask, So what else is new?

Bauman admits that there can be democratic or pluralistic modernisms. But if so, modernity as such does not explain why dictatorships that are ruled by ideologically obsessed power elites come into existence. Because the United States and Britain were no less modern than Nazi Germany, factors other than modernity must explain why a Hitler regime arose in Germany and decided to murder the Jews. But if Bauman talks about dictatorships, what about Italy? Why didn't the Italian dictatorship and its bureaucracy, the Italian army, and even parts of the Fascist Party join in what the German bureaucrats were doing? Bauman rejects the *Sonderweg* (discrete path) explanation, that is, the view that a uniquely German way led to Nazism and World War II. The problem was not Germany, he says, but modernity, which we have just shown is no explanation at all. But if the problem was not Germany, how does one explain Italy? Or, how does one explain that the Japanese rejected the Gestapo suggestion to murder the 18,000 or so Jews in the Hongkew ghetto in Shanghai? Could it be that in both Italy and Japan there was no "ideational" push against the Jews? Italian fascism did have a push against Black Ethiopians, and Japanese ideology a push against Chinese and Koreans. This would mean that the ideational or ideological push was the crucial and decisive element—which takes us back to Bauman's earlier argument, already disposed of. His analysis, brilliant though it is, is ultimately unsatisfactory and contradictory.

Bauman's definitions are vague. When he talks about genocide being the product of modernity, he includes the Stalinist purges and the deportation of the kulaks among the genocides, thus making a hash of the concept, because he contradicts not just the U.N. definition of 1948 but any suggested definition of genocide, without offering one of his own. Generally, he appears to draw fairly close parallels between the Stalinist and the Hitlerite regimes, yet he insists on the "uniqueness" of the Holocaust. In the end, with Bauman, every mass murder becomes a genocide; from his imprecise use of the term one gets the impression that he has no clear idea what genocide is. Thus, when he talks about genocides being the products of modernity, he mentions the mass murders committed by the Mongols as horrors committed as part of invasions aimed at pillage, not genocides, because they were not bureaucratically planned destructions of populations. I doubt whether Genghis Khan would have agreed that his conquests did not include planned destructions of populations—in Isfahan, Persia, for instance, and other places. Pillage was a by-product (as with the Nazis), the main purpose being control of territories and exploitation of riches.

Or one might take the total annihilation of the Caribs, mentioned in the previous chapter, as an example. A large proportion died from diseases, but a significant remnant were worked to death and murdered after suffering terribly. This was obviously counterproductive from a purely rational point of view, because the Spaniards needed laborers for their plantations and mines. Yet it was for these very "modern" reasons that the Spaniards worked them to death, against their own best interest. On the other hand, there is no doubt that the motive of maximizing profits was at work in an exclusivist power structure. Are we then to say that modernity was active in producing genocide in the sixteenth century? Was there no ideology at all, Christian, say, that gave part of the "push"? So we have a genocide, in a supposedly premodern era, produced by modern, largely economic motivations, directed by a bureaucracy, and justified by a totalitarian religious ideology. Bauman's conclusion, according to his own analysis, should really be that the Holocaust was not unique at all. And if it was, it was not because of the arguments that he offers.

Bauman repeats Hilberg's analysis of the reaction of the victims. The moment that Jewish leadership groups accepted positions of responsibility under Nazi supervision, they objectively became part of the machinery that destroyed the Jews of Europe. There is no value judgment involved. They could have been very worthy individuals trying their best to handle an impossible situation. Bauman relies on Isaiah Trunk's work of the late sixties and early seventies, completely disregarding anything that followed. The famous pictures of starvation in Warsaw and Łódź are taken as the only norm. The fact that there was no starvation in Czestochowa, Kaunas (Kovno), Siauliai (Shavli), Bialystok, Grodno, and so on, is ignored, and the fact that Judenräte in many of the Polish and Lithuanian ghettos were not asked for and did not deliver lists of Jews is mentioned only in passing. Hannah Arendt's conclusion that had there been no Judenräte, the Germans would have faced serious problems is restated despite the fact that many of the Soviet territories had no Judenräte, and the destruction was even more efficient there than in Poland. Yet Bauman says that the Judenräte "secured the smooth flow of the annihilation process by appointing the objects of its successive stages, delivered the selected objects to the sites from which they could be collected with a minimum of fuss."[22] The implication is that all the Judenräte did this, which is true of Łódź but not, for instance, of

Warsaw, where the Judenrat disintegrated after the suicide of its head,
Adam Czerniakow, at the beginning of the deportation, and the collaboration was done by the much hated Jewish police, which then itself was
deprived of its power by the underground. Elsewhere, for instance in
most east Polish ghettos, the Judenrat had no part in the deportation,
because the Germans handled it themselves. In many smaller places the
Judenräte refused to cooperate at all in any way.

From Bauman's description one would assume that the German bureaucratic machinery was efficient and "modern." It wasn't. It often
was a fumbling, ineffective, contradiction-ridden machine, where each
fiefdom in the Nazi state had its own interests and fought against everyone else to preserve them. The functionalist historians whom Bauman admires have indeed shown us how inefficient the bureaucracy
was, precisely because it acted in the framework of a dictatorship; the
unique efficiency they showed in destroying the Jews, often for pseudopragmatic reasons, really showed the remarkable impact of ideology on
them. They did not need schooling in antisemitism in order to conclude
that the annihilation of the Jews was a primary aim of the regime with
which they enthusiastically identified. Bauman's book appeared before
the total collapse of the Soviet regime, but he could today show how the
dictatorship there collapsed under its own weight. Because of total
German military and police dominance, the Nazi dictatorship overcame
problems of inherent inefficiency by using brute force, not unlike the
Mongols in the thirteenth century. It is the combination of modern
means and brutal inefficiency that is so characteristic of much of the
Holocaust.

In the end, what matters to Bauman is the result: German bureaucracy won out, and the Jews were murdered; but we don't have to go to
the trouble of doing research to know that.

Of course, Bauman—and Hilberg, who is Bauman's teacher in this—
are quite correct in saying that the Judenräte became part of the machinery of destruction simply because they were established in the
framework of a Nazi-ruled Europe. But Bauman ignores two major con-

siderations. One is the non-Jewish context: In all the countries directly controlled by the Germans, local administrations were established or their existence confirmed. By operating in a German-controlled framework they became part of the German machinery of domination. In the non-Jewish cases the aim was subjection, enslavement, exploitation, control, though accompanied by brutal repressive measures escalating to mass murder (in the East, especially). In the Jewish case the aim in the end was total physical destruction. The Judenräte were founded in 1939–1941, *before* the annihilation was decided upon. Bauman does not make the comparison, although this is exactly what his discipline of sociology should have caused him to do. How many French, Belgian, Dutch, Polish, Czech, and other mayors, local bureaucrats, police chiefs, and others, even if they were personally opposed to Germany, rebelled against the Germans or openly contravened their orders—even though disobedience did not always bring direct deadly danger? Why should Bauman and Hilberg apply a yardstick to the Judenräte that differs so radically from what they would apply to non-Jewish administrations? And, when one considers the amount of coercion applied in both types of cases, were not the Judenräte in a much worse position, which made outright opposition a suicidal project? And yet outright opposition did take place in many cases.[23] Thus, for instance, the Minsk Judenrat, under Ilya Mishkin, joined an organized underground resistance group in the Minsk ghetto led by Hersh Smolar when that was established. Minsk was the fourth largest ghetto in Eastern Europe, with over 80,000 inmates at the beginning. I know of no parallel non-Jewish municipal or local government that engaged in a similar activity under German occupation.[24]

The second objection applies to another sphere altogether. The intentions and the policies of the victim elites have to be dealt with no less than their role in the German bureaucratic machine. The attempts of many of the Judenräte to defend the Jewish populations in a rational way were in part motivated by a mixture of rational and moral considerations. The reactions of Judenräte ranged from massive resistance to

total submission, from cynical disregard of the welfare of the people
they represented to total commitment—all of which is no less worthy of
analysis than is the objective fact of their becoming part of a machinery
of destruction whose aims they recognized too late, if at all. Thus, of a
total of 146 Polish Judenräte examined by Aharon Weiss because a
sufficient number of testimonies about them are available, 73.3 percent were unanimously evaluated positively by survivors. The Judenrat
heads resigned because they were unwilling to acquiesce in Nazi policies, or they were removed by the Germans for not carrying out orders,
or they refused to surrender the names of Jews and were therefore
killed, or they committed suicide, or they had connections with the
underground, or they combined more than one of these characteristics.[25] Bauman, who appears to be unaware of these problems, presents
a one-dimensional picture of hapless, collaborating sheep led to the
slaughter by an efficient bureaucratic machinery. Both sides of his equa-
tion are simplistic.

A fascinating example of the dilemmas faced by the Judenräte and
their collaborators in the Polish ghettos is provided by a case analyzed
by Shaul Esh in the 1960s.[26] An anti-Nazi German by the name of
Friedrich Hielscher wanted to find out what the Nazis were doing with
the Jews. He managed, on the flimsiest of pretexts, to get permission to
visit the ghetto of Łódź twice—in the fall of 1941 and in the spring of
1942. He briefly met with the head of the ghetto, Chaim Rumkowski,
and had important encounters with Leon Rosenblatt, the head of the
police, and Rabbi Yosef Feiner, both of them Rumkowski's collaborators.
In his postwar testimony, Hielscher quotes Rosenblatt as asking him
whether what he was doing was morally right. "I have to report each
week, when a new group of Jews arrives, on the number of Jews to be
transported out to—" He stopped talking, and Hielscher said: "To be
gassed." "You know?" asked Rosenblatt. He continued.

> All right, then. Good God, each day we ask ourselves, Is this true? But it
> is true. And I have to choose the people for this. If not, I will be shot.

That for me would be a simple solution. What will they do then? The
S.S. already told me: Then *they* will choose. That is, the strong ones,
the pregnant women, the Rabbis, the learned ones, the professors, the
poets—they will be the first for the oven. But if I stay where I am, I can
take the volunteers. Often they demand to be taken, and sometimes I
have as many as I have to deliver, and sometimes they are few, and then I
take the dying, that Jewish doctors tell me about, and if these do not
suffice, I take the seriously ill. If these, too, are not enough, what shall I
do? I can take the criminals—and, merciful God, who is not a criminal
here? . . . Who will be the judge? . . . Mr. Hielscher, I am but a miserable
Jew, from Lwów. I learned my business. I knew how to command my
artillery unit [as an Austrian officer in World War I]. I did not learn
what I have to do here. I asked the heads of the community, the Rabbis,
the learned people; all of them said: You did the right thing by staying at
your post . . . all of them agreed with me; nevertheless, I don't want to
live, Mr. Hielscher. I am asking you for God's sake, the God in whom you
believe: If you know a better way from the one I found, tell me, and I will
bless you day and night. And if you do not know a better way, then tell
me—should I remain on my post, or should I prefer to be killed.[27]

Hielscher answered after he had talked with the rabbi, who was of the
same opinion as Rosenblatt. This is what Hielscher said, according to
his testimony: "You did the right thing, so help me God. Carry on like
that. If you do that, you will have done the right thing before God, and I,
too, would not have done any differently."[28]

There are two problems here. The first is purely methodological: Can
one rely on Hielscher's testimony? No one was more meticulous in such
matters than Esh. He compared Hielscher's testimony with documentation about Łódź, as well as with other testimonies, and found that
Hielscher was reliable. Of course, the dialogue that Hielscher quotes
cannot be accurate. After all, Hielscher's book appeared twelve years
after the events he described. But it is more than probable that the
gist of the question and answer correspond to what transpired. When
Hielscher wrote down his account, and when his book was published, no
one talked in those terms—no one used them.

The second problem is substantive: One cannot talk in the terms that

Bauman uses without distorting historical reality. In the moral dilemma
that the Judenräte faced, no simple answers could be given. Rosenblatt
was much hated in Łódź. Rumkowski has been generally described as
something of a Jewish war criminal, who decided to play God and
knowingly delivered Jewish children to be murdered by the Nazis. I
myself tend to share that view. But he did have a point. Was he or was he
not right in assuming that by following the policy of accommodation, he
had a greater chance of ensuring his survival than if he had tried to
oppose, with utter powerlessness, the absolute local power that he had
to contend with? In fact, there is a higher percentage of survivors from
the Łódź ghetto than from most other places because, thanks in part to
Rumkowski's draconian policies, the Łódź ghetto was the last one in
Eastern Europe to be liquidated—the final murder occurred in August
1944. The people who were transported, in the last stages, to Chelmno
were all killed, but of the majority, who were deported to Auschwitz, a
large number were taken to the concentration camp to be slave workers
and thus had a higher chance of survival. Who is right—Rosenblatt,
Hielscher, and Rumkowski, or Bauman (and myself) and the vast majority of historians? Again, one has to warn against what Saul Friedländer
so aptly called closure. We are faced with insoluble (but perfectly explicable) dilemmas.

The last part of Bauman's book is devoted to a fascinating and valuable discussion of a possible sociology of morality. That is a different
discussion, though related to the one here, and I don't have enough of a
sociological background to comment on it.

In the end, then, Bauman does not deliver on his promise. He does not
offer a consistent explanation of the causes of the Holocaust because he
retreats from an untenable position: that modernity caused the Holocaust. His statement that modernity enabled the Holocaust to happen is
not new at all. He dismisses antisemitism and ideology as leading causes
only to come back to them half-heartedly, attributing the Holocaust to a
combination of ideology and modernity. He considers the Holocaust to
have been a unique case of genocide, but for what appear to be the wrong

reasons. Like some others, who will be discussed later, he never mentions the term *consensus*. It is clear, however, that he is aware that a murderous consensus was created in German society. Who, then, or what caused this consensus to emerge within the framework of modernity? Why in Germany and not in France? Why the Jews, and not the proverbial *Radfahrer* (bicycle riders, as in the famous German joke: Who is responsible for the ills of the world? Answer: The Jews and the bicycle riders. Question: Why the bicycle riders? Answer: Why the Jews?). Is there something special about Nazism *within* modernity? What is it?

Bauman's insistence on the German state as the vehicle through which the murderous bureaucracy exercised its rational choices is, in my view, flawed in principle. The dream of German Nazis, the ideological dream, was to establish a *Volksgemeinschaft* (folk, or national, community) based on a *Volkswille* (folk, or national, will) embodied in the Party and the Führer, but the legalistic ways of the modern state were in the way. A famous agreement between Nazi Justice Minister Otto Thierack and Himmler (September 18, 1942), which practically barred the judicial system from dealing with most acts that were considered crimes in Nazi Germany and left such matters in the hands of the S.S., is a good example of this tendency.[29] The Prussian bureaucratic state became a hindrance to this attempt to realize a utopia; in essence, the Nazis turned against the state.[30] The conclusion that Bauman could not reach because he failed to grasp the core of the Nazi attempt to rebel against Western culture may well be that a bureaucracy that becomes the slave of an elite group imbued with an anti-state ideology may be just as efficient in pursuing genocidal aims as is an ordinary state bureaucracy. Herein lies, I think, one of the main differences between Nazism and Italian fascism. Italian fascism idolized the state; National Socialism wanted to degrade it in favor of its *Volksgemeinschaft*. The customary term for the Nazi regime in Germany, *Faschismus* (fascism), which is a throwback to Marxist interpretations, is erroneous. Had Nazism been only a *Faschismus*, events might have developed differently.

My colleague and friend Hans Mommsen has criticized these observations of mine by arguing that I seem to be defending the Prussian state. I seem to be arguing in favor of the German state as against the Nazi ideal of the *Volksgemeinschaft*, which gives ammunition to contemporary German nationalists. I beg to differ. One does not have to be an ardent defender of the Prussian-German bureaucracy to realize that the Nazis wanted to put an anti-normative norm, the Party's free-floating and arbitrary rule that the Führer's wish was the law, in place of *any* norm, even one laid down through Nazi laws—they did not want to be fettered by any legal restraints. As Uta Gerhardt wrote : "The intent of the Nazi rule was not to respect the tradition of the incorruptible and upright civil service but to destroy it and replace it with an ideological party bureaucracy."[31] The way Hitler undermined the relative autonomy of the Wehrmacht is—contra Mommsen—an excellent example. But I do not mean to say that Prussian bureaucracy—autocratic, closed, antisemitic, ultraconservative, imperialistic—was anything but what it was.

Jeffrey Herf's comments on the same problem provide a series of insights that for a historian, again, may not be that new, but that are, at least in large part, consistent with our knowledge of the development of industrialized modern states. He says that in Germany industrial development and a weak liberal tradition were in a unique combination, which formed the background for another combination: of an aesthetically conceived technological culture with a romanticist, racist, and nationalist approach harking back to a supposed golden age and looking forward to a global hegemony, also conceived in aestheticized formulations. I am not at all sure that this combination that Herf describes, I think correctly, is so unique to Germany. There are interesting similarities—and differences as well—in the development of modern Japan. There, a combination of the southern aristocracy (the daimyo), who had maintained a rebellious attitude toward the Tokugawa shogunate for centuries, combined with samurai elements to produce a new ruling class looking back to traditional Japanese culture and forward to a technological revolution guided by a subservient bureaucracy using the same rational methods as those described by Bauman. One might even mention the not unsuccessful prerevolutionary tsarist efforts in Russia to combine modern industrialization with traditional aristocratic rule guided by a reactionary ideology as an additional possible parallel.

Nazism, says Herf, sought the triumph of the spirit and the will over reason (*Triumph of the Will*, the name of Leni Riefenstahl's wildly successful documentary on the Nazi Party Congress of 1934, is the classic example of Nazi propaganda), of the free creative spirit, guided by the healthy *volk* instincts, over bourgeois morality. Nazism attempted to reach beyond morality in the belief that aesthetic experience alone justifies life. The racial soul was expressed in aesthetically conceived trains and highways. An irrational ideology guided rational decision making. The interesting point here is that this system resulted in technological backwardness, including failures in producing and utilizing necessary innovations even in the development of the weaponry needed in the pursuit of war. Romantic technology as "the flaming illumination of reality" failed in the end. Contrary to Bauman, whose description of Nazi Germany is, ultimately, that of a technically successful system, Herf points out that Nazi Germany's modernisms were, in many cases, total failures.

Hitler talked about the synthesis between the Greek spirit and Germanic technology, but the synthesis did not work from a purely utilitarian, rational point of view. Nazi modernism, then, was rational and, in Bauman's terms, modernistic, but only in appearance. Actually, it was an antimodern modernism because it was guided by a reactionary ideology. Herf explicitly supports the intentionalist interpretation of Nazism and the Holocaust because he considers the politics of Nazism to have been the central decisive element in the regime; and politics were guided by Nazi ideology. This combination of technology and irrationalism was not inherent to modernism, capitalism, or the Enlightenment; rather, it was a variation that was peculiar to an authoritarian, antiliberal and enlightenment-less nationalism. The destruction of the Jews would, in Nazi eyes, remove the two main evils of modernity—

capitalism and communism—and bring about the realization of the Nazi utopia.

Herf, therefore, comes down heavily in favor of an interpretation of Nazism as being the result, first and foremost, of a certain ideological approach taken by an elite that attained rule over a modern industrial society. I am much closer to Herf than to Bauman. Bauman either re-states the obvious or leaves us with vague formulations. In the end, he does not come down decisively in favor of interpreting Nazism and the Holocaust as a result of modernism, because then he would have to explain why the only modernist state or society that produced the horror was the German variation. He has to say that a combination of modernism and ideational processes, that is, ideology, won out. The ideological perspective of the ruling elite was antisemitic. How tradi-tional antisemitism became the racist variety, where the continuity lies and where the novel elements, neither Bauman nor Herf discusses. But all those who want to divorce the Holocaust from antisemitism arrive at a dead end. Love of Jews or indifference to them did not produce the Holocaust.

A final observation is in order about the concept of modernism itself. It is unclear, contradictory, and to my mind useless. How useless it is, is demonstrated unintentionally by Bauman himself.

Another attempt at a general analysis of the Holocaust is presented in a book by the preeminent German historian Goetz Aly. Aly is an aca-demic outsider—he never received a permanent job at a university, al-though his qualifications are more impressive than those of many who populate the German academia. His book is called *Endlösung* (Final Solution).[32] The title is misleading: *Endlösung* deals not with the Holo-caust but with the decision-making process leading up to it. In this, the presentation is in line with most of German historiography, which in a way avoids the murder itself and instead agonizes over who decided what and when regarding the murder of the Jews. Aly deals with the period between the outbreak of war in 1939 and the massive acts of murder in 1942 as the time during which the decision to exterminate the Jews was taken. His conclusions are novel and instructive and based on as impressive an array of documentation as one may imagine. He argues that the annihilation of the Jews fitted in with the Nazi attempt to reorganize the ethnic map of Eastern Europe in accordance with their ideas. They wanted to transfer all the ethnic Germans from the Baltic states, from eastern Poland (Volhynia), and ultimately the Balkans and the Soviet Union back into an expanding Reich. They wanted to add to the mix landless German peasants (especially the younger sons of small peasants) in order not to cause the splitting of farms into nonviable agricultural enterprises. These millions would receive land on the new eastern marches of Germany, thus ensuring the spread of Germandom and with it the supremacy of Germany in Europe. This was the practical translation of the Nazi dream of *Lebensraum*—living space—for the German people. The resettlement meant the displacement of non-German populations—mainly Polish, but also Jewish and Roma.

Aly describes, in impressive detail, the unsuccessful attempts of the Nazis to find land and jobs for the returning Germans—in the first instance, those from the Baltic states. The Jews were initially affected less by the deportations than were the Poles, because they were not, by and large, peasants, and they owned little land. The Roma who were to be deported were all the Sinti and Roma from Germany. But there was nowhere to push these hundreds of thousands of Poles, Jews, and Roma, not to mention the millions called for in maximalist German plans. The only place to which they could be sent was the rump area of Poland, the Generalgouvernement (G.G.), ruled by the Nazi lawyer Hans Frank. Aly describes the evolution of German policy vis-à-vis the G.G. Very soon, in the interest of rational colonial exploitation, Frank came to regard these deportations negatively: they disrupted the economy, and created chaotic conditions, making economic and social planning impracticable. He got the support of Göring. In the struggle between the fiefdoms, Hitler had to yield and permit two of his satraps, Frank and Göring, successfully to resist the third, Himmler. The process was slow and arduous and involved the suffering of huge numbers of people, who were, despite Frank's objections, shoved into the G.G. Many tens of thousands of Jews were included among hundreds of thousands of Poles. There was nowhere to put these Poles, and the "natural" solution was to crowd the Jews into ghettos to make a place for the Poles—and for the large numbers of German officials and army personnel who descended upon the Polish territory.

Aly weaves into his masterly description of a bungling German administration the horrors of "euthanasia," referred to earlier—the planned murder of about 100,000 German handicapped persons, some three-quarters of whom were killed prior to August 1941, when officially their murder was stopped because of protests by the churches and Party members (the rest were murdered after that, in stealth). In east Germany and the annexed territories, the murder of handicapped people created space for German settlers from the Baltic states and were in part motivated by this consideration. But it did not solve the problem of where to put the large number of settlers.

Ultimately, the decision to murder the Jews resulted from the pressure of the middle stratum of German officials: the population experts, the economists, and local governors. They did not know what to do with the masses of Jews now crowded into ghettos. These ghettos had been established as purely temporary solutions to the Jewish "problem," because it was expected that all Jews would be removed from the German Reich—and, later, all of Europe—after the German victory. But the temporary situation slowly became a permanent one, because Britain did not surrender, and the war continued. The Jews became an economic burden, because all possibility of gainful employment had been taken from them, and their utilization as forced laborers who were fed starvation rations proved counterproductive and was abandoned after thousands of Jewish laborers died. The ghetto inhabitants thus became a surplus population that, in accordance with the increasingly brutal and murderous Nazi mind-set, had to be annihilated. The Final Solution, then, resulted from an impasse into which an expansionist and imperialist policy had maneuvered the Nazi empire.

Aly is—or perhaps was—an extreme functionalist, at least until Gold-hagen apparently convinced him otherwise. He explains that there was no overall plan, no central decision to murder the Jews. The logic inherent in the bureaucratic failure to rearrange the ethnic map of Eastern Europe led inexorably to the murderous solution, which was enthusiastically accepted in the upper and middle strata of German society. Racist ideology generally, and antisemitism particularly, is an essential part of the background, but it cannot explain the Holocaust by itself. For Aly, the technological intelligentsia and the bureaucrats were responsible for the murder, and they were motivated by rational considerations. The rulers agreed with their recommendations, and German society accepted the idea of removing all those who did not fit the racist ideals. The direct cause of the Holocaust was the failure of the clerks to achieve demographic change.

Aly, even more than Bauman, sees only the perpetrators. Poles, Jews, and Roma are treated as passive victims. As with Bauman, there are no foreign powers, no churches, no history, not even an analysis of Nazism. In 1939, Nazism existed, and Aly does not ask how it came to be.

Aly's contribution is important. He adds an element that was missing from the picture: the demographic plans of the Nazis, the failure of their implementation, and their possible impact on Nazi anti-Jewish policies. Yet even within the narrow focus of his thesis, serious problems arise. If the problem of German resettlement in the eastern marches of the Reich was the motive for the murder of the Jews, why did the Germans deport to their death the Jews of Corfu and Rhodes, or those from Narvik in Norway and Bayonne in France? Why did they want to murder the Jews who had found refuge in Shanghai? Because they wanted to settle Germans in the Poznań (Posen) district? Hardly. And if they wanted to evict Poles in Poznań to make room for Germans, and if there was no place for the Poles unless Jews were forced into ghettos and later killed, why kill the Jews and not all bald-headed men and red-haired women? And why did the murder campaign begin, not in Poland, but in the occupied areas of the Soviet Union, including the Baltic states, which the German settlers had already left? Surely not to resettle them. Why, on the other hand, did the Nazis leave the Jews in the Łódż ghetto alive, in the midst of the territory in which they planned to settle Germans, when they found they could not deport them to the G.G.? Why did they allow them to survive until the summer of 1944, long after all the other Polish ghettos had been liquidated?

Here is another problem: Nowhere in the book does Aly convince us that the rulers in Berlin really listened to their minions in Poland. Since his book appeared in 1995, Sarah Bender has published her monograph on Bialystok (1997).[33] In a detailed analysis of the relationship between the Judenrat there, headed by Ephraim Barash, and local and regional German offices, she shows convincingly that the local German officials and economic experts did everything in their power to prevent the destruction of the ghetto. Their motives were both general—the economic advantage of using underpaid Jewish labor to produce essential goods with a wide profit margin for the Germans—and personal, such as the bribes provided by the Jews, which helped produce a good life, and the fear that with the annihilation of the ghetto many of them might be sent to serve at the front. Clearly, the decision to mass-murder the Jews in the ghetto was an ideological decision made in Berlin. The local middle bureaucrats would never have made it.

Research by Michal Unger on Łódż has uncovered basically the same story. In 1943 and 1944 the last thing the local and regional bureaucrats and experts wanted was the destruction of the ghetto. The Jewish workers produced goods, mainly textiles and carpentry products, for the army and the German economy generally. Orders for deportations from Łódż to the death camps came from the center; they were not initiated by the local officials. The final deportations, to the death camp at Chelmno in June 1944 and to Auschwitz in August, originated in Berlin. The local German officials would have been content to leave the ghetto in existence, for reasons much like those in Bialystok.

Christopher Browning has apparently come to similar conclusions. In some recent publications and lectures, he shows that after a struggle within the German bureaucracy in Poland, those who preferred to use the Jews for labor, in an economy that increasingly required workers, gained the upper hand. That meant slightly improved treatment of the Jews so that they could do the work demanded of them. The trend in Poland in early 1942 was toward improvement when orders came to kill them. The orders, again, came from Berlin and were motivated by anti-pragmatic ideology. In fact, all recent findings make hash of the extreme functionalist argument. Local officialdom slowly moved toward keeping the Jews, at least the "useful" ones, as work slaves; but the ideologically motivated center decided to murder them.[34]

Recent research in Germany has provided what may be a more persuasive answer. In a brief summary published in 1998, a group of mainly German and mainly youngish historians present a synthesis of intentionalist and functionalist arguments, based on detailed research on the murder of the Jews in Belarus (Belorussia), eastern Galicia, Lithuania, the Generalgouvernement, and France.[35] The basic argument as presented by the editor of the volume, the Freiburg historian Ulrich Herbert, says that in all these places the initiative for the murder was pseudopragmatic, with supposedly economic, demographic, and political (especially in France) motivations, and came largely from local officials and the German army. However, there was a constant dialogue with the center in Berlin, and a mutual readjustment in the direction of increasing radicalization. All these motivations grew out of a consensual ideology that was based on the radical, though not necessarily murderous, antisemitic convictions of students and university-trained intellectuals in the previous decades. The Nazi regime organized these preexisting elements and effected a transition to a murderousness that snowballed: more and more radical solutions were more and more easily accepted. Whether this transition to extreme evil was as easy as the group around Ulrich Herbert indicates, or whether it was accomplished with difficulty, as Henri Zukier suggests, remains open to debate.[36] Equally unresolved remains the problem of how the arrangements between the ideological center in Berlin and the local officials worked. But these German historians have gone a long way to settle the issue of local versus central initiatives: not only were the initiatives complementary, but they were based on a commonly held ideology.

For Aly, ideology, including antisemitism, exists as a necessary background against which the various Nazi extermination plans were developed. But the very plans that he so persuasively describes were not motivated by pragmatic considerations. They were the practical result, or the practical translation, of a racist ideology. The thesis holds true: when you want something badly, you try to translate your desire into reality. That is precisely what the Germans did: they were possessed by a racist ideology, and they enacted it, which is why they tried to restructure the ethnic and national map of Eastern Europe. So even if we fully accept Aly's analysis, we have to see that the motivation was not bureaucratic but ideological.

Aly's whole theory breaks down as far as the Jews are concerned. What is left is nevertheless important: a major addition to our detailed knowledge of the zigzags in German policy in Poland between 1939 and 1942.

chapter five

Overall Interpretations: Daniel J. Goldhagen,
John Weiss, Saul Friedländer

No book on the Holocaust has caused the kind of public controversy that Daniel Goldhagen's *Hitler's Willing Executioners* has. Hundreds of thousands of copies have been sold in the United States alone. Translations of the book have appeared in a number of languages. The number of reviews has amounted to a near deluge. In Germany, a major public discussion took place in major papers, chiefly but not exclusively in the intellectual weekly *Die Zeit*, and in overflowing lecture halls. In Israel, on the other hand, peculiarly perhaps, little attention has been given to the book. It was clear from the outset—from the first symposium held at the U.S. Holocaust Memorial Museum in April 1996—that in North America, at least, the book would appeal to many. The public reaction in the United States has been overwhelmingly positive; the less a commentator knows about the subject matter, and the more he or she is emotionally involved, the greater the enthusiasm. The professional historians, with some exceptions (notably, Gordon A. Craig in the English-speaking world and Yisrael Gutman in

Israel), and more especially the historians who deal with the Holocaust directly, have been overwhelmingly critical of the book.

Although the book or discussion about it has by now presumably been read by most of those interested in the subject, let us remind ourselves of the salient points. The central argument is that the Nazi policy to annihilate the Jews was carried out owing to a certain type of murderous antisemitism (*eliminationist* is Goldhagen's favored term), which so penetrated the minds of the German people that the vast majority became willing and enthusiastic followers from among whom it was very easy to recruit the actual murderers.

Goldhagen, arguing against some who say that the extermination was the work mainly of the S.S. and some other special groups, tries to prove his thesis about the willingness of ordinary Germans to commit the most horrendous crimes by concentrating on three case studies: the battalions of the Order Police, who were engaged on the mass killing operations in Eastern Europe; the slave labor camps; and the death marches at the end of the war. In all three cases he analyzes the participation of ordinary Germans who went through no special schooling in antisemitism and who were essentially interchangeable with any other Germans chosen at random. He concludes that the willingness, indeed enthusiasm, for murder, the penchant for humiliating the victims, and the endless sadism, were special to German society. He tries to explain why this should have been so, arguing that eliminationist antisemitism dates from the Middle Ages and was prevalent in the nineteenth century.[1] There were several types of eliminationism: first, a very moderate and liberal type, as with the German progressives who thought the Jews were a foreign element in Germany but one that could be assimilated and become truly German through the adoption of German culture generally and Christianity in particular. This meant the elimination of the Jews by assimilating and converting them, and Goldhagen quotes here the work of Uriel Tal.[2] The second type of eliminationism was the more radical antisemitism of those nationalists who wanted to restore the situation of the Jews in Germany to what it had been before Emancipation and the granting of equal rights. The third type was even more radical, espoused by those who wanted to expel the Jews in the manner of the medieval potentates in Western and Central Europe.[3] The murderous type of eliminationism that developed into twentieth-century Nazism is the last he describes, in great detail. He explains that almost the whole German people participated willingly, passively or actively, in the project of annihilating the Jewish people because of the pervasiveness of these types of eliminationist antisemitism in German society.[4]

An assumption underlies his thesis: he believes the Holocaust to be explicable and not, as Elie Wiesel and many others have stated, a mystery to which we can never know an answer. Goldhagen's defense against mystification is cogent, although many historians, including some of the most important ones, will disagree with him on this issue. I do not, as I have already discussed at length.

The second salient point in Goldhagen's book, which has to be stressed, is that Goldhagen places antisemitic ideology at the center of his explanation of the Holocaust. Again, in principle, I agree with him rather than with those, such as Hans Mommsen and the functionalists, who emphasize the social stratification in a crisis situation, the political and economic background, and the bureaucratic machinery.[5] In recent years, many authors dealing with the subject have followed the functionalist approach. Thus, for instance, as we have seen, Zygmunt Bauman has tried to explain the Holocaust by holding "modernity," not antisemitism, responsible. Goetz Aly thinks that the explanation lies in the self-created constraints of the Nazis, a result of their decision to reorganize the ethnic composition of Eastern Europe in 1939–1941. The background, he says, was their racist ideology, but the real reasons were the pragmatic calculations of middle-range intellectuals turned bureaucrats. Other historians take a more differentiated view and no longer subscribe to an extreme functionalism.

All these authors, including those I do not agree with, have made important contributions to our knowledge, and their findings have to be taken into account—which Goldhagen refuses to do, because he has an overbearing attitude toward the work of others. He offers a monocausal explanation: eliminationist antisemitism. But however erroneous such an exclusivist position is, the renewed emphasis he puts on the ideological, antisemitic factor is useful. Aly, Bauman, Mommsen, even Raul Hilberg, cannot explain *why* the murder happened. Hilberg has stated often that he preferred not to ask the big questions because he was afraid he would come up with small answers. His own masterly analysis of the German bureaucratic machinery that sent the Jews to their deaths does not explain why the bureaucrats set it up. We have seen the problems that Aly's interpretation encounters, and the failure of Bauman to explain why German modernity attacked Jews, whereas Italian modernity attacked Ethiopians but rescued Jews, by and large. One does not have to take Goldhagen's explanation as the last word in Holocaust scholarship in order to see that antisemitic ideology played a central part. In other words, Goldhagen's redirection of attention to antisemitism has to be valued positively. It is to his great credit, as my colleague and friend Yisrael Gutman has said, that the discussion following publication of his book had to deal again with that key issue. The commercial success of his book has had this salutary effect.

What makes Goldhagen's explanation simplistic? Let me begin by repeating what some other commentators have said: that Goldhagen ignores the social and economic traumas that afflicted German society in the wake of World War I. These were many, including the destruction of the social fabric of pre-1914 Germany, with the attendant loss of personal, economic, and psychological security and identity—this applied mainly to the aristocracy, the bureaucracy, and the middle class. There were wartime losses: millions of mothers lost their sons and wives their husbands—and many others had to care for the wounded and the crippled. France and Britain lost proportionately similar numbers, but they were the victors, and it seemed to some that the sacrifices had been worth it. Others protested bitterly at the pointlessness of the slaughter. But the conclusion that was generally drawn on the winning side was to study war no more. Pacifism spread. In Germany, however, the defeat added to the general feeling of despair, and one of the escape routes from despair was into a burning, chauvinistic desire for revenge. The inflation in the early Weimar years caused further social disloca- tions, with the loss of savings of the middle class and the peasants. Six years after Germany had emerged from this first bout with economic disaster, the Great Depression hit a country that had already had its fill of national catastrophes, and it hit hard. None of this finds a place in Goldhagen's description. After his book was discussed in Germany, Goldhagen apparently revised his position somewhat and admitted that he should have considered the social and economic traumas more than he did. But it is not the case that he has to improve his statements on these issues—quite simply, the book barely deals with them at all.

Critics have argued that Goldhagen does not explain how an anti- semitic norm translated itself into the actual murder. Here again I have to come to the defense of Goldhagen: surely if there is a norm in society that requires the elimination of a group of people, then if the structure of society provides a rationale for the killing, it will be done. The addition of structural factors, ignored by Goldhagen (but which most inten- tionalists no longer deny), to a basic motivation does provide a sufficient answer. If the general motivation exists, if accepted social structures sanction it, and if an order is understood to have been given—whether or not it was or not becomes immaterial—then a consensus will emerge, and genocide will be the result.

Another problem then has to be faced, namely, that the vast majority of a people among whom had developed one of the most advanced and humane civilizations overcame a traditional moral reluctance to commit mass murder or condone it—or, in other words, accepted as good what until then had been understood as evil. Reaching consensus involved education, preparation, and propaganda based on the utilization of pre- existing forms of rejection (not necessarily eliminationist antisemitism) of the populations that now became targeted for murder, partial or wholesale. The Nazis were successful in all these tasks, and the question

How could they? How does ideology turn into bullets, knives, clubs, or poison gas? is precisely the kind of naive, even mindless, question that enables genocide to happen. Humans, *all* humans, are the only kind of mammals that have within themselves the potential ability to annihilate their own kind.

The question that one has to ask of Goldhagen is to what extent there indeed existed an exterminationist antisemitic norm in German society from the mid-nineteenth century, if not from earlier, as he asserts.

Here Goldhagen stumbles badly. He does not seem to be acquainted with some basic developments in German society in the nineteenth century. Certainly, there was what he calls eliminationist antisemitism, and its impact increased as the century matured. In fact, any historian could add many quotations to the ones he presents. But antisemitism came in different forms, and Goldhagen puts all antisemitism in the same basket, including the liberal type that wanted to see the Jews disappear by assimilation and conversion. He quotes Uriel Tal, but Tal never said that liberal efforts to assimilate the Jews were the same as extermination programs. Despite Tal's trenchant critique of German liberalism, he knew very well how to differentiate between someone who wanted to change a person's identity and someone who wanted to kill that person instead. Nor would Tal have subscribed to the idea that the liberal form of anti-Jewishness *inevitably* led to a murderous hatred of Jews. There were gradations between these two positions, not a deterministic progression from less radical to more radical hatred. The vast majority of German antisemites did not wish to abolish formal Jewish emancipation. Goldhagen makes much of the radical antisemitism of the Conservative Party in Germany; but in 1893, it obtained less than 10 percent of the votes, whereas the National Liberals, among whom there were a number of former Jews, were much more numerous. Goldhagen ignores this and makes the counterfactual statement that "conservatives and Volkish nationalists in Germany . . . formed the vast majority of the population."[6] By 1912 the Social Democrats, with an explicitly anti-antisemitic program, were the largest party in the German Reichstag, and the Progressives ran very strongly as well. In Goldhagen's book there is, surprisingly, no discussion of the attitude toward Jews held by Social Democrats, members of the largest political party in the Germany of the Kaiser and the Weimar Republic. Formally at least, the Jews had been fully emancipated with the establishment of the German Empire and, although they were kept out of certain influential occupations, enjoyed extraordinary prosperity. They were accepted in middle-class circles, and they flocked to Germany from normatively antisemitic East European societies. Germans intermarried with Jews: in the 1930s some 50,000 Jews were living in mixed German-Jewish marriages, so at least 50,000 Germans, and presumably parts of their families, had familial contact with the Jews. Goldhagen himself mentions that a large proportion of the Jewish upper classes in Germany converted to Christianity in the nineteenth century. In a society where eliminationist norms were universal and in which Jews were rejected even after they had converted, or so he argues, the rise of this extreme form of assimilation of Jews would hardly have been possible.

A book that appeared at the same time as Goldhagen's but was almost totally (and unjustly) ignored, John Weiss's *Ideology of Death*, provides a much more cogent answer to the problem of the impact of antisemitism in Germany and Austria.[7] First, Weiss differentiates between the two countries, which Goldhagen does not, and shows that the Austrian version of Jew-hatred was much grimmer than the German. Second, he argues that radical antisemitism—often but not always racist and murderous—became pervasive among the German and Austrian elites: aristocrats, industrialists, academics, professionals, and bureaucrats. I do not think the court and the aristocracy in Austria were as antisemitic as in Germany, but I see the other elements as being there. Whether or not Weiss exaggerates somewhat, it is indisputable that antisemitism, much of it radical, became fashionable among the German and Austrian elites.

Weiss does not ignore the Social Democratic Party (SPD), which, though originally based on theories with strongly antisemitic overtones (expressed by such nineteenth-century socialist and anarchist thinkers as Pierre J. Proudhon, François Fourier, Karl Marx, and Michael Bakunin), became the main bulwark against antisemitism in Germany. The 1912 elections were critical, because they seemed to threaten the imperial establishment with the possibility of an internal revolution by ballot. A coalition of Social Democrats and Progressives might, it was thought, achieve a majority at the next election and make Germany ungovernable by the right-wing pro-imperial parties. Weiss implies that imperial Germany's contribution to the outbreak of war in 1914 may have been influenced by the fear of such a development.

What this means for the discussion of Goldhagen's thesis is that a majority of German voters were prepared to vote for parties that were explicitly opposed to antisemitism—but that would have been an unlikely eventuality if an eliminationist antisemitic norm had pervaded German society and formed a central social and political issue for the German population. There simply was no general murderous, racist, antisemitic norm in Germany in the nineteenth century. There was a strong and growing antisemitic influence among the elites, but even here it is difficult to talk of unanimity. True, there were latent and overt popular antisemitic feelings, though not necessarily eliminationist or radical, among the masses of Germans, just as there were in other European countries, and we have all learned from George Mosse about these phenomena.[8] But to speak of an eliminationist norm is wrong. Goldhagen's thesis does not work.

But that is not all. Despite pervasive antisemitism (not necessarily eliminationist) among the elites, Jewish participation in World War I was accepted. Hitler's commanding officer, a lieutenant by the name of Hugo Gutman, who recommended Hitler for the Iron Cross, was a Jew. Anti-Jewish propaganda, which led to a government-inspired investigation into how many Jews were serving in the German army, was attempted but had only a small impact. And the German army was enthusiastically welcomed by Polish and Russian Jews because it protected them from the antisemitic terror enacted by the Russian forces and because the incoming soldiers behaved in a friendly and civilized manner. The Yiddish expression *der Daitsh* (the German) was one of respect and sympathy. Where was Goldhagen's norm just over one decade before Hitler came to power?

The Weimar Republic opened the gates for Jewish participation in politics and academia—though not the army. The Weimar constitution was written by a Jew (Hugo Preuss), and individual Jews achieved great prominence, especially in intellectual and cultural fields. How could this happen in a society permeated by eliminationist antisemitism? Until 1930 anti-antisemitic parties (Social Democrats, Communists, Democrats) formed a clear majority in the Reichstag, along with non-eliminationist parties, such as the Catholic Center Party, which favored a Catholic, "moderate" antisemitism, one that aimed not at the abolition of Emancipation but at the reduction of "Jewish influence." Antisemitism of this non-eliminationist kind was much stronger in Poland, for instance, than in Germany. The Nazis had been reduced to a small splinter group by 1928 (2.6 percent of the popular vote), and the German Nationalist Party, the party of the traditional, often radical antisemitic elites, was a definite minority. Where was Goldhagen's norm?

The last free elections in pre-Hitler Germany were held in November 1932, at the height of the economic crisis. In these elections, the Nazis lost 2 million votes and 34 seats in the Reichstag. In a Reichstag of 584 members, the Social Democrats, Communists, Democrats, and Catholics together held 50.2 percent, or 293, of the seats; the Nazis and their German Nationalist allies held 41.9 percent, or 248, with the rest held by right-of-center splinter groups. In other words, a slight majority supported parties that were either explicitly non-antisemitic or "moderately" antisemitic, but certainly not eliminationist, or exterminationist. This applies especially to the Catholic Center Party (Zentrum), which was not friendly to the Jews but whose attitude cannot be described as antisemitic in any sense that Goldhagen uses. This does not contradict the statement that a very large segment of the population, including the Social Democrats, both leaders and supporters, were "moderately" anti-Jewish. Their attitude might best be described as "unease" in connection with the Jews. But we see evidence of no political antisemitism, certainly no eliminationist anti-Jewishness. Yet Goldhagen is absolutely right when he insists, contra his critics, that by 1940–1941 German society had become a reservoir for willing executioners.

My analysis points to an important difference between Hilberg and Goldhagen. Hilberg argues that German bureaucrats were comfortable using their considerable skills and creative initiative to put genocidal policies into practice as a matter of bureaucratic routine. He sees in them—rightly, I think—the crucial element in the execution of the genocidal project: ordinary people were guided by the bureaucratic machine. Goldhagen does not deal with the bureaucrats, because for him the personal, physical confrontation between the actual murderers and their Jewish victims in the ghettos, labor camps, and death marches is the key issue. He is right to emphasize this aspect because not enough has been said about it—apart from Israeli historians whom Goldhagen cannot read because of the language barrier and apart from a deluge of memoirs in English, which he can read and use but doesn't. To his credit, he reminds historians and others to look beyond generalizations and analyses into the abyss of day-to-day cruelty and horror that was the Holocaust. Others have done this, but they did not have his commercial success, and in this case commercial success has to be valued very positively. Still, Goldhagen's extreme position is untenable. The murder became an actuality not because some German policeman wanted to kill Jews but because political and administrative structures promoted the murder. The policemen, guards, and so on, executed directives, as he himself shows, though not necessarily direct orders. Contrary to Goldhagen's, Hilberg's analysis of German bureaucracy is well-nigh faultless and, indeed, paradoxically, explains why Goldhagen is right, insofar as he is right, because it explains how bureaucracy directed the immediate perpetrators to commit murder.

Goldhagen has an argument with Christopher R. Browning over what percentage of Germans were potentially or actually willing to participate in the genocide. Browning believes that the percentage of policemen examined who were opposed to murder was 10 to 20 percent; Goldhagen says 10 percent of all Germans were opposed. In either case, the statement that the vast majority of the German population were willing to be recruited for the murder of Jews stands. This has been said time and time again by a number of historians, Yisrael Gutman and myself included, and Goldhagen's disregard for the fact that he is not the first to say so is neither here nor there. The point is that he is right.

The real question, then, is this: If, in 1933, the Nazis and their radically but not murderously antisemitic allies were supported by some 43 percent of the electorate, non-Nazi parties by 57 percent, including outspoken opponents of Nazis who were either anti-antisemitic or only moderately anti-Jewish (that is, they opposed even the relatively moderate step of disenfranchising the Jews), how did it happen that by 1940–1941 the overwhelming majority of Germans became a reservoir of willing murderers of Jews? *That* is the problem. Goldhagen's discussion about norms that did not exist is useless. He does not ask the question, and when one does not ask a question, it is somewhat difficult to provide an answer.

I believe that the question has an answer, which I tried to elucidate in Chapter 2. To provide this answer one has to get rid of the ideology of anti-Germanism and give up notions of pervasive eliminationist antisemitic norms in Germany. Yet one also has to recognize that any valid explanatory model must show why the Holocaust sprang from German society and not, despite murderous antisemitism, in Russia or elsewhere. In other words, one has to deal with German specificity, the Sonderweg . Goldhagen's effort constitutes an attempt to describe such a Sonderweg.

Such an attempt is not new. Immediately following the war Friedrich Meinecke, the eminent anti-Nazi German historian, who, however, held antisemitic views himself—as did so many of the intellectual German elite (see John Weiss's book for information on that)—thought that Prussian militarism is what had brought on the German "catastrophe." The functionalists, with Hans Mommsen as their chief spokesperson, showed that the overwhelming majority of the German population embraced the Nazi utopia. The functionalist interpretation, largely influenced by a left-leaning political agenda totally different from Meinecke's, had to do with the structure of German society. Ideologies, in their scheme, formed the background to the genocidal policies of the regime. They tried to show that a specifically German development—a Sonderweg—led to the genocide.

Intentionalists, too, like Eberhard Jäckel, explained the rise of Hitler and the Nazi Party in terms of a specific German history. They emphasized that the main motive for the Holocaust was ideology, although modernism or bureaucracy were important additional factors. Even Ernst Nolte, the ultranationalist, almost revisionist German historian, has said that "Auschwitz was contained in the principles of the Nazi racist theory like the seed in the fruit." Goldhagen says almost the same thing: that genocide was "immanent in the conversation of German society."[9] In Israel, Yisrael Gutman, Otto Dov Kulka, and myself, among others, have been arguing for a position not dissimilar, in this respect, from Goldhagen's own: we think that the relative primacy of ideology, the centrality of radical antisemitism, and the specific German development made the rise of Nazism an unprecedented event in human history. For Goldhagen to say that he was the first to have discovered that a specific German way led to the Holocaust, a way shaped by radical antisemitism, is not credible.

Let me repeat here, in a condensed form, the model I have already presented as a possible alternative to Goldhagen's interpretation.

It appears that when an intellectual or pseudo-intellectual elite with a genocidal program, whether explicit or implicit, achieves power in a crisis-ridden society for economic, social, and political reasons that have nothing to do with the genocidal program, then, if that elite can draw the intellectual strata to its side, genocide will become possible. By intellectual strata I mean what John Weiss describes as elites: upper-class social groups, army officers, church leaders, bureaucrats, doctors and lawyers, industrial and commercial elites, and especially the university professors who provide all the rest with the necessary ideological tools. A social consensus will be created with the help of these elites; the consensus will provide a justification for ordinary folks to participate in the genocidal program. This is what appears to have happened in Germany after the elimination and silencing, by murder and terror, of tens of thousands of opponents of Nazism in the 1930s. The concept of a consensus is absolutely central to this line of explanation. It also makes the behavior of, for instance, police battalions, such as Battalion 101, around which Browning and Goldhagen wrote their books, much more intelligible.[10] It is worth remarking that *consensus* is not Goldhagen's term, although everything he says indicates that that is what he is driving at. The prevalent latent or overt nonmurderous antisemitic attitudes in the general population, the result of Christian antisemitism that had sought to dehumanize the Jews for many centuries— though never translated into a genocidal program by Christian society—prevented any serious opposition to the Nazis once they had decided to embark on the murder of the Jews.

Some parallels may also be worth examining. No one will argue that in 1926 or 1927 the overwhelming majority of Soviet citizens were ardent supporters of Bolshevik rule. Yet in 1941 and 1942 millions of Soviet soldiers went into battle with the cry *"Za Stalina"* (For Stalin), and most citizens wholeheartedly supported the Communist regime for mainly nationalistic reasons. Similar examples can be cited from other places and other times. The steps leading to these quick changes in perception by large numbers of people have not been properly researched.

In effect, by arguing for a widespread social norm of murderousness focused on the Jews, Goldhagen lets off the hook the specific groups that did advance radical antisemitic views: the academics, clerics, and, finally, the Nazis themselves. After all, if all these, and others, were the victims of a culturally inherited social norm, they cannot be blamed for drawing the logical conclusions, can they?

So much for eliminationist antisemitism as a general norm in German society.

Many critics have already said that the book lacks a European context. To explain why the Holocaust happened in Germany and not in France or Russia, one must compare the situations in these countries. If I understood Goldhagen correctly, he argues that comparisons were moot precisely because the Holocaust happened in Germany, and therefore only Germany was relevant to his project. This argument sounds peculiar coming from a social scientist and is the basis of my criticism of his Harvard tutors, who failed to draw his attention to these grave methodological errors; they should have known better. After all, Germany is located in the center of the European continent, and its whole history is one of interaction with its neighbors—in the intellectual and ideological sphere as well as in others. In addition, as I have tried to show, his thesis does not work as far as nineteenth-century Germany is concerned, so a comparative approach becomes even more necessary. If Goldhagen knows languages other than English and German or is acquainted with more than basic European history, the book contains no evidence of it. What he calls eliminationist antisemitism was much more in evidence in Russia than in Germany in the nineteenth century. The views of the elites there, and the attitude of the population at large, all pointed in the direction of eliminationist antisemitism. Why did the Holocaust therefore not happen in Russia? Well, one might argue that it almost did, but that the rise of communism in Russia may have prevented it. In any case, if one argues the way Goldhagen does, one must relate to the problem of comparisons, and he does not.

We find much the same situation in at least two other European countries—France and Romania. In France, in the last part of the nineteenth century, a truly eliminationist antisemitism became a distinguishing mark of the violent nationalistic mind-set. In Romania, the murderously antisemitic forces came into power in 1938 and again in 1940, and the result was the mass murder of some 260,000 Romanian Jews and more than 100,000 Ukrainian Jews by Romanian forces, albeit in alliance with Nazi Germany; this occurred in parallel with the murder of Jews and Roma by the infamous Einsatzgruppe D under Otto

Ohlendorf, whose victims are not included in the above figures. Lithuanians, Latvians, Ukrainians, and others participated in brutal killings in other places in Eastern Europe. Their participation, according to Goldhagen's thesis, would indicate the existence of an eliminationist antisemitic norm in those nations. For Romania, this may not be far from the truth. But if so, the Germans are not so unique. Others had these eliminationist impulses as well, yet "Death was a master from Germany," not elsewhere.[11] Again, Goldhagen's theory fails: one has to look for the special reasons why it happened in Germany in a much more sophisticated and differentiated manner.

I don't want to linger over the three parts of his book where he produces factual material to substantiate his argument that there were large numbers of willing executioners. In fact, I think there were many more such people than he imagines, including large numbers of ordinary Wehrmacht soldiers. His examples are in part, as others have already said, repetitions of what Browning has shown in his *Ordinary Men*. Goldhagen does more of the same. But his view that not ordinary men but ordinary German men were involved has some merit, as I have tried to show, except that his attempt to show what made Germans more adept at murdering Jews than Italians, French, or Russians were fails.

One problem with his analysis has not really been taken up in the many critiques of his book: he deals with the Order Police battalion because, he claims, they were typical ordinary Germans. In fact, Battalion 101 was partly composed of Luxembourgers, not Germans, so German eliminationist antisemitism hardly applies. A second, more weighty point is that Goldhagen wants to show that the murders were committed not by elite troops but by ordinary Germans. But Battalion 101 of the Order Police, like the Order Police generally, was part of the S.S., the Nazi elite formation. The question of how these policemen were recruited is still not quite clear. One theory has it that in 1933 the Nazis got rid of many ordinary policemen because they were members or sympathizers of the Social Democratic Party. They recruited Nazi sympathizers instead. They built up a reserve of such people, and it was this reserve that was recruited into Reserve Order Police battalions, of which 101 was one. If this is true, Goldhagen's purpose, to deal with ordinary Germans, is again thwarted. But even if it is not, he could have done what Hannes Heer and others have done in Germany and what Omer Bartov has done in the United States: he could have dealt with Wehrmacht units that committed horrors against Serbs, Poles, Greeks, and Russians as well as Jews and shown there what he tried to show with his Order Police, namely, that ordinary Germans (and ordinary others) committed mass murders of the worst kind.[12]

His example of slave labor camps suffers from the same weakness, because the camps he deals with were within the S.S. orbit. All three cases that he described were in or near Lublin: Majdanek concentration camp, Lipowa prisoner-of-war camp, and the *Flughafenlager* (Airport Camp). All three were S.S.-controlled.[13] But did not Goldhagen promise to present us with proof that ordinary Germans, and not the Nazi S.S. elite, were willing executioners? He took the wrong examples and flunked his own test. Had he taken slave work camps run not by the S.S. but by, say, the Hasag Company of Leipzig, he could have proved what he was out to prove.[14] The critics seem to have missed this point. On the other hand, his description of the death march from Helmbrechts is the best part of the book.[15] Little is new in the overall description, but the details and the way he analyzes the attitude of the murderers is powerful and convincing.

One overarching problem in Goldhagen's book is worth pondering. I alluded to it in that famous Washington symposium of April 1996: his thesis might boomerang. Sooner rather than later it will become obvious, beyond the circle of experts, that his explanation for the phenomenon of masses of willing executioners is mistaken and that the anti-German bias of his book, almost a racist bias (however much he may deny it), leads nowhere. Others may, in response, attempt to deny the very fact that such masses of murderers were easily recruitable from the German population. When people realize that his attempt to explain the Holocaust in terms of German eliminationist antisemitism is equally erroneous, the response to that may be a denial that antisemitism is indeed the central element in understanding the Holocaust. At that point the question may be asked—it has already been put by some critics, but it did not receive the kind of attention it deserves—What, in the end, is the difference between the murder of the Jews and the murder of all the others? Is it not the same thing? After all, the Germans did not murder only Jews but Poles, Roma, Russians, Ukrainians, Serbs, Czechs, and later Italians and French in huge numbers, as well as their own people. In many number of cases, the brutality and sadism with which all these people, Jews or not, were treated were not really different in kind. Obviously, such behavior toward non-Jews cannot be explained by antisemitism, eliminationist or otherwise. This point alone would invalidate the whole eliminationist thesis advanced by Goldhagen; further, some people could utilize his book to do the exact opposite of what he intended: "prove" that antisemitism was not the central motivation for the Holocaust.

In other words, Goldhagen is right when he points to the central role of ideology, but its central role cannot be explained the way he does it. A differentiated approach that recognizes the special position of antisemitism in Nazi ideology but sees the connection of that antisemitism with the Nazis' racist and nationalistic program of reordering the map of Europe is essential. Such a connection would explain why the Jews occupied such a key role in Nazi ideology and why, therefore, the Nazis' attitude toward the Jews was indeed different from their attitude toward others; it would, at the same time, clarify the reasons why horrible mass slaughter was committed against other populations as well. A logical link could be established between the murder of the Jews and the murder of others, without negating the central role the Jews played in Nazi ideology. The fate of individual victims, it would then become obvious, was the same, whether they were Jews, Poles, or something else, although the Jews were tortured and humiliated beyond anything the others had to suffer. The Nazis' attitude toward the different groups, murderous though it was in every case, was different in the case of the Jews. Goldhagen's approach prevents him from being able to explain that.

Last, one has to ask why the book has been such an outstanding success. Publicity efforts by the publisher cannot be the sole reason. Nor can one be satisfied with the explanation that for many Jews, as for many veterans of World War II, the book is a godsend: we always knew, many are saying, that the Germans were no good; here at last comes a gutsy young man who says it loud and clear. Yet Jews and war veterans are, after all, not so numerous that they account for the bulk of the purchasers of the book. I believe the real reason is the simplistic quality of the argument, its Manichean (black and white) character. A complicated phenomenon is seemingly explained thus: The Germans killed the Jews because they wanted to; they had wanted to since the Middle Ages. And that's all there is to it. People don't like complicated explanations; they don't want differentiated analyses. They want simplicity, even mindless simplicity. And Goldhagen gave it to them.

In Germany, the book answered needs that were at least partly different: the need to create distance from previous generations, which is particularly strong among young people, and the need for catharsis, the psychological advantage brought by wallowing in guilt. Germans read Goldhagen's book, agreed with every word, beat their breasts, and came out cleansed and reborn. The fact that it was an American Jew who took the place of the father confessor, a real-life Harvard professor who dressed his message like an academic exercise so beloved of many Westerners, including Germans, made the whole experience even more satisfying. Again, it was the simplistic nature of the message that made it so palatable.

Goldhagen, and some of the members of the public in Washington in April 1996, were angry when I said that Goldhagen had unfortunately failed to show that humility that a researcher should when approaching the Holocaust. I cannot recollect that Salo Baron or any of the great historians approached their colleagues with the superciliousness that

Goldhagen evinced when dealing with his peers. A student of a subject does not usually claim to have the final answer to a complicated problem. As the Hebrew proverb says, "Let the stranger laud you, not your own mouth."

Readers comparing this chapter with some of my previous statements about Goldhagen's book may notice a change in tone. I have consciously moderated my criticism, largely because of the violent attacks on the young Harvard scholar. In Israel, I defended him publicly against vicious personal attacks and invited him to a closed discussion at Yad Vashem with Israeli scholars who held various views on his work. I believe that academic discussion should be honest and open; criticism, even sharp criticism, should be voiced, but I am opposed to witch-hunting. I think that controversy should be civilized, and I believe that Daniel J. Goldhagen is a gifted scholar. I do not think his book will make it into the Pantheon; but his faulty thesis provoked a discussion about essentials, and for that at least he should be thanked.

In all the books discussed so far, books that claim to have unlocked the secret of the Holocaust—to explain what caused it and provide a picture of that cataclysmic event—certain major deficiencies become obvious, and the fact that they are common to all the books makes one wonder. In all of them, the Jews are passive victims, and the Churches, the Allies, the host nations, the neutrals, do not exist. Bauman, Herf, Aly, Goldhagen, Weiss, whatever one may think of them, are not uninformed observers. Quite the contrary. Goldhagen claims that he writes in the name of the victims, but apart from a couple of testimonies, the Jews in his book are just objects of German fury.[16]

The question arises, Why did the Nazis attack the Jews and not some other group? The answer "Antisemitism," though correct in itself, also begs the question. Why antisemitism and not some other group-hatred? No answer can be given without an analysis of the development of Jewish history, including the dimension of Jewish–non-Jewish relations.

Furthermore, the victims are, in principle, no less—arguably even more—important than the perpetrators. Telling about the Holocaust from the perspective of the perpetrators is no less biased than telling about it from the perspective of the victims—arguably even more so. The basic issue of Holocaust history is to tell it in such a way as to advance the prospect, dim though it may seem, to prevent genocides, Holocaust-like events in particular. In terms of prevention, the behavior of the victims of the Holocaust is of universal moral, social, and political importance, not to mention philosophical or theological considerations (for those who believe that these are of importance). That the overarching attempts in these books do not deal with the Jews except as murdered victims distorts the picture completely. What we see here may be an unconscious treatment of the Jews as the quintessential Other. If they are the Other, they need not be described as a people with a history, a culture, and conflicting individual identities. If they are not "people," the Holocaust becomes utterly inexplicable: the main character has been omitted.

The other problem common to all the books discussed is that a cogent history of the Holocaust cannot be written without assimilating into it analyses of the policies and behavior patterns of the "bystanders." That is the inaccurate term encompassing the non-Jewish populations of Nazi-occupied Europe, the Allies, neutrals, Jews in the "free world," and many others. Many monographic studies on all these indirect participants are available, but a synthesis is difficult to achieve, and none of the authors of the books discussed so far has attempted to do it. One exception is Leni Yahil's textbook, which is really much more than a textbook, because it offers a panorama of all the complicated aspects mentioned here.[17]

Another attempt was published in late 1997: volume I of Saul Friedländer's *Nazi Germany and the Jews*.[18] It is this book that may presage a more comprehensive and exhaustive treatment of the vast subject of the Holocaust.

In 1988 an exchange of letters between Saul Friedländer and Martin Broszat, director of the Munich Institute of Contemporary History (Institut für Zeitgeschichte), who has since died, was published, in English, in the Yad Vashem Studies series.[19] Broszat was one of the fore-most historians on the Holocaust. Like most, if not all, of his German colleagues at that time, he was interested in the perpetrators. In his letters he argued for a "historicization" of the Nazi period, for consider-ing it an integral part of the flow of German history. In his view, the pre-Nazi period was linked to the period that followed the twelve years of the National Socialist regime, with developmental lines that traverse the Nazi era. Apart from the criminal policies of the regime, which formed a major subject of Broszat's historical writings, Broszat dealt with social history, economic history, and local and regional develop-ments, much of which was not necessarily influenced by Nazi ideology or administration. Fitting the Nazi period into a general flow of events ought to be a major challenge to the historian, he thought, because this kind of history was real social history, the history of the individual, the family, and the neighborhood.

Friedländer did not deny that many lines of development led from imperial Germany through the Weimar Republic and the Nazi regime to postwar democratic Germany. But he focused on the meaning of the term *Alltagsgeschichte* (the history of daily life), on the mundane stories of ordinary people, those who have no discernible influence on their social environment and who, in effect, do not control their own lives, the ones who are anonymous cogs in a social machine. Friedländer argued that the Nazi period was unlike other periods and other regimes in that, during those short twelve years, studded with crises that hardly have any equal in human history, the important story was not the fate of ordinary German people living their ordinary lives but the cataclysmic events that influenced the lives of whole nations. The crucial issue was the criminal nature of the regime, its crimes against humanity, against target populations, first and foremost the Jews. To concentrate on what Broszat called everyday life would be to deal with marginal themes, not main ones, thus creating a historical distortion; it would mean ignoring the extraordinary character of Nazism, which lay in its criminality.

The first volume of Friedländer's work, which covers the years 1933 to 1939, is the book being discussed here. It deals with the National Socialist policy toward the Jews during that period. The second volume, not yet published, is to be called *The Years of Extermination*; it will cover the three years from the outbreak of war and until the peak of the murder campaign in 1942.

Friedländer's volume appears to be a continuation of his debate with Martin Broszat, an attempt to turn the tables on his colleague and opponent. Friedländer is not particularly concerned about either chronological developments or German (Nazi) history. He mentions these things and sends the reader to the specialized treatments of these issues. His is a combination of intellectual-cultural history and social history, mainly of the Jews but also of Germans and thus actually deals with their daily life, their *Alltagsgeschichte*, but their everyday life under a criminal regime. He details that history on the basis of both Jewish and Nazi sources. This is not a history of German Jewish liberalism, the view of the majority, who in the main remained attached to a German-patriotic ideology until 1938 while remaining loyal to their own version of Jewishness. Nor is it a history of German Zionism or German Jewish orthodoxy, of those minority movements that built on the idea of Jewish separateness. In other words, this is not an internal history of the Jewish minority in Germany but the story of the persecution of that minority as seen through Jewish and German eyes.

After providing the necessary background in terms of the antecedents of the Nazi accession to power and the accession itself, Friedländer devotes a seminally important chapter, chapter 3, to what he appropriately calls redemptive antisemitism. The original chapter title was "Redemptive Anti-Semitism in Its Epoch"—an obvious challenge to Ernst Nolte, the near-revisionist German historian whose later writings prompted the famous German "historians' controversy" (*Historikerstreit*), which began with a bitter discussion between him and Friedländer. Nolte's most famous, and still influential, book, *Three Faces of Fascism*, was originally published under its German title, *Der Faschismus in Seiner Epoche* (Fascism in Its Epoch).[20]

Friedländer's whole approach is an antithesis to Nolte's. The crucial thing in the history of Nazi Germany was not German fascism but the criminality shown in the Nazis' pseudo-messianic ideology. What Friedländer understands by the term *redemptive* is a novel mutation of anti-Jewishness, which places emphasis on the presumed spiritual, moral, and physical redemption of "Aryans" by cleansing the individual and society from the contaminating presence of Jews. It is only then that the Aryans can gain control of themselves and of human beings at large—which is what Aryans exist for.

Friedländer discusses two types of racist antisemitism: one that is based on the pseudo-scientific, quasi-rational findings of the late nineteenth-century, as in the fields of racial biology, Social Darwinism, and eugenics; and one, redemptive antisemitism, that is based on a "decidedly religious vision" in which "the struggle against the Jews is the dominant aspect of a worldview in which other racist themes are but secondary appendages."[21] The second type sprang from a fear of miscegenation and from old messianic views, from an anxiety about Jewish penetration into the German polity, and from dreams of a German renaissance that would happen upon liberation from the Jews by expulsion or worse. The elements of continuity and discontinuity in German ideology over time are encapsulated in Friedländer's formulation of the Nazi variety of racist antisemitism as a combination of Christian messianic hopes and traditional Christian antisemitic themes into an immensely potent anti-Jewishness, to which was added modern racist pseudo-science, which was not, by the way, exclusively German by any means. The messianic type appears in the form of a promise of total redemption; readers will be reminded of Friedländer's characterization of National Socialism as a pseudo-religious ideology in his early works.

The question is, How did this ideology penetrate into the German populace, and to what extent did it impact on the events of the Nazi era? There is no point in repeating here the arguments previously advanced to the effect that antisemitic ideology was a prime mover of Nazi anti-Jewish policies. What is important, however, is to emphasize the conjunction of the utopian hopes of a population in crisis with the established view of the Jew as the quintessential non-German, a view that has been discussed by many historians. Friedländer's redemptive antisemitism appears to be much more convincing than Goldhagen's compulsive eliminationist norm embraced by most, if not all, of German society for hundreds of years. Friedländer does not claim that redemptive antisemitism was a universally held belief, but he says, on the basis of the history of the latter nineteenth and the early twentieth centuries, that it gained ground, especially during the Weimar years, in segments of the German public. When we add John Weiss's insights regarding German elites, redemptive antisemitism becomes a key term in understanding not only Nazi ideology itself but its tremendous appeal both for German elites and for the population at large. By joining messianic hopes and expectations to old Christian antisemitic ideas and Social Darwinist perversions of modern science, National Socialism forged a powerful tool in its struggle for the souls of the German people. Nor was it just a tool. The Nazis really believed what they were saying; their ideology was not simply a matter of political instrumentalization. It is necessary to emphasize that although racist antisemitism, including its redemptive version, was associated with the intellectual elites in the hundred years preceding the Nazi rise to power, it was a marginal phenomenon, rejected, for instance, even by the first president of the imperialist Pan-German League, Ernst Hasse.[22] It was produced, as Friedländer and others point out, by a series of social, economic, and political crises in the context of the religious antisemitism that preceded it.

Friedländer notes that a nonradical, certainly nonmurderous anti-Jewishness was widely spread among the German population. Though not ubiquitous, it formed the basis for consensual approval for the antisemitic steps of the Nazi regime until 1938, steps aimed at excluding the Jews from German society and that went a long way toward dispossessing and stigmatizing them. In a parallel development, an intensive propaganda campaign managed to turn redemptive antisemitism, in a very short time, from a quasi-religious belief held by a small minority into a belief that was accepted by ever larger numbers of people, because of the moderate antisemitism that was so common. Friedländer has no explanation for how this speedy transformation took place, but his descriptions of the development itself are persuasive.

Friedländer's method combines a view from "above"—the political leadership—with one from "below," of Germans and Jews alike—a real *Alltagsgeschichte* approach. Paradoxically perhaps, it is exactly the detailed view from below that shows us the role of the dictator and the way his charismatic personality and the adoration accorded him by more and more Germans made it possible for the redemptive myth to be accepted by growing numbers of people. Friedländer avoids simplistic intentionalism, instead identifying the redemptive mythology in Hitler's own approach: Hitler saw in the Jew the embodiment of Satan, who had to be "removed" (*entfernen*, to use Hitler's famous expression of 1919). The Holocaust was not the result of a plan prepared in the 1930s, and Hitler's famous speech of January 1939 (in which he threatened that the European Jews would be annihilated in a future world war, supposedly caused by them) was not accompanied by any preparations to execute the threat. That threat was an expression of the radicalizing impact of the dictator and a clear expression of redemptive antisemitism.

Only recently was an overview of Jewish history in Nazi Germany produced, in Hebrew, although a very large number of monographic works are available that describe particular groups, events, contexts, and places.[25] Friedländer's book is not a general history of German Jews under the Nazi regime but the history of the persecution of Jews by the regime viewed from a synthetic perpetrator-victim-bystander perspective. The approach is definitely new: the book is a view of ideological, political, and social influences that molded the attitude of the persecutors to the persecutees; a social and cultural history of the Jews in the German social and cultural context; a review of the attitudes of churches and the outside world; and a composite of personal stories, included to make the whole period come alive. The persecutors are not the subject and the Jews merely objects, but both are subjects reacting to each other. This is the kind of history that needs to be written.

Criticism can be voiced, however, regarding what is missing from the book: intra-Jewish tensions and controversies, the intellectual reactions to important Jewish ideological trends, the story of the drive toward emigration, the attempts to reorient people to occupations in which they might survive in Germany or be accepted in foreign countries, and the way Jews met the economic challenges, social welfare problems, and other such issues of life under a Nazi regime. Friedländer deals with the Christian churches' attitude toward the Jews but not rabbinical responses. One cannot deal with everything, of course, certainly not in a relatively small volume. But of one thing there can be no doubt: Friedländer is the first historian who has managed to present an overarching history of the Nazi policy toward the Jews and the Jewish reactions to it that does not stumble over the difficulties mentioned earlier regarding the other attempts. It is, in fact, the first guide to how to write such a history by combining different perspectives and yet remain eminently readable.

Presenting overarching pictures of the Holocaust that make sense should be a goal of historians. The major challenge is how to write from above and below at the same time, weaving in the Jewish victims, the various influences from within Nazi Germany, the large social organizations, the outside forces, and present not just a description but an explanation. Germany occupied most of Europe: How does one tell the whole story, dealing simultaneously with France and Poland, with the Soviet areas and Germany, and so on, without giving up the main task—analysis and explanation of how and why events happened? I can only wish that Friedländer will continue to produce the kind of history that he provided in the first volume and hope that others, too, can go on to write general histories of the Holocaust.

chapter six
Jewish Resistance—Myth or Reality?

Jewish reaction to Nazi policies has been addressed many times before, although much of the material is available only in Hebrew and Yiddish.[1] Are there still new insights to be gained? I think so.

Twenty years ago I defined Jewish resistance as "any group action consciously taken in opposition to known or surmised laws, actions or intentions directed against the Jews by the Germans and their supporters."[2] I am no longer sure that that definition is valid, because it avoids dealing with individual acts of resistance, armed or unarmed, which have to be taken into account as an expression of the will of at least segments of Jewish communities or groups. Nor do I think referring to "Germans and their supporters" is appropriate; I now prefer saying "Germans and their collaborators."

Individual acts of resistance constitute a slippery and awkward topic, because what to include and what to exclude is difficult to determine. The problem cannot be ignored, however, and I shall come back to it below. A second problem is captured by the question of why one says "Germans," not "Nazis" and "collaborators," not "supporters." Here the answer has to take into account the findings, already discussed, that the vast majority of the German population supported, participated in, or at least condoned the genocidal murder of Jews and many others. It is therefore appropriate to speak of Germans, even though a minority opposed the regime and its works. The difference between "supporters" and "collaborators" is that some groups and political organizations, as well as some individuals, may not have supported the genocidal attacks but may have collaborated with the Nazis on some level or other.

Beyond these matters of definition, two basic concepts have to be discussed. The first is manifested in the Hebrew term *amidah*, which is almost impossible to translate. In this context it means literally "standing up against," but that does not capture the deeper sense of the word. When I speak of resistance, I mean amidah, and that includes both armed and unarmed actions and excludes passive resistance, although that term is almost a non sequitur, because one cannot really resist passively. When one refuses to budge in the face of brutal force, one does not resist passively; one resists without using force, and that is not the same thing.

What does amidah include? It includes smuggling food into ghettos; mutual self-sacrifice within the family to avoid starvation or worse; cultural, educational, religious, and political activities taken to strengthen morale; the work of doctors, nurses, and educators to consciously maintain health and moral fiber to enable individual and group survival; and, of course, armed rebellion or the use of force (with bare hands or with "cold" weapons) against the Germans and their collaborators.

A second concept of great importance is "sanctification of life," a term reputedly introduced by Rabbi Yitzhak Nissenboim in the Warsaw ghetto though actually used in previous eras.[5] It was taken to denote *meaningful* Jewish survival and probably includes most of the instances mentioned above, but not armed resistance or the use of force generally. I am not sure that it includes, for instance, smuggling food, although one could argue that it does when done consciously for physical survival. In the case of major smugglers whose aim was simply to make money, there may be a justifiable doubt, even though, arguably, without them, those in the ghetto would have perished before the major murder operations. A view is gaining ground in Israel—not necessarily among historians—that would label every struggle for physical survival "sanctification of life." But in the conditions created by the Germans to facilitate murder, the victims were often forced to choose between death and survival at the expense of others—a moral dilemma that makes survival not necessarily a matter of sanctification of life.

Let us, for purposes of clarification, briefly return to the example mentioned above, in Chapter 3, of the German anti-Nazi in the Łódź ghetto, Friedrich Hielscher. Most observers would probably not exonerate the head of the ghetto police, Leon Rosenblatt, from bearing a heavy moral responsibility for providing the Germans with the lists of deportees to a known death despite his putative moral qualms. He did not engage in the sanctification of life but in the rationalization of collusion in murder.

Or, another example: an inmate of a concentration camp who, to survive, stole bread from his or her neighbor. Most of us would not condemn such a person, because it was not he or she who was responsible but the Germans who created conditions in which such horrific choices had to be made. The ancient Jewish rule "Judge not your neighbor until you have reached his place"—or, we might say, stood in his shoes—applies here. A judgmental attitude is very much misplaced. But the choice does not represent sanctification of life.

In another example these dilemmas come to the fore. The Israeli dramatist Yehoshua Sobol wrote a play, *The Ghetto*, which was staged successfully in Israel, the United States, and Germany. The play deals with the theater in the Vilna ghetto, which was established with the full support of the head of the Judenrat, Yakov Gens, in order to raise the morale of the inmates and provide a means of livelihood for actors and other theater workers. The play is largely based on the diary of Herman

Kruk, a cultural activist in the prewar Warsaw Bund (the Jewish socialist party in Poland) who had fled to Vilna.⁺ In the Vilna ghetto he
worked at the archive and library of the Yiddish Scientific Institute,
which the Germans wanted to use to document Jewish culture after the
destruction of the Jews themselves. Kruk was opposed to armed rebellion as advocated by the underground youth movements (including
members of his own Bund party), and though critical of Gens, he saw
some value in Gens's policies as head of the ghetto. He organized in
Vilna an effort that paralleled that of Emmanuel Ringelblum in Warsaw,
who organized the "Oneg Shabbat" group of devoted coworkers to
establish a large underground archive documenting life in the ghetto.
Some of the material Kruk collected has survived.

In the diary and in Sobol's play, Kruk is opposed to the establishment
of the theater: one does not stage performances on graves, he says. He
could have called it blasphemy (he was an atheist), but certainly not
sanctification of life. Yet Gens supported the theater for life's sake,
to raise morale, just as he had supported schooling, and music, and literary evenings, much of which Kruk approved of. The partisan underground—FPO, the Farainikte Partisaner Organizacie, or United Partisan Organization—especially its second commander, the poet Abba
Kovner, were not opposed to the theater or to the other cultural activities, although the argument could have been put forward that such
activities were liable to lull people into illusions of permanency and
normalcy. Did this type of sanctification of life stand in contradiction to
resistance, or did it advance the cause by strengthening morale, or was
it morally unacceptable when mourning the tens of thousands of Vilna
Jews who had been murdered before the ghetto had come into existence,
as Kruk maintained? Are we with Kruk, who supported Gens and opposed armed resistance *and* the theater, or with Kovner, who opposed
Gens, thundered against having any illusions about German intentions,
but supported cultural activities, including the theater? Did the theater
sanctify life or rationalize escapism of the worst kind?

One could start the story of the sanctification of life in the 1930s, when German Jews developed an unprecedented number of cultural activities—Jewish studies, music, theater, studies of German literature, publications—consciously designed to preserve their morale.[5] But persecution and the threat of forced emigration is not the same as the wartime danger of physical annihilation. The reaction of German Jews can serve as a paradigm for what happened later, in the sense that most people refused to give in to despair and acted out their amidah—their resistance—by turning inward and discovering aspects of their Jewish heritage, whether religious or secular or antireligious. Yet it is perhaps more correct to speak of amidah and sanctification in the context of the war itself.

The examples that are usually given to underpin the sanctification of life argument are from some of the large ghettos—Warsaw, Łódż, Vilna, Kovno, Piotrków Tribunalski, Czestochowa.[6] Much less evidence comes from places like Cracow, Tarnów, Kielce, or the towns of eastern Galicia. The cases cited are all legitimate and persuasive, however. The case of Warsaw is symptomatic and well known. There were attempts to provide education for elementary school children in 1939–1941, when education was forbidden.[7] The community set up *complets*, small groups of children meeting clandestinely with a teacher, whose salary usually consisted of a very little food. The local Jews had two underground high schools, the more important of which was the school organized by the Dror underground socialist-Zionist youth movement.[8] Ringelblum talks of 600 *minyanim*—groups of at least ten males necessary for organized religious observance.[9] We know of ultraorthodox groups that tried to maintain at least minimal religious studies in Warsaw—and we have evidence of the disintegration and moral collapse of some of these. Out of one of these groups of the faithful comes the collection of sermons by a great chassidic thinker Rabbi Kalman Klonymus Shapira, the Rabbi of Piaseczna, which was found in Warsaw after the war and published under the title *Esh Kodesh* (Holy Fire).[10] Another chassidic thinker was

Rabbi Issachar Teichthal from Slovakia, who wrote a book—*Em Ha-banim Samecha* (The Mother of the Sons Is Happy)—justifying Zionism from a messianic point of view, against his ultraorthodox environment.[11]

Works of nonreligious literature and poetry were written to add meaning to the lives of the victimized people. Yitzhak Katznelson, in the Warsaw ghetto, for instance, wrote prose and, chiefly, poetry and taught young people at the Dror high school.[12]

Another, very important example is the massive work of the Warsaw house committees, more than one thousand of them grass-roots groups, mostly elected democratically by their neighbors. Many but not all of these committees provided opportunities for small children's education, organized social help for indigent neighbors, tried to protect neighborhoods from the so-called delousing campaigns (in which rapacious Polish and Jewish officials looted property and exposed people to life-endangering health hazards), organized cultural activities—from concerts to lectures to debates—and provided some cover for illegal political activities. These house committees were themselves organized under the coordinating umbrella of Zetos, a body established by the Warsaw branch of the American Jewish Joint Distribution Committee (JDC) and run by Emmanuel Ringelblum. They acted to preserve the morale of the ghetto inhabitants.[13] The JDC also had a hand in the running of ghetto hospitals, as well as the school for nurses run by an extraordinary woman, Luba Bilecka.[14] A system of orphanages was run by Centrala Opieki nad Sierotani (CENTOS), an organization from the prewar days that took care of orphans, headed by Adolf Berman.[15] Initiatives like that of the great Polish Jewish educator, Janusz Korczak, who headed his own children's home, continued from prewar days.[16] Other initiatives dealt with agricultural work (the name of the organization was TOPOROL), and there was much else.

Apart from these initiatives, there was a whole network of underground political organizations, most importantly of youth groups, representing various, largely left-wing Zionist trends, the Bund, and small groups of Jewish Communists. Many adults were grouped in political parties that maintained a tenuous existence until the Warsaw ghetto rebellion; they were largely organized around soup kitchens supervised either by the Judenrat or by the JDC. A very large underground press existed; it published in three languages, Polish, Yiddish, and Hebrew.[17]

More problematic, as already mentioned, is the economic self-help, mainly smuggling, and the establishment of illegal workshops that produced mainly for "export"—for smuggling to the Polish side of the ghetto wall. The famous cases of smuggling by children would fit under the sanctification of life concept, as would the daily economic struggle for existence, for the Jews thought, rightly or wrongly, that it was the Germans' purpose to starve them to death.

Parallel examples could be adduced for other ghettos in Poland, as well as in some of the Transnistrian ghettos, such as Shargorod and Mogilev, where Jewish initiatives enabled quasi-industrial production to take place, which saved many people's lives.[18] In countries and areas where no ghettos were established, certain modalities of action might well be described as examples of sanctification. Thus, Romanian Jews, themselves very hard pressed and their property largely expropriated, attempted time and again to help the Jews deported to Transnistria; they finally managed to send delegations there (under Fred Sharaga) with material help of life-saving importance.[19] The Slovak Jewish leadership organized three labor camps to prevent deportations to Poland— it is a matter of contention whether these camps did not play into the hands of the Nazis when they occupied Slovakia in September 1944. There were widespread cultural and illegal political activities in these camps.[20] Networks to rescue Jews, especially children, were established in Belgium and France; in these, Jews and non-Jews collaborated closely.[21] Youth movements all over Europe, largely left-wing Zionist in approach, held underground seminars, organized houses of refuge (France, Hungary), and later organized or joined the armed resistance (France, Slovakia).[22]

In considering resistance it is important to deal with Jewish cultural activities in the camps, both in the transit camps (Westerbork in

Holland, Malines in Belgium, Drancy in France) and in concentration camps proper. In all these there is credible evidence of study circles, cabarets, musical performances (Western Europe), all of them conducted to preserve morale; there are many instances of performances from memory (Auschwitz), religious observances made on a fairly large scale, and so on.[23] For instance, *Die Fledermaus* was performed in a subcamp of Gross-Rosen from memory by a group of young women.[24] On roughly the festival of Hanukkah (the Festival of Lights), in December 1944, a group of five Jewish men, all of them nonreligious, managed to light pieces of carton in their ice-cold barrack and sing the Hanukkah song.[25] Jewish women deported via Auschwitz to a slave labor camp at Altona, a suburb of Hamburg, in 1944 organized study circles, and each woman was asked to write down from memory poems by Romanian, Hungarian, and French poets on pieces of paper and with pencils recovered, with great difficulty, from the ruins of bombed-out buildings, where they had to work. "After a few days we sat around in a circle and wrote, and after some more days we had our first evening reading session. We invited guests from other barracks and read out poems so that we almost forgot where we were. Thus we continued evening after evening. After some time we also dared to present poems and little stories we wrote ourselves that gave expression to our own literary inclinations. We started to utilize our hidden talents; one knew how to draw, another had been a theater actress, and we tried to entertain each other so as to forget our hunger."[26] Things like that happened among non-Jews as well, as the literature on the camps testifies. But Jews were, as we know, the lowest of the low in the camps and needed special spiritual and mental strength to try and preserve their morale.

There was, and still is, a controversy about what commentators call "meaning." For the religious Jews as for the others, suffering and mass death had no intrinsic meaning. Any meaning in the concentration camp universe was a Nazi meaning, because for the Nazis that universe had a purpose. For the victims it had none. This is a difficult thing to say, especially to survivors, but any other response would not be truthful.

The Jews fell victim to a crime motivated by an evil fantasy; that fantasy could have no meaning for them. But humans need to find meaning in their lives, so the victims introduced meaning themselves, whether by strategies like that of Viktor Frankl, who insisted on his humanity against all odds, or by a strong desire to survive against all odds, or by a religious belief asserted against all evidence of divine indifference to suffering, or by political convictions that promised a better future after the horror ended.[27]

Two cases of Jewish cultural activity are well known: one concerns Jewish cultural activities in the camps established by the French Vichy regime in the south of France, mainly for Jews and Spanish Republicans. A great number of drawings, poems, and so on survived from these camps.[28] However bad the conditions were, and they were bad, these camps were not Nazi concentration camps. The other case is Terezin, a ghetto-camp in which special conditions existed. Despite severe starvation and the constant threat of deportations "to the East," tremendous cultural activity flourished there. The composition of the camp explains some of this: the pick of Czech Jewish intellectuals and many of their peers from Germany and Austria and some other countries were forced to live there and mostly die either there or at Auschwitz. Paintings, poems, musical compositions, concerts, children's "wall newspapers" and poems, drawings, theatrical performances, and academic lectures by brilliant speakers—all these were encouraged and produced with the same aim in mind as that of the Warsaw house committees: to preserve morale against the threat of annihilation.[29]

The literature that emphasizes active, unarmed Jewish response—amidah—has therefore a great deal to be said for it. Yet I fear that the picture is overdrawn. A reader might get the impression that while there was suffering, the majority of the Jews were busy educating, learning, putting on plays or making music or painting, giving or listening to lectures, publishing illegal newspapers, and so on. Let me state therefore, in unmistakable language, that life was hell, that people were starving to death, and that when survivors tell us that inmates of the Łódź or

Warsaw ghetto made attempts to educate their children, for instance, these attempts were heroic, but they did not encompass all or even most of the children, and they were part of a constant struggle against impossible odds. The same applies to the Judenräte, to which we now turn.

The historical literature on the behavior of the Judenräte is voluminous, and yet the subject is far from being exhausted. Two basic approaches can be discerned. One is represented by Raul Hilberg, who has analyzed the Judenräte with the tools of the social scientist. He says, in effect, that the moment these Jewish leadership groups accepted nomination at German hands, they became, willy-nilly, cogs in the destruction machine that the Germans developed to annihilate the Judenräte's own charges, the Jewish people. The Judenräte facilitated the murder, even when they did everything in their power to extricate themselves from that role. When they established hospitals and cured sick Jews, they made more slave workers available to toil for the Germans until the Germans decided to kill them. Whether or not Judenräte collaborated with the ghetto police forces, which usually served as German tools, their very existence as bureaucratic machines executing German orders made them a part of the murderous system. Hilberg does not pass a value judgment; he emphasizes that some of these Jewish bureaucrats may have been morally impeccable and that their disastrous role was the result of their objective situation; they "were *not* the willful accomplices of the Germans."[30]

Hilberg's analysis is valid in terms of a politological perspective.

The alternative view was first proposed by Aharon Weiss several decades ago, and some other historians, including myself, have accepted his analysis and tried to develop it.[31] Essentially, this alternative view does not oppose Hilberg's perspective but sees it as insufficient.[32] A historian cannot judge historical events only by their outcome but has to take intentions and attitudes into account. By this criterion, Judenrat policies failed: evasion, bribery, and establishment of workshops and factories that operated on behalf of the Germans, so that the workers and their families should be protected because they were economically useful to the perpetrators, were ultimately useless, as Hilberg rightly points out. The Judenräte indeed, as he argues, became part of the German machinery of murder. But if all we need to know is whether the final result was murder, we don't have to engage in historical research—we know it was. The problem goes deeper: What were the intentions of the Judenrat members, and what did they try to do to fulfill those intentions when protecting their communities was the goal? How did they stand up to the oppressors? How did they relate to their public—were they corrupt officials just trying to save themselves at the expense of others, or did they try to protect their public at the risk of their own lives and those of their families? I must repeat: we know they failed. But *we* know they had to fail; *they* usually knew that only when it was too late; but—did they try to protect their communities even after they knew the situation was hopeless? We judge them with hindsight, and that is always a much more knowledgeable view. So we have to ask whether in a totally immoral world they tried to maintain elementary morality, whether their strategies were designed for the common good, and not whether their actions were successful. Finally and most importantly, we have found that generalizations about their behavior put forward by Hilberg, and in a different and more extreme form perhaps by Hannah Arendt, are inappropriate, because no Judenrat behaved in quite the same way as any other Judenrat.[33] Each Judenrat presided over a hell, and similar though these hells were to each other, they were at the same time quite different.

Aharon Weiss's investigation was an eye-opener. He asked survivors of Polish ghettos what they thought of the Judenrat in their locality. The answers reflected their perceptions of the moral worth and decency of their official leaders—their good or bad intentions, not their success in preventing disaster. Weiss looked at "first," "second," and "third" Judenräte. By "first" Judenräte, Weiss meant those nominated at the beginning of the German conquest; in most cases they were replaced, often precisely because they did not fulfill the aims of the Germans. Then, a "second" Judenrat was nominated and often, later, a "third."

Of the 146 "first" Judenräte in Poland with a sufficient number of responses, 30.9 percent of heads of Judenräte were judged by the survivors
to have been "good" leaders (they assisted the community, refused to
carry out German financial directives, warned of approaching *Aktion*).
An additional 37.7 percent resigned because they were unwilling to
carry out German orders, were removed by the Germans because of
such refusal, or were murdered because they refused to hand over Jews
to the Germans. Another 9.1 percent committed suicide, or had connections with the underground, or died after taking office. The evaluation
of another 9 percent was ambiguous, and 14.3 percent were judged
negatively. At least 86.6 percent of these heads, according to Weiss, did
not go beyond a limited, forced cooperation with the authorities and
were thought by the survivors to have been devoted public servants.
Second Judenräte were often obedient servants of the German authorities. With them, the positive evaluation dropped to 30.6 percent. The
third Judenräte were judged negatively by an overwhelming number.[34]

To analyze these findings, Weiss established a grid of five types of
behavior, in the middle of which he drew what he called a red line, which
meant handing over Jews to the Germans at the latter's request. If a
Judenrat declined to hand over Jews or engaged in other types of sabo-
tage or resistance to German demands of lesser import, it was judged
positively. Delivering Jews into German hands and active collaboration
of other kinds placed the Judenrat below the red line and into the
negative columns.

But these are generalizations, and a more detailed look at the various
communities shows the differing behavior of each set of human beings
who had the unenviable task of leading a Jewish community during the
catastrophe. Weiss's analyses and figures throw light on one possible
aspect of the tragedy, but in a way they hide another—the irresolvable
dilemmas these Judenräte were faced with. To gain a sense of these
dilemmas, let us look at a hypothetical case centered on Łódź and its
notorious "Jew Elder," as the Nazis put it, Mordechai Chaim Rumkowski, and then at some cases that really occurred.

Rumkowski was without any doubt a brutal dictator. He handed the children of the ghetto over to the Germans. He not only knew what their fate would be; he even made a speech, which has been preserved, telling the inhabitants of the ghetto why he was doing it: if he did not, the Germans would take young people as well as the children and the old people. If the young people did not survive, there would be no hope for the future; if they did, they would give birth to new children.[35] Job, we will remember, had lost his wife and children in the game played by God and Satan; having proven his steadfastness, Job then was rewarded by God with another wife and other children.[36] The former ones died for no sin of their own. Rumkowski, originally a childless bachelor, was forcing others to play Job. He became an accessory to massive child murder. He turned the ghetto into a slave labor camp producing goods for the Germans, which he said was the only way the young and the strong would survive. We have seen the defense of his policy in the Hielscher-Rosenblatt document mentioned in Chapter 3.

The ghetto had 160,000 residents in June 1940 and only about 69,000 in late July 1944. Łódź was the only ghetto left in Poland at that time because there were strong local and military German interests that had prevented its destruction. The local Germans—and the obvious example is Hans Biebow, who was the German responsible for the ghetto—had a vested interest in its survival. Not only did it provide each of them with a sizable personal income and prevented many of them from being sent into the army to fight the Soviets, but it also provided essential goods for the Wehrmacht and for the German economy generally. And it provided a nice income for Artur Greiser, the Gauleiter of the area. In other words, Rumkowski's gambit seemed to be paying off. Then, in the spring of 1944, the decision to murder the ghetto residents came—from Berlin, from Himmler, not from local authorities. Some 7,200 were murdered in Chelmno, in June and July. In August the ghetto was finally liquidated and the remaining 69,000 people were sent to Auschwitz.

In the meantime, the Red Army was advancing toward western Poland. In July 1944 it reached the Vistula River, and there it stopped, for a combination of military and political reasons that need not concern us here, except that they had nothing to do with Jews, or with Łódź. The Soviets restarted their offensive in January 1945, and it took them three days to cover the distance to Łódź: exactly 100 kilometers (60 miles) as the crow flies. They found several hundred Jews there, who had been left behind in August to clean up the ghetto and ship abandoned properties to Germany. All these Jews were liberated because the Germans had other worries during those three days than to bother about them.

The hypothetical situation is this: Had the Soviets decided in July to stop their advance not then but three days later, not on the Vistula but 100 kilometers farther west, they would presumably have liberated most of the Jews still in Łódź. Rumkowski's policies would have been vindicated, and he might have been the only ghetto head who had rescued a sizable portion of his people. If so, would we have erected a statue in his memory, as a hero of the Jewish people, or would we have sentenced him to death for having knowingly caused the murder of thousands upon thousands of helpless Jewish children, old people, and sick people? The moment we raise the question, we instinctively pass judgment, even though we might say that we have no right to judge. Frankly, I would vote for the gallows, not the statue; but I realize that there are two sides to the story.

Most of my colleagues will be up in arms against this presentation. After all, historians are supposed to deal with what happened, not with what might have been. But I have never accepted that deterministic methodology. It implies that because something happened, it had to happen—but that is demonstrably false. Any event is the result of the interaction of an infinite number of causal chains; a distinction can be made between marginal influences and more central ones, and one of the main tasks of the historian, if not *the* main one, is to try and make that distinction. But the very fact that the number of causal chains is infinite, and that they interact and constantly change positions—old Heraklitos was right—means that there are choices; and it is people who make the choices. The view that if we knew all the causes, we could know all the results is off the mark, for there is not even the theoretical possibility of knowing an infinite number of causes. Anything could have happened differently from the way it did.

I have already suggested that if the Western Allies had reached an agreement with the Soviets in June 1939, to establish an armed coalition against Hitler's Germany, the Holocaust quite possibly would not have happened, at least not in the way it did. Other turning points in the 1930s are equally obvious. Even the personality of Hitler is of some importance: had he been killed as a valiant German NCO in World War I, the murder of Jews, Roma, and Poles might not have been so central in any racist-biological ideology guiding a German regime. Beyond some point, of course, other options and choices are shut out. In 1941, given complete German control over most of Europe, the weakness of the Allies, and the increasing radicalization of German anti-Jewish policies, the Holocaust of the Jewish people could not have been avoided by the West or by anyone else.

Historians should ruminate about unrealized possibilities in the situation that pertains before such final points of decision are reached—possibilities that realistically lay in the situations—or they miss their vocation completely. The example given here is realistic: the Soviets hesitated over whether to continue their quick advance into Poland until they reached the Oder in the west and the Beskide Mountains in the south, thus utilizing their victory over an increasingly demoralized German army on the run, or whether their lines of supply and communications were already so overstretched that they could not risk a second "miracle on the Vistula," as Poles called the defeat of the Red Army at the hands of the Poles near Warsaw in August 1920. Stalin's desire to let the London-directed Polish Home Army bleed to death in a futile attempt at armed rebellion against the Germans also played a role from early August on. But in July the choice was a real one, and the decision made might have been different.

The dilemma presented is far from being the only one. Minsk was the site of another dilemma. There was no Jewish community because the

Soviets had destroyed it after the Bolshevik Revolution, but there were Jews, and the ghetto contained 84,000 inhabitants. A Judenrat was appointed, with a Minsk trade employee by the name of Ilya Mishkin as head; his only qualification was that he spoke German. But from the first day he collaborated with a Communist underground, led in the ghetto by a Jewish Communist refugee from Warsaw named Hersh Smoliar. How could Mishkin do both: obey German orders (otherwise he would be removed and killed) and support the underground, supplying partisans in nearby forests with medical aid, clothing, and other equipment and helping to smuggle some 7,500 Jews out of the ghetto and into the forests? But he did it, and when he was murdered after relying on a supposedly anti-Nazi German officer, his successor, Moshe Yaffe, a refugee from Vilna, followed an identical policy. Yaffe was killed in July 1942 because he had warned the assembled ghetto inhabitants that they were going to be murdered. At one point, the Germans found out that Smoliar—they knew only his cover name—was the head of an underground organization in the ghetto and demanded that he be handed over to them. The alternative: they would destroy the ghetto. Yaffe solved the dilemma by giving the Germans the corpse of a Jew whose face the Jewish doctors had disfigured and in whose pocket they put Smoliar's false ghetto identity card.[37]

Most of the Judenräte in Europe were somewhere between Łódź and Minsk in the degree to which they yielded to the Germans. Some of them obsequiously obeyed German orders in the hope of "avoiding worse," as the Amsterdam Jewish Council repeatedly said, behaving in a kind of anticipatory compliance (Raul Hilberg's appropriate term)—that is, obeying orders before they had been given. Other Judenräte staged armed rebellions (Lachwa, Tuczyn, Zdzieciol [Zhetl], etc.).[38] Mostly, however, they did neither. Many acted with amidah—trying to preserve their dignity as long as possible, trying to obtain food, trying to preserve health, protect the children and the infirm, support cultural activities and other morale-building projects—and ultimately failing. A typical example is Dr. Elkhanan Elkes in Kovno, who tried to preserve a ghetto of some

16,000 inhabitants, facing the Germans with tremendous personal courage (supervising clandestine efforts to rescue children, support resistance, and so forth). No survivor of the Kovno ghetto is likely to regard Elkes with anything but the greatest admiration. He sanctified life.[39]

Then there is the case of Kosów Huculski, a small shtetl near the foothills of the Carpathians, in eastern Galicia. It had 2,500 Jewish inhabitants, who made up more than 80 percent of the total population, and another 1,500 Jewish residents from nearby villages who were forced to move to the town. After the German invasion of the Soviet Union, the Hungarian army occupied the town; then the Germans came, and a Judenrat was established, led by Chaim Zwi Steiner. There was no fenced ghetto. In the winter of 1941, in a major *Aktion*, 2,088 Jews of Kosów were murdered on a nearby hillside. The survivors knew what to expect. People dug hiding places or tried to arrange for refuge with friendly Ukrainians or Poles. During the Passover festival in 1942,

> All of the police were on their feet, and masses of German and Ukrainian police came from other places. All the Jews realized immediately that something was bound to happen and that one had to try and hide. All of them did, in cellars, in the forests, or with friendly peasants. On the second day [of Passover] not a soul could be seen in the town, except for four members of the committee [Judenrat] who decided not to hide. They thought that if the bandits [the Germans] came, there had to be someone who would negotiate with them. Perhaps something could be saved [by talking]? If there was no one there, they [the Germans] would set fire to the houses and everyone would be burned to death. The four discussed this with their families and then sat down to wait in the committee room, knowing that they would be the first victims. The phone rang. The Pole Zborowski, who worked at the Labor Office, announced that the "guests" had arrived. He meant the Gestapo. One of the four went very pale. So the other three told him to go and hide, because he was too weak. He left, and only the other three remained, silent, because they knew what they could expect.[40]

It is almost superfluous to comment. The three men of Kosów did not engage in armed resistance—there was no such possibility in Kosów.

They were willing to die to protect their community in the only way they could: by holding up the Germans for another, probably very small amount of time. Perhaps they could prevent people being burnt to death, although they were going to die themselves. This is hardly passive resistance. It is active, unarmed amidah at its most heroic. They even sent their colleague who could not stand up to the situation (would we?) home to his family.

How do we know what happened in the committee room in Kosów? The answer comes in the next sentence: "After about half an hour, the phone rang again, and the same Pole announced that the 'guests' had driven off" to Kitov, another hamlet, whose inhabitants were murdered that day. The Kosów Jews were killed half a year later, in September 1942.

We can see that the concept of amidah as an unarmed Jewish response in the sense of "sanctification of life" applies to the behavior of large numbers of Jews in many communities both East and West. To this must be added armed resistance, which I have written about extensively. Here I will summarize the findings to date in brief.[41]

Contrary to a widely held belief in the immediate postwar period and the 1950s, there was a great deal of armed Jewish resistance throughout Europe. Contrary to a widely held belief later on, it was not—it could not be—massive; quantitatively speaking, it was marginal. And contrary to widely held beliefs today, it was qualitatively an important series of events and is an important component of collective Jewish memory—quite rightly so. In the primeval forests of eastern Poland, Belarus, and the northern Ukraine, probably some 30,000 Jews fought against the Germans, with inadequate weapons. Most of them were killed. It is only now that we are able to reconstruct their stories, with the help of freshly opened Soviet archives.

In Belarus there were more than sixty small ghettos, mostly in former Polish areas, in which there were Jewish underground groups.[42] The resisters generally tried to fight in the forests. In Poland (including

Bialystok), seventeen or eighteen ghettos had such armed groups.[43] Some members of the resistance managed to escape into the forests; some died fighting in the ghettos. The most famous armed rebellion took place in the Warsaw ghetto; other such attempts at fighting occurred in Bialystok, Cracow, Bedzin, Czestochowa, and elsewhere. In Lithuania, the attempts at armed resistance in Vilna (Vilnius), Kovno (Kaunas), and Sviencian (Svencionys) are well known. In almost all of the Polish and Lithuanian ghettos the Jewish population at large did not side with the rebels; in many of the small Belarus ghettos they did, as they did in Warsaw. The main reason seems to have been that in Poland and Lithuania working with the underground could not offer a real chance of survival, just a different type of death. The exception in Warsaw was clearly due to two chief factors: one, the knowledge of the mass death at Treblinka of those who had been deported (before the resistance movement became an effective organization) did not leave a viable alternative to resistance; and two, the elimination of the Judenrat and of Jewish Gestapo agents by the underground made the underground the effective ruler of the ghetto. Belarus, on the other hand, had forests, which offered a slight chance of survival, as well as the real possibility of taking revenge, which probably explains the much greater support the rebels received from the Jews in the nearby ghettos.

Armed resistance sprang up in Western and Southern Europe as well, especially in France, where specifically Jewish groups existed and where Jews also served in general movements and units. A small Jewish unit operated in Belgium, but there and in Italy most Jews in the armed resistance fought in the ranks of general anti-German organizations. Several thousand Jews fought in Tito's army in Yugoslavia—a very high percentage of the remnants still alive out of the original 75,000 Jews in that country. Hundreds of Jews served in the left-wing ELAS-EAM forces in Greece.

How do we distinguish conceptually between Jewish armed resistance and the armed resistance of Jews, where the former indicates special Jewish units and organizations and the latter, Jews in basically non-Jewish units? This problem is easier to deal with in the East, because there the ethnic differences were clear-cut. Ghetto fighters were necessarily Jews, although Jewish Communists and Bundists hoped for a socialist utopia where national differences would disappear. Jewish partisan units existed. In Poland Jews had to join the Communist Armia Ludowa underground if they wanted to survive, because the "official" Polish underground, the Armia Krajowa, would not accept them. In the Soviet areas at least a few Jewish units existed despite the Soviet policy of forced assimilation, which aimed at disbanding Jewish partisan units and merging them with non-Jewish ones. Some Soviet units were overwhelmingly Jewish, however. Other Soviet partisan units were not only infested with antisemitism but engaged in the murder of Jews, especially unarmed groups in so-called family camps, especially early on, in 1941–1942. Other units accepted Jews only if they came with arms, and rejected women. Others welcomed Jews. The position of Jewish women was precarious, and most of them could survive only by forming sexual liaisons with commanders and ordinary partisans in the units.[44]

Among these thousands of Jewish partisans were, to be sure, some convinced Communists who were fighting not for the survival of the Jewish ethnic community but for the socialist Soviet Union. This was especially true for some of the cadres trained in the "free" Soviet Union and infiltrated into enemy territory. However, among the Soviet partisans, Jews overwhelmingly fought because they were Jews. In Poland, a few Jews were in Armia Krajowa units pretending they were Poles; even among the Armia Ludowa members, Jews preferred not to be identified as such. Whatever their understanding of themselves, therefore, Polish Jews fought as Jews, not Poles, and their fate as Jews determined, to a very large extent, their participation in the resistance.

In other European countries, in contrast, most of the Jews fighting against Germany fought in the framework of the national movements of their host countries. This was true in France, Belgium, Italy, Yugoslavia, Slovakia, and Greece. The question arises, however, whether their participation in the fighting was not the result of their special

situation as Jews and whether this did not have an effect on their identity during and especially after the war. The case of France is instructive. The main Jewish fighters' organization was not Jewish at all: it was
the Main d'Oeuvre Immigré (MOI), a Communist movement of foreigners living in France. Jewish participation was very marked, however, both among commanders and among the ordinary members. Jewish Communists published much of their propaganda in Yiddish, and
Jewish symbols, such as the Bar Kochba rebellion (135 C.E.) were utilized to mobilize the membership. After the war most of the survivors
joined specifically Jewish groups, increasingly non-Communist.[45]

One could argue that these people acted out of specifically Jewish
motivations, whether they admitted it or not. The same applies in the
Belgian, Yugoslav, and Greek cases, less so in the Italian one, where
up to 2,000 Jews fought in Italian units that made no differentiation
between Jews and non-Jews. Yet one wonders whether, without anti-
Jewish persecution, many of these Jews would have joined the resistance. In Slovakia, some 1,600 Jews fought in the underground, even
though there was also a specifically Jewish unit (commanded by a Jewish Communist).[46] Certainly, many Jewish individuals had no wish to
identify with specifically Jewish causes and saw their fight as an anti-
Nazi activity, pursued in the name of general ideals, whether Communist, socialist, or national-local. We must respect their self-identification
and conclude that theirs was resistance by Jews, but not Jewish resistance. But the majority of Jews in the resistance, including those
serving in general units, appear to have been motivated to a large extent
and consciously by their Jewishness.

Another significant form of resistance occurred in the concentration
and death camps. Some of it was unarmed, some armed. The most
famous were the rebellions in Sobibor (August 1943) and Treblinka
(October 1943).[47] In Sobibor the rebellion caused the Nazis to stop
using the camp. Treblinka stayed in existence a few months longer after
its rebellion and was then destroyed by the Germans. A rebellion of the
Sonderkommando (the inmates who were forced to work in the gas

chambers and the crematoria) took place in Birkenau on October 7, 1944, but was put down. Of the actual rebels, none survived, but some who saw it at first hand did.[48] It did not apparently affect the murder policies of the Nazis. Earlier uprisings took place at Sachsenhausen (unarmed), and attempts were made at organized breakouts in some smaller camps. It is interesting—and understandable—that the only rebellions and mass breakouts in concentration, slave labor, and death camps were staged by Jews. After all, their situation was the most hopeless.

To measure Jewish armed resistance in terms of the numbers of Germans killed, or the effect it had on German policies, or even on chances of survival is futile. All such results were negligible. Instead, the measuring rod has to be the effect this type of resistance had on those who engaged in it and on postwar Jewish consciousness. The motivations of the rebels were several. Some young people desired revenge, pure and simple. They had had their nearest and dearest murdered, often in front of their own eyes, and would not have the chance of building a life for themselves because they would die at a young age at the hands of brutal murderers for reasons that made absolutely no sense. Other rebels wanted to escape if possible, as in Belarus and the northern Ukraine. Others wanted to participate in the fight against what they saw as a monstrous and murderous regime; or to identify with their non-Jewish neighbors in a fight for the liberation of their common homeland; or to make a moral and political statement as Jews by taking up arms against the murderers of Jews. This last motivation was especially strong among members of the Zionist youth movements, who played a central role in some of the better-known ghetto rebellions. They understood their resistance as an expression of protest against what was happening to their people. They understood it also, quite explicitly, as a message to Jews in the free world and humanity as a whole. The message for the Jews sometimes included the notion that they were defending Jewish honor, as in the famous words of Dolek Liebeskind of the Zionist underground in Cracow: "For three lines in history that will be written about the youth who fought and did not go like sheep to the slaughter it is even worth dying."[49]

Of one thing the resisters were sure: their struggle was not going to win the war. On the contrary, repeatedly they voiced their view that few of them, if any, would survive. That was also the weakness of their position vis-à-vis the Jewish population: except for the very problematic chance of surviving in the forests, they could offer no life-promising alternative to the frightened and desperate Jews. In any case, few places in Europe had forests near Jewish populations.

Whether or not local Jews were supportive, the surrounding populations in Eastern Europe were not supportive of, and in many cases were actively hostile to, Jewish fighters. Jews qua Jews had no access to arms insofar as arms were available for anti-Nazi activities by the underground organizations of the nations under German rule; and these underground organizations had no wish to supply Jews with arms. Nor were Jews organized or prepared for armed struggle. No central commands existed, no experienced officer corps, no support from the Allies, who dropped supplies and arms to undergrounds they recognized, and no Jewish underground was ever recognized.

In the forests of Eastern Europe a Soviet partisan movement developed, but it did not become effective until the spring and summer of 1942, after the establishment in May of that year of a Partisan High Command on unoccupied Soviet territory under Panteleimon Ponomarenko (general secretary of the Belorussian Communist Party), who himself was no great friend of the Jews. Until then, scattered Soviet soldiers and Communist cadres and other adventurous types established small units whose members acted partly as robbers and criminals and partly as anti-German partisans. Some of them killed Jews; others did not. After May 1942 some efforts were made to curb antisemitism in partisan units, but not always successfully. The tragedy was that when Soviet partisan detachments became better organized and disciplined, from the fall of 1942, the Jews had already been murdered. Before that, when the Jews in what later became partisan territory were looking for aid from such units, none existed. To put it succinctly, the Soviet partisans came too late.

By rights, Jewish armed resistance all over Europe should never have occurred. That it did, and on a fairly large scale, needs an explanation. Raul Hilberg's statement that Jews had traditionally, because of their history, abandoned the art of communal self-defense and that therefore no significant armed Jewish resistance took place during the Holocaust is based on an error: there was a great deal of Jewish armed resistance, very much more than could have been expected. It must have sprung up from different traditions. There were, after all, quite a number of instances of Jewish armed action in premodern times. Also, there were perhaps newer traditions, such as those created when Jews became soldiers in large modern armies in the nineteenth century; or perhaps a latent preparedness for physical resistance was embodied in Jewish traditions but suppressed until a time of dire need. In any case, the history of modern Israel shows that Hilberg's assumptions are wrong. The issue still awaits serious research.

This review of active Jewish responses to Nazi oppression could be summarized in an almost triumphalist fashion: there was unarmed resistance, there was sanctification of life, there was armed resistance. But the summary would give a completely skewed picture. It would show a nostalgic, sickeningly sweet dreamworld, not the reality of the Holocaust. There would be no traitors in it, no desperate leadership groups trying to bribe and cajole the murderers even after they knew the situation was hopeless, no masses of disoriented, frightened people, numbed multitudes who gave up hope and therefore became easy prey for the murderers. There would be no account in it of illusions that gave people hope against hope and then faltered on the rocks of mass death. Other elements must be integrated into the picture for it to conform more closely to reality.

chapter seven

Unarmed Resistance and Other Responses

Historians describing Jewish reactions in the Holocaust have often concentrated on the Judenräte to the exclusion of other centers of power in the beleaguered Jewish communities.[1] Jewish police are mentioned, to be sure—almost always as traitors to the Jewish people because of their role in cooperating or collaborating with the Germans in delivering Jewish victims to the Nazi murder machine. Jewish ghetto police were established by German orders in almost all East European ghettos. They were nominally under Judenrat supervision but became in many places units of traitors collaborating with the Germans. In fourteen ghettos, however, the police were a part of the Jewish resistance.

Only in some of the larger ghettos were the Judenräte forced to provide the Germans with lists and cooperate in the handing over of victims. In most places this never happened; the Germans and their helpers marched in and took the victims themselves, in the most brutal way possible. Sometimes the police cooperated, even when the Judenrat was not forced to do so. Sometimes—often—both the police and the Judenrat were treated like other Jews and did not participate in the roundup in any way. The role of the Warsaw Jewish Ordnungsdienst (Order Service—that is, police) in the deportation of the Warsaw Jews to Treblinka in the summer of 1942 was different: they played a major role, as helpers to the Germans, and this has been described by Yisrael Gutman.[2] The similar role of police forces in Łódż, Cracow, and elsewhere, has also been the subject of more or less detailed descriptions. Isaiah Trunk devotes many pages in his *Judenrat* to these matters.[3] Aharon Weiss's detailed and comprehensive doctoral dissertation on the Jewish police in Poland during the Holocaust, which is available only in the Hebrew University collection, in Hebrew, provides valuable corrective information which should be published.

Weiss's summary makes for unpleasant reading, but he says that whereas most police forces cooperated with the Germans, fourteen did not. In Kovno, for instance, the police were actually at the heart of attempts at armed resistance and attempts to smuggle young people into the forests to participate in partisan fighting. The police commander was Moshe Levin, a right-wing Zionist (however, as in Vilna, there was a united leadership, with the Communists, led by Chaim Yelin, playing an important part as well).[4] In Warsaw, on the other hand, it was only the assassination or attempts at assassination of police commanders that enabled the underground to achieve undisputed control over the remnant of the ghetto between the time of the big deportation in the summer of 1942 and the Ghetto Rebellion in April 1943.[5]

In postwar Israel, a number of Jewish policemen have been brought to trial under the law decrying the Nazis and their henchmen. The important and unique memoir of a Jewish policeman from Otwock (near Warsaw), Calek Perechodnik, tells the story of handing over his own wife and daughter to the murderers and his subsequent pangs of conscience.[6] Collaborating Jewish police were hated and despised—the few exceptions were admired and noted—and this finds its echo in the many thousands of testimonies of survivors. The reasons for joining the police were obvious: hope for food, hope for exemption from deportation, expectation of status. In Warsaw, but not only there, police were recruited from among the intelligentsia, including lawyers and students of law.[7]

Yet Judenräte or police commanders who believed in a German victory and were therefore ideologically prepared to collaborate with the Germans were rare, if they existed at all. It may be argued that Moshe (Mietek) Merin, head of the regional Judenrat of Zaglebie (Sosnowiec-Bedzin) in southwest Poland, was such an individual, but conclusive proof is lacking, although he certainly belonged to the category of cooperating Judenrat heads to which Rumkowski and the two Dutch Jews, David Cohen and Abraham Asscher, also belonged. Merin's views are not authenticated by any credible evidence beyond public and private statements, most of which were designed to answer current problems of one kind or another; yet it is also true that he, along with Rumkowski in Łódź and Gens in Vilna and others, saw themselves as almost messianic figures, who would emerge from their present tribulations strengthened and steeled and would transfer the strong-arm policies learned under the Nazis to a powerful Jewish state in the future.[8]

We do have detailed and credible information about at least one group of collaborators with the Nazis; this information has been analyzed in Hebrew and Yiddish (except for that in Yisrael Gutman's book, which has been translated into English). The group was known as the Trzynastka (The Thirteen) because its headquarters was at 13 Leszno Street in the Warsaw ghetto. Its head was a man called Abraham Gancwajch.[9]

Gancwajch, a past Zionist activist, had come to Warsaw from Łódź. He had been in Vienna during the period of the Anschluss, and unsubstantiated rumors had it that he had served the Nazis there. Upon the collapse of Poland, he moved to Warsaw. His history up to his first appearance in Warsaw in April 1940 is not clear. In retrospect, his later political line was already then evident. Ultimately, he emerged as a Gestapo informer and contact. He had developed an ideology in which he seems to have believed: the Germans would win the war, and the only hope for Jewish survival was for Jews to collaborate with them, be useful to them, and slowly become a sort of low-level ally. In the ghetto he established a police force that paralleled that of the Judenrat and served the Gestapo. The Thirteen were supposed to fight the black market. To gain the support of the ghetto population—presumably thereby proving to the Germans that he was of use to them—he established departments that in part paralleled those of the Judenrat. He supported members of the intelligentsia, provided what he called legal help to ghetto inhabitants, and intervened with the Gestapo to obtain minor advantages for individuals who paid him sizable sums of money. His main usefulness to the Germans was in providing them with detailed reports about the internal life of the ghetto, especially about underground and illegal activities that he became aware of. A bitter struggle developed between Adam Czerniakow, the Judenrat head, and Gancwajch; Czerniakow was fully aware of the danger of the ghetto falling under the leadership of a Nazi collaborator. In the end, Gancwajch was abandoned by his Gestapo superiors (probably of the S.D.—the Sicherheitsdienst, or Security Service), perhaps because it was easier to control the Jews through a person like Czerniakow, who was representative of the ghetto population, than a lackey like Gancwajch—but these are guesses, and there is no documentary evidence available as to German thinking on this issue.[10]

Gancwajch disappeared from the scene in the spring of 1942, only to reappear after September, after the big deportation. But he was of no further use to the Germans, and rumor has it that he was shot sometime in the early spring of 1943.

The importance of this episode lies partly in the integrity of the Jewish leadership in the Warsaw ghetto and the struggle for supremacy there and partly in its being the only known case of a Jewish group, small though it may have been, trying to accommodate the Germans on an ideological basis. In other places in Europe, the Nazis likewise tried to use individual Jews, split the Jewish communities, and undermine the Judenrat heads whom they themselves had appointed, but these traitors did not act on the basis of an ideology. The Nazi purpose, in those cases, also seems to have been to establish a direct line of contact to the Jewish communities through people whom they could fully control.[11]

The tactic did not always work. Yakov Edelstein, the Zionist leader from Prague and the head of the Theresienstadt (Terezin) ghetto administration, and his colleague Richard Friedmann were sent to Amsterdam to "teach" the local Jews how to organize an effective Judenrat. Instead, he warned them not to collaborate with the Germans—a warning they did not heed. Two Jews were also sent to France for the same purpose. It seems they acted in a roughly similar manner. Another go-between in Amsterdam also failed to act according to the Nazis' intent.[12] Elsewhere the Germans simply deposed (and usually murdered) the head of the Judenrat and put a more pliant individual in his stead.

The Thirteen was the only group throughout the Nazi Empire that collaborated with the Germans because its members believed in (although they may not have been happy about) a German victory. Outside Nazi-controlled Europe there was one other such group, in Palestine: the Lohamey Herut Yisrael (Fighters for the Freedom of Israel), or LHY, also know as the Stern Group, led by Avraham Stern. Stern, originally a leader in the Irgun Zvai Leumi, or National Military Organization—Irgun for short—formally headed by Ze'ev Vladimir Jabotinsky, the leader of the Zionist Revisionists, had split off from the main organization to found his own group in 1940. Whereas Irgun followed a pro-British policy, declaring that it would not harm British interests for the duration of the war against Nazi Germany, Stern saw Britain as the main enemy of the Jewish national movement and vowed an unremitting struggle against the British Empire. His following was small (about one hundred members in 1941, possibly fewer) but determined. (It included Yitzhak Yezernitzky, who changed his name to Shamir and became commander of the LHY after Stern's murder at the hands of a British police officer in February 1942 and, decades later, prime minister of Israel.) In January 1941, Stern sent an emissary (Naftali Lubinczik) to Beirut to meet a German intelligence officer by the name of

Otto von Hentig and present him with two memoranda in German in which LHY offered a partnership with Nazi Germany in taking Palestine from the British if Germany allowed the European Jews to emigrate to Palestine and establish a Jewish dictatorship there, under LHY's auspices, on the basis "of a common worldview" shared by LHY and the Nazis.[13] LHY was a tiny group at the time, hunted not only by the British but also by practically the whole of the Jewish population in Palestine—the Yishuv—and it was reduced to impotence after the murder of their leader. LHY regrouped in 1943, largely as a result of the despair in the Yishuv in the wake of the terrible news of the Holocaust. Both the Thirteen and the LHY believed in a German victory and a willingness to accept the Nazi worldview, if only for tactical purposes.

Isaiah Trunk differentiates between two types of submissive Judenrat reactions to Nazi policies: *cooperation* is the term he used for unwillingly yielding to superior force, often in concert with trying to protect the people the Judenrat was supposed to represent; *collaboration* is the term he used to describe a collusion based on identical ideological premises or a conviction that the Germans would win the war. There was no collaboration with the Germans by Jews, except for the marginal case of the Thirteen in Warsaw; but there was forced cooperation unwillingly engaged in by large numbers of Judenräte. Such cooperation, and indeed sometimes policies much closer to collaboration, were followed by most non-Jewish local and municipal authorities in all the countries conquered by the Nazis. The Jewish police cannot be included here, because they were simply frightened people who served the Germans to save their own lives.

Members of the Jewish police were not the only ones who served the Germans; some Jews acted as Gestapo spies and agents throughout Europe. Their numbers are unknown; they were not many, but they caused tremendous damage.

Emphasizing amidah, or resistance, does not conflict with recognizing that the experience of Jews, as individuals and as communities, during the Holocaust was hell and that the pressure brought to bear was such that part of the population did not behave in a heroic manner. It is easy, and right, to condemn the behavior of Jewish policemen and others who yielded to the temptation of betraying even their closest kin in order to have a chance of survival; the rest of us can only hope that we would have acted differently. But there is no justification for turning Holocaust history into a hagiography of the victims. It is wrong to demand, in retrospect, that these tortured individuals and communities should have behaved as mythical heroes. The fact that so many of them did is a matter of wonderment.

A different yet connected issue is the spread of amidah. Was amidah all-embracing? Did it occur in all or in most places in Western and Eastern Europe? Did most people under the Nazi boot react nobly, or stubbornly, or morally? I have tried to check this in the only way a historian can, by examining available evidence. I have found differences and important deviations from the usual picture that has been painted.

To illustrate a difference, let us look at a place in Eastern Europe and see what happened there: Brest-Litovsk, a town on the Bug River, today in Belarus, whose Yiddish name is Brisk De-Litta and whose Polish name is Brześć nad Bugiem. Brest has been in existence since about the tenth century, and it has always been a frontier town between Poland, Lithuania, and Russia. The castle was built in the twelfth century, and Brest became Lithuanian in 1316. The Uniate Church, loyal to the bishop of Rome but following Eastern traditions and liturgies, was founded in Brest in 1594.

Jews have been living in Brest since at least the middle of the fourteenth century. A letter of tolerance dated 1388 attests to their presence; at that time, economic and financial affairs of the Lithuanian principality were largely in Jewish hands. In 1495 they were expelled from town, and their synagogue became a church. They were allowed to return and reestablish their house of prayer in 1503. Abraham Osipowicz, a local Jew, became Lithuania's minister of finance and converted to Christianity, whereupon he was ennobled. His brothers, Michael and Yitzhak, were official tax collectors and remained Jewish. In

1514, Michael became the "Head of Lithuanian Jewry" and was ennobled without having to convert.

Houses in Brest were built of wood, and fires were frequent, so the synagogue was rebuilt a number of times. In the late sixteenth century Saul the son of Judah Wahl of Padua, a major merchant, became a tax collector and built the first talmudic academy (yeshiva) in Brest. His descendants were very prominent in the traditional Jewish community until the twentieth century. A famous rabbi, Shlomo Lurie ("the Maharshal"), was active in Brest. The town was represented in the autonomous self-government of Jews in Poland and Lithuania, the "Committee of the Four Lands," in the sixteenth and seventeenth centuries. In 1623, Lithuanian Jews split off from the Committee and established their own Committee, consisting of representatives from Brest and two other places. Brest was responsible for thirty out of the forty-five Lithuanian Jewish communities, including Minsk, Slutzk, and Slonim. We are not dealing, therefore, with a historically marginal Jewish center, but with one of the major Jewish settlements in Eastern Europe.

There were tensions between Jews and the Catholic Church, especially when a Jesuit college was established in Brest. In 1637 a pogrom took place. In 1648–1649 the great Cossack rebellion against Poland, led by Bogdan Chmelnicki, broke out; Brest was overrun, and some 2,000 Jews were killed by the Cossacks. After Chmelnicki's defeat, the Jews were allowed to return and received a Letter of Protection (1655). In 1660, in a Polish-Russian war, Brest was temporarily conquered by the Russians, who evicted the Jews. As a result, only 133 Jews lived in Brest in 1672. Under Polish King Jan Sobieski the Jews were assured again of the government's protection (in 1669 and 1676), and a century later, in 1776, Brest had 3,175 Jewish inhabitants.

Brest became Russian in 1793, in the Second Partition of Poland. Even as late as 1900 there were only 81 stone houses in the town, out of 2,386, so the constantly recurring fires were a serious problem. The tsarist government opposed the industrialization of Brest, apparently because it wanted to preserve Brest as a garrison town, and forbade the building of factory chimneys. Instead, and because of its strategic location, Brest became an important commercial center in the nineteenth and early twentieth centuries. It also remained a garrison town, with an impressive fortress that was built in 1837. Close to 10,000 Jews lived there at the end of the nineteenth century, of whom 40 percent engaged in crafts and industry—mostly in crafts—and 35 percent in commerce (which meant that they were shopkeepers and itinerant peddlers).

Brest continued to be a center of rabbinical learning. The central figure was Rabbi Chayim Soloveitchik, the rabbi of the town between 1892 and 1918, an orthodox anti-Zionist, some of whose descendants emigrated to the United States to become the acknowledged leaders of the orthodox community there. A pogrom occurred in 1905, during the first Russian Revolution; a Jewish self-defense group, under Dr. Xavery Steinberg, a military surgeon, tried to defend the Jewish quarter. Two Jews from Brest were sent as representatives to the first Zionist Congress in Basel in 1897. Brest also became a center of the Zionist movement: the families of Menachem Begin and Ariel Sharon, of the Israeli right wing, as well as the family of Yakov Chazan, leader of the major leftist Zionist Mapam Party in Israel, hailed from Brest. A major branch of the Bund Party was represented in Brest, as were all the various Zionist factions.

During World War I, Brest suffered. The Russian general Leming ordered the evacuation of all civilians in August 1915, and the town was burned down by the Cossacks. The Germans occupied Brest and turned it into a military garrison and a POW camp. After the war the civilian population, including Jews, returned. Brest became part of the Polish republic, and in the 1926 elections seventeen out of thirty-one representatives on the City Council were Jews: five were orthodox, four were leftist (Zionist), five were representatives of craftsmen and merchants, and the rest were independents. The elections were annulled by the antisemitic Polish authorities, but they reflect the internal composition of the Jewish population, except the disenfranchised poor. Out of a total of 18,945 Jews in the town, 9,588 were entitled to elect candidates. The number of Jews in the town was estimated at 30,000 by 1939. As time progressed, the orthodox element grew weaker. However, owing to an alliance between the ultraorthodox element and the authoritarian Polish regime, the chairman of the Jewish community was always an ultraorthodox Jew. During the interwar period the deputy mayor was also generally a Jew. In 1931–1932 the Polish authorities terminated all support for Jewish institutions in the city, even though 80 percent of the taxes were paid by Jews.

After the death of Marshal Jozef Pilsudski in 1935, the policy of the Polish government veered further to the right and became more outspokenly antisemitic. A wave of pogroms in 1936–1937 reached Brest on May 13, 1937. The Polish police aided the pogromists, and only a direct appeal to Warsaw stopped the outrage.

In the 1930s economic dislocation became more marked. Jews were mostly employed in small Jewish-owned workshops (1,959 workmen were employed in 892 "establishments" in 1938). Craftsmen made a living with great difficulty—the JDC reported that only 50 out of some 300 Jewish shoemakers earned a reasonably sufficient income in 1929, and it established a Free Loan Bank. At the same time, however, cultural and political life and education flourished. The religious community, led by Rabbi Yitzhak Ze'ev Soloveitchik, maintained a yeshiva, two elementary schools, and other institutions, including twenty-seven houses of prayer, not counting the numerous small prayer groups (*shtiblach*). There were four Jewish nonreligious schools and two high schools. The Zionists taught in Hebrew, the Bundists in Yiddish, and both languages were used in some Polish state schools. There was a Jewish hospital; there was a local Jewish newspaper. Zionist political groups were active—the right-wing Revisionists; the left-wing Hechalutz; youth movements of all hues and colors, from the left-wing Hashomer Hatzair to the right-wing Betar. In 1938 a branch of the right-wing Palestinian armed underground, the Irgun Zvai Leumi, was established. And in 1939 the 1,532 people who had paid their membership dues voted in the elections to the Zionist Congress (which was boycotted by the Revisionists).

Brest was home, therefore, to a vibrant community, poor but not impoverished, active, and by no means small.

The story of Brest during the first two years of World War II parallels that of many other places. It was bombed by the Germans on the very first day of the war and occupied on September 15, 1939. The Germans maltreated the leaders of the Jewish community, and the local inhabitants instigated a pogrom; a Jewish self-defense group tried to stop them, to little avail. In accordance with the Ribbentrop–Molotov pact, Brest was handed over to the Soviets on September 22 and remained in their possession until the German invasion of the Soviet Union. In December 1939 the leaders of the Zionists and the Bund were arrested and sent to Siberia, and the wealthier Jewish citizens soon followed them. A wave of Jewish refugees from German-occupied Poland came to Brest, and most of them who refused to accept Soviet citizenship were deported eastward, which, paradoxically, saved most of their lives, because they were not murdered later on by the Germans.

On June 22, 1941, the German army gained control over the bridge across the Bug and conquered the city. The fortress, occupied by Soviet troops, refused to surrender, and some soldiers held out in the German rear (toward the end, the Red Army soldiers were reputedly led by a Jewish NCO, Zalman Stanski, a fiddler by profession). When the Soviet troops finally surrendered, almost all were murdered. Some claim that this heroic story is Soviet war propaganda.

Immediately upon the town's occupation by the Germans, dozens of Jewish men, mainly from among the intellectuals, were led away and murdered at a distance from the city. Between July 13 and 18, many more men—4,435 (according to Jewish sources, 4,870)—were arrested, led to the same place, and shot by the Order Police (Battalion 307 under the supervision of Sonderkommando 7b of Einsatzgruppe C).[14] According to postwar testimony by the Higher S.S. and Police Leader Erich von dem Bach-Zelewski, whose area of control included Brest, he had received an order from Himmler to kill these men, supposedly in retaliation for looting; but Bach's testimonies have to be viewed with skepticism. It is much more logical to view this murder action in the framework of the mass killings of Jewish men (women and children were added later) at the start of the "Barbarossa" campaign by the Einsatzgruppen and their helpers.

In August 1941 a Judenrat of twenty men was established, headed by Hersh Rosenberg, a merchant. Nachman Landau was his deputy. A popular doctor, Dr. Kagan, also served. We know very little about these men, except that before the war they had been mid-range community workers. A Jewish police (Ordnungsdienst) was set up, headed by Moshe Feldman, a man from another town (Biala Podlaska). Feldman had been a loyal servant of the Polish and then the Soviet regimes and was by all accounts a despicable character. The small but very unpopular police force consisted largely of recently arrived refugees from other places who had no local roots. Postwar testimonies accused them of cruelty and of close collaboration with the local Gestapo. Apparently, the Judenrat had little control over the Ordnungsdienst, and the Germans, according to some of the survivors' testimonies, used Feldman's police to introduce Jewish traitors and Gestapo spies into the ghetto. The police shared the watch over the gates to the ghetto with Ukrainian collaborators. No Germans held the gates. The Germans could rely on Ukrainian and Jewish policemen to aid them in starving out the Jewish population.[15]

The community was pressured into making a "contribution" to the Germans of two million marks (or four million rubles), and the members of the Judenrat were arrested as hostages to ensure that the sum was paid. According to an important testimony, one of the Catholic priests in Brest organized help for the Jews and collected money for them to help pay the huge sum.[16] The Jews were marked at first by a white armband with a blue star of David and later by a yellow badge and had to perform forced labor, in most cases without any remuneration except an occasional piece of bread or some watery soup.

Brest became, in September, part of the General-Bezirk (a territory roughly equivalent to a county) Volhynia-Podolia within the Reichs-kommissariat Ukraine. Until June 1942, when the General-Kommissar of the Bezirk, Heinrich Schöne, moved to Lutzk, he had his seat in Brest. On November 15, 1941, the Jews were forced to move into a ghetto on the shores of a Bug tributary, the Muchavetz, in the poorest part of the city. The ghetto was closed off, and the Judenrat established a primitive hospital (the original Jewish hospital in the city had been taken over by the Germans). The few survivors heap praise on the Jewish doctors who worked there, in impossible conditions. The Judenrat also opened a public kitchen that distributed soup twice a day to the needy—most of those in the ghetto. The Judenrat even managed to distribute small amounts of money to the poorest. The daily allocation of bread was 150 grams (5.3 ounces), later reduced to 100 grams (3.5 ounces), and it is no surprise that many died of starvation.

Quoting from a testimony will bring home what the starvation rations meant. "To write about life in the ghetto . . . it would be wiser and more truthful to write about the death in the ghetto. . . . Every expression of human life, of joy, or of creativity disappeared completely. . . . Indifference, lack of feeling, not even desire for revenge, existed. . . . They ceased to have any willpower. . . . No sound of song, no laughter of children, could be heard in the ghetto." The final, shattering statement reads: "Those who are sentenced to die do not smile." This description is borne out by the results of the postwar German investigation of surviving German and Jewish witnesses: "Only persons capable of working had the right to receive bread, which in any case was doled out in tiny rations. The rest . . . were exposed to death by starvation."[17]

People worked both inside the ghetto, in workshops, and outside it, and the workers received cards that were supposed to protect them from harm. Outside work was preferred, because sometimes food could be obtained there. There were even, here and there, workplaces where something approaching humanity could be observed in the behavior of a few Germans (staff at the city hospital, for instance, or an occasional German supervisor at the railway station). One survivor testified that she was warned by a good-natured German on the eve of the final destruction of the ghetto; the German soldier offered to protect her if she remained outside the ghetto. She refused because she would not abandon her parents in the ghetto.[18] A few other Germans tried to save Jews. Generally, however, it was a story of beatings, humiliation, and backbreaking work. The German authorities ordered the Jews to fill out registration forms, which have miraculously survived. They were found in the postwar municipal archive of the town and are now located at Yad Vashem in Jerusalem: 12,260 filled-out questionnaires, complete with passport photos of people who stare at us from the distance of time, unaware, when they were photographed, that they had been sentenced to death.

There were attempts at organizing resistance. One centered on a group of former students at the Hebrew and Polish high schools, and it seems to have had no concrete basis. We know next to nothing about that group, except that it probably existed. A second, apparently much larger one consisted of Communists and Soviet Jews who had come to Brest during the Soviet occupation and who were joined by others, mainly young Zionists. This group had some contacts with Communists in the city and also, it seems, with a Polish underground (led by a Jew pretending to be Polish)—whether Armia Krajowa or Communist, we do not know. The group managed to collect quite a few arms, bought from Italian soldiers or stolen from German arms stores. Reputedly, it even had some machine guns, or possibly the testimonies do not differentiate between machine guns and submachine guns. In any case, there seem to have been five or six such weapons in the ghetto. The names of the leaders are not known.[19]

The group was organized in a conspiratorial network of threesomes only one of whom knew the heads of other threesomes. The plan was to stage an uprising when the Germans came to liquidate the ghetto, and more or less force the ghetto inhabitants to participate in a breakout that would take them into the nearby forests to the south. In the course of these preparations, the group killed a Jewish traitor from among the Jewish policemen, and the Judenrat had to cover up for the killing and pay a large sum to the Germans as a bribe.

The uprising did not take place. Two of the testimonies indicate that the Germans withdrew from the city on the eve of the final liquidation (October 14, 1942), and that caused the members of the underground, who had been alerted, to return the arms to the caches and disperse. On the night of October 15–16 the ghetto was surrounded, and in the early hours of the morning, the Germans burst in, taking the underground by surprise. It had no time to organize the rebel force. Also, the Germans immediately cut one street off from the other so that no concerted action could take place. It is clear from the accounts that the potential resisters were inexperienced and naive. For three days and nights the Germans systematically cleared out the ghetto. Afterward, for weeks, the Germans and the local inhabitants uncovered Jews hiding in cellars and attics and murdered them—one report says, about 70–80 people daily— and looted what was left of the property.[20]

Most of the Jewish ghetto inhabitants were marched to the railway station and transported a short distance to a place called Bronnaya Gora, where peasants had been recruited earlier to dig a series of deep trenches. A large number of Germans, whose identity is not quite clear, unloaded each train and forced the Jews to march to the trenches, where they were forced to undress and were shot. The weak, old, and sick were killed in the ghetto itself, at a spot on Dluga Street.[21] Remnants of the resistance groups tried to reach the forests in order to join a unit supposedly set up by a character known as "Sashka with the gold teeth." This turned out to be a group of bandits, who overpowered the small groups of escapees who went into the forests, killed them, and took their possessions. Only a very few Jews from the ghetto managed to reach Soviet partisan units. After Brest was liberated by the Soviets on July 12,

1944, a total of nineteen Jewish survivors emerged from the forests to come back to the city. They dispersed—some stayed in the Soviet Union, but most left for Palestine and, later, Israel.

Let me first of all clear up a number of points that are not central to our argument. One of them is the problem of who the perpetrators were. Brest is an excellent example of participation by a large variety of German and local collaborationist elements in the murder of Jews. The murder started with the Einsatzgruppen units, aided by Order Police Battalion 307, in July 1941, during the first wave of murders in the occupied areas of the Soviet Union. The Einsatzgruppen units were RSHA (Reichsicherheitshauptamt—Main Reich Security Office) forces commanded by Reinhard Heydrich and were part of the S.S. The Order Police battalion that took part in the July murders was part of the Order Police commanded by Kurt Daluege and was a different part of the same S.S.

The Einsatzgruppen became the core of stationary S.S. and police posts, organized according to the geographic divisions of the German civilian authorities. At the Bezirk (county) level, at Rowno, there was a SIPO (Sicherheitspolizei—Security Police) station, which included the criminal and political police (Gestapo) and the S.D., the S.S. intelligence agency. The Rowno post was commanded by Ernst Berger and later by a Dr. Pütz. In Brest, which was subordinate to Rowno, there was an S.S. and police command post, which also controlled the local police—the SCHUPO (Schutzmannschaften—the ordinary police)—and the Belorussian and Ukrainian Supplementary Police (officially called Schutzmannschaften, or Civilian Protection Units, and unofficially called Hiwis [Hilfswillige, or Helpers]).

The 1942 orders to murder the Jews must have come down from the commander of the S.S. and police for Volhynia and Podolia, Oberführer Willi Günther, via the Bezirk SIPO to the local SIPO, included in the local S.S. and Police command. Other units were then added by consensus as a matter of course. The Wehrmacht was cooperative. The German civilian authorities—the mayor, the county leader, and others—

helped.[22] The dispute so dear to some German and American historians—whether the initiative was local or central—becomes almost irrelevant. There was an open consensus that the Jews had to be killed, and sooner rather than later. Local interests may have acted against this, but in the end they acted within the consensus, so there was only a matter of timing. It is doubtful that an order came from Berlin, nor was one needed. The commander of the S.S. and Police for the Ukraine wanted to show that in his area the Jews had "disappeared." The local S.S., police, army, and civilian authorities were eager to be part of the action. There was no need to teach them antisemitism; the consensus was antisemitic and racist-biological. The action would be applauded by the higher-ups and certainly by Berlin. Central and local initiatives complemented one another perfectly.[23]

In Brest, as in most places, there was a central figure among the perpetrators who probably pushed for radical anti-Jewish policies culminating in mass murder. In Brest he was Major Friedrich Wilhelm Rohde, born in 1893, about whose background I could find no details. Rohde was the *Standortführer* (local commander of the police) and, as such, was lord of the ghetto. He was totally corrupt, and the Judenrat tried to prevent the tightening of the screws at each turning point by supplying him with "gifts" of various kinds, brought to him by pretty young Jewish girls. There is more than a hint that the Judenrat called for volunteers to take on this awful mission and that four girls did; it seems that they were raped, although this is not stated explicitly, and that they were viewed in the ghetto as heroines.[24] Rohde plied the Jews with all kinds of promises, which were then broken. During the final murder, he personally commanded the action at Dluga Street. But no Jewish eyewitnesses survived, and the one German eyewitness who described him did not know his name at the time the massacre occurred. In 1965, after an exhaustive investigation by German judiciary authorities, he was let off scotfree.

The final tragedy was perpetrated by a number of German units apparently commanded or directed by Berger. Among them was a special police company, "Nürnberg," which had been established in August 1941 using police reservists, S.S. men, and others. It was commanded by Josef Eisele, who later became a SCHUPO captain, and was subordinated to the S.S. and Police commander of Volhynia. A subunit, the Service Department of SCHUPO, Brest-Litovsk (Schutzpolizei-Dienstabteilung Brest-Litovsk), the police post at Brest under Lieutenant Ernst Deuerlein, a motorized police unit under Hermann Heise, and possibly others also participated.[25]

Another question that needs clearing up is whether any help was extended to Jews. Several stories of aid to Jewish escapees are associated with the final liquidation action. One concerns a Belorussian engineer by the name of Ignacy Kuryanovitch who saved Moshe Smolar, who had hidden in the ruined ghetto from October 1942 to early January 1943. Kuryanovitch rescued him not once but several times after Smolar managed to escape from the ghetto. Kuryanovitch was an older man whom Smolar had employed in the orphan home that he ran before the war, and they had become friends. Smolar was aided by a Polish engineer, Kowalsky, who received him in a friendly manner a number of times and tried to help him get papers that would enable him to leave for Germany as a Polish laborer, but Kuryanovich, largely for religious reasons, decided to rescue his friend by building a tiny cell for him in his house, 80 centimeters by 130 by 80 (roughly 32 inches by 51 by 32). Had he been caught by the Germans, he and his wife would undoubtedly have been murdered. Later he gave Smolar the papers of a Soviet laborer, and with these Smolar managed to go to Germany as an *Ostarbeiter* (eastern laborer).[26]

Another testimony is that of Leah Ben-Chorin, who was rescued by a former Social Democratic German from Hannover by the name of Willi Friedrichs, a soldier, who hid her and another Jew and his daughter probably for a combination of humanitarian and political reasons and then enabled her to escape from Brest to another town in the vicinity (Kobryn) and from there to the Soviet partisans.[27]

A third case is, again, that of a Belorussian, a woman by the name of

Polenia Golovchenko, who rescued a small Jewish child, the son of a Jewish woman who had given Golovchenko medicine against abscesses some time before. The Jewish woman cried out to her son to run to Golovchenko while she herself was being taken away to be murdered.[28]

We might perhaps add the name of Oswald Cornelissen, the German eyewitness who testified in the 1960s against Rohde. There were others, but the conclusion must be that these were exceptional cases, not representative of the general murderous indifference of the local inhabitants—insofar as they did not actively participate in the murder of Jews.[29] Equally rare were the cases of German personnel who helped Jews in one way or the other, although one must reemphasize that there is at least one credible testimony, cited above, that tells us about the decent behavior of Germans running the city hospital where Jews were used as laborers.[30]

What is important about the story of Brest is the comparison it affords with other ghettos. Some 17,000 Jews lived in the Brest ghetto, maybe more.[31] In Vilna, there were about 20,000; in Kovno, there were about 18,000. Though in a different league from the large ghettos, like the ones at Warsaw, Łódż, Lwów (Lviv), Cracow, and Bedzin-Sosnowiec, Brest must be considered substantial in size, on a par with the Lithuanian ghettos and larger than most ghettos in eastern Poland. The number of survivors was very small, but the story of the Brest Jews could be reconstructed with their help and with that of the German investigative authorities in the 1960s, even though none of these investigations led to trials, never mind convictions.

What is crucial from our perspective is the fact that, apart from the attempt at organizing resistance, there was very little of what we have called amidah—no attempts at organizing education, no underground political life, no social welfare efforts apart from the Judenrat's soup kitchen for those who had nothing. There is some evidence of religious observance, which is not surprising, considering the past history of the Jewish community in Brest. Credible evidence about Rabbi Simcha-Selig Dayan (born in 1864) tells of his setting up a soup kitchen, apparently in addition to the one run by the Judenrat, and organizing clandestine prayer meetings on Jewish holidays, to the extent of setting up a *sukka* (traditional booth for Sukkot, the Festival of Tabernacles).[32] His efforts could have affected only a very small proportion of the ghetto inhabitants.

The survivors are unanimous in praising the Judenrat and condemning the police. On the Judenrat, Sheindel Winograd writes: "In contrast to other ghettos such as Vilna, Łódź, etc., the members of the Judenrat behaved well. They did not betray the Jews, as happened in other ghettos. When they had to provide cash in the forced levy [demanded by the Germans], they did it honestly and straightforwardly." The Judenrat head and his deputy (Rosenberg and Landau) could have lived outside the ghetto like most physicians (because they were useful to the Germans), but they refused and preferred to stay with the other Jews in the ghetto. Rosenberg's privileged position did not prevent the Germans from brutally beating him.[33] Brest appears to offer a typical case of a Judenrat that failed in its efforts to help and protect the community but that received high marks from the community because it tried.[34]

The descent into despair proceeded by stages. At first, there was unimaginable naïveté. One testimony, of a person who eventually joined the resistance group, tells us that when the July 1941 murder of close to 5,000 men took place, he and a friend of his saw that men were being taken somewhere on trucks. "We ran after the vehicles, and the Germans shouted: Where are you running to? Go back, go back!"[35] This first major murder action effectively reduced any chance of active, unarmed or armed resistance by killing off most of the young males. The resistance movement encountered opposition from those ghetto inhabitants who were aware of it—as in places like Vilna and Czesto-chowa.[36] The families left after the murder of most of the men in July were broken and dispirited—and hungry. Amidah was unlikely in such circumstances, and it must remain a wonderment that armed resistance was attempted.

The question is, Was Brest was an exception, or was it typical in some way? Research done in a seminar at the Hebrew University over a number of years focused on the following towns in prewar Poland: Rokitno, Tarnów, Przemysl, Kolomyja, Hrubieszów, and Baranowicze. The research found obvious similarities between them and Brest-Litovsk regarding the question of amidah. There are also divergences, as in Baranowicze, where the community managed much more of an organized unarmed response, and Tarnów and Hrubieszów, where the youth movements tried to maintain an organized life. Overall, however, I would argue that what is justly described as amidah in a number of outstanding instances mentioned in the previous chapter did not exist, or existed only in embryonic fashion, in the places studied.

What might be the reasons for these contradictions? One might be the destruction of Jewish organized life by the Soviets in the areas they occupied in 1939–1940. This would apply to Baranowicze and Brest. But Vilna, Kovno, and Shavli were also under Soviet rule, and these are places where amidah took place. It seems that a major reason for the different responses was the cruelty of the German administrators, which varied from place to place. In Brest the impetus for resistance came from the murder of nearly 5,000 men right at the beginning of the German occupation and, later, from starvation, which apparently impacted on people in opposite ways. In some places the policies of the Judenrat might be blamed, but Brest is rather typical in that its Judenrat received high marks for self-sacrifice and unstinting work for the community. One might also mention Kosów Huculski, discussed in the previous chapter, where no typical amidah activities took place either and where the Judenrat was also praised by most, though not all, survivors.

It is therefore important to qualify the picture usually painted of Jewish reactions in the face of murderous German policies; that includes my own published statements in the past. It is not that amidah did not take place or that it was not a centrally important element in Jewish reactions to Nazi policies and to the life-endangering situation that developed because of them. What has to be understood is that a sustained effort at keeping up morale and maintaining a halfway meaningful life

under the destructive policies of the Nazis was possible—at least to the
extent that it happened, even in places like Warsaw, Vilna, and Kovno—
only when certain minimal conditions allowed for its appearance. True,
starvation was prevalent in Warsaw as well, but although about a third
of the Warsaw ghetto population was starving, others were not, or were
at least better fed. Łódź residents, too, faced terrible starvation; but the
ghetto was much larger, hence a greater variety of responses was possible. The ghettos where amidah undoubtedly was a factor also had traditional political and social leadership groups, which seems to have
helped—although such groups seem not to have been lacking in Brest,
either. Again, what seems to have been very important in decreasing the
likelihood of amidah was the character of local German rule. The combination of totally ruthless exploitation, starvation, and the mass
murder of young men right at the beginning of the German occupation
seems to have been the deadly mix that differentiated towns such as
Brest from other places. The exact parallels between the Brest ghetto
and other ghettos still have to be elucidated.

Is there a qualitative difference between Poland, the Baltic states, and
the former Soviet Union, on the one hand, and countries in Western and
Southern Europe, on the other hand? Was amidah universally prevalent
in these other countries? The conditions were different in different
areas, of course, but what made France, Greece, Italy, the Low Countries, Hungary, and Slovakia in some ways similar were the forms that
the Nazi onslaught took there, as opposed to the East. Starvation of the
kind that spread in Łódź, Warsaw, and Brest was absent. The Jews were
not concentrated in ghettos—the ghettos that the Germans established
in Hungary for a short period, in the spring of 1944, were holding
camps before deportation to Auschwitz; the ghetto in Budapest at the
end of that year was a last attempt by Hungarian Nazis to effect a radical
antisemitic policy. The only other ghetto outside Eastern Europe was in
Theresienstadt, which was a unique combination of ghetto and concentration camp. There were no ghettos anywhere else. Romanian-
organized ghettos existed only in Transnistria, the Soviet area occupied

by the Romanians. Starvation affecting the general population, in beleaguered Budapest or in Greece outside Saloniki, for example, affected Jews as well, but it was the result of the war and general German policies and not specifically anti-Jewish measures. In all these countries, elements in the Jewish population engaged in what we have called amidah to one extent or the other: efforts at mutual help, morale-building cultural activities, underground operations, religious life, efforts at obtaining more food through social efforts. Romania is a separate case. Although the leaders of Romanian Jewry, headed by Wilhelm Filderman, provided prime examples of amidah under impossible circumstances, and although in at least two of the ghettos in Transnistria conditions developed that made some kind of amidah possible, amidah was absolutely impossible in the Transnistrian death traps of Berezovca, Acmecetka, and Vapniarka, or in holding camps and Ukrainian villages where the remnants of the Romanian Jewish population tried to survive.[37]

An unrealistic view of the fate of the Jews during the Holocaust needs to be corrected, for it might give rise to a distorted, almost nostalgic attitude. At the same time, amidah is not a myth. The conditions under which it took place require an answer to a very simple question: How was amidah possible at all? One might argue that the Jews made an effort, unorganized and unplanned, to continue civilized life in conditions imposed by a force that had abandoned any previously held humanistic traditions altogether, an effort based on an instinctive urge to carry on, whether with the traditional, religion-bound way of life, or, as in most cases, with older traditions combined with modern humanism, liberalism, or socialism. That instinctive urge made the organization of amidah by groups and individuals possible. Wherever amidah was possible, Jewish society stood the test; where amidah was not possible, it simply could not.

Finally, Raul Hilberg's contention that Jewish armed resistance was almost nonexistent because the Jews lacked a tradition of resistance fails on at least two counts: first, armed resistance did exist, and to a surprisingly large extent; and second, to leap ahead a bit, if he were right, the rise of the State of Israel would be a mystery.

The explanation that I suggest for unarmed resistance holds for armed resistance as well: it took place wherever there was the slightest chance that it could, which did not happen too often. Hilberg's argument that the lack of military tradition among Jews was the prime cause for a large number of failed attempts contains some truth, however. In these many cases, a lack of military tradition was one of a combination of factors that led to failure. One factor was the naïveté of the resisters and their failure to realize that German policies were based on excellent intelligence work. A second factor was the opposition they encountered from the Jewish population, to whom they rarely offered anything but another form of death. To women, children, and old people they could offer nothing but hopelessness, for those groups would in any case be abandoned to be murdered by the enemy. A third factor, which has been stressed many times over, was the resisters' lack of arms and lack of knowledge about how to use them. A fourth factor was the lack of sympathy on the part of most East European nations for Jewish resistance. A fifth factor was the lack of contact between Jewish groups in Nazi Europe and any Allied government that would lend them support. Brest was not the only place where resistance was planned but never happened, because the Germans were quicker and more sophisticated. Baranowicze and Czestochowa are less well-known examples.

It is important to strike a reasonable balance between nostalgic hero worship of Jews during the Holocaust and attempts to downplay all forms of amidah. The importance lies, among other things, in the need for truthful analyses of reactions of victims of genocide generally to further the educational process that may provide at least an outside chance of preventing future tragedies like the Holocaust or other genocides. To quote what Raul Hilberg has said many times: "We historians are in the truth business and have to judge ourselves by that standard."

chapter eight

The Problem of Gender:

The Case of Gisi Fleischmann

              The fate of Jewish women and the problems they had to face have so far just barely been touched upon in the Holocaust literature. From the research that has been done to date, there seems little doubt that in some ways their fate and their problems were indeed different from those of Jewish men. And if all human experience has a gender-related agenda, as women's studies tells us, the Holocaust can be no exception. Indeed, it seems to me that the problems facing women as women and men as men have a special poignancy in an extreme situation such as the Holocaust. In dealing concretely with the role of women we must differentiate between perpetrators and victims and possibly some of the people inaccurately described as bystanders. Here I wish to deal with the fate and role of Jewish women during the Holocaust by discussing a particular case.

Others have dealt with the traditional role of women in the Jewish family since the Enlightenment, including its development and its crises. I do not pretend to say anything new when I emphasize that the place of women in the public arena in traditional Jewish Central and East European orthodox families was definitely inferior to the place of husbands, fathers, and brothers. The entry of European Enlightenment ideas into the environment of those families began in the nineteenth and early twentieth centuries, creating an acute social, ideological, and gender-related crisis. Although orthodox Jewish women were economically active in some areas, especially when they were the family providers, their husbands devoting their time to Torah studies, their role in social and political life was secondary at best and nonexistent for the most part. They were politically absent not only in the orthodox world: none of the major Jewish political movements—Zionist, Bundist, Autonomist—had any noticeable female leadership. Only in revolutionary circles—socialist and later Communist—were there a very few exceptions to this general rule. At the very outset of the Enlightenment period, in Germany and to an extent in Austria, wealthy Jewish women had been active in intellectual and artistic life; and a few women had been writers of literature. But all these cases were, I think, exceptions, with outstanding individuals who had succeeded in using loopholes in the patriarchal structure of both European and specifically Jewish society to make their presence felt.

Jewish society, especially the tradition-bound parts, was even more inhospitable to female leadership or even meaningful female participation than general society was. Women, as we all know, had circumscribed roles as daughters, wives, and mothers, and participation in social and political decision making was not among them. According to Talmudic law (halakhah), women cannot be witnesses at law, they cannot fulfill any official functions in religious life (being called to read the Torah, serving as rabbis, and so on); the voice of a woman is an abomination (the Hebrew expression is *erva*, the word for female genitals). These are just some indicators of a basically misogynistic attitude.

During the first three decades of the twentieth century, changes occurred. The suffragist movements in Western Europe registered their first successes, and women began penetrating, slowly and painfully, into the public domain. In Jewish society, wealthy women, often wives and widows of important male figures or spinsters who were somehow considered eccentric personalities with what might be thought of as fools' privileges, began to be active in groups responsible for social welfare. In societies that considered themselves to be revolutionary in some respects, women's participation developed much further. In revolutionary circles in Russia, as well as in the pioneering Zionist groups in Palestine, the role of women was much more prominent. Mania Shochat, Rachel Yanait-Ben Zvi, Rachel Katznelson, and Beba Idelson are some of the names that come to mind in the latter case.[1] Yet these and other women were the exception even in Jewish Palestine.

In the Zionist movement in Europe, women became prominent in activities relating to social welfare. The framework for this was provided by the Women's Zionist Organization (WIZO) and similar groups, which paralleled the growing Hadassah Organization in the United States. By the 1930s Hadassah had become a powerful political organization, but its leaders were still part of a political leadership headed by men. In Palestine, the leader of the American Hadassah, Henrietta Szold, became the director of Youth Aliyah but not a member of the Jewish Agency Executive.[2] In Europe, too, WIZO had no political power. In the early 1930s women who were part of WIZO or WIZO-like groups came to prominence as the problem of refugees became urgent and their experience in social welfare work became useful. In Holland, Gertrude Van Tijn (Cohen) became a controversial figure. Van Tijn was the secretary of the Dutch Committee that dealt with refugees, largely from Germany. The leader, David Cohen, was later cochairman of the Amsterdam Judenrat. The practical work was done by Van Tijn.[3] In Berlin, Recha Freier was the founder of Youth Aliyah, the group that Szold headed in Palestine, Cora Berliner came to prominence as an important member of the German Jewish leadership, and there were others.[4] In Czechoslovakia a group of women arose who knew each other fairly well and who became responsible for matters concerning refugees. Marie Schmolka, Irma Polak, and Hannah Steiner were all connected with WIZO and Jewish refugee work in Prague.[5] In Bratislava, Gisi (Gisela) Fleischmann came to prominence.

Typically, female participation in leadership roles in Jewish society in Poland prior to the Holocaust was practically nil. Women could be teachers in schools and activists in local social welfare causes, but their public role was generally limited to influencing their husbands when they had the urge to do so and when the husbands were willing to listen. With very few exceptions it was the men who filled leadership positions. The force of Jewish traditions and their impact on even non-religious Jewish circles was considerable, especially in the area of traditional gender roles.

The Nazi invaders of Poland brought with them an antifeminist ideology that relegated German women to three areas: *Kinder, Küche, Kirche* (children, kitchen, church). The Nazi leadership did not, in fact, translate this ideology into practice in Germany. In line with this extreme form of reactionary modernism, to borrow Jeffrey Herf's term, women were supposed to stay at home and not work in the marketplace.[6] Yet the modern German economy demanded female participation, the family's economy required that women work, and during the war female labor became essential to the maintenance of the German war machine. As a result, very large numbers of German women joined the work force, and the number of women doctors and women in other professions did not decrease, ideology and their subordinate role in the German medical world notwithstanding.[7]

As far as subject peoples were concerned, such as Poles, or perceived enemies, such as Jews, female labor posed no ideological problem to the Nazis. The institution of slave labor for Jews, and increasingly for Poles, was an immediate consequence of the German conquest. At first, mainly men were drafted, but as time went on, women were taken for slave labor as well. Loss of life accompanied slave labor, and because it was mainly men who died, women became family providers, and not only, as in the past and for quite different reasons, in the ultraorthodox sector.

The Nazis decreed that only Jewish males should constitute the forced leadership groups known as Judenräte or Ältestenräte. As a result, with one minor exception, Jewish women did not participate in these bodies. Their functions in Polish, Belorussian, and Baltic ghettos were the traditional ones of social work, education, wherever possible, and artistic life, whenever *that* was possible. A certain degree of contradiction is evident in the fact that whereas more and more families were led by women after the death or disappearance of the male heads of families, their input on the level of group leadership was practically nonexistent.

In women's concentration and slave labor camps, minor positions of power in the camp prisoners' hierarchy could be attained by Jewish women. The one exception is the position of a female Jewish camp leader in Camp C of the forced labor camp of Skarzysko-Kamienna, which was held by an unsavory character by the name of Fela Markowiczowa.[8]

It was in the unofficial and rebellious circles that female leadership became possible. The main social welfare organization of Polish Jewry, the Warsaw-based JDC office, consisted of males only. But the Oneg Shabbath group led by Emmanuel Ringelblum had some women collaborators, including the influential Rachel Auerbach.[9] More important were the underground political parties, especially the left-wing ones. The Left Poalei Zion had some outstanding women leaders. But the chief participation of women at the group level was in the underground resistance, though less perhaps on the communist and Bundist side than on the Zionist left.[10]

The problem of gender equality did not arise among these groups, who accepted women leaders as a matter of course, or so it seems at first glance. Dror in Poland had Zivia Lubetkin, Frumka Plotnicka, and many others; Hashomer Hatzair had Tosia Altmann, Ruzhka Korczak, Vitka Kempner, Chaika Grossmann, Haika Klinger, and others. In Cracow, Akiva had Gusta Davidson, and the communists, Mira Gola, who was their leader.[11] Other examples can be cited. In Vilna, after the tragic death of the communist leader, Itzik Wittenberg, the communist underground was led by women, with Chaine Borowska as the head.[12] Because

Jewish men were marked by circumcision, Jewish women could more easily move around in Nazi-occupied Poland, which meant that they filled the centrally important role of emissaries between the ghettos; Vladka Peltel-Meed of the Bund, Tosia Altmann and Frumka Plotnicka of the Zionists, and many others did this work.[13] Under the exceptional circumstances and the pressure of new conditions the old taboos were set aside, and female political and even quasi-military leadership became acceptable.

It is against this background that Gisi Fleischmann emerged.

Gisi Fleischmann was the daughter of Julius and Jetty Fischer, owners of a hotel and restaurant in the old Jewish quarter of Bratislava.[14] Jetty Fischer was the aunt of Rabbi Shmuel David Halevi Ungar, who became the acknowledged leader of Slovak Jewish ultraorthodoxy, with his seat in the town of Nitra. Gisi grew up in an orthodox environment, and being the first cousin of the famous rabbi played a part in her activities during the Holocaust.

She and her younger brothers, Desider and Gustav, became Zionists while in their teens; in her twenties, Gisi married Josef Fleischmann, a merchant, with whom she had two daughters, Alice and Judith, born in 1917 and 1920, respectively. The family restaurant became a meeting place of Zionists, probably at an early date. The meetings must have been held in German, possibly Hungarian, because those were the languages of the Jewish intelligentsia—Slovak was the "dialect" spoken by the peasants. Bratislava was still Pressburg, the Habsburg city, or Poszonyi, its name as an ancient Hungarian stronghold. Gisi's Zionist friend Oskar Neumann, a native Viennese, had no Slovak either. It is doubtful whether Rabbi Ungar's son-in-law, Gisi's chief collaborator during the Holocaust, Rabbi Michael Dov Ber Weissmandel, knew more than a bare minimum of Slovak. The language difficulties increased for Jewish leadership groups with the establishment of the Czechoslovak republic, which united two ethnic groups, the Czechs and the Slovaks.

The Slovaks had been developing a national consciousness since about the middle of the nineteenth century. This was the type of European nationalism that tended toward exclusiveness. Because Slovak Jews, like many other Eastern European Jews, were inclined to adopt the urban culture of the reigning power—in this case, the Austro-Hungarian monarchy—their Slovak neighbors perceived them as a Germanizing and, chiefly, Magyarizing factor. In the late 1930s, there were 136,000 Jews among some 2.5 million Slovaks, and they constituted a large part of the merchant and industrial middle-class, as well as of the artisan population. Slowly a Slovak intellectual class emerged, in competition with Germans, Hungarians, and Jews; and the radical nationalist elements among them grew as the crises of the interwar period revealed the fragile structure of Slovak society.

Zionism was weak in Slovakia at first but gained strength in the late 1920s and 1930s. Most Slovak Jews were orthodox, at least nominally. Orthodoxy in Slovakia was not of just one type. Ultraorthodox strongholds—Nitra, Topolčany, and some other places—boasted of yeshivot or strong orthodox communities. But orthodoxy was easygoing in many places and coexisted with a pro-Zionist tendency. The minority neolog group, roughly similar to modern-day American Conservatism, became more and more Zionistic. Zionist youth movements flourished in the 1930s under the influence of neighboring Polish movements. On the fringes were extreme assimilationist groups and a small but important number of converts to Christianity. The communists formed a strong movement in Slovakia, led by indigenous leaders, and many Jewish youths joined them or inclined in their direction in the 1930s. The top communist leadership included no Jews. Caught between the orthodox establishment, assimilation, and communism, the Zionist movement did not have an easy time.

By the mid-1920s, Gisi Fleischmann was a young mother and was no longer an orthodox or observant Jew, although she always maintained a respect for religious tradition. She cofounded the Bratislava branch of WIZO, the women's Zionist organization, and became its second president. Her political involvement in Zionist life became more and more intense, and in 1937 she attended the Twentieth Zionist Congress in Switzerland. In 1938 she became the head of the Bratislava branch of HICEM, the agency that dealt with emigration to countries other than Palestine—which indicates that although European Zionists were concerned with emigration to Palestine, their commitment to that goal was not exclusive.

In 1938–1939, Fleischmann moved into formal leadership roles. She became a member of the Slovak Central Refugee Committee and, as such, a member of the Joint Committee, which advised the local JDC representative, Joseph Blum (father of Yehuda Blum, Israeli ambassador to the United Nations and professor of international law at Hebrew University). There was no love lost between Blum and Fleischmann, but in 1939 or 1940, Blum moved to Budapest, although he remained responsible for JDC operations in Slovakia as well as in Hungary (together with his American colleague S. Bertrand Jacobson, who was active in Romania as well). With his departure, Fleischmann became, to all intents and purposes, the JDC person in Bratislava.

In the spring of 1939 she traveled to London with Oskar Neumann of the Zionist Organization and Robert Fueredi, chair of the Central Refugee Committee, to try to persuade the British to help get Jewish refugees out of Slovakia. Their mission was a failure. In the summer she attended a JDC conference in Paris, chaired by Morris Troper, European head of the JDC, at which representatives of JDC committees from all over Europe discussed refugee questions. The results were negative: on the day the conference ended, war broke out in Europe with the German invasion of Poland. Fleischmann returned to Bratislava by a circuitous route. She had been invited to remain in London, but she would not leave her family and her community.[15]

Radical changes occurred in her private life as well. She had sent her two daughters, Judith and Alice, to Palestine—Judith before and Alice just after the outbreak of war—with immigration certificates, the ones for children and pioneers going to Palestine. Her husband was sickly, and after her father died, she had to look after her frail mother. Her refusal to leave Bratislava was, I think, more a question of family responsibility to her husband and mother than one of communal responsibility. I do not think that she would have refused to follow her two daughters had it not been for her family in Bratislava.

In late 1939 and 1940 she became involved with illegal emigration transports that were organized partly by the Mossad and Revisionist representatives in Austria but later mainly by Bernhard Storfer, a Jew who had been recruited by Eichmann to push for increased illegal emigration to Palestine. In an abandoned munition factory on the outskirts of Bratislava and in another location nearby, many hundreds of refugees were waiting for ships to take them down the Danube to the Black Sea. But it was not until early September 1940 that ships finally came to take the main group of refugees away. Up to then, the Central Refugee Committee, now under Gisi Fleischmann, had to take care of them, with but little help from the JDC or anyone else. That meant raising large funds from an increasingly impoverished Jewish community and then distributing them to the refugees.[16] According to testimonies collected by Joan Campion for her biography of Gisi Fleischmann, *In the Lion's Mouth*, Fleischmann personally delivered and distributed food, cared for children, and organized cultural activities for the refugees. It was that rare combination of organizational talent, intellectual ability, and personal, emotional involvement, together with a great deal of political savvy, that made Gisi Fleischmann's personality so unique.

Slovakia became autonomous in October 1938 and declared its independence, at the bidding of Nazi Germany, in March 1939. The clerical-fascist government of the country, now a German protectorate, was led by the fascist Hlinka party, headed by the Catholic priest Jozef Tiso. Anti-Jewish pogroms followed; during one, Gisi Fleischmann's brother, Gustav, was injured, and he died soon afterward. A program of so-called Aryanization set in, in the course of which Jews were deprived of their property. An attempt by the Zionists, whose leadership now included Gisi Fleischmann, to establish a Jewish umbrella organization in Slovakia was aborted by the opposition of the ultraorthodox. A Slovak

Judenrat was established as early as September 1940, at the instigation of Dieter Wisliceny, who had been sent by Adolf Eichmann to be the Adviser on Jewish Affairs with the Slovak government just prior to its establishment.

This Slovak Judenrat, called the Ústredňa Židov (ÚŽ), or Jewish Central Office, was the first Judenrat outside Germany and Poland. To be the head of this body the Slovaks nominated a respected orthodox official, Heinrich Schwartz. The Zionists, after some hesitation, joined the body, but opposed Schwartz. Against this background, Blum in Budapest complained to the JDC parent body in the United States about the unreliability of the Zionist leadership in Bratislava, even though one of the people mentioned, Dr. Ernst Abeles, was of the same political persuasion as Blum—namely, Zionist orthodox. Blum named Fleischmann as one of the unreliable Zionists. The U.S. JDC, however, had no way of intervening in local disputes even had they wanted to; and as time went on, Gisi became known as the local JDC representative. Help from the United States was insignificant, and it fizzled out by the end of 1941, when the Japanese attack brought the United States into the war.

The Final Solution was the result of a stage-by-stage development during 1941. In July 1941 mass murder of Jews in newly conquered Soviet territories began at the hands of the S.S. and the German regular army. The Wannsee conference of January 20, 1942, dealt with some of the administrative aspects of mass murder, and its protocol reflects some of the internal discussions among the Nazi leaders. They expected no obstacles by the Slovak regime to the murder of the Jews. In fact, Slovakia turned out to be the only country in Europe whose local puppet government actually asked the Nazis to deport the Jews. The Slovaks could not fulfill their commitment to the Germans to supply them with a large number of Slovak laborers for Germany, so they suggested deporting 20,000 Jews instead. It immediately became clear to them, however, that deporting productive workers would leave them burdened with their families, and they therefore asked the Germans to accept the families as well. Eichmann at first did not want the families—in early 1942 only one extermination camp (Chelmno) was working, and that was busy murdering the Jews of the annexed west Polish territories. Auschwitz was not yet ready. But Eichmann accepted the challenge and decided to transport most of the families to the Lublin region in Poland; the young people and a part of the families were sent to Auschwitz. The young workers were employed in building up the camp—especially the women, who built the women's camp at Birkenau.[17]

Slovak Jews heard rumors about the impending deportations. Both the ultraorthodox and the neolog-Zionist leadership pleaded with the government heads, including Tiso, to desist from deporting the community. Parallel pleas for intervention were made to the Vatican. The Vatican did intervene, on March 14, 1942, but to no avail. The deportations started on March 26, with a transport of young girls and women. From then until October, some 58,000 Jews, out of a community of 90,000, were deported to Poland.[18]

From the early days of the ÚŽ, the Slovak Judenrat, Gisi Fleischmann was a member. As far as I know, she was the only woman to be a member of a major Judenrat in Europe, with the possible exception of Cora Berliner in Germany. She headed the Department of Emigration, a natural consequence of her prior involvement with HICEM and the JDC. We have no real evidence of what she thought and did during the period up to the deportations, except that we know she tried desperately to get as many Jews as possible out of Slovakia. She must have belonged to the Zionist leadership group that worked within the ÚŽ against Schwartz, only belatedly realizing that the head of the Judenrat had done his best to stand up against the demands of the venal Slovak officials.

The threat of the deportations caused Neumann to send some of his young coworkers from the Zionist youth movements by rail to Slovak townships and communities and to warn them, not of murder, because that they did not know about, but of the life-threatening deportation to Poland. By and large, leaders and even youth groups and individuals in the communities refused to listen and decided that it was best to report to what they thought would be forced labor in order to avoid reprisals against their families.[19] As the deportations proceeded, a sizable minority became convinced that it was better to run away. Led by the orthodox leadership around Rabbi Ungar and by the Zionist youth groups, with fair numbers of ordinary, unorganized people joining in, at least 7,000 people, about 8 percent of the total number of Jews, fled to Hungary despite great obstacles.[20]

As the spring months went on, an underground leadership crystallized at the ÚŽ. The members of the group used to meet in Fleischmann's office. They were all opposed to the second head of the ÚŽ (who took office after Schwarz's flight to Hungary), a frightened and ineffective schoolteacher by the name of Arpad Sebestyen. The composition of the group varied, but the core consisted of Gisi Fleischmann; Oskar Neumann; Wilhelm Fuerst, a banker who became the treasurer of the group; Tibor Kováč, an assimilationist; Andrej Steiner, an engineer vaguely connected with the prewar Social Democrats; and a number of other people who worked at the ÚŽ or were involved with it on the fringes. They were soon joined by Rabbi Michael Dov Ber Weissmandel, the son-in-law of Rabbi Ungar and Gisi's second cousin by marriage, who was and remained outside the ÚŽ organization. The group called itself the "Working Group" (Pracovná Skupina) or the "Parallel Government" (Vedlejší Vláda) or, in Weissmandel's reports written in rabbinical Hebrew, the "Hidden Committee" (ha-Va'ad Hamistater).

According to all the documentation we have, especially the book Weissmandel wrote after the war, testimonies by Steiner, Kováč, and Neumann, and Fleischmann's letters, it is clear that Fleischmann headed the Working Group. For an ultraorthodox man like Weissmandel it was no doubt a radical departure for a woman, and a Zionist to boot, to head a group of which he was a member. He explains it by referring to her strong personality, her commitment, and her wisdom in heading the heterogeneous group; it was precisely because she was a woman, he says, that the individuals who otherwise would have quarreled with each other accepted her leadership. I think that Weissmandel's explanations are a combination of true feelings and rationalization. He does not mention what must have been decisive for a halachic Jew: that Gisi was a relative, not a strange woman, which neutralized in this case the traditional attitude of fear and superciliousness toward women. In addition, because he consulted Rabbi Ungar on everything, he must have consulted him on the leadership question, and Ungar must have decided that Fleischmann, his cousin, was the right person to head the group. The testimonies of the others indicate a great admiration for her steadfastness, courage, and altruism but mainly for her sharp intelligence and general qualities of leadership.

At first the group dealt with legal rescue, trying to obtain certificates for individuals showing them to be economically important for Slovakia, and so on. Then, apparently in late June, Weissmandel suggested bribing Wisliceny, who was supervising the deportations on Eichmann's behalf. The only Jew who was in contact with Wisliceny was a Jewish traitor by the name of Karel Hochberg, who headed a department for special tasks at the ÚŽ and who helped Wisliceny and the Slovak fascists by giving technical help and information regarding the Jews to be deported (although his group did not prepare the actual lists). After some hesitation the group decided to approach Wisliceny through Hochberg. This apparently happened some time in July 1942. A sum of money—Weissmandel claims it was $25,000—was handed to Hochberg on August 17, and a second sum, toward the end of September, after Yom Kippur (which occurred on September 21 that year). The fact that there were only two transports to Poland after that— deportations did not restart until September 1944—convinced the group that their bribes had stopped the deportations.

The attempt to bribe Wisliceny was accompanied by determined attempts to bribe corrupt Slovak officials. Kováč, Steiner, and Fleischmann herself were very active in this. The funds at their disposal were obtained in part from the JDC in Switzerland, and it was Fleischmann who was in touch with Saly Mayer, the JDC representative there, and with Nathan Schwalb (Dror), the Hechalutz emissary—Hechalutz was an organization of leftist pioneering youth with its headquarters in

Palestine. I have written extensively on all the above and do not wish to
repeat the story here.[21] What interests us here is the personal involvement of Gisi Fleischmann. She was the one who phoned and sent letters
through emissaries, and she also went to Hungary to try and convince
the local Jewish leaders, especially the wealthy neolog leaders, to help
their Slovak brethren. She failed miserably—the Hungarian Jewish leaders were concerned about their own legal status and refused to engage
in what they feared would be illegal operations.

That the deportations meant not only great suffering and mass mor-
tality but the total murder of every Jew as a planned operation dawned
on the Working Group gradually. They tried to send non-Jewish persons to the Lublin area, where some of the transports had been sent and
from where they also received occasional postcards from the deportees.
They organized the sending of parcels to Lublin, and then, in the summer, they learned that the people had been deported "beyond the Bug"
river. They were not heard from again. In late August a letter from
Fleischmann to Switzerland says, "I almost despair of believing that we
shall ever see any one of our friends again." I emphasize this, because a
respected colleague in Canada, John S. Conway, has accused the Working Group of being collaborationists who betrayed their community by
negotiating with Wisliceny; even more important, he says that they
knew about the mass murder and failed to inform their community in
order to preserve their own skins. Nothing could be further from the
truth. They warned the community not to report for the deportations
months before they knew what the German plan was. They encouraged
the flight to Hungary, and they negotiated to stop the deportations.
Moreover, they apparently did not become aware of what we know of as
the Final Solution until August, after which they increased their efforts
to have the deportations stopped.[22]

They were mistaken, as we now know. It was not the bribing of
Wisliceny by Hochberg that stopped the deportations but the bribing of
the Slovak officials. In addition, so many Jews were protected by various
documents that only a relatively small number were left for additional

transports. And the Vatican intervened again, in June, and a directive from Berlin agreed that there was no point in pressing for the deportations of the last Jews at that time, given these conditions. When the deportations ended, 24,000–25,000 Jews were left alive in Slovakia.

Because the Working Group thought they had succeeded in stopping the deportations by bribing Wisliceny, they embarked immediately on a much larger program: trying to reach Himmler through Wisliceny and bribe the murderers to stop the trains to the extermination camps from all over Europe, perhaps even stop the murder altogether. This was known as the Europa Plan. Apparently only Fleischmann and Weissmandel pressed hard, within the group, to make the effort. The others did not think there was much of a chance. Nevertheless, a first contact was made in November 1942. Repeated talks were held with Wisliceny, and money for the bribe was solicited from abroad, both from the JDC and from the delegation of the Palestinian Yishuv who had established themselves in Istanbul. Contrary to a great deal of misinformation, much of it originating from Weissmandel, most of the initial $200,000 required for a down payment was transferred to Bratislava, illegally, during the spring and early summer of 1943. But, as we now know, Wisliceny was inventing the conditions and the sums of money. In November he had received the approval of Himmler to conduct negotiations, but after that, because he received no further instructions, the negotiations lacked a concrete basis. Himmler's initial agreement to negotiate appears to have been connected with his desire to open options for negotiating with the Americans, in case the Führer should want to do so or in case it should become necessary in some other way. The Jews were, from his standpoint, a logical conduit for such contacts. In the summer of 1943, Himmler ordered Wisliceny to stop the talks, perhaps because he thought he had found alternative routes to the Americans.[23]

What is amazing in this story is that the underground leadership of a remnant of a Jewish community in a satellite state should have tried to rescue not just itself but all the Jews in Nazi-occupied Europe in a daring plan of ransom negotiations with the murderers. In the light of traditional attitudes it is significant and interesting that this effort should have been led by a woman, at the head of a group in which practically all the divergent ideological Jewish trends of our times were represented.

While the negotiations around the Europa Plan continued, the danger of renewed deportations arose again, especially after March 1943, when Slovak antisemitism was ignited by German reminders that there were still Jews in Slovakia. The Working Group mobilized all its resources to avert the danger through massive bribery—and again they succeeded. Led by Fleischmann, they were managing to provide a responsible leadership for the remnant of Slovak Jewry.

At the end of 1943, Neumann became the head of ÚŽ, and the Working Group became, in effect, the official leadership of Slovak Jewry. Fleischmann was arrested in early 1944 because an attempt to bribe a centrally important official misfired, and the Germans traced the bribe to her. For four months she was in prison while her friends tried by every means to pry her loose. They succeeded and offered her an escape from Slovakia. She had refused a certificate of entry to Palestine prior to the closing of the exit gates at the beginning of the war. She did the same now. Her husband had died a natural death in 1942, but she had her sick mother to look after, and this time it seems that her feeling of responsibility for the community, along with her worry about her mother, again prevented her from accepting the offer.

From her letters and from the memoirs of the surviving members of the group, it seems clear that they all feared a deterioration of the situation in Slovakia prior to liberation, whether due to ravages during a German retreat or due to a rebellion in Slovakia that would invite a German invasion. In the end, it was the latter contingency that occurred. Elements in the army, as well as in that part of the underground that was loyal to the Czechoslovak government-in-exile in London, and the communist underground, which was already active in partisan detachments in the mountains—all pressed for a rebellion. The Slovaks supporting the reestablishment of Czechoslovakia, especially the Slovak army officers, wanted to rehabilitate Slovakia in the eyes of the Allies; the communists wanted to help their Soviet mentors—their leader, Gustav Husak, actually advocated annexing the country to the USSR. The preparations went awry, however, and the rebellion broke out prematurely, on August 29, 1944. German troops immediately entered Slovakia to suppress it. In their wake came an Einsatzkommando of the S.S., who took action against the Jews. Shortly afterward, Alois Brunner, one of Eichmann's most ruthless henchmen, who now lives peacefully and happily in Syria, came to oversee the Final Solution of the Jewish question in Slovakia.

The Working Group, under Fleischmann's leadership, tried to use bribery again in the new circumstances. They did not call upon the Jews in the western parts of the country to escape to the territory held by the rebels. They went to the Nazis and offered them goods in return for ceasing to concentrate Jews in the camp at Sered, which the Nazis had begun to do. The S.S. people who were negotiating with Reszoe Kastner in Hungary at the time actually warned the Working Group not to conduct negotiations with Brunner, but Fleischmann and her colleagues did not listen. When they were told to ask the Jews of Bratislava to report for deportation to Sered, they obeyed. When the police took their community list, they complained to the S.S. about it but did not spread word to the community to hide. Consequently, toward the end of September 1944 most of the Working Group members were arrested and put into Sered. Fleischmann was arrested in early October and interrogated at Sered in a brutal fashion by Brunner personally. She reportedly broke down and pleaded for her life, but to no avail. On October 17 she was shipped to Auschwitz, along with a letter from Brunner telling the S.S. at Auschwitz to liquidate her. There, on October 18, she was separated from the rest, and she was not seen anymore. No one knows how she was killed.

The activities of the Working Group in the month of September, right before the group ceased to exist, do cast a dark shadow over all of them, and on Fleischmann as their leader. They knew; they had been forewarned; they could have had no illusions. But still they acted just like some of the other Jewish Councils did: they could have warned and they didn't; they could have refused the demands of the Nazis—it would have made no difference in any case—but they didn't. But we were not in their place, and we don't know how we would have acted.[24]

What is one to say in conclusion? Does the gender-studies approach provide us with an additional perspective on a case study like this? Does the story of a woman who resisted, who tried to sanctify life through her actions, tell us something about the problems of the Holocaust that are uniquely connected with gender? I think the answer to both questions is yes. The feminist perspective is, surely, a secondary perspective, the chief one being the story of an underground group and its attempts to rescue Jews within the context of the Slovak fascist state and the German policies toward the Jews, policies that did not differentiate between the fate of women and the fate of men.

In terms of the social history of the Jews, however, the story is significant: a woman and a leader climbed the ladder of traditional female involvement in Jewish welfare and migration matters to become the political leader of the only Jewish underground—the only underground anywhere in Europe—that united all the political factions of a country (with the exception of the communists) and was the only group anywhere in Europe that tried to rescue not just itself but Jews of other countries. The case of Gisi Fleischmann should be addressed as an important manifestation of the development of Jewish society and of the role of women in it. A brave woman, a brave leader, a person who wanted to enjoy life, who had a happy family around her, chose to stand at the head of a group that tried to save a community. I don't know of any other woman who did something similar during the Holocaust or, indeed, before it.

Paradoxically, the case of Gisi Fleischmann is so exceptional that it seems to prove that women had almost no chance to show their leadership qualities. Given the constraints of the period, only men were called upon to lead Jews. Her acceptance by the ultraorthodox, her contacts with aid organizations outside her country, her unique ability to manipulate and persuade individuals with opposing ideological and political perspectives—none of these attributes could be easily repeated elsewhere.

It must be remembered, too, that she was in charge of a group representing a whole community and not, like some women resisters, of a small segment of a community. That women headed some of the resistance groups, or at least were equal partners with young men in that leadership, again shows how exceptional Fleischmann's case was, because the resistance groups were youthful and acted, in most cases, against the wish of the adults.

When we speak today about the role of women in society and transpose our attitudes to the period of the Holocaust, we are doing something ahistoric. When we point out the heroic role, or the leading role, or the tragic but special role, of Jewish women at that time, we tend to endow them with a consciousness that they did not possess and assign them a role that they were not aware of. They did not see themselves as fighting for their status as women in a male-dominated society; rather, they fought for the survival of their group, for revenge, for Jewish honor, for their own survival. They could do that because of the collapse of Jewish patriarchal society under the blows of the Nazis. Jewish society would not have allowed them such a position in times of peace; they would have been shunted back to their traditional roles, and all but a small minority would have accepted that. The Holocaust engendered a special fate for Jewish women, to be sure, just as it did for men. We should investigate it, because it says something to us today. In that sense, Gisi Fleischmann's story is important. When reading her letters, one is overwhelmed by her personality, intelligence, drive, and leadership qualities. I think she did her best, and I think she should be recognized as a role model, despite her terrible mistake at the end. She was a brave, resourceful, self-sacrificing, generous woman who acted to save lives.

chapter nine

Theology, or God the Surgeon

Jewish theological explanations of
the Holocaust offer a variety of justifications for God's action or inac-
tion at the time (*tzidduk ha'din*—"justification of [God's] judgment"),
some more and some less grounded in Jewish religious tradition. That
tradition has the concept of an all-powerful Being who cannot be asked
for any explanation because humans are too puny to understand his
leadership (*hanhaga*) of the world. His ways are not our ways. God, then,
can be removed from the argument altogether in consideration of Job's
submission at the end of his struggle with the Almighty: Job admits
God's infiniteness and his own incapacity to understand it. Indeed, with
Job, God ultimately acts outside human morality; in other words, he is
the ultimate cosmic power, beyond good and evil. Regarding the Holocaust, this might appear to solve the problem.

Most orthodox commentators (and many nonorthodox ones as well)
are right to then ask the counterquestion: Don't ask where God was,
because you cannot grasp his ways; instead, ask, where was Man? The

ball is, so to speak, in the human, not the divine, court. Of course, after having said that we cannot understand God's actions, Jewish (and many Christian) religious thinkers then desperately try to do just that—namely, to understand them. According to a second argument, all evil is grounded in the freedom that God has given humans to choose between good and bad. Punishment for evil was, in the Psalms, promised to the evildoers in this world. Later, punishment was transferred to the next world. In any case, evil is again a human choice, not a divine one. There is a tension, even a contradiction, between the two arguments; the first says that we cannot question God's leadership of the world (because we are too puny), and the second says that there is no need to question it (because he decided long ago to give freedom of choice to humans, and he will reward and punish us in due course).

The second argument again creates a problem. If Man is given the freedom to choose between good and evil (and a God-fearing Jew knows what good is: to obey the 613 commandments of Jewish Law—halakhah), the freedom to choose may well apply to the Nazis: they chose, and they chose evil. Did the victims have any choice? Hardly. And if they chose what generally accepted standards would categorize as "good," were they saved? Were they saved if they were observant Jews and followed all the commandments? Were they saved if they were not observant Jews? Survival rates indicate the contrary of what the religious argument would suggest. Among the largely nonorthodox Jews of Western Europe—in France, Belgium, Italy, and Denmark—a relatively high proportion of Jews survived, whereas among the orthodox Jews of Poland the proportion of survivors was minimal. *Vehadra kushia le'dukhta*—"the question returns to its beginning," to use a phrase common in talmudic discourse. In other words, the objection is not answered.

As to the first argument, orthodox thinkers, in contradiction of their own view (the "we are too puny" argument), still wonder what God's purpose might have been, because obviously it is he who rules the world and who determined that the Holocaust should happen. After all, according to tradition, God occasionally told humans why he did what he did. Is not the whole Jewish tradition based on the assumption that it was inspired by God, if not more than that, and that if the moral commandments it contains come from God, was he not more than just a neutral cosmic power—is he not obliged to act in accordance with his own decreed morality? Serious ultraorthodox or *haredi* thinkers—I use the term they use to describe themselves: *haredi* (*hared* means "[God]fearing")—addressed the question, and this is what they said and wrote after the Holocaust.[1]

The argument goes around in circles. If Man had the freedom to act, if Man alone was responsible for evil, was God relevant in any real sense? If the ball is in the human court, what do we need God for? If Man is responsible, what is the point in praying or the point of serious religious observance beyond perhaps the need to convince oneself?

Another basic, but contradictory, Jewish religious tradition holds that everything, evil as well as good, comes from God, is designed by God. So evil is also part of God's plan, whose ultimate goal is always the good, which means that evil, misfortune, horrors—all of these are only seemingly bad, and they ultimately lead to the good. That this answer is opposed to the others does not matter—orthodox Jews live with these contradictory ways of thinking and integrate them into views that turn from one argument to the other as occasion demands. In the end, for traditional Judaism, belief in God is self-understood, but is of less importance than the observance of the commandments (*mitzvot*). What is important is what one does, not what one believes; what one declares one believes in is even less important.

Attempts to escape these contradictions are not lacking. In contemporary religious philosophy one finds the strengthening of a well-known argument: To ask questions relating to theodicy does not require recourse to the Holocaust. Any child that is run over in the street arouses the same questions of evil in the world as the Holocaust does. The murder of millions for no apparent reason makes the issue more dramatic, but in principle there is no difference at all. In other words, the Holocaust as such does not create any problems for a theodicy; the problems exist regardless. The theological problem is one of day-to-day religious observance: Can a Jew carry on his or her religious life after the Holocaust?[2]

This argument may be convincing from a philosophical point of view, but it is exactly from the viewpoint of the ordinary believer who sees God as an omnipotent, omnipresent force for good that the Holocaust presents a major problem. The very magnitude of the event compels people to ask questions that they can perhaps ignore or explain away in their daily life.

Another explanatory strategy is based on the mystical, kabbalistic tradition, which includes thinkers opposed to vital elements of organized religion, such as Martin Buber. Essentially, they propose *tzimtzum* (contraction), or the voluntary removal of God's presence from the universe. In some interpretations he removed himself to permit the world to exist, because if God's presence were all-pervasive, the world could not function. God withdrew from the world so that human free will could assert itself, for good or evil. The Jewish worldview (like the Christian and Muslim worldviews) is orbocentric; that is, it sees our earth—a tiny speck in a vast universe with trillions upon trillions of suns, planets, and other bodies—as the center of attention of a universal God. It is also anthropocentric; it sees humanity—which has been on this earth for perhaps a couple of million years out of the several billion years of the planet's existence—as being at the center of God's attention and everyday care. And it is Judeo-centric; it sees the Jews—today, 13 million out of several billion humans—as the center of the universal God's attention. All these views contradict the idea of tzimtzum, because it is difficult to see how a God that frees the world from his presence would nevertheless be tremendously interested in what Jews— a fraction of humanity, itself a new arrival on one of trillions of heavenly bodies—eat for lunch. And yet orthodox Jews believe that God is attentive to the slightest detail of Jewish daily religious observance. If God is the God of our forefathers, of Abraham, Jacob, and Isaac, and if he is just, omnipresent, and omniscient and nevertheless the Holocaust happened, then, it is said, the answer must be tzimtzum. God has hidden his face (*hester panim*) as a punishment to humanity, especially the Jews, for not having observed his commandments.

Just because God has hidden his face does not mean that he has given up his power—that is one of the things God cannot do without ceasing to be God. That in turn means that being all-powerful may enable him not to exercise his power; but he cannot give up being an all-powerful God. He may be the *deus absconditus* (the God who runs away), but he cannot abdicate. Hiding his face means that he may intervene, but normally does not do so, even when he disapproves of what humanity, especially the Jews, choose to do. Withdrawing, hiding his face, is in fact a punishment because thereby the forces of evil, which he created by creating Man and giving him free choice, are free to act without let or hindrance.

Various versions of this theological explanation can be perused in works by non-haredi thinkers such as Eliezer Berkovits and Emil Fackenheim, but even more so by quite a number of very serious figures in the haredi world.[5] Without going into a deeper analysis of these theories, I will say two things, which will bring us nearer to our central topic. First, these theories are, like any theological speculations, just that—pure speculations, *human* speculations, running up against the first argument ("we are too puny to understand God") and against the logical argument that if God is hiding his face, such speculation is not God-inspired unless a miracle has occurred and God has "shown" his face in order to inform the theologians of the divine truth, which does not seem very likely. Second, if God is hiding his face, the question of his relevance to humanity comes up again. An absent God is a God who decided to be absent, and he is not likely to listen to prayers, and even if he does, he will not react to them. An absent God is basically a callous God, a God who has ceased to be interested and is therefore no longer relevant. Yet he is still all-powerful; he *could* intervene because he is omniscient and therefore knows what humans do, hence his responsibility is in no way lessened. By *choosing* to be absent, he may be held

responsible for the evil he permits, and we can call it evil by setting it
against the moral standards he himself supposedly decreed.

A great contemporary Jewish thinker, Rabbi Irving "Yitz" Greenberg, has addressed the problem from a modern orthodox perspective in
an original and innovative way. Greenberg is confronted by the dilemma
that if God is both just and all-powerful, the Holocaust is inexplicable in
religious terms, because hiding his face does not prevent his knowing. If
God is all-powerful and omniscient, he cannot be just, because by his
own moral standards he should have prevented the Holocaust, which he
did not do, and hiding his face cannot be his excuse; if he is just, he
cannot be all-powerful, because if he were, he would have prevented the
Holocaust. Greenberg feels he has to choose between these explanations, and he chooses the second: he rescues the idea of the Jewish God
of justice and compassion and declares that God could not save the Jews
because he is not, or is no longer, all-powerful. Whether he once was all-
powerful is beside the point; clearly he is not so now. God, then, is a
weak God, who needs the cooperation of humans to redress the ills of
the world. This, by the way, is an old Jewish tradition: Man cooperates
with God in bringing good to the universe. For Greenberg, the Holocaust has shaken the very basis of the Covenant between God and the
Jews because it has called into question the existence of the Jewish
people. The only way out is to redefine the Covenant to allow for a real
partnership between the Jews and God, a partnership in which Jews are
called upon to take a much more active role than they have up to now.
This, as has been noted, is not a new idea in the Jewish tradition, and it
could be viewed as another version of the "hiding the face" argument.*

The problem with this explanation, apart from its being no less of a
speculation than the others, is that if God is weak, who needs him in
moments of crisis and danger? What is the point of praying or of ob-
serving the commandments? Are the Ten Commandments only ten
suggestions, or are they—what a thought!—human precepts that can be
approached merely from a human perspective? Greenberg, however,
goes beyond these explications and argues that the Holocaust has

shown up the essential brokenness of Judaism, Christianity and, indeed, nonreligious thought as well. This argument seems to reflect the kabbalistic concept of the broken vessels, that is, the idea that with the exile of the Jews the exile of the Spirit of God (*shekhina*) has taken place. In effect, the world itself is broken, and it is the task of the Jews to gather the pieces of light from the hard crust of the material world and reconstruct a meaningful world. For Greenberg, the brokenness of the religious world should be a cause for a nonfinal approach to all ideologies, or, as he puts it, for a pluralistic openness to thought and action. One may believe what one believes, but one should not deny the possible validity of other, even opposing ideologies. This conclusion appears to represent a break in traditional Jewish thought, but not many orthodox—or many other Jews—seem to follow Greenberg, at least so far. An acceptance of his ideas would go a long way toward healing heated intra-Jewish controversies and might even point the way toward a neutralization, though not a solution, of the theodicy problem.[5]

Beyond these and similar attempts to explain where God and Man were when the Holocaust occurred, there is a major problem of the Jewish tradition from the times of the prophets on: whether all the disasters that have befallen the Jewish people came about because they had sinned against God's commandments. Originally God was a tribal deity. When Egyptians, Assyrians, and Babylonians proved stronger than the Jews, and their gods seemed to be stronger than the Jewish God, the prophets found a brilliant explanation: God was universal, and he was using the surrounding empires to chastise his people who had failed to do what he had ordered them to do. His people may have been fairly meticulous in bringing sacrifices to the temple (or temples), but they had reneged on the social and personal moral obligations that God had imposed upon them. *Mipnei khata'einu*—"because of our sins"— became the general explanation for all the disasters of Jewish history. This is interpretation of the universe in terms of magic: If only the Jews obey God, they will influence him and, through him, history, because then God will do what is good for the Jews. They therefore have real power over their own fate, for if they obey the commandments, they will prosper. Basically, Christianity and Islam have taken over this predisposition of the Jewish teaching toward magic.

This kind of explanation has tremendous value for a minority group constantly threatened with persecution by the majority and often faced with real and continued suffering. The magic explanation returns power to the persecuted group: They are actually more powerful than their persecutors because they can change history by their behavior, and they know perfectly well what the behavior desired by God is. Magic is real, prevents despair, and enables the minority group—the Jews, in this case—to overcome disasters.

It is this explanation that forms the basis for an orthodox interpretation of the Holocaust. It is grounded in the classic Jewish writings and in their medieval, early modern, and modern interpretations. Does that make Hitler another Nebuchadnezzar, sent by God to punish his people? Orthodox tradition pulls believers to accept just that, and it is hardly possible to avoid that conclusion. In fact, as early as November 30, 1942, the Chief Rabbi of Palestine, Yitzhak Halevi Herzog, declared, in a speech to the protest meeting of the General Assembly of the Yishuv—the Jewish population in Palestine—after the arrival of detailed information about the Holocaust—that the disaster had come as a result of the sins of the Jews. This diatribe was repeated several times, in various formulations, by the orthodox (not the haredi) establishment. It meant that the sins of the Jews were so terrible that they warranted the death of close to six million Jews, including at least a million children under thirteen, which is the age of bar mitzvah (the rite of passage from childhood to adulthood—for boys only, as girls do not really count). We may ask: What sin or sins were so terrible?

Ultraorthodoxy, increasingly powerful and increasingly aggressive in today's Jewish world, searches for concrete sinners. Thus, some of the haredi rabbis claim that it was the Reform movement in Central Europe that diverted Jews from the straight and narrow path of strict religious observance. Reb Yoel ("Yoelish") Teitelboym, the Satmarer Rebbe (he

came from Satu Mare in Romania—Satmar in Yiddish), a Holocaust
survivor, accused the accursed Zionists. Others hold Bundist socialists
or Zionist secularists, Reform or Liberal synagogues, or others responsible. Many think that the Enlightenment diverted the Jews from their
tradition, with fatal consequences. Many see modernity as the main
culprit: nonreligious Jews followed the ways of modernity and thereby
sinned. Different authorities assign different degrees of responsibility
to various Jewish nonorthodox movements.[6]

The chief difficulty with all this lies in the fact that the primary
victims of Nazi murder were the East European Jews. While it is part of
the accepted and inaccurate nostalgic belief that East European Jewry
was largely orthodox or ultraorthodox (haredi), in fact by 1939 it most
emphatically was not—it is true that the proportion of the "keepers of
the commandments" (*shomrei mitzvot*) there was very much higher than
among Western or Central European Jews. As I mentioned earlier,
many more Eastern European Jews were murdered than Western or
Central European ones: 90 percent of Polish Jews were murdered (and
among the 10 percent who survived, the orthodox were a very small
minority), whereas of the half-a-million-plus German Jews, a majority
survived, as did two-thirds of the Jews in France, about 60 percent of
the Jews in Belgium, and almost all the Danish Jews. The same holds
true of Italian Jews, though not for the Jews of the Netherlands or the
Czech countries. Haredi thinkers devote a great deal of their work to
explaining why God punished the "innocent," that is, those who followed the commandments, and rescued or facilitated the survival of
the sinners.

Some of the more serious orthodox thinkers, especially modern ones,
but also some profound haredi thinkers, rebel against the dictum of
mipnei khata'einu—"because of our sins." A just God must not be accused of blatant injustice; in fact, such an accusation might even be
considered blasphemy (*khillul hashem*). Lord Immanuel Jacobovits, the
former Chief Rabbi of Britain, argued that a direct causal connection

between Jewish sins and acts of God can take place only in the Land of Israel, but he also published other interpretations.[7]

The way out of the dilemma is often a return to the argument of "we are too puny." Not so Kalman Klonymus Shapira, the chassidic Rabbi of Piaseczna and author of a collection of sermons given on Sabbaths in the Warsaw ghetto in 1940–1942; he himself did not survive.[8] For him, the suffering of the Jews was the suffering of God himself; it was certainly not caused by their sins—though sinful they surely were—but by God's plan for humanity in general and his Jews in particular. The question for the Rabbi was whether the suffering was not so great that it endangered God's master plan by annihilating God's people. This should have been enough to produce a miraculous intervention—but it did not. Mipnei khata'einu was rejected in this instance. But the Rabbi of Piaseczna and other great thinkers and moral authorities do not represent the thinking of most haredi teachers of the post-Holocaust generations. Rather, people like Yoel Teitelboym and, as we shall see, the leader of Habad are more typical and much more popular.

Another, perhaps more logical and appealing way to deal with these dilemmas is that taken by a number of orthodox thinkers and teachers (such as Walter Zvi Bacharach, a survivor of Auschwitz, in a public radio program in Israel), who say that they are angry at the Lord of the universe and might even argue with him, but they believe in him, because there had to be a God of Sinai. This line of argument, which has deep roots in the Jewish tradition, seems to be directed against all theologizing about the Holocaust.

One of the fastest growing Jewish religious movements—some may call it a sect—is Habad, whose name is the Hebrew acronym for *khokhma, binah, da'at* ("wisdom, understanding, knowledge"); it was founded by the sage Shneur Zalman of Lady at the end of the eighteenth and early in the nineteenth century. Habad is also known as the Lubavitch movement, and its Rebbe (chassidic rabbi) as the Lubavitcher, after the Ukrainian village in which the Rebbes of the movement resided during the

nineteenth century. Habad, a chassidic sect, is an aggressively missionizing movement with a dynamic, messianic ideology that develops and
changes as occasion demands. It advocated settling in the Holy Land but
opposed Zionism, which it saw as a secular distortion of the Jewish
dream. Ironically, the third Israeli president, Zalman Shazar (Shneur
Zalman Rubashov), a secularized Labor leader, was a member of the
Rebbe's dynasty.

Under the late incumbent, Menachem Mendel Shneersohn, Habad
underwent a revolution. Among other things, modern technology was
harnessed, mainly for propaganda. In the movement today, Torah study
is pursued with verve, and great emphasis is placed on missionizing
activities. The ultramodern techniques used to recruit believers are
obviously copied from Protestant fundamentalist movements in the
United States. Discipline under the late Rebbe was strict, and obedience
was hierarchical, even more so than with other chassidic sects, although
these, too, are generally disciplined and hierarchically organized. The
Rebbe was the ultimate authority for everything from very personal
decisions to public policy. Until recently, Habad intervened in Israeli
politics in the interests of the extreme Right and influenced the election
of Benjamin Netanyahu as prime minister in May 1996. Its main opponents in the haredi camp are the Lithuanian yeshivot (talmudic academies) under the leadership of Rabbi Eliezer Shach. An apocryphal story
has it that when Shach was asked to identify the religion that is closest
to Judaism, he said, "*Efsher* ["possibly"] *Lubavitch.*"

The Rebbe, who died in 1995, set out to convert Jews to Habad beliefs
(the equivalent of being "reborn" among Christians), especially in Israel. He refused to go to Israel, however, saying that if he went there, he
would have to stay, in accordance with Jewish Law (So what? one is
inclined to ask).

The missionizing drive has a purpose, laid out in Habad ideology:
observance of the commandments will prevent another catastrophe
and assure the miracle of divine intervention, which will peak with
the coming of the Messiah. The Hebrew acronym of the Rebbe's name

is *Mamash*, which means "truly," or "really," with the connotation of "now." Habad supporters saw, and many still see, the promised Messiah in Menachem Mendel Shneersohn. Stickers on cars read, "We Want Moshiach [Messiah] Now" or "We Want Mamash Now." Even though he is dead, many Habad supporters continue to see him as the Messiah, who could not reveal himself because the world ("the generation") was not yet fit to accept him. Many believe that he will rise from the dead and reveal himself as the Messiah in due course.

It is quite safe to predict that there is not going to be another Lubavitcher Rebbe—one cannot have a Rebbe after the Messiah. All this makes Habad into a Christological movement, which also has roots in Jewish traditions; after all, Jesus was proclaimed as the Messiah by devout Jews of his generation. According to the Gospels, Jesus, when confronted with the question of whether he was the Messiah, did not deny it, but neither did he make the claim explicitly. Menachem Mendel Shneersohn acted likewise. On the other hand, one could see in Habad a direct continuation of the tradition of supporting false Messiahs, of whom there were quite a number in Jewish history, the most famous being Shabbatai Zvi, who caused a tremendous upheaval in the Jewish world of the second half of the seventeenth century before he converted to Islam.

A fascinating aspect of Habad's Messianism is the link between it and the Holocaust. Unanimously, chassidic haredi thought sees the modern age, especially the twentieth century, as the *Ikveta Di'Meshikha*, loosely translated as "the beginning of the Messianic age." That age is to be preceded by convulsions (again, the parallel with Christian fundamentalism is obvious), and for the chassidic haredi world of the 1940s and early 1950s, without exception, the Holocaust was the well-nigh unsurpassable climax of these promised times of trouble. The immediate coming of the Messiah would be the result. Was Shneersohn not a logical choice, both as an individual and as the timely fulfillment of an expectation? This chronology makes the wide acceptance of the Rebbe as the Messiah more understandable. In the wake of the Holocaust, God *had to*

send his Messiah, and he did, as wide circles within Habad believed and
continue to believe.

Rabbi Shneersohn did not address the issue of the Holocaust directly
for many years. He himself, the son-in-law of the previous rebbe, fled
from occupied France. In 1971 and 1973 he addressed the faithful, in
Yiddish, in the traditional form of the *shut* (acronym for *she'elot ve'tshuvot*,
pronounced "shoot"), or responsa. His responsa were popular and were
not directed to the Torah-educated elite. They were published by the
Habad publishing house in Kfar Habad, Israel, in 1980, in a booklet
entitled *Mada Ve'emunah* (Science and Belief).

Before we analyze pages 115–124 in the booklet, it is important to
note that Habad propagandists (but not the Rebbe) denied that these
were the Rebbe's words. At first, the argument was that the Habad
publishing house was not the official or legitimate producer of Habad
texts, an odd argument indeed for a publication that appeared under the
Habad imprimatur and saw the light of day in Kfar Habad, the center of
the Habad movement in Israel. Then it was said that the Rebbe spoke in
Yiddish, with his faithful taking down his words, but they made errors
or misunderstood his message. This argument is equally odd, because
the Rebbe himself must have gone over every text that emanated from
him, especially in such a theologically important publication as a booklet of responsa—even though they were directed at the general public,
or perhaps precisely because of that.

Some people might think that these prevarications were a way for the
Rebbe to distance himself from the statements he had made, without
actually saying so. That, however, would hardly be typical of a man who
made no bones about his views. In fact, he did stand behind the passages
in the text, in a letter written in response to an article published in the
Israeli left-wing daily *Al Hamishmar* on August 22, 1980, by a Member
of the Israeli Knesset, Chaika Grossman. The Rebbe wrote her a letter
on August 28 and not only signed it but corrected some words and
passages in his own handwriting. Grossman had attacked him for what
was written in the booklet, and the Rebbe, obviously disturbed by the

attack, replied. Grossman, after all, had been the commander of the remnants of the ghetto rebels in Bialystok during the Holocaust; she was a symbol of Jewish armed resistance during the Holocaust, and her attack stung him.[9] In the letter Shneersohn explicitly acknowledges and defends the statements in the booklet, although he says that the language is an adaptation of his actual words (see below).

His responsum was part of the process of popularization that Habad has been engaged in since the 1940s. Menachem Mendel Shneersohn was a brilliant scholar of the classical Jewish heritage, and he was also extremely well versed in general knowledge (he was a student at a technical college in Paris before he came to the United States), besides speaking and reading a number of languages. No less important is the strength and genuineness of his moral convictions. He was a devout follower of his predecessor and relative, an original thinker and leader, Yossef Yitzhok Shneersohn (Menachem Mendel suffered the stroke that began his long and painful descent to death while visiting Yossef Yitzhok's grave).

It was Yossef Yitzhok who led Habad during the Holocaust years. Originally, like many other haredi ideologues, he saw in the experiences of those years the sufferings that would precede the coming of the Messiah and the ultimate redemption of the Jews and, through them, of humankind. In fact, he was convinced that the persecutions in Europe were but a prelude to even more severe persecutions that would strike the United States because of the sinful behavior of the Jews there. When that did not happen, he nevertheless remained certain that the Messiah would come soon, depending upon the return (*tshuvah*) of the Jews to their religious roots. God was waiting for that return in order to make his presence felt again—hence the need for radical and immediate popular action. Menachem Mendel did everything in his power to realize his predecessor's vision, and the spread of Habad's ideas in popular form was a central strategy.[10]

The first statement in the responsum is the axiom that God punishes in proper proportion to the transgression. The question asked is,

How can one explain the Holocaust "as well as other persecutions in which the punishments were so extreme"? (The translations are mine throughout.) The very question, the Rebbe says, implies, first, that God is all-powerful *and* just; second, that he is omniscient and knows everybody's transgressions; third, that as the supreme judge, his justice is absolute, hence the conclusion that he punishes according to the severity of the crime; and fourth, that the Holocaust is not unique—he sets it within the framework of other persecutions of Jews. Decades of research showing that the Holocaust was unprecedented—in the Nazi aim of total annihilation, in the racial definition, in the impossibility of escaping by converting—are ignored.

The Rebbe avers in his responsum that the questioner understands that God is both creator of the universe and supreme judge, for if that were not so, there would be no point to the question, because there would be no one with whom to raise objections. Anyone who does not recognize God in the same way has to "contend with a world which is a jungle and in which a mad goy [Hitler] has been let loose to murder people."

Shneersohn, with his full awareness of Jewish sources, knew the traditions regarding the great Jewish apostate and heretic of talmudic times, Elisha ben Avuya (called Acher, or "The Other"), who arrived at an atheistic conclusion based on his own thorough knowledge of the Jewish heritage, when he said: *"Leit Din Veleit Dayan"*—"There is no Law and there is no Judge." The Rebbe implies that accepting Acher's position makes no sense. If there is no God, who let loose the mad goy? If one assumes, like Acher, that the world has no extrahuman judge, it follows that no one sent a mad goy; humans alone are responsible for their actions. But if one follows the logic of the Lubavitcher Rebbe, then the inevitable conclusion is that Hitler was sent by God—not a pleasant thought. The same conclusion, as we have shown above, could be derived from the statement by Rabbi Herzog, made as early as 1942, and by many other orthodox authorities. One might add that an atheist or agnostic speaking to the Rebbe would not question God's justice but would deny the existence or the relevance of God, to which the Rebbe's reply about a mad goy would in turn be irrelevant.

In his letter to Grossman, the Rebbe says that the "contents [of the booklet as quoted by Grossman] are in general correct. And I am not, God forbid, coming with any complaint that you failed to act correctly with the quotes [from him] in your article." God was "also the leader of all creatures at the time of the Shoah."

The Rebbe's answer in the responsum moves into the traditional "we are too puny" argument. God is omniscient, all-powerful, and just, and he "manages all the affairs . . . of some four billion people. Is it then possible to doubt His integrity and contend that 'His conduct is unjust because it is incompatible with what I think'? Is it possible for the created to understand the Creator?"

Had Shneersohn stopped there, as some orthodox thinkers do, his argument would have been cogent: we cannot understand, hence no explanation is possible. But he continues. Having just denied that an explanation is possible, he proceeds to search for answers—specifically, a response to the question of whether "perhaps there is still an explanation."

In Jewish tradition, rabbis sometimes do not wait for questions to be asked. A responsum comes in reply to a question the sage asks himself, and this seems to be what happened here. The method is the same as before: the Rebbe starts with some axiomatic statements. First, it is certain that "evil does not start from on High." From that it follows, second, that "in the very pain and suffering there is also lofty and spiritual good"—and, knowing that this statement may arouse tremendous opposition, he adds—"although the human mind may not be able to grasp this." The solution follows, in a kind of synthesis: "There is a possibility that a physical catastrophe [he uses the term Shoah, which means "catastrophe"] may be a spiritual benefaction because the bounds of the body and the soul are not necessarily coterminous. Body and soul have contradictory characteristics."

Shneersohn's assumption is that of Jewish fundamentalism generally: God is absolutely good and absolutely just, hence he cannot be the source of ultimate evil. What is its source? Shneersohn does not answer that question directly, but it may perhaps lie in the theory of tzimtzum (contraction) mentioned above. God withdraws from the world to permit free will to be active, and free will opens up the possibility of choosing to be evil. The usual continuation of this line of argument in orthodoxy (not only Jewish) is that the reward of the just is not in this world but in the next (although some biblical texts say the opposite). To reach that point in the argument, Shneersohn explains the difference between body and soul. By body he means physical existence in the physical world; this clearly is on a lower level than the existence of the soul, which is the eternal spiritual quality in humans and which alone is worth saving. He can then say that what is good for the soul may not be good for the body. The conclusion that one may draw from this distinction in relation to the Holocaust is that basically the Holocaust was a good thing because God is good, and he must have ordained it to save many souls at the expense of their bodies.

This argument is a popularization of Rebbe Yossef Yitzhok's differentiation not only between body and soul but also between the "animal soul" and the "human soul." Another great sage said something similar. Rabbi Avraham Hacohen Kook, no advocate of Habad-like solutions, was the justly revered first Chief Rabbi of Palestine until his death in 1935. Kook, too, made the differentiation between two types of souls, arguing that the difference between the Jewish spirit (he seems to have meant only the spirit of men, in line with the antifeminist character of monotheistic religions) and the souls of non-Jews is greater than the difference between the souls of non-Jews and the souls of animals. The "animal soul" (non-Jewish) is concerned with this-worldly affairs, whereas the "human soul" (Jewish) directs itself toward God and his commandments.

Not content with this generalization, however, the Rebbe proceeded to invent a chassidic parable, which is worth quoting from the booklet in full.

Imagine, for example, a person who happens to be in a hospital and enters an operating theater. He is confronted with a frightening spectacle: a person tied down to an operation table is surrounded by ten or so people, their faces covered with masks, knives in their hands. They are about to remove one of his limbs. If the "visitor" knew nothing about modern medical practice, he would be sure that he was witnessing a cannibalistic practice. He would surely start screaming and would call for help to "save" the "victim" from the "criminals." His reactions would be due to his lack of knowledge of medicine and of the past, present, and future condition of the patient. Had he known that the limb to be removed was hopelessly poisoned and that its removal was necessary to save the patient's life and that to save his life the doctors and the professor at their head have to operate and remove the affected limb, he would have reacted differently. . . . God, like the professor surgeon, understands the situation and knows what is good for Israel. Thus, everything that happened was for the good. Had the behavior been that of a mortal being, there would have been room for doubts and objections to his actions. However, when God is the "specialist surgeon," there can be no room for questioning.

The parable is self-explanatory and perhaps self-condemnatory. Contrary to classic chassidic parables, in which God usually appears as the King (because he is "the king of the kings of kings"—*melekh malkhei hamlakhim*), here God is a professor, or a specialist surgeon. "No hurt has occurred," adds Shneersohn, because the pain was only physical, not spiritual.

In the letter to Grossman, Shneersohn repeats the story, thus authenticating it: "As to the 'operation'—I never heard anyone say that operating on a patient is a punishment to him; the opposite is true. . . . Of course, an operation that is done to someone is done, first of all for his own good. . . . And as to the rhetorical question in your article asking who the surgeon is . . . surely, there is no need to explain, and the axe should not show pride as against its wielder." This could be interpreted to mean that a Hitler (the axe in the hand of God the surgeon) should not be seen as anything but a tool, and that is indeed what Grossman deduced from the passage. Then Shneersohn continues: "But it is clear that man is not a chisel or an axe, but a person who can choose and who is responsible for his actions. . . . As to the 'task' of Hitler, may his memory be damned, what I said is not something I invented; it is rooted in our Torah . . . in connection with the destruction of the First Temple," and Shneersohn quotes from Jeremiah 25:9 about "Nebuchadnezzar My slave" and from Isaiah (10:5), who saw Assyria as God's rod of punishment. And then Shneersohn returns to the example of the surgeon, writing that "in our generation I must say that it is a matter of an 'operation,' that is, a matter of a *tikkun* [lit., "correction"; the return of the individual, the society, and the world to a divine order], and it must be emphasized that the *tikkun* is made for the good of the person who is operated on, and the *tikkun* goes to such lengths that the suffering does not nearly equal the *tikkun* that is achieved." The fact of death is immaterial, because a devout Jew believes in resurrection.

The important element in Shneersohn's letter lies in his acknowledgment that the metaphor of the surgeon and the operation is his and that he used it to show that the Holocaust was an act of God, done to make a *tikkun*, or, in contemporary language, to redeem Israel, the Jewish people, by eliminating its weaknesses and pointing out its sins so that it can return to its role as God's people, which is what the Rebbe wants—and what the Rebbe thinks God wants.

Needless to say, there are some problems with this. Hitler becomes a Nebuchadnezzar, a scourge of God (one may wish Hitler would have been as considerate as Nebuchadnezzar). This has the corroborative implication that God is directly responsible for the Holocaust, and the Lubavitcher Rebbe does not flinch from that conclusion. The Holocaust saved the people of Israel, because it amputated the poisoned limb. So we are back to the mipnei khata'einu argument. Yet nowhere does the Lubavitcher say explicitly what the sins were, where the poison was, where the gangrene had set in. The sins surely must have been horrendous, because the "operation" excised close to six million people, among whom were the children. . . .

The suffering was not as horrible as one may think, according to the Rebbe. In the booklet, Shneersohn says that "the suffering and pain of those pure and holy ones was only temporal, and there is no value in the temporary anguish of the body compared to the eternal life of the soul." This sounds almost like a Jewish Monroe Doctrine: the next world is recruited to redress, as it were, the balance of this one. This view is built on the traditional speculation about an afterlife. It has always been the last refuge of bigotry and religious fundamentalism to speculate that all suffering is purely temporary, and that if the soul is saved, it will ascend to heaven. The chief inquisitor of Spain, Tomás Torquemada, would have nodded enthusiastic agreement: the argument is an excellent way to assure the calm behavior of the victim being led to death.

Shneersohn develops this approach even further. For an orthodox Jew, sanctifying the Name of God (*Kiddush Hashem*) through martyrdom is the highest degree of religious observance, and the martyr will thank the Almighty for having been given the privilege of being a sacrifice. Shneersohn sees orthodox Jews who were killed in the Holocaust as dying on Kiddush Hashem, a great privilege. Saying so seems to be intended, in part at least, to answer the objection, not yet raised in the responsum, that many orthodox Jews were victims. Not at all, says Shneersohn. They were not victims; they died on Kiddush Hashem, the highest privilege of all. The parallel with Muslim fundamentalism, which sees Muslims killed in a holy war as *shuhood* (martyrs) seems obvious, although shuhood are not passive victims but armed fighters. In both cases, there is the promise of the world to come.

Orthodoxy generally has appropriated not only the orthodox victims of the Holocaust but increasingly all the Jews who died in it, considering them all believing Jews who died on Kiddush Hashem. This represents a certain subtle change in the concept used. The classical examples—the great sage Rabbi Akiva, who was tortured and killed by Roman soldiers for his beliefs, and the many pious Jews who died rather than convert or commit other cardinal sins during the course of later anti-Jewish persecutions—do not apply to the Holocaust. In the Holocaust, Jews were not

killed for what they did or did not believe, and they could not escape
death by conversion, apostasy, or change of ideology. They were murdered for being Jews, that is, for being descended from three or four
Jewish grandparents. There was absolutely no element of personal decision in their fate: they were murdered for having been born. Their
forebears, too, were killed for being Jewish, but traditional Jewish martyrdom had an important moral element—voluntariness—which was
absent in the Holocaust. There, all Jews were killed, including people
who had chosen Christianity or communism and people who were loyal,
law-abiding citizens of their communities and countries, as well as Jewish criminals. If they died on Kiddush Hashem, if they were martyrs,
they were involuntary martyrs. But all martyrdom is voluntary by
definition. A person who does not want to be a martyr and is killed
anyway is the victim of murder, not martyrdom. I therefore cannot
agree with my much admired friend Emil Fackenheim, who says that *all*
Jews killed in the Holocaust are *kdoshim* (holy people), because they died
on Kiddush Hashem. That is, increasingly, the orthodox argument, and
I find it unacceptable.

Here Shneersohn gets tangled up in a contradiction. On the one hand,
nonorthodox Jews are supposed to be the reason why God the surgeon
punished the Jewish people, and on the other hand, they are supposed to
have died on Kiddush Hashem.

Having answered part of the question, Shneersohn asks it explicitly:
How can one explain the death of so many pious Jews? To propose an
answer, he uses a parable current in orthodox circles.

> A person may receive a slap in the face for a misdeed he has committed,
> although that misdeed was done with his hand. This is so because pun-
> ishment is not a form of revenge, God forbid, but a means of making him
> correct his ways. . . . In order that the punishment be effective and
> influence the man's ways, it is administered as a slap on the face, which is
> a person's chief feature. This is what happened to Israel [the Jewish
> people]. Besides being given a heavy punishment quantitatively speak-
> ing (six million victims), the punishment was increased manyfold by

hitting the group that was the pride of that generation [that is, the orthodox population generally and its sages especially].

The elitist thinking so typical of ultraorthodoxy (and of extreme left-wing Jewish thinking) is easily apparent. The rabbis and their academies (yeshivot) were the "face" of "that generation." People are not really equal in the eyes of God or Man. Some, as with Orwell, are more equal than others. And, of course, women are never mentioned in the responsum; they are dumb objects—of wrath, of murder, of sin. The language is masculine throughout. In Shneersohn's thinking, women are a necessary appendage to men and need not be mentioned when the fate of a generation is discussed, except sometimes as co-victims. Pragmatically, as well as according to accepted halakhic rulings, scholars are rescued before their pupils, and their pupils before their families.[11]

There is another aspect to Shneersohn's argument. He implies that the "face" was slapped because of the sins of others. In other words, not only were the nonorthodox responsible for the Holocaust, and specifically for the murder of the orthodox, but it is they who by their sinful actions may yet produce another such catastrophe; and it is they who by their very existence prevent the arrival of the Messiah. As with all the other points in Shneersohn's discourse, parallel statements can be quoted from other haredi sources. All agree, therefore, that the highest priority must be to missionize nonorthodox Jews—not for some abstract ideological reason but for two interrelated practical reasons: one, because they endanger the lives of everyone else by not believing, and two, because their conversion to orthodoxy will hasten the coming of the Messiah. This, of course, is what God wants, and Shneersohn has his own way of knowing exactly what the Divinity desires.

The Rebbe cannot be content with what he has explained so far. Ultraorthodoxy, certainly the Habad version of it, has a dialectical approach to reality. On the one hand, it fully expects the coming of the Messiah and believes in an afterlife. On the other hand, it is this-worldly. There is a deep-seated belief in the magic power of prayer and of the observance of commandments. Shneersohn refers to this, quoting God via the Bible: "If you obey My laws, I shall give you rain on time." The result of proper religious conduct is a good life in this world, and a long one.

It is not easy to fit the Holocaust into this scheme. However, there is a way out. The Rebbe quotes from *Pirkei Avot* (The Words of the Fathers): "One hour of repentance and good deeds in this world is worth more than the entire life in the world to come." Shneersohn interprets this figuratively, not literally, and argues that a person acquires credit for the afterlife by carrying out the commandments in this world. Conversely, with each act of disobedience, such as not laying *tefillin* (phylacteries), a person (a man is always meant) accumulates a debit for the afterlife. Jewish fundamentalism, Habad style, can here be seen to parallel the Christian version. For Shneersohn this argument for credits and debits in an afterlife was important because he not only had to protect his mission to the Jews from doubt but also had to give a determined push to the major undertaking, the missionizing program—in this case, using the fire and brimstone strategy so popular with his Christian counterparts. In line with this, Habad sends its missionaries to street corners, houses, and airports to persuade Jews to lay tefillin, just a little, just once, because then the person will have less of a debit in the afterlife, and, conversely, the missionary will add to his own credit.

Following the commandments was what chassidic Jews all over Nazified Europe desperately wanted to do, precisely because of the terrible situation they found themselves in, but the Holocaust prevented them from doing so. They wanted to please the Lord, but very often they could not. Shneersohn quotes one of the great examples of religious Jewish humanism when he reminds his readers that it is a commandment to desecrate the Sabbath if there is the slightest chance that thereby a life may be saved—a Jewish life, not a non-Jewish one, apparently.

But if this is God's command, and if the high priest may desecrate the Day of Atonement to save a Jewish life, why did God not save millions of lives? Shneersohn's answer is to return to the "we are too puny" argument with which he started and which he abandoned. We don't know the secret of God's conduct in this case, says the Rebbe. Instead, he returns to another important humanistic religious tradition, namely, that it is "incumbent upon us to cry to the king and beg God to remove from us all heavy persecutions." We are encouraged to protest because protest carries with it the desire to follow God's laws. The best-known examples were the stories told about the famous Rabbi Levi Yitzhak of Berdichev, who lived at the beginning of the nineteenth century and reportedly argued with God in favor of the poor and the unfortunate in his community. It is a moot point as to whether these interventions had any results, but it is clear that Shneersohn was too canny a pedagogue not to realize the psychological value of a protest, however useless, against an inexplicable fate.

The Rebbe then returns to his first parable, explaining that it is a parable, not an exact analogy. A surgeon may have to remove a limb, but God, had he so chosen, could have prevented the Holocaust and brought spiritual health to the Jews, Shneersohn style, without making them undergo the horrors. Shneersohn has no answer as to why God chose otherwise; all he can suggest is to protest to God and to obey the commandments; there is no contradiction there, he says.

The argument does not lack internal logic: God is all-powerful, he could have prevented the murder, and no other explanation is possible but to say that we do not know God's ways—except that Shneersohn just explained why God did it, and put the blame on the nonorthodox Jews.

In the last portion of the responsum the Rebbe deals with the rebellion of the nonbeliever against God. Quoting Habad lore, he tells the story of a supposed rebel. The Rebbe who confronted the rebel told him that if he, like Acher, had acquired full knowledge of the Jewish religious tradition before rejecting it, he would indeed have been a rebel, because he would have known what it was he was rebelling against. But most of our present-day rebels are ignoramuses, says Schneersohn, and what motivates them is not rebelliousness (because they don't know what they are rebelling against) but laziness and sinful desires. This argument is wonderful, and it is partly true; every Catholic, Protestant, and Muslim fundamentalist preacher makes it as well.

Again, the Rebbe's line of argument is flawed. To reject a philosophy of religion, or any complicated set of ideas or beliefs, does not require immersion in the depths of the constructs. It is quite sufficient, it would seem, to acquire a good understanding of the main principles and the general outlook. Indeed, one could argue the contrary to the Rebbe's line of thought: If one were convinced of the validity of such a belief system, at least prima facie, one would then and only then be justified in studying it carefully and in depth before finally adopting it. Otherwise, the finer points of such a construct are immaterial, because the principles are unacceptable.

Likewise, as has already been mentioned, a heretic does not question the way God works, as Shneersohn seems to assume; he denies the existence of God altogether or, alternatively, the existence of an all-powerful God who is also just. Shneersohn did not deal with that possibility.

What can we make of all this? First and foremost, we should understand, with empathy, the deep emotional and intellectual convulsions among orthodox and ultraorthodox Jews, specifically chassidic Jews, as a result of the Holocaust. In this respect, all Jews, religious or otherwise, were and are in the same situation. Attempts to deal with the trauma abound, as do attempts to deal with the questions of personal belief. Any reader can sense in Shneersohn's often tortured and contradictory, but genuine, soul-searchings the upheaval and the mental anguish of an honest believer who tries to find answers to impossible and unanswerable questions. There is therefore no place for an emotional response upon reading the responsum. Yet the responsum, because it is basically self-condemnatory, is a rare statement to come out of the world of Jewish fundamentalism. Shneersohn's words are important not only because of the central position of the Habad movement in the fundamentalist world (and in Jewish and Israeli politics) but also because the

Rebbe said, or strongly hinted, what other haredi leaders may have feared to say: that the Holocaust was the act of a just God, that it was caused by Jewish sins, and that Hitler was God's scourge, an extension of God's arm, or, in other words, his messenger. The acceptance of such an ideology would make redundant all Holocaust research and all attempts at explaining what occurred.

Are we too puny to understand God's plan—does that argument hold water? At least one million Jewish children under the age of thirteen died in the Holocaust, and no one will argue that they were responsible for their deeds or misdeeds or that they could have sinned, at least according to the Jewish interpretation of sin. True, one tradition visits the sins of the fathers (what about mothers?) on their sons (what about daughters?), but more decisive is the tradition that says that each person is responsible for her or his actions and therefore also for any transgressions.

Why the children were killed is the most bothersome question of all. In the haredi interpretation they were killed because God did not intervene, although he undoubtedly could have, and of course he knew that they were going to die. If the answer is that we can never understand God's intentions, the obvious and trite—but arguably true—reply is that we have no wish to know God's intentions or reasons, whether we might understand them or not, because *any* reason, divine or human, for not preventing the murder of a million children when that murder might have been prevented is evil. It can be judged evil by the very code of morals supposedly derived from divine inspiration. Otherwise, God becomes Satan, and Jews do not want to believe in Satan.

Neither Menachem Mendel Shneersohn nor other, highly intelligent and, in many cases, morally admirable personalities in the haredi world had an answer to the question of why children were killed. Unless somebody gives a more satisfactory explanation, maybe, from a religious point of view, the answer of Walter Zvi Bacharach is not so bad: to be angry with God but to believe in him anyway. From a nonorthodox point of view, even more so from a nonreligious point of view, theology does not yet seem to have come up with any answers to the Holocaust. Historical, sociological, psychological, and maybe even philosophical explications have been more productive. Some might even doubt the relevance of the theological answers altogether, so far. That, indeed, is my own position. The theology of the Holocaust is fascinating, but it is a dead end.

chapter ten

Rescue Attempts: The Case of

the Auschwitz Protocols

Could the Jews murdered in the Ho-
locaust have been rescued? That question has caused and will continue
to cause innumerable sleepless nights. Possible answers have to be formulated with great circumspection. Historians are not supposed to ask
such "what if" questions, although most historians in fact do so.[1]

The Holocaust could have been prevented, as could World War II,
which provided its context, had the Great Powers stopped Nazi Germany when it was still weak. But no one knew then that a Holocaust
would happen. Nobody knew that a Holocaust was even possible, because nobody knew what a Holocaust was; the Germans had not decided
on anything like it in the 1930s. The future Allied Powers did not stop
Nazi Germany and ended up suffering hecatombs of casualties. The
Western Allies accepted as few Jewish refugees from Central Europe as
possible, because these bothersome and traditionally unpopular minority people were trying to enter labor markets blighted with unemployment in the midst of an economic crisis.

Once the war began, Poland, defeated and divided between Germany and the Soviet Union, was beyond the reach of France and Britain. After the defeat of France, Britain stood alone against the Germans and was fighting for its own survival. No help for the Jews, of all people, could be expected. The only exception was Palestine, where Jews could have fled had the British agreed to let them in. I do not wish to go over the well-worn tale of the closure of Palestine to Jewish immigration.[2] The British government did not let in even those whom they had officially agreed to have enter: 75,000 Jews over five years. When the Jewish Agency Executive (JAE) tried to get permission for 29,000 children to enter after information about the mass murder of European Jews reached Palestine in November 1942, very few received immigration certificates. The rationale for this policy, repeated over and over again in British governmental papers, was that if Jews came into Palestine, the Arabs would turn to the Axis Powers, and Britain would lose its hold over the Middle East.[3] British politicians argued that Indian Muslims, especially the ones serving with Indian units of the imperial forces, might become disaffected, with disastrous results for the conduct of war. Historians have examined whether these were genuinely held views or reflections of anti-Jewish sentiment. A second question is whether the threats were real.[4]

Whatever the worth of these opinions, I believe they were genuinely held. This does not mean that the officials of the London government were lovers of Jews. Not at all. Many of them, perhaps most of them, were at least mildly disapproving of Jews in general and of Zionists in particular. But that was not, I would argue, what decided their attitudes and their policies. Rather, they really believed in what they were saying.

Arab disaffection was the result, mainly, of the fact that the British were the foreign rulers of much of the area, and Arab nationalists wanted to get rid of them. Zionist settlement in Palestine added to that burning desire, for the Jews in Palestine were seen as a foreign population put there by the British.[5] But the Arab threat was long-term, not short-term. The one Arab attempt at rebellion against the British—the takeover of Iraq by the pro-German Rashid Ali el-Ghailani in the spring of 1941—was suppressed with amazing ease by a tiny British force.[6] No serious Arab underground was active against Britain during the war. There was some anti-British propaganda, and there were small groups of officers, especially in Egypt, who were hoping for an Axis victory, but there was never any real danger to the British position in the area from these quarters. The activities of the Mufti of Jerusalem, Hajj Amin al-Husseini, an enthusiastic supporter of the Nazis, who had a hand in the execution of the Final Solution, was certainly important, and he was considered by most Palestinian Arabs to be their legitimate leader. But his interventions had a negligible impact, for the Palestinian Arabs were still smarting from the brutal suppression of their rebellion against the British in 1936–1939.[7]

A review of long-term policy gives a different view. Britain was trying to maintain its predominant position not only against the Axis but also against the United States and France, with the threat from communist Russia always in the background. After the war Britain would have a limited armed force in the Middle East and would have to rely on Arab friendship. The problem, seen from the perspective of a wartime Britain still intent on keeping its empire, was real. The Zionists, it was felt, were a millstone around Britain's neck, because they could not defend themselves against the Arab world, so it was thought, and would have to rely on Britain. An Arab Palestine with a Jewish minority whose rights would be protected by the empire was thought to be the best solution, and the fewer Jews there were, the better. Hence, no or very little Jewish immigration. Therefore, no rescue from the Holocaust.

From the Jewish perspective the situation looked different. At the very moment when immigration to Palestine became the only hope for tens of thousands, the British turned their backs on the Jews in contravention of their undertakings to them, in effect sentencing those who might otherwise have reached Palestine to death. As it turned out, Jewish military prowess proved to be more efficacious than the Arab variety—but that happened three years after the end of World War II.

Before that, the British estimate was that militarily the Jews were weak and the Arabs potentially strong, or at any rate stronger than the Jews.[8]

Heated controversies have developed on the question of the attitudes of the Jews in Palestine to the Jews in Europe during the Holocaust. New scholarship has shown, I think convincingly, that the Jewish Agency Executive leadership under David Ben Gurion and his two close allies, Moshe Sharet (Shertok), head of the Political Department, and Eliezer Kaplan, the treasurer, was very much engaged in rescue attempts. Practically all of these failed, however, because the Palestine Zionists were a small group (about half a million) ruled by the British, who used the country as a military base during the war—one with a very large garrison. There were no direct communications with London and New York. The Yishuv, the Jewish population of Palestine, had no armed forces to use; its underground groups could act in Europe only with Allied support, and that was not forthcoming. Undoubtedly, more might have been done, but without Allied consent, breaking down the walls separating European Jewry from their Palestine brethren was impossible.[9] As it was, slightly more than 50,000 Jews managed to get to Palestine during the war, mostly from the Balkans, Hungary, and the Soviet Union; by no means all of them were refugees from Nazi Europe.[10]

Let us come back to the dismal chronology of rescue attempts. In June 1941, Germany invaded the Soviet Union, and the mass murder of Jews in the occupied Soviet territories began. The Soviets were in full retreat, and it was only at the gates of Leningrad (St. Petersburg), Moscow, and Stalingrad that the German advance was stopped, at a tremendous cost in Soviet lives. Did the West know what was happening? Well, historians, especially Richard Breitman, have found that British decoders of German radio messages had read German Order Police messages from occupied Soviet territories between July and September 1941. The decryptions documented the killing of many, many people, and in a number of cases, Jews were explicitly mentioned. There is proof that these messages reached Churchill's desk. In one instance, an officer analyzing the reports concluded that a campaign to exterminate the Jews was going on: "The fact that the [German] Police are killing all the Jews that fall into their hands should now be sufficiently well appreciated."[11] The messages dried up after mid-September 1941, after an order from Berlin forbidding the transmission of sensitive details about murder actions by radio.

Two questions arise. First, did the British continue to analyze the decoded messages or, indeed, take their analyses seriously? Was it even possible to deduce from the material at the disposal of the British that a Europe-wide extermination of Jews was being conducted? Recent German research indicates that in the summer of 1941 the decision to kill all European Jews had not yet been taken.[12] How could the British divine that the Nazis would later make that decision? Breitman has shown that some of those analysts who read these messages had reached the conclusion that Soviet Jews were being annihilated. The problem is that these analyses did not reach the Foreign Office; they had no measurable impact on British policy because they were unknown except to a very few people. Churchill used the information in a speech on August 24, 1941, for propaganda purposes, as Breitman shows, but there it ended.[13]

The second question is even more serious: If the British government, and not just a few analysts, had drawn the conclusion that what they were witnessing was a genocide (the term had not yet been coined), what could they have done to save the millions of victims? In the summer of 1941 the Soviets were in full and hasty retreat, the British forces had just been roundly defeated in Greece and Crete, and the battle of the Atlantic was not going well for Britain. The United States was neutral. The British could have done nothing, even if they had wanted to, to save the European Jews from annihilation, but clearly they didn't want to. They could have done important things on the margins: they could have permitted more Jews to escape from the Balkans to Palestine—which they refused to do. They could have made public declarations of policy. A year later they could have permitted illegal transfers of funds through Switzerland to West European countries. Practically speaking, their options were limited, as was their realization of what was going on, even though that one British officer, more intuitively than otherwise, analyzed the situation correctly, as we know with hindsight.

Could the British have warned the threatened Jews in the fall of 1941? In the Soviet areas, Jews had no radio receivers that could tune in to London—under Soviet rule no such receivers were permitted; and once the Germans invaded, Jews who had radios had them confiscated. Mass murder commenced immediately, first of men and soon thereafter of women and children; Jews no longer needed to be warned, because most were victims, and those who were not, saw with their own eyes what the Germans were doing. Whether the British could have used their knowledge of what was happening on Soviet territory to extrapolate on German policy in Western and Central Europe is a further question. Even assuming they could have done that—a very large assumption—would they have been believed? On the strength of what we know today about attitudes of Jews and non-Jews toward German policy, this is extremely unlikely.

On the other hand, had the British, and not just the occasional intelligence analyst, believed what they were reading, they might well have found a way of publicizing the material without endangering their decoding operation. In that case—and the putative dilemma arose often during the next three years—they could have shown they cared. The question is therefore a moral one, not a practical one. Morality aside, I have argued many times that the information may have been there, but not knowledge—not an understanding of what the information meant. Here, probably only a few attained that knowledge, and they did not manage to convince others.

Information snowballed as the months went on. In November 1941, Richard Lichtheim, the JAE representative in Geneva, wrote to Palestine that what was happening was mass murder on a vast scale; his outlook for the future was pessimistic.[14] On March 27, 1942, at the instigation of the German army commanders in France, the first French Jews were sent to "the East"; now we know it was to Auschwitz, where the first steps were being taken to establish the machinery that would murder more than a million Jews. Information about the deportations seeped through to Switzerland. The Swiss government did not need to be informed: they had received detailed information about the mass murder of the Jews from the medical officers whom they had sent to German hospitals on the Eastern front in November 1941 as a goodwill gesture to Germany. The doctors were forbidden to tell anyone of their experiences.[15]

In June 1942 a report from the underground Bund Party in Poland (which was a major socialist, anti-Zionist, anticommunist, and anti-religious Jewish political party), was received in London and published in late June and in July. Radio broadcasts from the BBC transmitted the information to Europe: 700,000 Jews had been killed in Poland, partly by gas. Extermination camps (but not Auschwitz) were mentioned. The impression was that Polish Jewry was the target, not necessarily all European Jews, nor even all Jews everywhere. American and Palestinian Jews did not believe it; neither did the British officials who published it.[16]

On August 8, Dr. Gerhard Riegner, a young World Jewish Congress representative in Geneva, sent off his famous cable to the WJC representatives in London and New York, which stated that three and a half to four million European Jews were threatened with imminent murder "in the East," in part by the use of prussic acid (the gas used in Auschwitz, known as Zyklon B, was based on prussic acid). The information had come to him, via intermediaries, from Eduard Schulte, an anti-Nazi German businessman, who had sat in on a meeting of high Nazi officials in Silesia who freely talked about the murder of the Jews. It is common knowledge that the U.S. State Department did not wish to inform Stephen S. Wise, the acknowledged leader of the Zionists in the United States, of the cable, although that was what Riegner requested. When Wise received the cable via London, he was told that he should not go public with the contents until the information contained in the cable was checked.

The Riegner cable was a turning point in the history of the Holocaust: for the first time, the outside world had received a clear indication that the Germans were going beyond localized mass killings and were planning the destruction of all European Jews. In American Jewish historiography especially, Wise has been accused of obeying government instructions, when what he should have done was to go out and arouse the public, Jewish and non-Jewish. Two comments are needed here because this is a crucial issue. The first comment is that Riegner's cable contained two sentences that were dictated by Riegner's local World Jewish Congress superior in Geneva, Paul Guggenheim. They read as follows: "We transmit information with all necessary reservations as exactitude cannot be confirmed. Informant stated to have close connections with highest German authorities and his reports generally speaking reliable."[17]

What should Wise have done when he was asked to wait until the information was checked, given that the cable itself expressed uncertainty? What if the information was mistaken? If Riegner expressed reservations, was it not the proper course for the government to investigate?

The second comment must be that Wise's position was not easy. Antisemitism was rising in the United States. A large and growing number of young Jewish men were in the armed forces, along with young men from the rest of the population, and the first worry of Jewish families was their husbands, sons, and brothers. The Roosevelt administration stood between American Jews and Hitler, on the one hand, and American Jews and local antisemitism, on the other hand. Arousing the public would have been difficult, and the government would have argued that the best way to help the Jews was to win the war. Could America have helped European Jews in the summer of 1942 if it had wanted to, which it did not? The Germans were making dramatic advances toward Stalingrad and the Caucasus in Russia and toward Cairo in North Africa (July 1942). American forces were fighting at Midway in the Pacific (June 4–7, 1942). Could America have prevented the Germans from murdering Jews? The answer is no. Yet Wise *did* inform the

American Jewish leadership of the cable's contents, and he did try to pass the information to the president.

Should Wise have acted differently? It is certainly valid to argue that after the worst fears were confirmed and the State Department informed Wise to that effect in November, the United States could have come out with a propaganda blast to show that it cared. Why it shied away from taking action in favor of European Jews has been stated time and time again: the preoccupation with a brutal and terrible war; the gap between information and knowledge, even after the information had been received; the fear of being accused of waging the war because of the Jews; traditional anti-Jewish sentiments on the part of Anglo-Americans; and what one might call ill will: the tendency to see in the Jews a bothersome minority asking for special consideration while others were—so most politicians thought—suffering equally.

The Anglo-American leaders, pressed by a mutinous British public that wanted the government to help the Jews and by Jews in the United States, devised a subterfuge based on lies: an Anglo-American conference on "refugees" (not Jews, God forbid) met in Bermuda, as far as possible from prying eyes. That this tragicomic sham started on the same day as the Warsaw ghetto rebellion (April 19, 1943) was an accident. That participants reached the conclusion that nothing should or could be done was no accident, considering who the participants were. That that conclusion was kept secret, supposedly for weighty security reasons, while statements were made that momentous decisions to help Jewish and other refugees had been taken—that was a web of lies to maintain the cover-up. "I am sorry to bother you about Jews," wrote Richard Law, the main British representative in Bermuda, to his superior, Foreign Secretary Anthony Eden, before the meeting (March 18, 1943). "I know what a bore this is."[18]

By 1943 the Western Allies could have helped. They were in no position to save the millions. Nor could they, in 1943, bomb the death camps in Poland, because they had no airfields from which to reach those areas—not until November of that year did they occupy the airfields at Foggia, in Italy, from which they could bomb Poland. But the Allies could do what Jewish organizations asked them to do: promise the neutrals to take care of any Jewish refugees who could reach those countries; accept in Palestine at least those Jews who were supposed to be able to enter under British restrictive laws; transfer funds to underground Jewish groups in occupied Europe; continue a war of propaganda in Germany. Breitman has shown that the British did drop leaflets on Germany informing the Germans of the Allied declaration of December 17, 1942, which acknowledged the fact that the Germans were murdering the Jews of Europe; if they did it once, they could have done it more than once, as could the Americans.[19]

Even if these measures, if taken, would not have saved millions, still, they might have helped some more people survive. Jewish tradition says that to save one life is to save a whole world. How many worlds could have been rescued—hundreds, maybe thousands, maybe more? Who knows. But again, no one realized the potential scope of this tragedy. Whether such a realization would have changed policy must be left open to question. The conclusion, at any rate, is that the Allies did not really care; and even if they had cared, it is doubtful whether large numbers of Jews could have been saved. So the question boils down to a moral question. (A historian is asking a moral question? I can see the eyebrows rise.)

At the basis, then, of the problem of rescue during the Holocaust lies the question of information: When did word of the murder reach the West, and to what extent was it believed? If it was believed, the question is, Who believed it, and were they influential enough to have an impact on political action? If so, there remains the problem of the military situation at each point and whether practical steps could be taken.

Breitman makes it clear that contrary to the views of historians who preceded him, the basic facts about Auschwitz were known before 1944. A Polish journalist by the name of Tadeusz Chciuk-Celt wrote in the fall of 1942 about mass executions at Auschwitz and the expansion of its capacity to absorb victims.[20] On November 27, 1942, information was distributed by the Polish government-in-exile that tens of thousands of Jews and Soviet POWs had been shipped to Auschwitz "for the sole purpose of their immediate extermination in gas chambers." On March 23, 1943, the underground Representation (Delegatura) of the Polish government-in-exile in Poland reported the building of a new crematorium in Auschwitz that could dispose of 3,000 victims a day and the intention to kill Jews there. Breitman quotes this from an important work by David Engel.[21] In May 1943, Polish intelligence reported in London that 520,000 Jews had been killed in Auschwitz, and in December, that 645,000 Jews had been murdered before June.[22] There can be no doubt that Polish intelligence knew about Auschwitz with all the details and that they reported what they knew to London, although they stressed the fate of the Polish internees and mentioned Jews in second place.

Why is there an impression that nobody knew about Auschwitz until the spring of 1944? It is the same old story: no credence was given to reports about the mass murder of Jews. Even well-informed people, such as Victor Cavendish-Bentinck, chairman of the Joint Intelligence Committee of the British government, dismissed them. "This gas chamber story" should not be believed. Poles and Jews—especially the latter— are "stoking us up," he said.[23] The British had the information, and they did not really believe it, partly, as Breitman argues—I think rightly— because of the precedent of World War I, when atrocity stories spread by the Allies turned out to have been fabricated for propaganda purposes, and partly because, paradoxically, the kind of information they were receiving was unprecedented—they were right about that—so they had a hard time convincing themselves that it was true. To be fair, we have to admit that it was difficult even for Jews deported to Auschwitz to believe what went on before their eyes. The S.S. guards who told the Jews that even if they survived, no one would believe what they were reporting had it right, too. As the title of a book by Deborah Lipstadt has it, the idea of a death factory was "beyond belief."[24] Breitman has shown that the information about Auschwitz was there, at least in general terms and in some of the details as well—and I am grateful to his meticulous scholarship for having corrected my view in this regard, because I also had maintained that Auschwitz was almost unknown until 1944, and I was wrong. But the information had not jelled into knowledge, and it was rejected by many—government officials, the military, and the general public, Jews and non-Jews alike—as preposterous.

At this point, I wish to introduce the problem of the Auschwitz protocols, the story of a rescue attempt involving Hungarian Jews in the late spring of 1944. It is useful for our purposes because it illustrates the elements of information, knowledge, and action. I have told part of that history in another book.[25] Here I want to establish the context.

The roughly 800,000 Jews in the area occupied by Hungary in 1944—including the converts to Christianity, that is, people defined as Jews by the Hungarian equivalent of the Nuremberg laws—were the largest surviving group of Jews in Europe before the occupation of Hungary by the Germans in March 1944. This is not to say, as some writers have argued, that Hungarian Jewry had not been hit, and hit hard, before that. The government was in the hands of an aristocratic oligarchy at the head of which stood the regent, Admiral Miklos Horthy, supposedly in lieu of a king (the Hungarian rulers did not want the Habsburgs to return but did not want to give up the pretense of a royalist regime). The oligarchy was predominantly antisemitic, although their antisemitism was not of the Nazi kind. It was wrapped in the ideology of Hungarian nationalism, and they accepted the presence, even the influence, of a small number of very wealthy Jewish families of industrialists, bankers, and landowners, some of whom had intermarried with their Hungarian counterparts and many of whom had converted to Christianity. Hungary was the only country where major parts of the industrial and commercial infrastructure were in the hands of Jews or converted Jews and their families. A Jewish upper middle class was tolerated, and Jews were very influential in the cultural life of the country. Antisemitic policies were exercised in the main against the lower Jewish classes—small traders, clerks, craftsmen, and farmers (there was a small

Jewish farm population in Hungary), who constituted the bulk of the Jewish population. Three consecutive laws were directed against the Jews, in 1938, 1939, and 1941, according to which Jews were severely circumscribed in their professional choices, their participation in the cultural life, and their economic opportunities as merchants. Some of the limitations could be circumvented, and many Jews found alternative means of economic subsistence.

In 1941, when Hungary joined with Germany in the war against the Soviet Union (and consequently, also against the West), some 16,000 Jews who did not have Hungarian citizenship papers for one reason or another were deported by the Hungarians and murdered near Kamenets Podolsk in the Ukraine by SIPO (security) units of the S.S., units of the Order Police (ORPO), and Hungarian troops. An additional 2,000 deportees managed to escape and return to Hungary, so information about the mass murder of Jews in the occupied Soviet territories was widespread among Hungarian Jews. Jews were also murdered, in much smaller numbers, in the areas of former Yugoslavia (Novi Sad) occupied by Hungary in 1941 in massacres that were directed primarily against Serbs. Another major blow was the recruitment to the forced labor battalions in the army of about 50,000 Jewish men of military age, who were sent into the Ukraine to clear minefields and do sappers' work without adequate food or lodging, initially in the Russian winter of 1941–1942. In 1943 the 5,000 survivors were returned to Hungary, and they told their story to families and friends. While it is therefore untrue to say that Hungarian Jewry survived unscathed until the German occupation, it is true that the majority of that community survived until then, and that was because of the policy of the government. Horthy's government, under Miklos Kallay, prime minister between 1942 and 1944, tried not to commit itself too deeply to the Germans, and it rebuffed repeated German attempts to persuade it to deal harshly with the Jews—and attempts by some Hungarian circles who supported such policies. As the fortunes of war turned against Germany with the Stalingrad defeat, which was accompanied by the total defeat of Hungarian troops fighting against the Soviets, the reluctance to turn against the Jews grew.

Hungary, because of its traditional friendship with Poland, had accepted the remnants of the defeated Polish forces that crossed its borders in September 1939 and had permitted a Polish organization to support additional escapees who crossed the border from Poland. Thus, many Jews who managed to flee from Poland were helped. Jewish organizations in Hungary, sometimes rather reluctantly, also gave support to Jewish refugees. It is estimated that 2,000–2,500 Jews fled to Hungary between 1942 and 1944. Many of them dispersed throughout the country and told their stories to anyone who would listen—but most people did not want to listen. I have stated elsewhere that this reluctance was not just a natural reaction to life-threatening news. It was also a reflection of hopelessness: potential victims had no way out of the situation. They were caught on an island in shark-infested waters, and they had no boat. If the island was flooded, they were doomed. Most people reacted, therefore, by closing their eyes to the dangers. One might add that in Hungary one could hear the BBC, and many listened; American intelligence reported that 800,000 radio receivers in the country could tune in to foreign broadcasts.[26] And the BBC, although it did not feed its listeners with too much information about the fate of the Jews, did repeatedly broadcast the facts of the mass murder in Hungarian. Hungarian soldiers and officers on leave told of their experiences, and this news also spread. Neutral newspapers could on occasion be procured. To say that Hungarian Jews had no inkling about what was happening in Poland and elsewhere stretches credulity much too far.

Then came the German occupation (March 19, 1944) and with it Eichmann's *Sondereinsatzkommando* (special action commando), who organized the deportation of some 437,000 Jews from the provinces to Auschwitz with the help of Hungarian pro-Nazis who had been put in positions of power under Horthy's government. Horthy did not intervene or even try to do so. While he watched, Hungarian citizens were deported to their deaths. Did he know that deportation meant murder? If not, it was because he refused to know: the information was there. Could he have stopped the deportations? He did, much too late, in early July 1944, after all the Jews from the provinces had been carried off, leaving only the Jews of Budapest, some 200,000 strong, and the men in the forced labor battalions, whom the Hungarian army did not want to hand to the Germans because they needed them for work. His intervention did save them from Auschwitz.

There was no Jewish community in Hungary. The Jews in Hungary were organized into mutually hostile groups: about one-third of Hungarian Jewry were orthodox, and about two-thirds owed some kind of allegiance to the neologs, who were roughly similar in belief to present-day American Conservatives. But most members of neolog communities were quite removed from religious Judaism. The top leadership, mostly the Jewish aristocrats, belonged to the neolog faction. But both the orthodox and the neologs were fervent Hungarian patriots and even refused to have organizational contacts with Jews outside Hungary. The Zionist movement in Hungary was a tiny minority of 5 percent or so.

Between 1938 and 1941, as a result of its alliance with Nazi Germany, Hungary annexed areas that had belonged to the Hungarian Crown until 1918, in southern Slovakia, Subcarpathian Russia (the former eastern tip of Czechoslovakia), northern Transylvania, and the Yugoslav Banat. In almost all these areas, orthodox Jews predominated among the local Jewish populations, so the annexations strengthened the orthodox element in Hungarian Jewry. However, especially in Transylvania, a strong Zionist element now became Hungarian as well. Cluj (Kolozsvar in Hungarian) had a strong Zionist movement, which included a young journalist, Reszoe (Rudolf) Kastner, who was not only a Labor Zionist activist but had also served as secretary to the Jewish parliamentarians in the Romanian parliament in Bucharest. Now, in 1941, he moved to Budapest, where he quickly became the leading light

in the very small Labor Zionist faction. He established good contacts
with the weak Hungarian social-democratic movement but was hardly
known outside a small coterie of intellectuals.

The most energetic leader of the Zionist movement was a Hungarian
war hero of First World War vintage, an engineer by the name of Otto
Komoly. In early 1943, together with Kastner and a small number of
like-minded Zionists, he established an Aid and Rescue Committee,
known as the Va'adah (Hebrew: committee). The Va'adah established
contact with a group of Palestinian Jewish emissaries in neutral Istanbul and received some funds, encouragement, and instructions of a sort.
Contact was maintained via a network of double agents, Germans and
others (including two Jews and a couple of "half-Jews"), members of the
Abwehr, the German military intelligence. The Va'adah was supposed
to prepare for armed resistance, and it collected a pitiful quantity of
arms and established a few caches. But Hungarian Jewry was unfitted
for such an adventure. They were law-abiding citizens and Hungarian
patriots who would not dream of taking up arms against a Hungarian
government and its police forces. Nor was there an organized Jewish
community or underground—apart from the few Zionists—who could
give impetus to such attempts.

One group did in fact consider the option of armed resistance. In
Slovakia, on the last day of 1943, in the town of Nové Mesto nad Váhom,
leaders of the underground left-wing Zionist Hashomer Hatzair decided that a group of them should go to Budapest to organize rescue,
rather than rebellion. They recognized that armed rebellion was not
feasible in Budapest, and they believed that rescue had more chance of
success. The enormous contributions of Zionist youth movements in
the Hungarian capital which formed the backbone of the efforts of neutrals such as Charles Lutz and Raoul Wallenberg sprang from that
meeting. The Zionist youth movements in Budapest were nominally
connected with the Va'adah, but in fact they guarded their independence
and kept their distance from Kastner and his friends, although they
maintained constant contact.[27] The various youth movements—Dror,

Maccabi Hatzair, Noar Tzioni, Bnei Akiva, Hashomer Hatzair—did not number more than a few hundred, and most of the members were young Slovak Jews who spoke Hungarian because their Hungarian colleagues had been called up for service in the labor battalions.

To understand the story of the protocols, one has to understand the Slovak background, described already in Chapter 8. The Slovak Working Group knew that the Jews were being murdered, but they had no information about Auschwitz and the methods of murder used there.

What, then, were the Auschwitz protocols? On April 7, two Auschwitz inmates, Slovak Jews, Rudolf Vrba (Walter Rosenberg) and Alfred Wetzler, hid in an unfinished part of the Birkenau camp, and after the three-day search for them ended, they headed, on the 10th, toward the Slovak border. After a series of adventures, they managed to cross into Slovakia on April 21. Between that date and April 27, the two escapees reported all they knew about Auschwitz to Oskar Krasniansky, a Polish Jewish activist who worked for the Working Group. The original report, written up in Slovak, contained the first authentic account of what was happening in Auschwitz—the gassings, the deprivation, the suffering, the camp organization, a rough plan drawn up from memory, and an (exaggerated) statistic of the number of victims.[28]

The two escapees had a burning desire to inform the world about Auschwitz—there can be no doubt of that. Their logic was simple: something unprecedented in human history was happening before their eyes, and their assumption was that if the "world" knew, it could not possibly permit a continuation of the horror. Their task, therefore, was to inform the world.

On May 27, 1944, two more Jewish inmates managed to flee from Auschwitz: Arnošt Rosin and Czeslaw Mordowicz, who reached Slovakia on June 6—D-day in Normandy. They had been witness to the first stages of the annihilation of the provincial Jews from Hungary, and their supplementary report was later incorporated into a second version of the Vrba-Wetzler report, which had been finalized in Bratislava on April 27, while Vrba and Wetzler were hiding in a small town,

Liptovský Svätý Mikuláš. On June 20, Vrba and Mordowicz, together
with Krasniansky, met with Monsignor Mario Martilotti, of the papal
nunciature in Switzerland. Martilotti had read the report (whether the
first or the second version is not clear), and stated that he would be
traveling to Switzerland the next day.[29] On June 25, the Pope wrote to
Horthy imploring him to prevent further suffering by the Jews. As the
Vatican still refuses, at this writing, to open its archives of the Nazi
period, it is not clear whether the information in the Auschwitz protocols had any influence on the Pope's intervention. Vrba and his friends
also met with Rabbi Weissmandel, and Vrba said, after the war, that he
thought the Rabbi was, at best, a clown in the hands of the Nazis.[30] At
worst, he was a collaborator, because of his negotiations with them to
rescue European Jews (see Chapter 8). That Vrba should repeat this
preposterous accusation against one of the real Jewish heroes of the
Holocaust is understandable in a bitter Auschwitz survivor. That it
should have been accepted by others is less understandable.

The crucial element here is the fate of the protocols: we need to track
how and when they reached Budapest and Switzerland. Knowing this
may enable to us to gauge the impact of reliable information on policies
and to see whether rescue efforts were influenced by the information.

The deportations en masse of Hungarian Jews, after a first transport
in late April, started on May 14, 1944. In the German essay quoted
above, Vrba says that he sent copies of the protocols to Hungary
through a friend of his in Bratislava named Josef Weiss. Weiss utilized a
number of young Jews who were among the "many Slovak Jews who
crossed the border into Hungary to join their families, who had gone
there in 1942."[31] This explanation by Vrba is not credible, for the concentration of Jews into ghettos in Hungary had already started in April,
and the flow of refugees was the other way, from Hungary into Slovakia.
It is not impossible, however, that a group such as the one described by
Vrba existed and that it smuggled copies of the protocols into Hungary;
but Vrba cannot tell us when that happened or who got those copies.
Logically, such a group would have received the report from the Work-

ing Group, in Bratislava—Vrba says he spent the weeks until late June in Liptovský Svätý Mikuláš, near Bratislava, and he does not say that he had a copy of the protocols with him. The person who could have organized the smuggling of the protocols would have been Krasniansky, who had taken down the protocols in the first place. After the war, Krasniansky made three partially conflicting statements about the way he smuggled the protocols abroad.[32]

According to one of Krasniansky's statements, Reszoe Kastner received a copy on April 26, when he was in Bratislava. However, the protocols were not ready until the 27th, so he could at most have seen an unfinished version and memorized the main points, or he could have heard those main points from his contacts in the Working Group. According to another statement, Kastner was in Bratislava on April 28. However, his colleague (and lover) in Budapest, Hansi Brand, denies that he visited Bratislava at the end of April.[33] He could not have traveled without a German guard, she says, and there is no evidence to indicate such a trip.[34] Hansi Brand testified that Kastner visited Bratislava only in August. Yet it is clear that Kastner had received the main points of the information contained in the protocols by the end of April or early in May, possibly through informants sent by the Working Group. It is most unlikely that the Working Group would have risked sending the actual protocols by such an uncertain route.

How do we know that Kastner had at least a general knowledge of the information in the protocols? In his postwar report, Kastner speaks about a piece of luggage (*"Koffer"*) containing protocols from "Auschwitz, Treblinka, and Lemberg [Lwów, today Lviv]"; he handed the luggage over, he says, to Josef Winninger, an Abwehr agent and a contact to the Zionist representatives in Istanbul. Despite his arrest by the S.S., Winninger managed to destroy the documents, according to Kastner. Randolph Braham assumes that the protocols must have been destroyed on May 10, because Winninger was arrested on May 11. But Kastner's text is clear: he mentions the Winninger affair in connection with the German occupation of Budapest on March 19, and it was then

that the luggage was handed to Winninger. Therefore, it could not have
included the Auschwitz protocols—Vrba and Wetzler had not yet escaped from Auschwitz.[35] Because, however, the surviving members of
the Budapest Judenrat claimed that they knew the basic message of the
protocols before they actually saw them, and because they may have
been informed as early as early May, one may assume, although there is
no secure source for such a statement, that Kastner could have been a
source of this information. After the war, Kastner obviously mixed up
the information he had about mass death in Auschwitz, Treblinka, and
Lviv (which he may have confused with Belzec) with the protocols that
he received much later. That such a mixup might have occurred shows
another important point: individuals like Kastner knew about Auschwitz in very general terms even before the Vrba and Wetzler report.

In early May, Weissmandel received information from an anti-Nazi
Slovak railway official that the Germans were preparing deportations of
Jews from Hungary (supposedly by means of 120 trains reserved for the
purpose). This came on top of information about the impending deportations from Vrba and Wetzler. He imparted the news to the chief
representative of orthodox Jewry in Hungary, Fülop von Freudiger, on
May 10 or 11. The protocols were not mentioned in their exchange, and
Vrba does not understand why. The reasons are simple: the protocols
and, through them, their authors could not be divulged in a letter sent
illegally from a Nazi satellite country to a Nazi-occupied one; it would
have been madness to do so.

In 1972, Freudiger told Braham that he had received the actual protocols between June 5 and 10, but he had been given the essential
information contained in them earlier.[36] Braham says that the Judenrat
got the information from Freudiger, who apparently got it from Weissmandel. Who gave Freudiger the protocols at a later date remains unresolved. Of course, by the end of the first week in June, when he got them,
310,000 Jews had already been deported. Freudiger fled to Romania in
August and wrote a memorandum that reached the West. In it he does
not mention the protocols. but it is likely that he indeed saw the pro-

tocols sometime in June. We have it on good authority that a central member of the Judenrat, Ernö Petö, handed the protocols to the Horthy family in early June,[37] which suggests that Freudiger, a member of the Judenrat, would have seen them then. At the same time, the Judenrat, somewhat heavy-handedly, as Braham says, also prepared to hand over the protocols to the Vatican—but we know that the Vatican had the information already.

What we know for certain is that the basic contents of the protocols reached Budapest at the end of April or early in May via non-Jews, who had less difficulty crossing the borders than Jews did. The actual protocols were brought to the Slovak-Hungarian border, most likely toward the end of May, and there were received by Geza Soos, a member of a small Lutheran resistance group called Jo Pasztor (Good Shepherd); Geza Soos took them to Budapest. This version of the protocols, in German, was then translated by Maria Szekely, a member of the group, into Hungarian, within eight days, as she testified. Five copies were made, of which four were handed to religious leaders of the Catholic, Lutheran, and Calvinist churches.

The fifth was supposedly given to Otto Komoly, the leader of the Zionist group in Hungary, by another member of the Lutheran resistance group, a Professor Geza Karpathy.[38] However, Komoly's daughter, Leah Komoly-Fuerst, testified that she translated the protocols from German to Hungarian for her father; in Komoly's own diary he notes, on June 14, that his daughter was translating the material received from Bratislava—which would make no sense if he had received a Hungarian version from the Lutherans. This strengthens the theory that Kastner had the information, but not the protocols, in early May and that the protocols reached Budapest some time in early June, too late to have any effect on the deportations, which started, let me repeat, on May 14.

This analysis shows the difficulty of documenting the really central events of the Holocaust, certainly from the Jewish side. It seems, then, that two copies of the protocols reached Budapest, probably in early

June: one, via Jo Pasztor, the Lutheran resistance group, which may
have been the copy that the Judenrat received; the second, probably via
Kastner. Whether Kastner's copy was transmitted by Vrba's friend
Weiss is unclear. That there were two copies emerges from Komoly's
diary, his daughter's testimony, and the testimony of Maria Szekely—
that is, there were two different translations, made at roughly the same
time, from two different copies. At the same time, all the available facts
indicate that Kastner and others had the general information before, in
early May.

Weissmandel wrote a letter, often quoted, on May 16 or 18 in which
he warned the West of the coming Hungarian deportations and asked
for the railway tracks to be bombed.[39] The letter reached Switzerland
and the Anglo-Americans and formed the primary basis for requests by
Jewish organizations to bomb the rails and Auschwitz itself.[40] It is,
again, not clear exactly when and how the letter reached Switzerland.
In any case, its arrival shows that the Slovak Working Group tried to
transmit the protocols to Switzerland and in the end succeeded. Weissmandel's letter, like his message to Freudiger, does not mention the
protocols, although it says enough for us to know that the author had
received the essential information in the protocols.

The protocols themselves appear not to have reached Switzerland
before June 10. On that day, Jaromír Kopecký, the Czechoslovak representative in Switzerland, says that he held the protocols—smuggled in
by the Czechoslovak underground from Bratislava—in his hands.[41] Another copy reached Switzerland from Budapest, through Mosze Krausz,
the secretary of the Palestine Office of the Jewish Agency in Hungary,
who was hiding in the Swiss legation. On June 18, Krausz says, he
gave the protocols to Florian Manoliu of the Romanian embassy, who
brought them to Switzerland the next day.[42] On July 4, the protocols
were distributed in Switzerland by George Mantello (Gyorgy Mandel),
a Hungarian Jew who was the honorary representative in Switzerland
of San Salvador.[43] It is very possible that a third copy reached the Swiss
press via the orthodox representatives in Switzerland, Recha and Isaac

Sternbuch in Montreux—they would have been Weissmandel's most natural conduit. What emerges, then, is that the Working Group tried its best to have the protocols reach both Budapest and Switzerland. Unfortunately, by the time that happened, the deportations were over halfway completed.

The first question to ask is whether possession of the protocols could have prevented the deportations. Kastner, and presumably others in leadership positions as well, had the information that anyone deported to Poland was threatened with death. This information, as we have seen, was very widespread; those who were ready to accept it as true did not need the protocols to convince them; everyone else rejected it. In any case, by the end of April most provincial Jews were already detained in ghettos, isolated from the surrounding population, and exposed to starvation, humiliation, and robbery. The Hungarian people were indifferent, and where they were not indifferent, they were hostile—the honorable exceptions were pitiably few. The Catholic Church, through its head, Cardinal Jusztinian Seredi, expressed extreme antisemitic views and during the deportations worried only about the fate of Jewish converts to Catholicism. The two non-Catholic churches were slightly better, but apart from offering some ineffective expressions of sympathy and half-hearted protests, did not act. Had the Jews accepted the information and refused to believe the cock-and-bull stories of the Germans, which were offered to ensure a quiet, trouble-free extermination, what exactly could they have done? Hide? Among a hostile population? Resist? Without weapons, without local support? Flee? Where? In fact, with the help of orthodox and left-wing Zionist underground groups, a few thousand Jews managed to reach Romania, and some Slovak Jews made it back to Slovakia. For the hundreds of thousands of provincial Jews, fleeing was no solution.

Vrba, in an understandably embittered and furious essay, argues that the Slovak and Hungarian Jewish leaders betrayed their fellow Jews by ignoring the protocols and not using them to warn others.[44] We can rely on Vrba when he reports what he saw and went through himself.

But his interpretations have to be the subject of an analysis, just like every document and every testimony. His point of departure is simple: he and his three friends passed on the information, and the leaders should have acted upon it; they did not, in his view, and therefore hundreds of thousands of Hungarian Jews died: they would not have entered the trains, had they known.

Many survivors share this view, and it is patently wrong. Large numbers of Hungarian Jews were aware of the mass murder in Poland, even if they did not know the ways the Germans killed Jews in Auschwitz. Even if they had known the details included in the protocols, the assumption that they would not have entered the trains is unrealistic—they would have been forced onto the trains by the Hungarian gendarmes. After all, large numbers of Polish Jews knew what awaited them in Belzec, Treblinka, and Auschwitz, and they saw no choice but to board the trains; they were forced to do so by Ukrainian and German guards, armed to the teeth, with dogs.

Kastner and his group, including the youth movements, differed from the Judenrat in their approach. Kastner was never a member of the Judenrat; but he got the youth movements an office in the Judenrat from which they sent out emissaries to major ghettos to warn the inhabitants not to board the trains. Given the hopeless situation of the Jews shut up in these ghettos, the leadership groups there reacted by evicting the young people as agents provocateurs. Almost no one wanted to believe them.[45] But these youth groups tried to warn Hungarian Jews—even before they had access to the protocols.

Vrba's strictures against the Slovak Jewish leadership are equally groundless. The very letter that he quotes and misdates, Weissmandel's missive of May 16, shows clearly that the writer was aware of the information contained in the protocols and used it, without of course betraying his source, to try and move the outside world to bomb the railways and thus stop the deportations. His warning to Freudiger has to be seen in the same way. And a third incident shows Weissmandel's policies (if that is the right term for what the Working Group, and

Weissmandel as part of it, did): in a letter to the Jewish community in Ungvar (Czech: Užhorod; Ruthenian-Ukrainian: Uzhgorod) he warned that under no circumstances was anyone to enter the trains. The local Judenrat, led by a Dr. Julius Lászlo, tried to keep the letter secret but failed to do so. Before responding to the letter, Lászlo turned to the Gestapo and asked whether what was written in it was true! He was arrested and executed, with his wife. The warning was sent to two other towns, Chuszt and Munkacz, but most of the Jews there refused to heed the warning.[46] We can see that the Working Group, and Weissmandel specifically, tried to warn people.

They also tried to send the protocols to Hungary and Switzerland, as we have seen. But one point remains unexplained: the protocols were written by April 27 but did not reach Budapest or Switzerland until early June. Why the hiatus of one month? The Working Group tried hard to get the material out of Bratislava—why did it take a month to succeed? The question has no satisfactory answer, although we know that the general contents of the protocols were transmitted to key individuals in May, and to Switzerland in Weissmandel's letter. Did the additional information provided by the two later escapees hold up the distribution until it was incorporated into the final version? How many letters were written and did not arrive, how many efforts at sending the protocols through trusted emissaries failed, we do not know. What is clear is that Vrba's accusations are groundless.

Let us backtrack one step. Kastner and apparently others were aware of the deadly threat involved in the deportations. Did they do anything to warn people? I have already mentioned the attempt to do so by the Zionist youth movements. The Judenrat, headed by members of the old Jewish aristocracy, did not warn people. But once the Auschwitz protocols were in their hands, they acted, through Petö, to transmit the material to Horthy's family. So, both groups did act.

In May 1944 what could a person like Kastner, the most active of the group around Komoly, do? He was a "foreigner," a Transylvanian journalist, unknown outside his own town, Cluj, and a fairly small circle in

Budapest. Jews were forbidden to go by railway, and Kastner could not
have traveled to dozens of ghettos; the young people who did, illegally,
failed in their task. How else could he have warned the Jews of Hungary? By radio? Through the press? By giving lectures? These questions are so ridiculous that they do not deserve an answer. Quite apart
from other considerations, the time anyone had to warn the provincial
Jews before the deportations started was about two weeks—between
the probable reception of the general information contained in the protocols by Kastner and/or the Judenrat in late April or early May and the
start of the deportations on May 14—and given the situation, it is
difficult to see how anything could have been done in so brief a span,
except by Horthy. But Horthy kept silent.

Horthy is the key element. The Germans had occupied Hungary, but
with relatively few troops. Horthy, as regent, had agreed that some of
the extreme right-wing radicals should become high officials in his
government and expressed no objection to the deportations. But he was
still in power, and the army was loyal to him. He could have acted. He
did not. But two weeks or so after he received the protocols, on June 26,
1944, Horthy, at a cabinet meeting, began preparing to withdraw from
his acceptance of the deportations. On July 9, after all the provincial
Jews had been deported, he forbade their continuation and thereby
rescued the rest—the roughly 200,000 Jews of the capital—from Auschwitz. Why the turnabout? Some reasons are obvious: Germany was
losing the war, and it was not a good idea to anticipate a separate peace
with the West (he still resisted, in June–July, the idea of a peace with the
hated Bolsheviks) by deporting Jews to their deaths. The point is that
through the protocols he must have learned details about what he had
already known in general—that with his connivance a mass murder was
being committed against Hungarian citizens. There is no doubt that the
well-known interventions by the Swedish king, the Pope, the chair of
the International Red Cross, and the warning issued by Roosevelt all
contributed to his change of heart.[47]

The documents published by Braham are the main source for Horthy's relations with the Germans, to whom he said, after the massive American bombing raid on Budapest on July 2, that he had to stop the deportations because of the bombing threat. Weissmandel's May 16 letter had been intercepted by—or was played into the hands of—Hungarian counterintelligence agents in Switzerland, and Horthy thought that the bombing raids requested in the letter had started with the Budapest raid, although we now know there was no connection at all.[48]

I would suggest that the protocols were an important factor in stopping the deportations. First, they had a direct impact on Horthy, who could no longer deny that he knew about the mass murder, and given the war situation, the protocols contributed to his decision to halt the deportations. Second, via Weissmandel's letter, the protocols created the false impression that the Allies cared about the deportations and would respond with bombardments, not just declarations of disapproval. The Slovak leadership and also Kastner—falsely accused not only by Vrba but also by authors such as Tom Segev and by other Israeli writers and journalists—emerge as people who tried to utilize the knowledge they had acquired for rescue.[49] All the odds were against them, but they nevertheless succeeded to a very small degree, and I have dealt with that elsewhere.[50] It may even be argued that Kastner and his group contributed considerably to the final rescue of most of the 200,000 Budapest Jews; it is more than likely that they had a hand in the rescue of the more than 10,000 Hungarian Jews who were deported to the area around Vienna (Strasshof) instead of to Auschwitz; and it is clear that Kastner succeeded in rescuing 1,684 people, including his family and friends, on the so-called Kastner train, who were brought to Bergen-Belsen and from there, in two batches, in August and December 1944, to Switzerland.

Vrba's complaint about the Hungarian Judenrat should also be revised: it was the Judenrat who transmitted the protocols to Horthy, who may well have been influenced thereby to stop the deportations.

Paradoxically, Vrba's despair and bitterness are overdone. Contrary

to what he says, the protocols that he and his friends prepared in order
to rescue people did have an important effect, and his and his friends'
readiness for self-sacrifice—their unqualified heroism—was not in vain.
Yet Vrba and the others wanted to achieve more. It is hard to see how
much more could have been achieved, however. Although the world did
not listen, there were results.

Why can the case of the protocols be presented as a case study in
rescue efforts during the Holocaust?

For any rescue efforts, the first precondition was information. The
information about Auschwitz was essential if anything was to be done
to facilitate rescue. The second condition was that the information
should be believed. The previous pieces of information produced by
Polish sources were not believed in the West—the Soviets had no interest in the murder of the Jews in any case—but the protocols were
obviously authentic, and by disseminating them in Switzerland, Mantello and others created a public opinion that could no longer be ignored. But the rescue efforts had a postwar life as well. In what some
may call a traditionally Jewish development, postwar commentators,
judges, politicians, historians and authors of fiction have vied with one
another to denigrate, attack, and accuse those who tried to help. To be
sure, Kastner, Weissmandel, Petö, Krasniansky, and, for that matter,
Saly Mayer, the JDC representative in Switzerland, were not perfect
people. Some were ideological fanatics, some were overweening and
superambitious political types,, some were inflexible do-it-by-the-book
types. But they tried to help, which is considerably more than their
postwar detractors have done. Ultraorthodox fanatics accuse all but
Weissmandel, who was an ultraorthodox fanatic himself, of betrayal.
Right-wing commentators attack the left-wing Zionists who tried to
rescue Jews. Left-wing fanatics see the moderate left-wingers of Holocaust times as collaborators with the Judenräte. Authors like Amos
Elon and Tom Segev distort historical evidence to prove a point—the
list is endless.[51]

The basic reason for the attacks is, I believe, a refusal to recognize the

condition of the Jewish people in World War II: nearly total helpless-
ness. American Jews could offer very little assistance, British Jews none
at all, and Palestinian Jews were a minority numbering half a million in a
Palestine occupied by large British forces. When visiting a contemporary Israeli high school, I am likely to be confronted with the question
Why did the Israeli air force not intervene? The Holocaust has caused
the development of a massive social trauma affecting the whole Jewish
world and, within it, the Jews of Israel. It prevents them from looking at
reality, because the real world of the 1940s is terrible and humiliating
for a Jew to contemplate. It is better and easier to accuse the Jewish
generation that is no longer alive of having failed to rescue their fellows.
It is the social trauma that causes Jews to accuse one another of Nazism,
that causes people to draw absolutely inappropriate analogies with the
Weimar or Nazi periods, and so on. The world at large absorbs antisemitic images when critics imply that during the Holocaust, Jews were
powerful and rich, and if they didn't help rescue other Jews, it must have
been because they did not want to, or because they were part of some
conspiracy. In effect, with these accusations they imply that the Jews
were responsible for their own murder. Ultraorthodox and quite a few
orthodox Jews say that God punished the Jews because the Jews supported Reform or Conservative or Liberal interpretations of the Jewish
religion.[52] Some secular commentators and Israeli anti-Zionists argue
that the wartime Zionist leaders were inept bunglers who are responsible for the failure to rescue the Jews of the Holocaust.

Yet rescue was attempted. Mostly the attempts failed—not because
those who tried were bunglers but because they lived in dire and desperate times, times that their detractors have no inner understanding of.
Here, too, paradoxically, just like during the Holocaust, we see that fatal
gap between information and understanding. Now, as then, it is not
information but understanding that is lacking.

chapter eleven
From the Holocaust to the State of Israel

In this book I do not memorialize the Holocaust. I ask questions about what happened and why.[1] I deal mainly with what happened during the war. But I do hold the view accepted by many colleagues that although the Holocaust itself occurred during the world war, the *period* of the Holocaust stretches from the rise of the Nazi regime in 1933 to the dissolution of the displaced persons (D.P.) camps in Central Europe after the war. In these camps, the core of the survivors lived until 1948. Most of them then emigrated either to Israel or to the West, where they restarted their lives as best they could.

One of the basic questions asked not only by historians but also by politicians, journalists, and ideologues of all kinds is, What was the impact, if any, of the Holocaust on the establishment of Israel? In a real sense, the question bridges the gap between an unconquered past tragedy and the hope for the resurrection of an almost mortally wounded people.

The importance, therefore, of dealing with the background to the establishment of the State of Israel is too obvious to be dwelled upon, and it fits in here as a question, as well as an attempt to answer it: Is there any sense in which the establishment of Israel can be seen as one of the outcomes of the Holocaust, as an epilogue to it? I will offer a brief overview, punctuated by attempts to deal with some major turning points in the history of the Jewish people in that short period between 1945 and 1948.[2]

As is usual in historical discourse, several schools of thought have developed, offering diverging interpretations of what happened between the end of the Shoah and the Israeli Declaration of Independence in 1948.[3] According to one interpretation, independence was achieved largely through the military activities of the underground movements in Jewish Palestine against the British. The emphasis is less on the Hagana, the main underground armed force, controlled by the Jewish Agency for Palestine, with its approximately 36,000 active members, and more on the Irgun Zvai Leumi, the independent right-wing armed opposition to the Jewish Agency, which in 1944 had about 1,500 passive and active members, and the extremist Lohamey Herut Yisrael (LHY), with its approximately 120 members. The reason for this emphasis lies in the fact that although the three organizations made an agreement in the autumn of 1945 to act against the British and maintained a certain level of cooperation until July 1946, Hagana then ended its participation in military attacks on the British and limited itself after that date to actions connected with illegal immigration. After that, the two right-wing armed groups were the only ones to mount armed attacks on the British in Palestine.

A majority of the Jews in Palestine—the Yishuv—supported Hagana but were reluctant to act against Irgun and LHY. Despite strong opposition to the tactics and strategy of the militant organizations and occasional collaboration with the British (which resulted in the handing over to the British of a number of members, especially of the LHY), the Yishuv thus provided a shield behind which Irgun and LHY could operate. The British forces, which were, after all, controlled by a Labor government, could not very well put up machine guns in the center of Tel Aviv because of world and British public opinion. The pinprick actions of these groups, it is argued, against the vastly superior British forces in Palestine, moved the British government to decide on withdrawal from the country in early 1947. So-called illegal immigration by sea, organized almost wholly by the Hagana, was an additional political burden on London. The survivors in the D.P. camps in Germany, Austria, and Italy exercised a certain amount of pressure, by their very existence. From a British point of view, the only escape from what was increasingly an impasse was to leave Palestine. The Holocaust, in this interpretation, motivated the underground movements in Palestine, as well as the survivors in Europe.

A second interpretation is that offered by the post-Zionist Israeli intellectuals, who argue that the period under discussion was shaped by the Arab-Jewish conflict. In this interpretation, which leans heavily on neo-Marxism and postmodernism, the Zionist movement was a colonialist movement that clashed with the interests of the local inhabitants, who, understandably, tried to defend their ancient property rights to the soil and their incipient development into an identifiable national community. The Zionists, disappointed in the help they had received from Britain until the 1930s, increasingly turned to the United States for support. Utilizing and instrumentalizing the Holocaust experience, they now had a moral weapon of some importance, which they wielded to gain control over Palestine, or at least key parts of it, driving out the resident Arabs in the process. The armed undergrounds are thus viewed as the arms of a colonialist and nationalistic political movement; and illegal immigration, as the exploitation of desperate survivors of the Holocaust by the Zionists to attain their political aims in Palestine. This interpretation stands out at Israeli universities and enjoys the support of some academics in the United States and in Britain.[4]

A group of other interpretations, offered by a number of historians, consist of attempts to combine different factors in a less ideological and more traditional historical framework. Many of the various interpretations changed, however, with the opening of the British archives in the late 1980s. It is now clear that the first view has some validity: the activities of the Jewish underground, especially the Irgun, had a much greater impact on the policies of the British Labor government than was formerly thought.

Until 1947, the British chiefs of staff saw Palestine as a possible military base in the event of a withdrawal from Egypt and the Suez Canal. The Jewish underground activities convinced at least some of them that Palestine could not serve as a secure base. But an interpretation relying almost exclusively on Jewish armed activities is not very convincing either. The policies of the British Labor government, which was elected to power in July 1945, were designed to maintain a presence in Palestine, withdrawal from India and, later, Burma and Sri Lanka notwithstanding. Without India, they realized, Palestine was much less strategically important than it had been before. They wanted to reach a pro-Arab compromise that would not break their relations with the Jews but would forge an alliance with the Arab countries, which were economically more important to the Western Allies than the relatively small Jewish population in Palestine. They tried to convince the Americans to take a similar view, and the State Department, and to a large extent the White House under both Roosevelt and Truman, agreed with them. In other words, the influence of world politics on the British, and especially their relationship with the United States, was much more decisive than local problems with the Irgun.[5]

Another salient element in the overall interpretation is a relatively new insight into the policies of the Truman administration. The notion that Truman supported a Jewish state has been shown to be erroneous. He supported the immigration of the Jewish D.P. camp inmates to Palestine but was wary of any commitment to Jewish independence. I shall discuss this further on.

Let me now backtrack to bring in what some historians, including myself, see as the major factor in the process that led to independence: the D.P. camp inmates specifically and the Holocaust survivors generally.

I estimate that at the end of World War II about 200,000 Jews emerged from the Nazi concentration and slave labor camps and had survived the death marches. Of these 200,000, a plurality, more than 70,000, were Hungarian Jews who returned to Hungary, Slovakia, and Romania, with only a small minority staying in the Jewish D.P. camps in Germany and Austria beyond the summer of 1945. Some of the survivors from Poland and Lithuania went back to look for relatives, but upon meeting extreme antisemitism from the local inhabitants, not to mention failing to find relatives, neighbors, and communities, returned to the Western zones of occupation in Central Europe. Survivors from Western Europe returned to their homes. What remained was a population, largely from Lithuania and Poland, that numbered about 55,000.

Most of these people were housed in D.P. camps, initially together with non-Jews, because the Allies refused to recognize Jews as a group entitled to separate treatment. Jews were, at first, a small minority among the 800,000 or so D.P.s, all of them from Eastern Europe, who had remained after the repatriation of the bulk of the original 11,000,000 D.P.s found in Germany and Austria at the end of the war. The Jewish survivors were soon joined by Jews who had hidden in Poland, by some Jewish soldiers in the communist Polish forces who were demobilized or who deserted, and by remnants of the Jewish partisans in Poland. Toward the end of 1945 and then in large numbers in 1946, some 176,000 Jews who had fled to Soviet Central Asia in 1941 or who had been released from Soviet Gulags returned to Poland as the result of agreements between the pro-communist Polish government and the Soviets. Because of local antisemitism and despite the blandishments of Jewish Communists and Bundists, who wanted them to remain in Poland, many of them fled to the D.P. camps in Germany and Austria, almost all of them to those in the American zones. An attempt by the Polish government and its Jewish supporters to settle these returning Polish Jews in Silesia seemed to succeed, with considerable help from American Jewry through the JDC, but in 1947 these Jews, too, began to join the exodus to the West. By the middle of 1947 there were 250,000 Jews in Germany,

Austria, and Italy, mostly in D.P. camps, and some 50,000 in France and the Low Countries, who had infiltrated there in the meantime or who had already left, illegally, for Palestine.

These survivors did not wait for emissaries from either America or Palestine. The first group of JDC representatives reached the D.P. camps in July 1945, three months after liberation, and they brought with them neither food nor medicines or clothes. American Jewish help did not become effective before the late autumn of that year. Jewish soldiers from Palestine had a critical impact on the survivors in Germany, but they did not stay, because their units moved on to Belgium. Jewish emissaries from Palestine arrived in Poland, illegally, in the early autumn; not until November did an official Jewish Agency group arrive in Germany. The reason for the belatedness of these arrivals was U.S. army opposition to having such groups come. The role of military rabbis was decisive here. They filled some of the gap, often by highly unconventional means, and helped in organizing the survivors as well as pressuring army authorities to provide better shelters and medicines.

That said, however, one must emphasize that the organization of the survivors was achieved chiefly by themselves, not by any outsiders; and their ideological direction was clearly, overwhelmingly, and right from the beginning, Zionist. In fact, the first Zionist paper, if it can be called that, was written in concentration camps in Bavaria even before liberation, and handwritten copies were passed around among Jewish inmates. A recent book published in Israel by one of the post-Zionist intellectuals—a philologist student of Noam Chomsky's, by the way—argues that a strong Bundist presence in the camps was suppressed by physical force, just as, later, force was used to force young people to "volunteer" for the Hagana and, later still, for the Israeli army.[6]

There is some truth in the allegation about the use of force by pro-Zionist survivors—the vast majority of survivors were pro-Zionist and were not too gentle in their dealings with Bundists. Also, coercion was undoubtedly used in a number of cases to make young people in the D.P. camps join the Jewish armed forces in Palestine. However, one can say with some certainty that although these things did happen, they were marginal. The overwhelming majority of the D.P.s were genuinely pro-Zionist. It is also true to say that the Bund became increasingly unpopular right from the beginning, for Jews who had gone to Poland to look for relatives came back and related stories of Polish antisemitism. After the autumn of 1945, with increasing physical attacks on Jews in Poland, and especially after the Kielce pogrom of July 1946, the Bund in the camps virtually disappeared. All it could offer to the inmates was a return to Poland to participate in the establishment there of a socialist state in which Poles and Jews would collaborate on the basis of friendly relations. But socialist Poland, the antisemitism there, and the developing communist dictatorship—that was exactly what the Jews had fled from. The Bund also proposed that those who left Poland go to other countries, not to Palestine—but Jews did not need the approval of the Bund to apply for U.S. or other visas.[7]

All in all, Zionism became what today would be called the civil religion of the D.P. camps. Elections were repeatedly held to select camp committees and central committees, first and foremost in the U.S. zone in Germany but also in the British and French zones and in Austria as well. These committees demanded virtually unanimously that the D.P.s be allowed to leave the camps and emigrate to Palestine.

U.S. policies were determined by several pragmatic and moral considerations. Feeding and supervising the D.P.s was an army task (although food rations were confiscated from the German economy), but the budgets, which had to be approved by the Senate, were not at all generous. The army therefore pressed to get rid of the remaining 800,000 D.P.s after the great repatriation in the late spring. The Jewish minority was a particularly difficult group for the army to handle. On the other hand, General Dwight Eisenhower personally and his chief of staff, Walter Beddell-Smith, who had Jewish family connections that were unknown at the time, were sympathetic to the Jews because of what they had seen in the Nazi camps that they had liberated at the end of the war. David Ben Gurion visited Frankfurt in October 1945 and persuaded the

Americans to agree not to close the borders of the American zones to Jews fleeing from the East, despite the food problems and despite the reluctance of many army officers to deal with the Jews while engaged in normalizing their relations with the local German population, which was not friendly to Jews. The American decision opened the American zones to Jewish refugees and increased the number of Jewish refugees, helping them become a real political force.[8]

Another determinant of U.S. policy was the White House. Truman sent a Philadelphia law professor, Earl Harrison, to investigate the situation in the camps, with special emphasis on the Jews, and Harrison's report, in late August 1945, was scathing in its condemnation of army policies, which had not allowed for Jewish camps to be set up and had not provided the Jews with adequate food or lodgings. Truman's sharp reaction, and Eisenhower's follow-up, which improved the Jewish situation radically, was undoubtedly motivated primarily by humanitarian and moral considerations. Separate Jewish camps were set up. An equal motive, one that increased in importance as time went on, was undoubtedly the realization that Truman's political situation was weak and that he desperately needed the Jewish vote in New York, Pennsylvania, Illinois, and California to maintain his administration and, chiefly, to have a chance of success in the congressional elections in 1946 and the presidential elections in 1948. When British Foreign Secretary Ernest Bevin accused Truman of pandering to the Jewish vote in New York, he was right. Truman was not in sympathy with Zionist political aspirations in Palestine; what he supported and what he tried to persuade the British to accept was the immigration to Palestine of 100,000 Jewish D.P.s, which Harrison had proposed. Allowing Jews into Palestine would be a truly humanitarian gesture, and it would ease the problems of the army in Germany, as well as serve the president's political interests at home.[9]

If the British had accepted Truman's demand for the immigration of the 100,000, Israel might never have arisen. It is not impossible that such a development would have taken the fire out of the D.P.s' demands, and all that the British would have had to do would have been to hand over Palestine to the Arabs with 100,000 more Jews than they had originally planned. There would still have been two-thirds Arabs and one-third Jews in the Arab State of Palestine. But, fortunately for the Jews, the British were adamant in their refusal to countenance any substantial Jewish immigration to Palestine.

The British persisted in their refusal even after an Anglo-American Commission of Inquiry, nominated by the two Western Powers to examine the situation of the Jewish D.P.s and the political situation in Palestine, had in the spring of 1946 recommended that 100,000 Jewish D.P.s be permitted to go to Palestine.

The British, who would have had full American support if they had accepted the 100,000, could easily have suppressed the Jewish armed rebellion. Without such support, they did not have sufficient public backing to do so. However, in the wake of the British refusal to accept the 100,000, the Americans found themselves in a quandary. They had hundreds of thousands of Jews on their hands, people who wanted to find new homes and had nowhere to go. The United States was closed to them, and Congress was on the whole very unfriendly to the prospect of Jewish immigration to the Unites States. It was only in 1948, and again in 1950, that the United States agreed to accept D.P.s at all, and Congress saw to it that Jews would be excluded as far as possible. Had the spirit of the congressional legislation been followed, very few Jews would have immigrated to the United States. What changed the picture was the intervention of some non-Jewish officials of the relevant government departments, which made it possible for a much larger number of Jews to utilize loopholes in the legislation and immigrate to America than Congress had intended.[10]

It was the refusal of the British to accept Jewish D.P.s in Palestine that caused the political situation to change when the Jewish Agency met in Paris in the summer and early autumn of 1946. Important members of the Jewish Agency who until then had opposed any idea of partition in Palestine and had insisted on the Zionist plan formulated in 1942 in the

Biltmore Hotel in New York—to turn all of Palestine into a Jewish state—now agreed to compromise, for the situation of the Jewish D.P.s had become intolerable, and a wave of despair and demoralization had swept the camps because escape from camp life in Germany and Austria seemed unlikely. It was therefore decided to send Nahum Goldman, a Zionist leader and a permanent resident of the United States, to Washington, with the idea that if the Americans proposed a partition plan, the Jewish Agency would consider it.

Truman had no intention of coming down in support of partition, but he was being pushed into considering solutions to the Palestine problem. Without a solution, he could not arrange for the 100,000 to go there, and he would be subject to virulent attacks by American Jews. On the eve of Yom Kippur, 1946, October 4, he therefore published a declaration saying that he would be in favor of a compromise between the British plans and those of the Jewish Agency. The American media wrongly interpreted this as supporting partition and catapulted Truman into a position he had not wanted to occupy—that of a supporter of Jewish statehood.

The British saw Truman's declaration as betrayal and as undignified pandering to Jewish voters. Despite no American support, increasing violence by the Irgun in Palestine, negotiations for a retreat from India in full swing, and the desperate economic situation in Britain itself, the British were at the end of 1946 still seeking a compromise that would be acceptable to both Jews and Arabs and that would enable Britain to continue its presence in Palestine. By that time, however, the British army no longer insisted on staying there.

Complicating the scenario was Jewish illegal immigration by sea. A long array of unseaworthy ships organized by the Hagana tried to reach Palestine, arousing sympathy among Eastern and Western European nations. People had not been compelled to board these ships; on the contrary, ever growing numbers of people desperately sought to be included. The post-Zionist arguments about Zionist manipulation of Jewish survivors appear to be completely counterfactual. The British tried to deter the D.P.s from joining the immigration by sending them to grim detention camps on Cyprus beginning in August 1946. But the knowledge that would-be immigrants could be detained on Cyprus did not deter them at all, and thousands wanted to get on the ships. Between 1945 and 1948 about 69,000 Jews—mostly D.P.s but with a large contingent of Romanian Jews in early 1948 and a fair number of North African Jews thrown in—tried to reach Palestine. All of them ultimately did after the rise of Israel.

British policy against illegal immigration was broken by the *Exodus* affair of July 1947. An American ship, the *President Garfield*, renamed *Exodus 1947*, was caught by the British on its approach to Palestine, and its D.P. passengers were forcefully transferred to deportation ships that took them back to the French port from which they had embarked. The British government thought that the people on these deportation ships would break and agree to land on French shores. When the people refused, despite the terrible conditions on board, they had to be taken to Hamburg; they had originally come from D.P. camps in Germany, and the north of Germany was the British Zone of occupation. Again, the British thought that returning full circle would teach the D.P.s and their organizers a lesson. The British Foreign Office had miscalculated. The *Exodus* D.P.s remained adamantly Zionist, even after they had been returned to Germany, which they hated, and their plight led to increased support for the Zionist cause in both Europe and the United States.[11]

Going on behind the whole immigration-Palestine show and debate was the illegal escape of Jews from Eastern Europe to Central and Western Europe. The Brichah, as it was called, was probably the largest organized illegal mass migration in the twentieth century: it brought a quarter of a million Jews to D.P. camps and other places. The Brichah was not originally organized from Palestine; rather, it was an initiative of survivors of Zionist youth movements and their comrades who had spent the war in the Soviet Union. Jewish emissaries from Palestine joined and took over at the end of 1945, when the original organizers moved out of Poland, the Baltic countries, and Romania-Hungary, and the Palestine emissaries stayed. The organization of this mass movement was exemplary and financially responsible: the Brichah participants smuggled out the money and jewelry of the escapees and returned every penny to them; they themselves lived simple lives and used money that came from the JDC to bribe officials and border guards and pay for food and transport for the refugees.

The Brichah was the organization that moved people from Eastern Europe to the D.P. camps and the shores of the Mediterranean on their way to Palestine. It is my contention that the people of the She'erith Hapletah, the Surviving Remnant, as the Jewish D.P.s were known, formed their own political organizations, which created pressure on the American army and government; that this pressure caused the United States to put pressure on the British to accept at least a portion of the Jewish D.P.s into Palestine; and that the refusal of the British to do so, because they were aggravated by the military activities of the Jewish underground in Palestine and further stymied by the resounding failure of British policies toward illegal immigration, caused them to abandon the idea of maintaining their presence in Palestine. The weakening of the imperial position in India and the Far East, combined with the economic plight of the United Kingdom, lessened the vital importance of the Suez Canal for Britain, and the importance of Palestine declined, too. These factors, and chiefly the unabating pressure of the United States, led, in February 1947, to a British decision to hand over the Palestine problem to the United Nations.

Was there a British conspiracy to maneuver the United Nations into returning the Palestine Mandate to Britain to do with as they would like? Not exactly. Rather, British policies were designed to have a majority at the United Nations declare the establishment of what would in effect amount to an Arab state with a permanent minority of Jews. Such a state would become a trustee territory of *both* Western Powers. Everything pointed to this happening. The United States was not hell-bent on a Jewish state—certainly not the State Department. The Vatican feared that Jerusalem and the holy places would fall to the Jews, and Catholic states in Latin America would hardly support a Zionist policy of partition. The Soviet Bloc was anti-Zionist and would support the Arab position, and the Dominions as well as Western Europe were certain to be inclined to support British policies.

It is at this point that another major factor has to be introduced: American Jewry. From about 1943, after the success of the radical right-wing Zionist Bergson-Kook group to mobilize Jewish and non-Jewish support for their causes on the same basis as other American political movements, the Zionists, under the leadership of Rabbi Abba Hillel Silver, created a grass-roots, typically American political movement. This was a vital breakthrough. It enabled them to mobilize American Jewry and receive massive support from the American public for Zionist aims.

American Jews were, in my view, motivated in large part by the information about the Holocaust and by guilt feelings about their behavior during the years of murder—whether the feelings were justified or not does not matter here. Zionism had become fashionable among many American Jews earlier, but it had always been a minority movement. Now, American Jews could support Zionist aims without becoming members of Zionist parties. At the end of the war, letters from Jewish soldiers in the U.S. occupation forces in Europe and reports by rabbi chaplains fed into a willingness to help. Again, the concrete situation of the Jewish D.P.s in Central Europe and the absence of a real alternative by emigration to other countries besides Palestine (before 1948) made immigration to Palestine the obvious solution. On this, as on the attitude of the American public, much more research is needed, and what I have said here is not properly grounded in such research but is more of a general hypothesis.

The support by the general American public for Rabbi Silver's movement came from a number of non-Jewish sources. It would be unwise to ignore the tremendous influence of Christian religious attitudes that accepted the Jews as the rightful owners of the Holy Land. Not only fundamentalists and evangelicals felt this way, but also, though to a lesser degree, some more liberal Christians. Most Democrats and Republicans supported the wish of an old-new nation to be independent and believed that the Arab-Jewish quarrel could be solved by some sort of compromise. For some of the politically minded, as well as for some who were not so minded, support for the Zionist cause may have been motivated by the thought that if the Jews went to Palestine, they would not come to the United States. The Jewish vote in New York and elsewhere was, as I have said already, of crucial importance for the administration. All this created a combination of forces that had a chance of success, as against important economic and political interests of the United States, such as the big oil companies, and much of the professional bureaucracy. The arguments of the anti-Zionists were well grounded, and in fact, for a variety of moral and political reasons, the Truman administration acted against the economic and strategic interests of the United States in supporting the Jews. But in all this, the input of American Jewry was absolutely central.

At the United Nations, British hopes went unfulfilled. The crucial development there was the speech of Andrei Gromyko, the Soviet representative, during the debate on Palestine in April 1947: he declared that the Soviet Union would support partition if there was no other choice, and created a sensation when he declared further that the Jewish people deserved to have national sovereignty after what had happened to them in World War II. The reason for this volte-face of the Soviets can, with hindsight, be explained without too much difficulty. They wanted to expel the British from the Middle East and thought that they had a chance to influence a future Jewish mini-state, for Jewish communists would help them organize an anti-imperialist front in the area. Mass emigration of Jews from the now Soviet-dominated East European countries would also help get rid of a potentially disruptive presence. We now know, for instance, that the Soviets even caused a mass expulsion of Jews from Soviet-controlled northern Bukovina and its capital, Czernowitz (Cernauti), to Romania in 1946, although generally they radically opposed the emigration of Soviet Jewish citizens. But they supported the opening of the borders between Poland and Czechoslovakia and Austria and, to a significant extent, the transition of Jewish refugees through their Austrian zone of occupation. They had no objection to the supply of Czech weapons—for cash dollars—to the Hagana in Palestine and later to the Israeli army. Their concern for what the Jews had suffered in the Holocaust was window dressing; the same, however, should not be said about the Polish and Czech communists, whose identification with the Jews was not simply political but was based, for some of them, on real sympathy. We have documentation to prove that.[12]

Be that as it may, the Soviets supported the Zionists at the United Nations. Surprisingly for the British, so did most of the Latin American countries, partly because of real sympathies for the cause and partly because of relentless pressure by Jewish interlocutors, who were organized by the Jewish delegation at Flushing Meadows under the leadership of Moshe Sharet (Shertok) from Palestine, Rabbi Silver, a fiery orator and by then the acknowledged leader of American Zionists, and their colleagues. Truman was wary and in effect agreed to a policy of nonintervention and neutrality favored by the State Department in the hope that a British-type compromise would finally be arrived at or that no decision at all would be made, which would leave the Anglo-Americans to decide on the future of Palestine alone. Under concentrated Jewish pressure, he changed this policy at the last minute before the U.N. decision on Palestine (on November 29) and instructed the American delegation to intervene in the favor of partition. The same pressure then led him to recognize the State of Israel, in opposition to his State Department and his secretary of state, George Marshall, on May 14, 1948.

The partition decision of the United Nations did not establish the Jewish state. That was done by the Yishuv and its military arm, which emerged from the Hagana. The Irgun contributed on the margins, and the LHY was too small to have any real effect. The Jewish-Arab War was almost lost, which Israeli historians know but which has to be understood outside that narrow circle. Contrary to the arguments of the post-Zionist commentators, the Jews were weaker in number and equipment than the Arab Palestinians and the other Arabs who joined in. In March 1948 the outlook was bleak for the Jews in Palestine. Roads had been cut, Jewish Jerusalem was under siege, and modern arms were lacking. Then and later, with the invasion of the Arab states in May—again contrary to some arguments now presented by various commentators—it was indeed the fight of a David against a Goliath, a weak Goliath, but no one knew the Arab weakness at the beginning of the War of Independence. Help came from communist Czechoslovakia. The supply of Czech arms turned the situation around, and the Palestinian Jews won that war.

At the end of that war the proportion of European survivors in the Israeli army was about a third; most of them joined relatively late in the hostilities because of the difficulties in immigrating to the country, although they did participate immediately upon arriving there. The brunt of the war in its first, decisive phases was borne by the Jewish youth of the Yishuv. The common story about the unprepared survivors who were sent in large numbers to die in an unsuccessful attack on Latrun, near Jerusalem, early in the war is simply untrue, as the Tel Aviv historian Anita Shapira has shown.[13] Most of the casualties in that particular battle were Israeli-born soldiers; twenty-three were survivors from Europe. Later on, new immigrants played an increasingly important part, sometimes a preponderant part, in the battles, and casualties among them increased, too.

It is probably clear from what I have said here that I do not support any of the alternative interpretations mentioned at the beginning of this chapter. I believe that the establishment of the State of Israel was far from being a foregone conclusion. It almost failed; it hung by a thread more than once. It was facilitated first of all by the survivors, both those of the Nazi camps and those who were in Central Asia during the war. They became D.P.s in Central Europe, and their presence and their organizations caused endless problems for the British and the Americans.

They were the basic reason for the American pressure on Britain that convinced the British to hand over the Palestine issue to the United Nations. The survivors were also the basic reason for the mobilization of American Jewry by the Zionists. This pressure was compounded by the activities of the armed underground in Palestine and by the illegal immigration organized by the Hagana. The survivors had a further decisive influence on all these activities, expressed in the vast Brichah movement organized by them and by Palestinian Jewish emissaries. If the United States had opened its gates to Jewish immigration, or even if the half-hearted congressional measures of 1948 and 1950 had occurred earlier, it is highly probable, in my view, that a much larger proportion of Jewish D.P.s would have gone to the United States than did. As it was, some two-thirds went to Palestine-Israel, and a third elsewhere, mostly to North America. Hypothetically, a different American policy might have changed the proportions. At the United Nations, the help of the Soviets in the final stages was crucial. The ambivalence of American politics was redirected by a grass-roots movement led by American Zionists that organized the pressure on the White House at critical moments.

Finally, a controversial issue has to be addressed, namely, the argument that Israel was created by the Holocaust. That is not what I think happened. On the contrary, if the German Reich had held out one more year, it is doubtful whether there would have been any survivors at all. More Holocaust would have equaled less chance for a Jewish State. The Holocaust prevented a Jewish State from coming into existence with, as new-minted citizens, the millions of Jews who were murdered. Indeed, because of the Holocaust, the attempt to establish a state almost failed. There were almost not enough Jews left to fight for a state. The ones who survived the Holocaust were central to that effort, and had there been more, the effort would have been easier and the outcome more certain. My answer, therefore, is unequivocal: The view that Israel was created by the Holocaust is erroneous. The opposite is true. But it is certainly correct to say that it was the surviving European Jews, especially those in the D.P. camps, who played a central role in the developments that enabled Palestinian Jews to fight for independence.

Another argument connecting the Holocaust and Israel says that in some mysterious way the rise of Israel was an answer to the Holocaust. I do not think I have to deal with this because the very line of thought is so repugnant. I think most Jews would have preferred saving the lives of the Jews who died in the Holocaust to establishing the state.

Another version of the argument states that guilt feelings about the Holocaust caused the United Nations to decide to partition Palestine. I did not find any evidence that would confirm this motivation for the United States, certainly not for Great Britain. The use of the argument by the Soviets was purely instrumental. Some Latin American states, and some small European states can be shown to have been influenced by the moral argument, but not by a guilt complex, which is not evident anywhere. By and large, the considerations that led the majority of the supporters of partition to vote for it were purely political. Jews would like it to have been otherwise, but Jewish sensibilities do not determine international politics, then or today.

What, then, is the link between the Holocaust and Israel? I think it is an indirect one. The survivors were a central element in the achievement of independence, but the Holocaust as such was a catastrophe that, apart from its other effects, also endangered the very struggle for independence. We find Israeli politicians of all hues and stripes claiming time and time again that had there been a Jewish state in 1939, the Holocaust would not have happened. The notion that a mini-state with one or two or three divisions would have stopped the German army that overran all Europe is sheer nonsense. Equally nonsensical is the notion that an Israel in 1939, in a partitioned Palestine (that was the only realistic possibility), would have been able to receive millions of Jewish refugees on top of the less than half a million Jewish residents already there in the midst of a world economic crisis. That serious people bruit such crazy notions shows that attitudes toward the Holocaust are shaped by a deep social trauma. More time must pass before even very thoughtful and informed people begin to understand what really happened. The State of Israel is, first and foremost, the creation of the generations that preceded the Holocaust and that created in Palestine a basis for the struggle for independence. Because of that foundation, the survivors could make an impact. Nevertheless, a bitter war, in which 1 percent of the Jewish population of Palestine died, was needed to make an actuality out of the possibility of statehood. In the United States there are, say, 250 million inhabitants. One percent would be 2.5 million. I need say no more.

As I said at the outset, the Holocaust has become a world issue. It has had an enduring impact on contemporary civilization and continues to shape, at least indirectly, the fate of nations. For its impact to effect mutual understanding, widespread peace, and active, full-scale opposition to genocidal events, we all have to rethink what happened then. That is what I have tried to do in this book.

Speech to the Bundestag

On January 27, 1998, the German Holocaust Memorial Day, I spoke to the Bundestag, the German house of representatives. What I said there is really the conclusion I can draw from everything I tried to say in this volume.

Mr. Speaker of the Bundestag; Mr. President of Germany; Mr. President of the Bundesrat [upper house of Parliament]; Mr. Chancellor; Ladies and Gentlemen; dear friends. On January 27, 1945, the Soviet Army conquered the Auschwitz complex of camps. Still, only some 7,000–8,000 people were liberated, of which the majority were ailing people whose lives had been miraculously spared by the S.S. The other 58,000 had left a few days earlier on a death march.

They were followed, during the four months leading to the end of the war, by many hundreds of thousands from almost all of the concentration camps, marking the last spastic and endlessly brutal impact of the cruelest regime that the world has ever seen. On January 27 the horror was still far from over, even though Auschwitz was no longer in the hands of the murderers.

Have we learned anything? People seldom learn from history, and the history of the Nazi regime constitutes no exception. We have failed as well to understand the general context. In our schools we still teach about Napoleon, for example, and how he won the battle of Austerlitz. Did he win it on his own? Maybe somebody assisted him in this? A few thousand soldiers perhaps? And what happened to the families of the fallen soldiers, to the wounded on all sides, to the villagers whose villages had been destroyed, to the women who had been raped, to the goods and possessions that had been looted? We are still teaching about the generals, about the politicians, and about the philosophers. We are trying not to recognize the dark side of history—the mass murders, the agony, the suffering that is screaming into our faces from all of history. We do not hear the wailing of Clio. We still fail to grasp that we will never be able to fight against our tendency toward reciprocal annihilation if we do not study it and teach it and if we do not face the fact that humans are the only mammals that are capable of annihilating their own kind.

The American sociologist Rudolph J. Rummel arrived at the conclusion that between the years 1900 and 1987 governments and government-like organizations murdered 169 million civilians, apart from the 34 million fallen soldiers. Who committed those crimes? Mainly nondemocratic regimes. Even though democracies committed crimes as well, they were responsible for only a fraction of 1 percent of the civilian victims.

These statistics are only partially useful. Actually, they do not reveal the tragedy but cover it up. We do know that it is people who were tortured and murdered, not statistics, but—it happened to an impossibly huge number of people who were just like you and me.

The war, which was instigated by National Socialist Germany, mainly for ideological reasons, cost the lives of about 49 million people, most of whom were civilians. If we adopt the definition of *genocide* used by the

United Nations, then what happened to the Polish nation and to the Roma, called Gypsies by others, was indeed genocide. The Polish nation as such was meant to disappear. The policy toward them was accompanied by mass murders: the Polish intellectuals had become the target for annihilation—universities and schools were shut down, the clergy were decimated, all the important economic businesses were confiscated, children of Polish families were deported to Germany to undergo "Germanization." The Sinti and the Roma of Germany were slated for disappearance by means of mass murder and sterilization. Nomadic Roma were supposed to be murdered wherever they were in Europe (those of them who were settled, would be tolerated). Millions of Russians and other Soviet peoples—but Western Europeans, Italians, Balkan peoples, and Germans as well—became victims of the regime.

Why? I think that we have to be clear that a radical revolution had been planned, a mutiny against everything that had been before. It was not a new order of social classes, of religions or even of nations that was envisioned, but a completely new hierarchy—one constructed of so-called races—in which the invented master race did not only have the right but the duty to rule over the others and to enslave or murder all those it considered different from itself. This was a universalistic ideology: "Today Germany belongs to us, tomorrow the entire world," as the Nazi song had it.

How was it possible for a people of culture who lived in the midst of Europe and who had developed one of the greatest civilizations ever, to subscribe to such an ideology, to instigate a war of annihilation because of it, and to stick to it until the bitter end? Terror was not the only reason, Ladies and Gentlemen. There was a consensus based on a promise of a wonderful utopia—a utopia of an idyllic community of people governing the world, devoid of friction, without political parties, without democracy, one that would be served by slaves. To achieve such a goal, it was necessary to revolt against everything that had been before: middle-class and Judeo-Christian morality, individual freedom, humanitarianism—the whole package of the French Revolution and the

Enlightenment. National Socialism was, in fact, the most radical of revolutions that had ever taken place—a mutiny against that which was, until then, thought of as humane.

The nucleus of the strategy to annihilate anybody thought of as different was the Holocaust, the project of the total annihilation of the Jewish people and the actual murder of all the Jews the murderers could lay their hands on. And the most horrible thing about the Shoah is in fact not that the Nazis were inhuman—the most horrible thing about it is that they were indeed human, just as human as you and I are. When we claim that they were different from us and that we can sleep in peace, with untroubled consciences, because the Nazis were devils and we ourselves are not devils because we are not Nazis, that is cheap escapism. Escapism of the same cheap kind is implicit when we say that the Germans were somehow genetically programmed to execute mass murders. Because most people are not Germans, many tend to think that whatever happened can never be repeated by anyone else and that it could have happened only in Germany. This is reverse racism.

All this happened almost sixty years ago. One would have thought that the famous bottom line should have been drawn long ago, that interest in this specific genocide would have petered out. Yet the opposite is the case. Hardly a week goes by without a new book being published somewhere in the world, or memoirs or a novel or a scientific debate, without plays being staged, without poetry appearing, without television programs or movies being released, and the like. Quite a lot of it might be kitsch, but a lot of it is of value. Again, we must ask why. Why is the Holocaust the central issue, and not Cambodia or the Tutsi or Bosnia or the Armenians or the Indians of North America?

I am not at all sure whether my answer to this very central question is better than any other, but I would nonetheless like to present it to you. I do not think the sadism and the brutality with which the victims were maltreated could offer an explanation, because suffering, agony, and torment cannot be graded. I have published, in English, the testimony of a Sinti woman who lost her husband and who saw her own three children die in front of her very eyes. How is it possible to compare this with the tragedy of a Jew or of a Russian peasant or of a Tutsi or of a Cambodian Khmer? It is, surely, impossible to say that the suffering of one person is greater or less than that of another, that one mass murder is better or worse than another. Such a statement would be repulsive. If so, is it the brutality and the sadism that makes the Holocaust so singular? Indeed, National Socialist Germany enriched this tragic repertory in an extraordinary manner, but brutality is no novelty in history. Is the distinguishing factor, possibly, the fact of its having been a state-initiated mass murder carried out with the aid of modern technologies and bureaucratic thoroughness? I do not think so. The genocide of the Armenians was carried out with the aid of the then available technological and bureaucratic tools, and the Nazis themselves carried out their crimes against the Poles and against the Roma with the same methods that they used against the Jews.

No, I think the answer lies elsewhere. You see, for the first time in the whole of history, people who were descended from three or four of a particular kind of grandparents—Jewish ones—were condemned to death just for being born. The mere fact of their having been born was in itself their deadly crime that had to be avenged by execution. This has never happened before, anywhere. A second characteristic of the Holocaust that was unprecedented was that anybody of Jewish descent was to be caught wherever in the world Nazi Germany exercised influence, be it directly or through allies—anywhere in the world, a world that tomorrow would belong to "us." The murder of Jews was not directed against the Jews of Germany or the Jews of Poland or even the Jews of Europe, but against all the seventeen million Jews scattered throughout the entire world of 1939. All other cases of genocide had been perpetrated on definite territories, although the territories may sometimes have been very wide, whereas the murder of the Jews was construed to be universal. Third, the ideology. Numerous colleagues of mine have analyzed the structure of Nazism, its bureaucracy, the day to day operation of the murder apparatus. All their findings are absolutely correct—but why did the bureaucrats, who were shipping German schoolchildren by train to summer camps and Jews by train to death camps with the same administrative means, do the latter? Why murder all the Jews who could be found and not, let us say, all the green-eyed people who could be found? To try and explain this away with social structures—although they may have been very important—is unacceptable, as far I am concerned.

The motivation was ideological. The racist-antisemitic ideology was the rational outcome of an irrational approach, an approach that was a cancerlike mutation of the Christian antisemitic ideology that had sullied Christian-Jewish relations all through their two millennia of co-existence. Nazi antisemitism was pure ideology, with a minimal relation to reality: the Jews were accused of a worldwide conspiracy, an idea stemming from the Jew-hatred of the Middle Ages, whereas in reality Jews were not capable of achieving unity, not even on a partial basis. Between you and me, they are still not capable of it. A conspiracy did exist, but it was not a conspiracy by the Jews; it was one by the National Socialists.

The Jews were accused of being revolutionary agitators as well as capitalists, which means that all the different phobia were reduced to one single denominator. Naturally, most of the Jews belonged to neither of these categories, but were in the lower or middle class. They did not possess territories, nor did they command military might, nor did they control any national economy, if only because they did not constitute any entity, but observed their tradition, as individuals, following mutually contradictory interpretations, within the framework of small religious-ethnic communities or, when secular or atheistic, did not even belong to formal Jewish communities.

In all the other cases of genocide known to us, the motivation was somehow pragmatic, as in the case of the Armenians, where there was a nationalistic motivation for their murder, or in the case of Rwanda, where there is a deadly conflict over power and territory. In the case of the Holocaust, the ideology underlying the genocide was, for the first time in history, pure fantasy.

One can add a fourth element to the unprecedented characteristics of the Holocaust: the concentration camp. The Nazis may not have invented it, but they surely brought it to a totally new stage of development. Not only the murder and the suffering in those camps should occupy our mind, but also the elevated level to which they brought the art of humiliation through the control they exercised over people through their physiological needs. This is without precedent in human history. True, the humiliations and the rest were not perpetrated against the Jews alone, but Jews were the ones on the lowest rung of that hell. What the Nazis achieved by subordinating Jews to that extreme, was not the dehumanization of the Jews but the dehumanization of their own selves. By establishing these horrific concentration camps they positioned themselves on the lowermost possible rung of humanity.

What did the Nazis leave behind? Where are their literary, their artistic, their philosophical, their architectural achievements? The Nazi Reich dissolved into nothingness. It left only one memorial: the ruins of the concentration camps and, crowning it, the only great achievement of Nazism—Auschwitz and the mass murder.

It is the lack of a precedent for the Holocaust that is beginning to be understood all over the world. A very special case of genocide took place here—total, global, purely ideological. It might be repeated—certainly not in the exact same form, but possibly in a similar, maybe even very similar manner, and we have no way of determining who will be the Jews and who might be the Germans the next time.

This menace is universal and at the same time—because it is founded on the experience of the Holocaust—very specifically connected with the Jews. The specific and the universal cannot be separated. It is the extreme character of the Holocaust that allows it to be compared with other cases of genocide and to be presented as a warning. It has in fact, been already copied, though not exactly. Should the warning be ignored? Should the Holocaust serve as a precedent for others who would like to inflict the same onto yet others?

How could it have happened? I think that one must look at that ancient tradition included in the book that comes from my ancestors. In that book it is written that humankind can choose between Good and Evil, between life and death. This means that humankind is capable of both, that both exist within the self—both God and the devil. Expressed in a more modern fashion, it means that the urge for life and the wish for death—our own or others', is inside us. Under certain conditions we might become either Eichmanns or rescuers.

For Germany, we are not discussing guilt; we are talking about the responsibility toward the future of the culture within which this monster developed. Because, Ladies and Gentlemen, you know very well that "Death was a master from Germany"—although the Jews were never enemies of the Germans or of Germany. Quite the opposite. German Jews were always proud of how much good they had achieved for German civilization.

So how can the Nazi regime be explained? I think that a pseudo-intellectual elite took over power in Germany, and it did so not because the masses supported their potentially genocidal ideology, but because there was a situation of a grave crisis which the potentially genocidal layer of leaders offered a way out of, in the form of a wonderful utopia. The determining factor was that the layer of intellectuals—the academicians, the teachers, the students, the bureaucrats, the doctors, the lawyers, the churchmen, the engineers—joined the Nazi Party because it promised them a future and a status. Through the fast-growing identification of these intellectuals with the regime, it became possible to have the genocide easily presented as an unavoidable step toward the achievement of a utopian future. When Herr Doctor, Herr Professor, Herr Director, Herr Priest or Pastor, Herr Engineer, became collaborators with genocide, when a consensus evolved, led by the semimythological figure of the dictator, it became easy to convince the masses of the necessity of the murders and to recruit them to carry them out.

Something similar could happen elsewhere, but in Germany, where at least some of the elite had absorbed a radical antisemitism in the course of the nineteenth century and where many of them added a general racist ideology, it proved easy for the genocidal Nazi layer of leaders to turn the majority of German citizens into accomplices. A major role was played by academics. I keep returning to the question of whether we have indeed learned anything, whether we do not still keep producing technically competent barbarians in our universities.

And what about the churches? The Holocaust has brought to light a profound crisis in Christianity. Nineteen hundred years after the Christian Messiah spread the Gospel of love, his own people were murdered by baptized heathens. The churches, insofar as they did not collaborate, kept their silence.

On the other hand, one definitely cannot say that within German society a radical antisemitic norm had prevailed. There was, however, a general queasiness regarding the Jews, even among the non-antisemitic or even anti-antisemitic mutually antagonistic mass movements of the Social Democrats, the Communists, and the Catholic Center that constituted the majority of the German voting population up to the end of 1932. This queasiness made it practically impossible for a general protest against the murder of Jews to develop. It was not as though the dictatorship was so fully totalitarian as to make protest movements totally impossible. This was demonstrated not only by the opposition to the murder of handicapped Germans that brought about the stoppage, in August 1941, of the so-called euthanasia program, at least partially, but also the demonstration of German women in the Rosenstrasse in Berlin, in February–March 1943, which led to the freeing of their Jewish husbands. The fragility of the famous German-Jewish symbiosis became apparent, as any mass movement for the protection of the unpopular Jewish minority was totally outside the sphere of possibilities.

It seems to me that yet another factor is involved. European culture has two pillars: Athens and Rome on the one hand and Jerusalem on the other hand. An ordinary citizen of two hundred years ago, if he or she owned a book at all, would probably have owned the Christian Bible, which, as we all know, is composed of two parts—the Old Testament and the New Testament. Both of them were written mainly by Jews.

Greek and Roman literature, law, art, and philosophy are and have surely been, as important to Western civilization as the prophets and the moral commandments of the Jewish Bible. Still, modern Italy and modern Greece do not use the same languages as in ages past; they do not worship the same gods, create the same kinds of art, or write the same kinds of literature. Different peoples live there now. But my granddaughter reads what the Jews wrote three thousand years ago, in the original, needing no dictionary. Try that with Chaucer—and he wrote only a few hundred years ago.

When the Nazis wanted to carry out their rebellion against Western culture, was it not the Jews, those still living reminders of one of the sources of that culture, that they had to annihilate? The Jews, whether they like it or not, are a central component of Western self-perception. This self-perception is diffused throughout the world by means of so-called Western civilization, as well as by means of kitsch culture—which also originates in the West.

There is an Auschwitz museum in a suburb of Hiroshima. Holocaust literature is read in South America. The Holocaust has assumed the role of universal symbol for all evil because it presents the most extreme form of genocide, because it contains elements that are without precedent, because that tragedy was a Jewish one and because the Jews— although they are neither better nor worse than others and although their sufferings were neither greater nor lesser than those of others— represent one of the sources of modern civilization.

The way I see it, a historian is one who not only analyzes history but also tells true stories. So let me tell you some stories. In Radom, in Poland, there lived a Jewish woman with two sons. Her husband had gone to Palestine in 1939 to prepare the way for his entire family to immigrate. The war broke the family apart. The husband became a

Palestinian citizen and tried to save his family by including them in an exchange with German settlers in Palestine.

In October 1942, when the woman already knew what awaited her and her children, a Gestapo man summoned her to headquarters and told her she was going to be exchanged. Within one hour she was supposed to turn up with her two sons at his office. Yes, said the woman, but my elder son is working outside the ghetto, and she asked how she was supposed to summon her son. That was none of his business, said the Gestapo man. They had to show up in one hour. And if not? The woman was desperate. Should she and her younger son share the fate of her firstborn? Or should she at least save herself and her younger son? She agonized over the decision back home. Her neighbor approached her and said: Look, you cannot save your son. Why don't you take my son in his stead? My son is the same age as your elder son. Shocked and in tears, the woman showed up at the Gestapo headquarters with two boys. On November 11, 1942, she arrived in Haifa. The two boys became, in time, prominent Israeli citizens, with children and grandchildren.

The woman spoke little after that. She was a proud person and would not live supported by the pity of others. [Her husband died soon after she joined him in Palestine.] Until the end of her life she ran a small stall opposite the great synagogue on Allenby Street in Tel Aviv. It was said that she was a survivor of the Holocaust. Had she really survived? I am not sure.

The Holocaust, along with all the other horrible things that the National Socialists perpetrated, shows not only the evil that Man is capable of but also—at the margins, so to speak—the opposite, the good. Oskar Schindler has become a controversial figure because of the well-known movie. But look, when you strip away the myth, something does remain. Schindler was not only a member of the Party; he had been a spy as well, a womanizer, an alcoholic, and a ruthless exploiter and liar. There are few people to be found on whom you could pin more negative characterizations. Yet he apparently contributed to saving the lives of more than one thousand people while risking his own safety. He or his wife carried severely sick and dying Jewish slave laborers from a freezing train to try to save their lives. He did not have to do that, but he did. He went to Budapest to warn the Jews there about the Shoah. He did not have to do it, but he did. Why? Because he was a human being—as bad as he was, he also was good.

His story shows that one could, even as a German, even as a member of the Party, behave in a different way from the executors of the Holocaust. Schindler and others like him, like Otto Busse in Bialystok, who supplied the Jewish resistance with weapons, show us that it was possible to save lives. The deeds of these people prove, on the one hand, the guilt of the others, but also, on the other hand, that hope is not lost.

You see, there is the story of Maczek. Actually, his name is Mordechai. His name is the only thing that he knows about himself. Before the war, at the age of three, he was handed over by his mother to a Jewish orphanage in Łódź. This is what he was later told. Then came the war, and he was raised in Cracow by a Polish woman named Anna Morawczika. Naturally he thought she was his mother.

At the age of six, while playing on the street, he was hit by accident by a car full of German soldiers. The soldiers wanted to take him to the hospital, but Anna Morawczika opposed it with all her might. She knew he would be murdered instantly if it was found out that he had been circumcised.

When the war was over, a woman presented herself at Anna's. Anna told Maczek that this woman was his mother. This time, both women took the boy and put him in a Jewish orphanage in Łódź. The mother disappeared, never to be seen again. Maczek was brought to Israel. Anna, who had saved him, passed away shortly thereafter. Maczek does not know to this very day who he is. All he knows is that a Polish woman saved his life because she loved him—a Jewish boy orphan.

There were the Annas and the Schindlers, but they were few, very few. And most Nazis were like the S.S. man in the next story. I do not know whether the story is true, but here is how it goes: An S.S. man told a Jewish woman that he would spare her life if she guessed which of his two eyes was of glass and which one was live. Without hesitating the woman pointed at one of the eyes and said, "This is the glass eye." "Correct," said the S.S. man, "but how did you find out?" The woman answered, "Because it looked more human than the other."

I now return to the question of whether we have learned anything. Not much, or so it seems to me. But hope persists, even among the traumatized people, a group to which I belong. You, Ladies and Gentlemen, just like members of other democratic parliaments, carry a very special responsibility—especially as Europeans, especially as Germans.

I do not have to tell you that what happened in Rwanda or in Bosnia happened right next door. To be reminded, as a consequence, of the Holocaust, constitutes only a first step. To teach and study about the Holocaust and everything that transpired during the Second World War and thereafter involving racism, antisemitism, and xenophobia— that constitutes our next responsibility. We Germans and Jews depend on each other in undertaking this responsibility. You cannot carry out the task of remembering without us, and we must be sure that here, where the disaster arose, a new, humane, better civilization is being constructed on the ruins of the past. Together we carry a very special responsibility toward the whole of humanity.

There might be one further step. The book of which I spoke earlier contains the Ten Commandments. Maybe we should add three additional ones: "You, your children, and your children's children shall never become perpetrators"; "You, your children, and your children's children shall never, ever allow yourselves to become victims"; and "You, your children, and your children's children shall never, *never*, be passive on-lookers to mass murder, genocide, or (may it never be repeated) a Holocaust-like tragedy."

I thank you for your kind attention.

notes

Chapter One
What Was the Holocaust?

1. Karlheinz Deschner, "Was ist Geschichtsschreibung, und was könnte sie sein?" in Hermann Gieselbusch, ed., *Über Karlheinz Deschner*, Rowohlt, Reinsbek, 1986, pp. 15–38.
2. Deschner, p. 22
3. See, e.g., Gordon A. Craig, *The Politics of the Prussian Army*, Oxford University Press, New York, 1964, pp. 499–500.
4. Eberhard Jäckel, *Hitlers Herrschaft*, Deutsche Verlagsanstalt, Stuttgart, 1986, pp. 105–122.
5. Nuremberg Trial Documents, NO-1880. For a more detailed discussion, see Chapter 4.
6. Hans Mommsen, "Realization of the Unthinkable," in Gerhard Hirschfeld, ed., *The Politics of Genocide*, Allen and Unwin, London, 1986, p. 100; Goetz Aly, *Endlösung*, Fischer, Frankfurt, 1995, pp. 390–394; and Goetz Aly and Suzanne Heim, *Vordenker der Vernichtung*, Hoffmann und Campe, Hamburg, 1991, passim.
7. Christian Gerlach, "Die Wannsee-Konferenz, das Schicksal der deutschen

Juden und Hitlers politische Grundsatzentscheidung, alle Juden Europas zu ermorden," *Werkstattgeschichte* (Hamburg), vol. 18, October 1997, pp. 7–44. Hitler said, according to Goebbels's diary, quoted there: *"Der Weltkrieg ist da, die Vernichtung des Judentums muss die notwendige Folge sein"* (The world war has come; the annihilation of Jewry must be the necessary result). My interpretation differs from Gerlach's, who thinks that the Hitler speech represents a decision in principle to murder the Jews (*Grundsatzentscheidung*) and that the Himmler note indicates a decision that all European Jews should be killed on the pretext that they are partisans. See Michael Wildt et al., eds., *Himmler's Terminkalender, 1941–1942*, Christians, Hamburg, 1999.

8. Ulrich Herbert, ed., *Nationalsozialistische Vernichtungspolitik, 1939–1945*, Fischer, Frankfurt, 1998. This slim volume contains contributions by Walter Manoschek, Christian Gerlach, Thomas Sandkühler, Dieter Pohl, Christoph Dieckmann, and Michael Zimmermann, of the younger generation of historians, and Goetz Aly and Christopher R. Browning, of the older group. Herbert himself has two extremely important chapters in the book.

9. Herbert, pp. 114–115: *"Die gesamte Umsiedlungspolitik wurde in der Zentrale am grünen Tisch geplant. Dort wurden die strategischen Entscheidungen getroffen, und dies war ohne Hitler nicht möglich."* Herbert speaks of the *"wechselseitigen Kommunikationsprozess zwischen Zentrale und Peripherie"* (a two-way process of communication between the center and the periphery).

10. Arthur A. Cohen, *Thinking the Tremendum: Some Theological Implications of the Death-Camps*, Leo Baeck, New York, 1974.

11. Saul Friedländer, *Nazi Germany and the Jews*, vol. 1, Harper Collins, New York, 1997.

12. E.g., in Saul Friedländer, "The 'Final Solution': On the Unease in Historical Interpretation," in Peter Hayes, ed., *Lessons and Legacies*, Northwestern University Press, Evanston, Ill., 1991, pp. 23–35.

13. Raphael Lemkin, *Axis Rule in Occupied Europe*, Howard Fertig, New York, 1973, pp. 79 ff.

14. Lemkin, pp. xi–xii.

15. Yehuda Bauer, "The Holocaust in Contemporary History," *Studies in Contemporary Jewry*, no. 1, Jerusalem, 1984, p. 204.

16. As in Frank Chalk and Kurt Jonassohn, *The History and Sociology of Genocide*, Yale University Press, New Haven, 1990, p. 23; Frank Chalk, "Definitions of Genocide and Their Implication for Prediction and Prevention," *Holocaust and Genocide Studies*, vol. 4, no. 2, 1989, pp. 149–160; Kurt

Jonassohn, "Prevention Without Prediction," *Holocaust and Genocide Studies*, vol. 7, no. 1, 1993, pp. 1–13.

17. Rudolph J. Rummel, *Democide*, Transaction Press, New Brunswick, N.J., 1992; Rummel, *Death by Government*, Transaction Press, New Brunswick, N.J., 1995. Rummel has been criticized for exaggerating the losses. Even if the criticisms were valid, a figure lower by 10 or 20 or even 30 percent would make absolutely no difference to the general conclusions that Rummel draws.

Chapter Two
Is the Holocaust Explicable?

1. Roy Eckardt, "Is the Holocaust Unique?" *Worldview*, September 1979, pp. 31–35, and elsewhere.

2. These lines were written, and the term "willing helpers" used, in an article I wrote with a title identical to the title of this chapter, which appeared in *Holocaust and Genocide Studies*, vol. 5, no. 2, 1990, p. 145, that is, in the pre-Goldhagen historical era.

3. Yehuda Bauer, *The Holocaust in Historical Perspective*, University of Washington Press, Seattle, 1978, pp. 30–49.

4. See Arthur A. Cohen, "The Holocaust and Christian Theology," in Yitzhak Mais, ed., *Judaism and Christianity Under the Impact of National Socialism*, Historical Society of Israel, Jerusalem, 1982, pp. 415–434. Even Saul Friedländer, who explicitly distances himself from any kind of mysticism, wrote: "The historian's paralysis arises from the simultaneity and the interaction of entirely heterogeneous phenomena: messianic fanaticism and bureaucratic structures, pathological impulses and administrative decrees, archaic attitudes within an advanced industrial society. We know the details of what occurred, we are aware of the sequence of events and their probable interaction, but the profound dynamics of the phenomenon evade us. And what likewise escapes us is the almost immediate disintegration of the political, institutional and legal structures of Germany, as well as the surrender of the moral forces that by their very nature ought to have been important obstacles to the Nazis in Germany, in other European countries, and in the entire Western world." See Saul Friedländer, "From Anti-Semitism to Extermination," in *Yad Vashem Studies*, vol. 16, Yad Vashem, Jerusalem, 1984, p. 50. For an analysis of the sociopsychological phenomena involved and invoked by Friedländer, see Erich Fromm, *The Anatomy of Human Destructiveness*, J. Cape, London, 1974; Elie Wiesel, "Introduction,"

in Abraham J. Peck, ed., *Jews and Christians After the Holocaust*, Fortress, Philadelphia, 1982, pp. ix–xi; and Emil Fackenheim, "The Holocaust and Philosophy," *Journal of Philosophy*, vol. 82, no. 10, October 1985; Edward Alexander, "The Incredibility of the Holocaust," in his *The Resonance of Dust*, Ohio State University, Columbus, 1979, pp. 3–30. On the question of speech versus silence, see, e.g., Lawrence L. Langer, *The Holocaust and the Literary Imagination*, Yale University Press, New Haven, 1975, pp. 1–30.

5. The massacre referred to here was that of the Albigensians and Waldensians by forces organized into a crusade by Pope Innocent III, in 1209. The pro-papal forces were under the command of Simon de Montfort. Massacres and persecutions continued until 1226.

6. Some of my colleagues have argued that the concept of "uniqueness" is devoid of any real meaning, because every historical event has unique features and is, in a very real sense, unique: it cannot be reenacted. In my view, this is a quibble. We compare events to each other, and when we find an element in one event that is not present in any other, then we are justified in claiming uniqueness. However, to avoid misunderstanding, and contrary to my usage in previous publications, I am now using *unprecedented* instead of *unique*.

7. See IMT (Nuremberg Documents), PS 1919.

8. The last ten words appeared in Bauer, "Is the Holocaust Explicable?" p. 150, and, again, predate Goldhagen.

9. Eberhard Jäckel, "On the Purpose of the Wannsee Conference," in James S. Pacy and Alan P. Wertheimer, eds., *Perspectives on the Holocaust*, Westview Press, Boulder, Colo., 1995, pp. 39–50; Kurt Pätzold, "Die vorbreitenden Arbeiten sind eingeleitet," *Aus Politik und Zeitgeschichte* (Berlin), vol. 1–2, January 1992, pp. 14–23; Christian Gerlach, "Die Wannsee Konferenz, das Schicksal der deutschen Juden, und Hitlers politische Grundentscheidung, alle Juden Europeas zu ermorden," *Werkstattgeschichte* (Hamburg), vol. 18, October 1997.

10. See Juergen Stroop, *The Stroop Report*, Pantheon, New York, 1979.

11. The main Polish underground group, Armia Krajowa, although it maintained a number of armed groups in Polish forests, especially in 1943 and 1944, did not engage in any major rebellions except for two: the *Burza* (storm) uprising in Volhynia (in eastern Poland before the war, now in western Ukraine) in 1944 and the Warsaw rebellion of August–September 1944. In both cases the Polish leaders wanted to assert their political claims, in eastern Poland and in Poland generally, against the Soviets. Both attempts failed.

12. Isaiah Trunk, *Judenrat*, Macmillan, New York, 1973, passim.

13. Aharon Weiss, "Jewish Leadership in Occupied Poland—Postures and Attitudes," in Yisrael Gutman, ed., *Yad Vashem Studies*, vol. 12, Yad Vashem, Jerusalem, 1977, pp. 335–366.

14. E.g., Rabbi Immanuel Jacobovits, "Some Personal Theological and Religious Responses to the Holocaust," *Holocaust and Genocide Studies*, vol. 3, no. 4, 1988, pp. 371–381.

15. Lucy Dawidowicz, *The War Against the Jews*, Weidenfeld and Nicholson, London, 1975.

16. Steven T. Katz, *The Holocaust in Historical Context*, Oxford University Press, New York, 1994.

17. This, again, is the exact version in my "Is the Holocaust Explicable?" p. 150—pace Goldhagen, who claims he invented this particular wheel all by himself.

18. Adolf Hitler, *Hitler's Second Book*, Grove Press, New York, 1961.

19. David Bankier, *The Germans and the Final Solution: Public Opinion Under Nazism*, Blackwell, Oxford, 1992; Otto Dov Kulka, " 'Public Opinion' in Nazi Germany and the 'Jewish Question,' " *Jerusalem Quarterly*, part I, vol. 25, Fall 1982, pp. 121–144; part II, vol. 26, Winter 1982, pp. 34–45, and elsewhere; Ian Kershaw, "German Popular Opinion and the Jewish Question," in Arnold Paucker, ed., *Die Juden im Nationalsozialistischen Deutschland*, J. C. B. Mohr, Tübingen, 1986, pp. 368–388; Kershaw, *Der Hitler-Mythos, Volksmeinung und Propaganda im Dritten Reich*, Deutsche Verlagsanstalt, Stuttgart, 1980; and Kershaw, *The Nazi Dictatorship*, Edward Arnold, London, 1985.

20. Peter H. Merkl, *Political Violence Under the Swastika*, Princeton University Press, Princeton, 1975.

21. Cf. Thomas Childers, *The Nazi Voter*, University of North Carolina Press, Chapel Hill, 1983; William Sheridan Allen, *The Nazi Seizure of Power*, Franklin Watts, New York, 1965, 1984; Michael H. Kater, *The Nazi Party*, Harvard University Press, Cambridge, 1983. Kater says: "The German intelligentsia still remained over-represented in the NSDAP [Nationalsozialistische Deutsche Arbeiter Partei, or National Socialist German Workers Party] until 1930. The first reason for this was that scores of intellectuals looked upon themselves as having been socially and politically displaced after 1918. They strove . . . for the social and cultural attributes of an elitist minority rather than of the mass" (p. 47) And: "The gradually improving relationship between the Nazi leadership and the Protestant church was undoubtedly instrumental in drawing academi-

cally trained professionals and intellectuals to the party in greater numbers after 1929" (p. 67). On the Protestant church, see Wolfgang Gerlach, *Als die Zeugen Schwiegen,* Institut Kirche und Judentum, Berlin, 1987, esp. pp. 21–36.

22. Victor Klemperer, *Ich will Zeugnis ablegen bis zum letzten,* vols. 1–2, Aufbau, Berlin, 1995.

23. Goetz Aly and Heinz Roth, *Die Restlose Erfassung,* Berlin, 1984, p. 105; also quoted in Goetz Aly, *Endlösung,* Fischer, Frankfurt, 1995, pp. 376–377.

24. Franklin H. Littell, *The Crucifixion of the Jews,* Harper and Row, New York, 1975.

25. See Helen Fein, *Accounting for Genocide,* Free Press, New York, 1979.

26. Konrad Kwiet and Helmut Eschwege, *Selbstbehauptung und Widerstand,* Hans Christians, Hamburg, 1984, p. 43.

Chapter Three
Comparisons with Other Genocides

1. Robert Melson has reached conclusions that are identical with mine, e.g., in his lecture entitled *On the Uniqueness and Comparability of the Holocaust: A Comparison with the Armenian Genocide,* Center for Comparative Genocide Studies, Macquarie University, Sydney, Australia, 1995. For a detailed presentation, see his *Revolution and Genocide,* Chicago University Press, Chicago, 1992, esp. pp. 33–39.

2. Erich Fromm, *The Sane Society,* Fawcett, Greenwich, Conn., 1955: "If I cannot create life, I can destroy it. To destroy life makes me also transcend it. Indeed, that man can destroy life is just as miraculous a feat as that he can create it, for life is *the* miracle, the inexplicable. In the act of destruction, man sets himself above life; he transcends himself as a creature. Thus, the ultimate choice for man, inasmuch as he is driven to transcend himself, is to create or to destroy, to love or to hate" (p. 42).

3. William Nicholls, *Christian Antisemitism,* Aronson, Northvale, N.J., 1993, passim. Few historians will deny this statement. Some Christian historians and thinkers will go even further, and say that there is a straight line of continuity between Christian antisemitism and the Nazi variety. I do not subscribe to that view.

4. Franklin H. Littell, *The Crucifixion of the Jews,* Harper and Row, New York, 1975; and Nicholls.

5. Uriel Tal has argued that whereas in Christian antisemitism the Jew was a *symbol* of Satan and satanic forces in the world, in National Socialism the

Jew *was* Satan. From being a symbol of evil, he became evil itself (or the Evil One himself), a major transformation. "The symbol itself underwent a total reversal of meaning and of structural function. The symbol itself was divested of its quality of standing for someone beyond, or of standing for 'the Beyond,' pointing to it, substituting for it, covering what can never be uncovered. . . . The symbol . . . now became identical with its own actuating source . . . the Jew no longer symbolized anti-Nazism; he was the incarnation, the embodiment of anti-Nazism" (Tal, "Forms of Pseudo-Religion in the German Kulturbereich Prior to the Holocaust," *Immanuel* [Jerusalem], no. 3., Winter 1974, p. 72). Judaism, the Nazis argued, was "the demon who became visible" (Tal, "Political Theology and Myth Prior to the Holocaust," in Yehuda Bauer and Nathan Rotenstreich, eds., *Holocaust as Historical Experience*, Holmes and Meier, New York, 1981, p. 63, quoting Alfred Bäumler [1943]).

6. See Yosef H. Yerushalmi, *Assimilation and Racial Anti-Semitism: The Iberian and the German Models*, Leo Baeck Memorial Lecture 26, New York, 1982.

7. My friend and colleague Raul Hilberg has, in my view, conclusively proved, over and over again, the central role that German bureaucracy played in the destruction of the Jews. He has studiously avoided applying himself to the question of *why* the bureaucracy did what it did. He is fond of saying that he did not want to ask large questions in case he came up with small answers; but surely one has to ask a question as obvious as that. Because he did not find an answer, his conclusion is necessarily mystifying: we will never know, some questions are unanswerable, and the like. In fact, the answer is, in principle, the same as for any other human action: people were motivated to act because there was an overarching consensus in society, expressed by a ruling ideology, to do so.

8. Saul Friedländer, *Nazi Germany and the Jews*, vol. 1, Harper Collins, New York, 1997.

9. See Robert Melson, "Revolutionary Genocide," *Holocaust and Genocide Studies,* vol. 4., no. 2, 1989, pp. 161–174; Melson, "Paradigms of Genocide," *Annals of the American Academy of Political Science*, 1996, pp. 156–168; Vahakn Dadrian, "The Armenian Genocide in Official Turkish Records," *Journal of Political and Military Sociology*, vol. 22, no. 1, Summer 1994, pp. 1–204. See also a collection of chapters on the Armenian genocide with contributions by Roger W. Smith, James J. Reid, Robert Melson, and others, in Richard G. Hovanissian, ed., *The Armenian Genocide*, St. Martin's, New York, 1992.

10. See Helen Fein, "Testing Theories Brutally: Armenia, Bosnia and

Rwanda," in Levon Chorbajian and George Shirinian, eds., *Problems of Genocide*, Zoryan Institute, Toronto, 1997, pp. 181–190; and a series of articles by various authors in *Der Überblick* (Hamburg), March 1994, September 1994, January 1996, March 1996.

11. Ben Kiernan, "Enver Pasha and Pol Pot," in Levon Chorbajian and George Shirinian, eds., *Problems of Genocide*, Zoryan Institute, Toronto, 1997, pp. 53–68; and Kiernan, *The Pol Pot Regime: Race, Power and Genocide in Cambodia Under the Khmer Rouge, 1975–1979*, Yale University Press, New Haven, 1996.

12. See Michael Zimmerman, *Rassenutopie und Genozid*, Christians, Hamburg, 1996, passim.

13. Friedländer, pp. 73–112.

14. See Göring's famous instruction to Heydrich, July 31, 1941, Nuremberg Trial Documents, PS-710, quoted in Chapter 2.

15. Cf. Yehuda Bauer, "Gypsies," in Yisrael Gutman and Michael Berenbaum, eds., *Anatomy of the Auschwitz Death Camp*, Indiana University Press, Bloomington, 1994, pp. 451–453.

16. Despite his protestations to the contrary, Daniel J. Goldhagen presents such a quasi-genetic explanation of German behavior in his *Hitler's Willing Executioners*, Knopf, New York, 1996.

17. I am indebted to Dr. Jean Ancel for showing me his manuscript on the Holocaust in Romania, which is going to be published by Yad Vashem in both Hebrew and English.

18. See below, Chapter 4, in the discussion of Zygmunt Bauman's *Modernity and the Holocaust*, Polity Press, Cambridge, England, 1989.

19. See Chapter 2, note 23, above.

20. Hermann Rauschning, *Hitler Speaks*, Butterworth, London, 1939.

21. See Jeffrey Herf, *Reactionary Modernism*, Cambridge University Press, New York, 1984. Herf argues that the German version of modernism was a combination of rapid modern industrial development with the continued rule of a reactionary, aristocratic social elite that managed to absorb the rising elite of industrialists and traders. Most of these members of the elite were driven by a backward-looking ideology. The liberal middle-class did not succeed in overcoming this force. I think Herf's analysis is convincing; the cases of Japan during and after the Meiji Revolution and of pre-Bolshevik tsarist Russia (which Herf does not mention) appear to present somewhat of a parallel. See also Goetz Aly, *Endlösung*, Fischer, Frankfurt, 1995, passim, for a partial description of the internal problems of Nazi bureaucracy. See also Chapter 4.

22. Maly Trostinetz, a death camp near Minsk, has only recently been described, and there is still much research to be done. The number of victims is probably near 200,000–230,000. Not only Jews were murdered there. See Yaakov Tsur, "Makhane Ha'hashmada Maly Trostinetz" (The Extermination Camp of Maly Trostinetz), *Yalkut Moreshet*, no. 59, 1995, pp. 31–50; and Christian Gerlach, *Kalkulierte Morde*, Hamburger Edition, Hamburg, 1999, pp. 768–770, which quotes a much lower figure—about 60,000.

23. A detailed description of the internal structure of the Nazi camps is provided in Yisrael Gutman and Michael Berenbaum, eds., *Anatomy of the Auschwitz Death Camp*, Indiana University Press, Bloomington, 1994.

24. Goldhagen is right in emphasizing this fact, even if others have stated it before him.

25. See Goldhagen, passim. I deal with the Goldhagen theses in Chapter 4.

26. Helmut Heiger, "Der Generalplan Ost," *Vierteljahreshefte für Zeitgeschichte*, no. 2, 1972, pp. 133–153; for full documentation, see Czeslaw Madajczyk, ed., *Generalni Plan Wschodni—Zbor dokumentów*, Institut Historii Polskiej Akademii Nauk, Warsaw, 1990, esp. pp. 71, 82–110.

27. Christian Gerlach, *Krieg, Ernährung, Völkermord*, Hamburger Edition, Hamburg, 1998; and Gerlach, *Kalkulierte Morde*, passim.

28. Hitler's statement on August 22, 1939. There is controversy about what precisely he said—indeed, whether he said it at all. The evidence, however, seems to indicate that he did utter something like the words attributed to him. See Kevork B. Bardakjian, *Hitler and the Armenian Genocide*, Zoryan Institute, Cambridge, Mass., 1985.

29. On September 22, 1919, in an interview with Major-General Harbord, head of the American Military Mission to Armenia, Mustafa Kemal complained that "only Turkey is held accountable for the massacre of 800,000 of its citizens"; and on April 20, 1920, the day after the inauguration of Turkey's new parliament, he spoke of "the massacres against the Armenians," describing them as a "shameful act." The Ittihadist chiefs and their accomplices "deserve the gallows. Why do the Allies delay having all these rascals hung?" Quoted in Vahakn N. Dadrian, "The Documentation of the World War I Armenian Massacres in the Proceedings of the Turkish Military Tribunal," *International Journal of Middle East Studies*, vol. 23, 1991, p. 549.

30. Sybil Milton, "The Context of the Holocaust," *German Studies Review*, vol. 13, no. 2, 1990, pp. 269–283; Milton, "Gypsies and the Holocaust," *History Teacher*, vol. 24, no. 4, 1991, pp. 375–386; Milton, "Nazi Politics Toward

Roma and Sinti," *Journal of the Gypsy Lore Society,* vol. 2, no. 1, 1992, pp. 1–18; Henry Friedlander, *The Origins of Nazi Genocide,* University of North Carolina University Press, Chapel Hill, 1995. Friedlander says: "I realized that the Nazi regime systematically murdered only three groups of human beings: the handicapped, the Jews, and Gypsies" (p. xiii). The fact that he concentrated on *German* Roma becomes clear only when he adds, "From the first, the regime excluded members of the targeted groups from the national community" (ibid.). This is absolutely true and not very relevant: one may add political and other opponents as well (homosexuals who were denounced to the authorities, Jehovah's Witnesses), although they were not excluded on a biological basis. Friedlander continues: "With the invasion of the Soviet Union in June 1941, the killings were extended to include Jews and Gypsies" (ibid.). He talks of the "annihilation" of the Gypsies. As will be shown below, many Roma were indeed murdered, but there was no planned "annihilation" of all Roma. Finally, on p. 295, Friedlander says: "One cannot explain any one of these Nazi killing operations without explaining the others. Together they represented Nazi genocide." Because he does not differentiate between different forms of genocide (including total annihilation), he can put all three cases in the same category, which, as I try to show, is an error.

Friedlander's very important work on the handicapped appears to have led him to lump the murder of the Jews with the murder of the handicapped. I do not wish to deal here with the murder of handicapped Germans. This was an internal "cleansing" action, to use an anachronistic term, most certainly not a genocide; it was a mass murder, not unlike the murder of political and other undesirables by communist regimes, although the motives were different. Hundreds, possibly more, of the handicapped Poles in the territories annexed to the Reich were also engulfed in the murder actions, but in their case, murdering them was a way to "free" institutions to harbor German settlers from the Baltic states and other places.

31. Tilman Zulch, ed., *In Auschwitz vergast, bis heute verfolgt,* Rowohlt, Reinbek (Hamburg), 1979, pp. 85–90, quoted in Bauer, "Jews, Gypsies and Slavs—Policies of the Third Reich," in *UNESCO Yearbook on Peace and Conflict Studies,* UNESCO, Paris, 1985, pp. 73–100. See also Bauer, "Gypsies," pp. 451–453.

32. Here and in what follows I rely on a relatively recent doctoral dissertation, now published as a book: Zimmermann, *Rassenutopie und Genozid,* pp. 300–301. Zimmermann's book is the only really comprehensive research

on the fate of the European Roma since Kenrick and Puxon's book, *The Destiny of Europe's Gypsies*, Chatto-Heineman, London, 1972, which is very much outdated and inaccurate. The author is extremely cautious and does not even provide a summary of losses in Roma lives (see below).

33. Raul Hilberg, *The Destruction of the European Jews*, Quadrangle, Chicago, 1961, esp. pp. 50–53, 268–277.

34. Zimmermann, pp. 13–15.

35. Zimmermann, pp. 255–257.

36. Zimmermanm, p. 261.

37. Zimmermann, pp. 263–264.

38. Zimmermann, p. 265.

39. Zimmermann, p. 271.

40. Zimmermann, p. 275.

41. Peter Witte et al., eds., *Der Dienstkalender Heinrich Himmlers, 1941/42*, Hamburg, Christians, 1999, p. 405.

42. Zimmermann, p. 283.

43. I am avoiding the term *Polish death camps* because of the totally erroneous implication it might have that the Poles had anything to do with these installations, which were established by Germans, not by Poles, on conquered Polish territory.

44. Zimmermann, pp. 288–289.

45. According to newspaper reports, the number of European Roma in 1997 was estimated to be between 6 million and 12 million. Serious research is needed, for all the reports offer no more than guesses and may be influenced by anti-Roma prejudices.

46. Witte et al., p. 405.

Chapter Four
Overall Interpretations: Zygmunt Bauman, Jeffrey Herf, Goetz Aly

1. Gerald Reitlinger, *The Final Solution*, Valentine-Mitchell, London, 1953; Joseph Tennenbaum, *Race and Reich*, Twayne Publishers, New York, 1956; Raul Hilberg, *The Destruction of the European Jews*, Quadrangle, Chicago, 1961; Karl A. Schleunes, *The Twisted Road to Auschwitz*, Illinois University Press, Chicago, 1990; Dietrich Uwe Adam, *Die Judenpolitik im Dritten Reich*, Droste, Düsseldorf, 1972.

2. Philip Friedman, *Their Brothers' Keepers*, Holocaust Library, New York, 1978.

3. Isaiah Trunk, *Judenrat*, Macmillan, New York, 1972.

4. Yisrael Gutman, *The Jews of Warsaw, 1939–1943*, Indiana University Press, Bloomington, 1982; Michael R. Marrus and Robert O. Paxton, *Vichy France and the Jews*, Basic Books, New York, 1981; Louis de Jong, *Het Koningrijk der Nederlande in de Tweede Wereldorlog*, RIOD, Nijhoff, The Hague, 1969–1991; Jacob Presser, *The Destruction of the Dutch Jews*, Dutton, New York, 1969.

5. Arthur D. Morse, *While Six Million Died*, Random House, New York, 1967; David S. Wyman, *Paper Walls*, University of Massachussets Press, Amherst, 1968; and Wyman, *The Abandonment of the Jews*, Pantheon, New York, 1984.

6. Joshua A. Sherman, *Island Refuge*, Paul Elek, London, 1973; Bernard Wasserstein, *Britain and the Jews of Europe*, Clarendon, Oxford, 1979.

7. Dina Porat, *The Blue and Yellow Star of David*, Harvard University Press, Cambridge, 1990.

8. An important recent book is Leni Yahil, *The Holocaust*, Oxford University Press, New York, 1990.

9. Zygmunt Bauman, *Modernity and the Holocaust*, Polity Press, Cambridge, 1989; Jeffrey Herf, *Reactionary Modernism*, Cambridge University Press, Cambridge, 1984.

10. Bauman, p. 13.

11. Bauman, p. 9

12. Bauman, pp. 17–26.

13. Bauman, p. 32.

14. Bauman, p. 38.

15. Bauman, p. 40.

16. Bauman, p. 42.

17. Bauman, p. 46.

18. Christopher R. Browning, *Ordinary Men*, HarperCollins, New York, 1992.

19. Bauman, p. 44.

20. Bauman, p. 104.

21. Bauman, p. 94.

22. Bauman, p. 118.

23. See Aharon Weiss, "Jewish Leadership in Occupied Poland—Postures and Attitudes," in Yisrael Gutman, ed., *Yad Vashem Studies*, vol. 12, Yad Vashem, Jerusalem, 1977, pp. 335–365.

24. Shalom Cholavsky, "The Judenrat in Minsk," in Yisrael Gutman, ed., *Patterns of Jewish Leadership in Nazi Europe*, Yad Vashem, Jerusalem, 1979.

25. Weiss, p. 363.

26. Shaul Esh, "Germani Be'Getto Lodz" (A German in the Łódź Ghetto), in

Joseph Walk, ed., *Iyunim Be'Heker Ha'Shoah VeYahadut Zmanenu* (Investigations into Holocaust Research and Contemporary Jewry), Hebrew University and Yad Vashem, Jerusalem, 1973, pp. 296–316.

27. Friedrich Hielscher, *Fünfzig Jahre unter Deutschen*, Vogel, Hamburg, 1954; and his correspondence with Esh, as quoted in Esh's article. My translation from the Hebrew.

28. Esh, pp. 307–308, 310.

29. Hilberg, p. 295.

30. A recent doctoral dissertation at Hebrew University, by Yakov Lozowick, which in the meantime has been published in German with the title "Hitlers Bürokraten" (Pendo, Munich, 2000), proves conclusively that the people around Eichman were an ideologically committed group of National Socialists and radical, murderous antisemites, not at all the faceless bureaucrats that Bauman, in Hannah Arendt's wake, considers them to have been.

31. Uta Gerhardt, in Hans-Ulrich et al., eds., *Systemrationalität und Partialinteresse: Festschrift für Renate Mayntz*, Nomos, Baden-Baden, 1994, p. 70, my translation.

32. Goetz Aly, *Endlösung*, Fischer, Frankfurt, 1995.

33. Sarah Bender, *Mul Mavet Orev* (In the Face of Lurking Death), Am Oved, Tel Aviv, 1997. An English edition will probably appear in 2002.

34. Michael Unger, "The Łódź Ghetto," Ph.D. diss., Hebrew University, 1999; Christopher R. Browning, *The Path to Genocide*, Cambridge University Press, Cambridge, 1992.

35. Ulrich Herbert, ed. *Nationalsozialistische Vernichtungspolitik, 1939–1945*, Fischer, Frankfurt, 1998.

36. I am deeply indebted to Professor Henri Zukier (New School, New York) for letting me read a summary of his highly important forthcoming volume, *Genocide and Identity*.

Chapter Five
Overall Interpretations: Daniel J. Goldhagen, John Weiss, Saul Friedländer

1. In *Hitler's Willing Executioners*, Knopf, New York, 1996, Daniel Goldhagen attributes the success of the anti-Jewish genocide "in the main to the preexisting, demonological, racially based, eliminationist antisemitism of the German people, which Hitler essentially unleashed" (p. 442). Genocide was "immanent in the conversation of German society . . . in the structure of cognition" (p. 449). The world of the concentration camps "reveals the

essence of the Germany that gave itself to Nazism" (p. 461). But all this is based on his statement that "in the middle ages and the early modern period, without question until the Enlightenment, German society was thoroughly antisemitic" (p. 30). "Antisemitism, albeit an antisemitism evolving in content with the changing times, continued to be an axiom of German culture throughout the nineteenth and twentieth centuries" (p. 32). His conclusion is "that antisemitism was endemic in German culture and society" (p. 48).

2. Uriel Tal, *Christians and Jews in Germany, 1870–1914*, Cornell University Press, Ithaca, N.Y., 1975, quoted in Goldhagen, p. 58. Also quoted: David Sorkin, *The Transformation of German Jewry*, Oxford University Press, New York, 1987.

3. Goldhagen, pp. 61–62 and elsewhere.

4. E.g., Goldhagen, p. 65. The differentiation between these types of anti-semitism, as described here, is precisely what Goldhagen does *not* offer— he links them together in a linear continuity. It is only when one reads his work carefully that one sees that he actually describes different types of anti-Jewishness. It is not that he does not see the differences; rather, he theorizes that all of them are expressions of the same underlying elimina-tionist mind-set.

5. Hans Mommsen, "Die Realisierung des Utopischen. Die 'Endlösung der Judenfrage' im 'Dritten Reich,'" *Geschichte und Gesellschaft*, vol. 9, 1983, pp. 381–420.

6. Goldhagen, p. 56.

7. John Weiss, *Ideology of Death*, Ivan R. Dee, Chicago, 1996. A justified criticism of Weiss's book could be that whereas all the other authors of overall explanations of the Holocaust based themselves on, or argued that they based themselves on, primary sources, Weiss's volume is essentially an interpretative essay using secondary literature exclusively.

8. George Mosse, *The Crisis of German Ideology*, Grosset and Dunlap, New York, 1964; and Mosse, *The Nationalization of the Masses*, Howard Fertig, New York, 1975.

9. Goldhagen, p. 449.

10. Christopher R. Browning, *Ordinary Men*, HarperCollins, New York, 1992.

11. In the German original, in the *Todesfuge* by the great Jewish poet Paul Celan: "*Der Tod ist ein Meister aus Deutschland.*"

12. See Hannes Heer and Klaus Naumann, eds., *Vernichtungskrieg—Verbrechen der Wehrmacht*, Hamburger Edition, Hamburg, 1995; Omer Bartov, *The Eastern Front, 1941–1945: German Troops and the Barbarization of Warfare,*

Macmillan, London, 1985; and Bartov, *Hitler's Army: Soldiers, Nazis and War in the Third Reich*, Oxford University Press, New York, 1992.

13. Goldhagen, pp. 293–316.

14. See Felicja Karay, *Death Comes in Yellow*, Harwood Press, Amsterdam, 1996. Hasag ran slave labor camps at Skarzysko-Kamienna, Radom, Czestochowa, Leipzig, and elsewhere.

15. Goldhagen, pp. 326–354.

16. I found four Jewish testimonies, three of them published, in his book, but I may have missed a couple. He also uses secondary literature, largely by Israeli historians (Yisrael Gutman, Shmuel Krakowski, Yitzhak Arad, and others), that relates to Jewish testimonies or documentation. But there were survivors from the mass murders committed by Battalion 101, and although I have not examined the Helmbrechts death march, there probably are more Jewish testimonies than the one he uses. This omission is the result of a general inclination to rely on German materials. One might even argue that Goldhagen, like many others, almost instinctively sees German materials as "real" sources, Jewish and Polish sources as less real.

17. Leni Yahil, *The Holocaust*, Oxford University Press, New York, 1990.

18. Saul Friedländer, *Nazi Germany and the Jews*, vol. 1, HarperCollins, New York, 1997.

19. Aharon Weiss, ed., *Yad Vashem Studies*, vol. 19, Yad Vashem, Jerusalem, 1988, pp. 1–47. The original German exchange was published in the same year in *Vierteljahreshefte für Zeitgeschichte*, vol. 36, no. 2, pp. 339–372.

20. Ernst Nolte, *Three Faces of Fascism*, Holt, Rinehart and Winston, New York, 1966; Nolte, *Der Faschismus in seiner Epoche*, Piper, Munich, 1963.

21. Friedländer, pp. 86–87.

22. See Geoff Eley, "What Are the Contexts for German Antisemitism?" in Jonathan Frankel, ed., *The Fate of the European Jews, 1939–1945*, Studies in Contemporary Jewry, vol. 13, Oxford University Press, New York, 1997, p. 122.

23. Abraham Margaliot and Yehoyakim Kochavi, eds., *Germania* (Hebrew), Yad Vashem, Jerusalem, 1998, pp. 761–838.

Chapter Six
Jewish Resistance—Myth or Reality?

1. The literature, even in English, is vast. I have tried to summarize it in my book *Jewish Reactions to the Holocaust*, Ministry of Defence, Tel Aviv, 1989, esp. pp. 110–163, and elsewhere. Here is a purely arbitrary choice of

a few salient titles from among the host of Hebrew and Yiddish research studies on the subject that have not been translated: Raffi Benshalom, *Ne'evaknu Lema'an Hachayim* (We Struggled for Life), Moreshet, Tel Aviv, 1977—on Hungary; Yisrael Gutman, *Ba'alatah Uvema'avak* (In Darkness and While Fighting), Moreshet, Tel Aviv, and Hebrew University, Jerusalem, 1985—on amidah and resistance; Lieber Brenner, *Widerstand un Umkum in Czenstochower Getto* (Resistance and Death in the Czestochowa Ghetto), Jewish Historical Institute, Warsaw, 1984; Shalom Cholavsky, "Minsk Bema'avaka Uvekhilyona" (Minsk: Its Struggle and Its Destruction), *Yalkut Moreshet*, no. 18, 1974, pp. 101–112; and Yael Peled, *Krakov Hayehudit, 1939–1945* (Jewish Cracow, 1939–1945), Kibbutz Meuchad, Tel Aviv, 1993. Cf. now Shalom Cholavsky, *Meri Velochama Partizanit* (Resistance and Partisan Struggle) on Belarus, Yad Vashem, 2001.

2. Yehuda Bauer, *The Jewish Emergence from Powerlessness*, Toronto University Press, Toronto, 1979, p. 27.

3. Natan Eck, *Hato'im Bedarkei Hamavet* (Those Who Lose Their Way in the Paths of Death), Yad Vashem, Jerusalem, 1960, pp. 73, 244.

4. Herman Kruk, *Togbuch fun Vilner Getto*, Yiddisher Wissenschaftlecher Institut (YIVO), New York, 1961.

5. Yehoyakim Kochavi, *Chimush Lekiyum Ruchani* (Armor for Spiritual Existence), Lohamei Getaot, Haifa, 1988. This thorough research into the cultural life of German Jewry in the 1930s has not been translated into English.

6. Again, it is hardly possible even to skim the vast literature that exists on the sanctification of life: Yisrael Gutman, *The Jews of Warsaw, 1939–1943*, Indiana University Press, Bloomington, 1982; Abraham I. Katsh, *The Warsaw Diary of Chaim A. Kaplan*, Colliers, New York, 1973; Dalia Ofer, "Everyday Life of Jews Under Nazi Occupation," *Holocaust and Genocide Studies*, vol. 9, no. 1, 1995, pp. 42–69. A great deal of material is contained in Lucjan Dobroszycki, ed., *The Chronicle of the Lodz Ghetto*, Yale University Press, New Haven, 1984, which is a shortened version of the full *Chronicles*, published by Yad Vashem in 1986. A recent doctoral dissertation (1999), in Hebrew, not yet published, by Michal Unger, presents a detailed and comprehensive picture of the Łódź ghetto. On Kovno, see Dina Porat, *The Kovno Ghetto Diary*, Harvard University Press, Cambridge, 1990. On Vilna, see Yitzhak Arad, *Ghetto in Flames*, Yad Vashem, Jerusalem, 1980. On Cracow, see Peled. On Czestochowa, see Brenner. On Tarnów, Kielce, and Piotrków memorial books and archival materials are available at Yad Vashem, Jerusalem.

7. Gutman, *Jews of Warsaw*, p. 84.

8. Gutman, p. 141.

9. In September 1940. Emmanuel Ringelblum, *Notes from the Warsaw Ghetto*, ed. Jacob Sloan, McGraw-Hill, New York, 1958, p. 47.

10. Kalman Klonymus Shapira, *Esh Kodesh* (Holy Fire), Va'ad Chassidei Piaseczna, Jerusalem, 1960.

11. Issachar Teichthal, *Em Habanim Samecha* (The Mother of the Sons Is Happy), Meshulam Katzburg, Budapest, 1943.

12. Yitzhal Katznelson, *Ktavim Achronim* (Last Writings), Kibbutz Meuchad, Tel Aviv, 1956.

13. See, e.g., Michel Mazor, "The House Committees in the Warsaw Ghetto," in Yehuda Bauer and Nathan Rotenstreich, eds., *The Holocaust as Historical Experience*, Holmes and Meier, New York, 1981; Ringelblum, passim; and Emmanuel Ringelblum, *Yoman Urshimot Mitkufat Hamilchama* (Diary and Notes from the War Period), ed. Yisrael Gutman et al., Lohamei Getaot and Yad Vashem, Jerusalem, 1993, esp. pp. 270–273, 305–308, 374–381.

14. Charles G. Roland, "An Underground Medical School in the Warsaw Ghetto," *Medical History*, vol. 33, 1989, pp. 399–419; Luba Bilecka, testimony in the Oral History Department, Institute of Contemporary Jewry, Hebrew University, Jerusalem, (47) 10.

15. Adolf A. Berman, "Goral Hayeladim Begetto Varsha" (The Fate of the Children in the Warsaw Ghetto), in Yisrael Gutman, ed., *Sho'at Yehudei Eropa* (The Holocaust of European Jews), Yad Vashem, Jerusalem, 1973.

16. Yisrael Gutman, "Janusz Korczak—Kavim Lidmuto" (Janusz Korczak's Personality), *Yalkut Moreshet*, no. 25, 1978, pp. 7–20.

17. Gutman, *Jews of Warsaw*, pp. 119–154.

18. The most detailed source for Transnistria will soon be Jean Ancel's monumental *Romania* (in Hebrew, but a short English version is planned), to be published in 2002 by Yad Vashem. See also Meir Teich, "Haminhal Hayehudi Begetto Shargorod" (The Jewish Administration in the Shargorod Ghetto), in *Yad Vashem Studies*, vol. 2, Yad Vashem, Jerusalem, 1958; Yeshurun Sharaga, "Ha'"Turantoria"—Mifal Ta'asiyati Yehudi Begetto Mogilev" (The "Turantoria"—A Jewish Industrial Enterprise in the Mogilev Ghetto), *Dapim Lecheker Tkufat Hasho'ah* (Research Contributions on the Holocaust Period), no. 5, Lohamei Getaot, 1987; Avigdor Shachan, "Gettaot Transnistria" (The Transnistrian Ghettos), Ph.D. diss., Hebrew University, 1981, published under the title *Hakfor Halohet* (The Sizzling Freeze), Kibbutz Meuchad, Tel Aviv, 1988.

19. Shachan, *Hakfor Halohet*, pp. 248–255, 265–269. See also Theodor Lavie,

Yahadut Romania Bema'avak al Hatzalata (Romanian Jewry in Its Struggle for Survival), Yad Vashem, Jerusalem, 1965; Chava Eshkoli, "Giluyei Ezrah Bekerev Yahadut Romania Basho'ah" (Aid Activities Among Romanian Jews During the Holocaust), *Gesher,* Winter 1997, pp. 83–99. But these references will become redundant with the appearance of Jean Ancel's book on Romania, mentioned above.

20. Gila Fatran, *Ha'im Ma'avak al Hissardut* (Was It a Struggle for Survival?), Moreshet, Tel Aviv, 1992, pp. 84–105.

21. Hillel J. Kieval, "Legality and Resistance in Vichy France: The Rescue of Jewish Children," *Proceedings of the American Philosophical Society,* vol. 125, no. 5, 1980, pp. 339–366; Debórah Dwórk, *Children with a Star,* Yale University Press, New Haven, 1991; Shlomo Kless, "The Rescue of Jewish Children During the Holocaust," *Holocaust and Genocide Studies,* vol. 3, no. 3, 1988, pp. 275–288; Jean Laloum, "L'UGIF et ses Maisons d'Enfants: Le Centre de Montreuil-sous-Bois," *Le Monde Juif,* vol. 116, October–December 1984, pp. 153–171; and Laloum, "Conference: Le Sauvetage des Enfants Juifs de 1940 a 1944," *Le Monde Juif,* vol. 137, January–March 1990, pp. 30–41; Nili Keren, "Hatzalat Hayeladim Hayehudim Betsarfat" (Rescue of Jewish Children in France), *Yalkut Moreshet,* no. 36, 1983, pp. 101–150. On amidah in France generally, see the now rather outdated article by Leon Poliakov, "Ha'amidah Hayehudit Bama'arav" (Jewish *Amidah* in the West), in Yisrael Gutman, ed., *Ha'amidah Hayehudit Bitkufat Hasho'ah* (Jewish *Amidah* During the Holocaust Era), Yad Vashem, Jerusalem, 1970.

22. Alain Michel, "Les Eclaireurs Israelites de France Pendant la Seconde Guerre Mondiale," M.A. thesis, Center de Recherche d'Histoire Sociale et Syndicale, University of Paris 1, 1982; Haim Avni, "The Zionist Underground in Holland and France and the Escape to Spain," in Yisrael Gutman and Efraim Zuroff, eds., *Rescue Attempts During the Holocaust,* Yad Vashem, Jerusalem, 1977; Lucien Lazare, *Rescue as Resistance,* Columbia University Press, New York, 1996; Ya'akov Ronen, "Tnu'ot Hano'ar Bemachteret Slovakia" (Youth Movements in the Underground in Slovakia), in Akiva Nir, ed., *Prakim Bekorot Sho'at Yahadut Slovakia* (Chapters in the History of Slovak Jewry's Holocaust), Moreshet, Giv'at Haviva, 1988; Avihu Ronen, *Hakrav al Hachayim* (The Battle for Life), Yad Ya'ari, Giv'at Haviva, 1994.

23. Jacob Presser, *The Destruction of the Dutch Jews,* Dutton, New York, 1969; Renée Poznansky, *Les Juifs en France Pendant la Seconde Guerre Mondiale,* Hachette, Paris, 1997; Louis de Jong, "Jews and Non-Jews in Nazi-

Occupied Holland," in Max Beloff, ed., *On the Tracks of Tyranny*, Valentine Mitchell, London, 1960.

24. Testimony of Chava Bin-Nun, Yad Vashem Archive, 03/3846.

25. Personal testimony of Joseph (Yossele) Rosensaft to me, 1974.

26. Hedi Fried, *Ressisei Chayim* (Fragments of a Life), translated from the Swedish, Eked, Tel Aviv, 1995, pp. 107–108. A great deal of similar material is available in a large number of sources. See Felicja Karay, *Death Comes in Yellow*, Harwood, Amsterdam, 1966; and Karay, *Pagazim Vecharuzim* (Shells and Verses), Moreshet, Tel Aviv, and Yad Vashem, Jerusalem, 1997, on the Hasag slave labor camps at Skarzysko-Kamienna and Leipzig and the efforts at cultural life that developed there.

27. Viktor Frankl, *Man's Search for Meaning*, Pocket Books, New York, 1973.

28. Poznansky, passim.

29. The literature about Terezin (Theresienstadt) is tremendous. Here only a few examples will be cited: Josef Polak and Karel Lagus, *Město za Mřížemi* (City Behind Bars), Naše Vojsko, Prague, 1964, esp. pp. 186–205; Frances G. Grossman, "The Art of the Children of Terezin," *Holocaust and Genocide Studies*, vol. 4, no. 2, 1989, pp. 213–230; Marketá Petrásová, *Theresienstadt in den Zeichnungen der Häftlinge, 1941–1945*, Staatliches Jüdisches Museum, Prague, 1983; Max Plaček, *Double Signature*, Yad Vashem, Jerusalem, 1994; Jarmila Skochová, "Theater im Konzentrationslager Theresienstadt," *Judaica Bohemiae*, vol. 19, no. 2, 1982, pp. 63–71; Josef Bor, *Requiem Theresienstadt* (Requiem for Theresienstadt), ed. Ruth Bondy, Moreshet, Tel Aviv, 1965; Ruth Bondy, ed., *Chayim Ke'ilu—Yoman Egon Redlich* (Pretended Life—the Diary of Egon Redlich), Kibbutz Meuchad, Tel Aviv, 1983; Nili Keren, *Ressissei Yaldut* (Fragments of Childhood), Kibbutz Meuchad, Tel Aviv, 1993; Nava Shan, "Lihyot Sachkanit Beteresienstadt" (To Be an Actress in Theresienstadt), *Yalkut Moreshet*, no. 43, 1987, pp. 95–108; Ruth Bondy, ed., *Kar'u Lo Chaver* (They Called Him "Comrade" [*Kamarad*—a children's wall newspaper in Terezin]), Yad Vashem, Jerusalem, 1998.

30. Raul Hilberg, "The Ghetto as a Form of Government: An Analysis of Isaiah Trunk's Judenrat," in Yehuda Bauer and Nathan Rotenstreich, eds., *The Holocaust as Historical Experience*, Holmes and Meier, New York, 1981, pp. 155–171 (the quotation is on p. 165; emphasis in the original); Hilberg, *The Destruction of the European Jews* (shortened version), Holmes and Meier, New York, 1985, pp. 293–305.

31. Aharon Weiss, "Jewish Leadership in Occupied Poland—Postures and Attitudes," in Yisrael Gutman, ed., *Yad Vashem Studies*, vol. 12, 1977, Yad

Vashem, Jerusalem, pp. 335–365; also, Weiss, "Ledarkam shel Hajuden-
ratim Bidrom-Mizrach Polin" (The Policies of the Judenräte in Southeast
Poland), *Yalkut Moreshet*, no. 15, 1972, pp. 59–122.

32. Yehuda Bauer, "Jewish Leadership Reactions to Nazi Policies," in Yehuda
Bauer and Nathan Rotenstreich, eds., *The Holocaust as Historical Experience*, Holmes and Meier, New York, 1981, pp. 173–192.

33. Hanna Arendt, *Eichmann in Jerusalem*, Viking Press, New York, 1961.

34. Weiss, "Jewish Leadership," pp. 363–364.

35. "Rumkowski's Address on September 4, 1942," in Yisrael Gutman, Yitzhak Arad, and Avraham Margaliot, eds., *Documents on the Holocaust*, Yad
Vashem, Jerusalem, 1981, pp. 283–284.

36. Job 42:10–15.

37. Yehuda Bauer, *A History of the Holocaust*, Franklin Watts, New York, 1982,
pp. 166–167. The history is based on Shalom Cholavsky, *Besufat Hakilayon*
(In the Storm of Destruction), Moreshet, Tel Aviv, 1988; Cholavsky,
"Minsk Bema'avaka Uvekhilyona"; and, chiefly, Hersh Smoliar, *Yehudim
Sovietiyim Me'achorei Gderot Hagetto* (Soviet Jews Behind the Ghetto
Fences), Sifriat Poalim and Tel Aviv University, Tel Aviv, 1984.

38. Dov Levin, "The Fighting Leadership in the Small Communities of Poland," in Yisrael Gutman and Cynthia J. Haft, eds., *Patterns of Jewish
Leadership in Nazi Europe, 1933–1945*, Yad Vashem, Jerusalem, 1977, pp.
133–150.

39. Avraham Tory, *The Kovno Ghetto Diary*, ed. Dina Porat, Harvard University Press, Cambridge, 1990; Zvi A. Bar-On and Dov Levin, *Toldoteha shel
Machteret* (History of an Underground), Yad Vashem, Jerusalem, 1962.

40. Meshulam Simcha, "Der Umkum fun Kossev" (The Demise of Kosów), in
G. Kressel and L. Olicki, eds., *Sefer Kosow* (The [Memorial] Book of
Kosów), Menorah, Tel Aviv, 1964: p. 290. A memoir published in 1998
contains the testimony of a member of the Judenrat, Jehoshua Gertner. It
mentions events that took place in April 1942 but has no reference that
might parallel Simcha's testimony, or for that matter contradict it: Jehoshua and Danek Gertner, *Der Untergang von Kosow und Zabie*, Wiener
Verlag, Vienna, 1998.

41. See Bauer, *Jewish Reactions to the Holocaust*; Bauer, *The Jewish Emergence
from Powerlessness*, Toronto University Press, Toronto, 1979, pp. 26–40;
Bauer, *History of the Holocaust*, pp. 245–278, and elsewhere.

42. Sixty-four ghettos, according to Shalom Cholavsky, *Al Naharot Haniemen
Vehadniepr* (On the Banks of the Niemen and the Dnieper), Moreshet, Tel
Aviv, 1982, pp. 333–337.

43. According to Shmuel Krakowski, *The War of the Doomed*, Holmes and Meier, New York, 1984, pp. 161–234.

44. Nechama Tec, "Women Among the Forest Partisans," in Dalia Ofer and Leonore J. Weizman, eds., *Women in the Holocaust*, Yale University Press, New Haven, 1998, pp. 223–233.

45. Adam Rayski, one of the main commanders of the MOI, is a good example. See Adam Rayski, *Zwischen Thora und Partei*, Herder, Freiburg, 1987; Rayski, "La Participation des Juifs à la Resistance," *La Lettre des Résistants et Deportées Juifs* (Paris), nos. 17–18, August 1944; Rayski, "Le Front Invisible—les Groupes de Résistance Juive Face à la Repression Policière," *Le Monde Juif*, no. 53, March 1969.

46. Juraj Spitzer, *Patřím k Vám*, Československý Spisovatel, Prague, 1964; and Fatran, pp. 244–249.

47. Arnold Hindls, *Einer Kehrte Zurück*, Deutsche Verlagsantalt, Stuttgart, 1965; Yitzhak Arad, "Jewish Prisoner Uprisings in the Treblinka and Sobibor Extermination Camps," in Yisrael Gutman, ed., *The Concentration Camps*, Yad Vashem, Jerusalem, 1980.

48. Jozef Garlinsky, *Fighting Auschwitz*, Friedman, Fontana, 1975; Lore Shelley, *The Union Kommando in Auschwitz*, Studies in the Shoah, vol. 12, University Press of America, Lanham, 1996; Filip Mueller, *Auschwitz Inferno*, Routledge and Kegan Paul, London, 1979, pp. 120–171.

49. Peled, p. 163. See also the testimony of Klara Wolf-Klein, *Opinia*, no. 33, Warsaw, April 19, 1948; testimonies (188)2—Simon Lustgarten, 7/2/1981; and (188)4—Rivka Liebeskind, 7/29/1982, all at the Institute of Contemporary Jewry, Hebrew University, Oral History Department.

Chapter Seven
Unarmed Resistance and Other Responses

1. Including myself, e.g., in my book *Jewish Reactions to the Holocaust*, Ministry of Defence, Tel Aviv, 1989, pp. 66–76, 138–149, and elsewhere.

2. Yisrael Gutman, *The Jews of Warsaw, 1939–1943*, Indiana University Press, Bloomington, 1982, pp. 204–211, 217, 237–240, and elsewhere.

3. Isiah Trunk, *Judenrat*, Macmillan, New York, 1972, pp. 90, 475–527.

4. Zvi A. Bar-On and Dov Levin, *Toldoteha shel Machteret* (History of an Underground), Yad Vashem, Jerusalem, 1962, pp. 97–107, 131–143, 188–200, 216–227, 352–355, and elsewhere.

5. Gutman, pp. 237–240.

6. Calek Perechodnik, *Am I a Murderer?* Westview Press, Boulder, Colo.,

1991. The book was edited to eliminate certain passages that describe negative behavior on the part of Polish neighbors and officials. I am grateful to Professor David Engel, who directed my attention to the original diary, which is deposited at Yad Vashem.

7. Gutman, pp. 85–90.

8. Trunk, p. 431, and elsewhere.

9. Gutman, pp. 90–94.

10. Details are in the article by Aharon Weiss, "Ha-13 begetto Warsha" (The Thirteen in the Warsaw Ghetto), *Yalkut Moreshet*, no. 21, June 1976, pp. 157–180. Gancwajch was born in 1904 in Czestochowa, had received rabbinical training, and had switched to left-wing Zionism. For a time he lived in Belgium, where he was active as a Zionist journalist. Then, in Vienna, where he lived until 1938, he wrote in the anti-fascist paper *Gerechtigkeit* (Justice), published by Irena Harand. Upon his return to Poland, he lived in Łódź, where he published a magazine, *Wolność* (Liberty), attacking antisemitism. From Łódź he moved to Warsaw, probably just before the Łódź ghetto was closed. In Warsaw he apparently contacted the S.D. as the brother-in-law of Moshe Merin, head of the Zagłębie Judenrat.

11. An example is the situation in Cracow: when the Germans sent 6,000 Cracow Jews to the Belzec death camp in June 1942, including the whole Judenrat, they nominated a man called David Gutter to be head of a new body called the Commissariat. He sent the ghetto police to hunt down resistance movement members and fully collaborated with the Gestapo. Typically, he was not a Cracow Jew but a refugee who had arrived in the city during the war and therefore had no roots in Cracow. Cf. Yitzhak Arad, "The Armed Jewish Resistance in Eastern Europe," in Michael Berenbaum and Abraham J. Peck, eds., *The Holocaust and History*, Indiana University Press, Bloomington, 1998, p. 598.

12. Livia Rothkirchen, "Czech and Slovak Wartime Jewish Leadership," in Abraham J. Peck and Michael Berenbaum, eds., *Holocaust and History*, Indiana University Press, 1998, p. 632. In France the emissaries were from Vienna: Israel Israelowicz and Wilhelm Biberstein; see my *American Jewry and the Holocaust*, Wayne State University Press, Detroit, Mich., 1981, p. 166.

13. Bundesarchiv Koblenz, Auswärtiges Amt, E234156; see also Werner-Otto von Hentig, *Mein Leben, eine Dienstreise*, Vendenhoek and Ruprecht, Göttingen, 1962.

14. Yad Vashem Archive (hereafter YVA), TR10/1142; Pinkas Hakehillot,

Brisk [Brest], p. 237; Zentralstelle Ludwigsburg, 204 AR 334/59. The area had been combed by Einsatzgruppe C. By October 1941, part of this group, Einsatzkommando 5, was stationed in Kiev and had sent an Aussenkommando (local command group) to Rowno, where in February 1942 a Dienststelle (service post) was organized under Obersturmbannführer Dr. Pütz. This became the Kommando der SIPO und S.D. Wolhynien. An Aussenstelle (local command post) of this Kommando was established at Brest, under S.S.-Sturmbannführer Ernst Berger. His *Judenreferent* was Paul Fischer, within Department IV (i.e., the Gestapo).

15. Moshe Smolar, *Ne'evakti Al Chayay* (I Struggled for My Life), Moreshet, Tel Aviv, 1978, pp. 63–64. The other testimonies quoted agree on the sorry role the Ordnungsdienst played; see, e.g., Roman Levin, *Mal'chik iz getto* (A Child from the Ghetto), Rossiskaya Biblioteka Kholokosta, Moscow, 1996, pp. 23, 30.

16. Smolar, p. 68. If this was really a Catholic priest, he was Polish. If he was a Catholic Uniate, he was Belorussian.

17. Zentralstelle Ludwigsburg, 204 AR 334/59: "*Anspruch auf Brot, das zudem nur grammweise zugeteilt wurde, hatten nur arbeitsfähige Personen. Der Rest . . . war dem Hungertod ausgeliefert.*" For the first quotation, see Smolar, p. 66.

18. Sheindel Ginsburg, YVA, 03/8236.

19. For much of what is in this and the next paragraph, see Smolar; and two testimonies, those of Sheindel Winograd (YVA, 03/8236) and Michael Omlinsky (YVA, 03/3637). See also Sheindel Winograd, "In di Teg fun Churbn" (During the Days of Destruction), in Eliezer Sheinman, ed., *Brisk-DeLitta* (Memorial Book of Brest-Litovsk), Enzyklopedia shel Galuyot, Jerusalem, 1955, pp. 571–582; Bertha Charlash-Bronstein, "Di ershte Groyel-Teg" (The First Days of Horror), in ibid., pp. 585–590; and L. Gluzman, "Zichroines fun an Entlofenen fun Brisk" (Memoirs of a Refugee from Brisk [Brest]), in ibid., pp. 549–572. Methodologically, some of these testimonies are fascinating. Smolar published his book in 1978. Omlinsky gave his testimony to Yad Vashem in 1969; he did not know Smolar, nor did Smolar know of him. Omlinsky thought that there was a woman survivor "somewhere in Natanya." Winograd, a citizen of Natanya, gave her testimony in 1995, and by that time Omlinsky had died. Clearly, the three individuals did not influence each other's testimony. They converge on the main issues: the existence of the underground and its armament, organization, and plans. There is a slight divergence regarding the reason why it failed (see in the text) and a wide divergence in

small details—the length of the stay in the bunkers and the like. Without these testimonies we would know nothing. With them, and because of their convergence, we have an inkling. On the resistance group, see also Levin, pp. 23–24. Gluzman has the story of one Asher Sheinwald, who claimed that he and another man had overpowered and killed a German and a Polish gendarme on the road between Brest and Kobryn (p. 562); no date is given.

20. Deuerlein monthly report, 10/31/42, Bundesarchiv, Koblenz, R94/7. "*In dem Stadtgebiet werden täglich ca. 70–80 bei der Bergung der jüdischen Sachen in dem jüdischen Stadtviertel aufgefunden. Dieselben werden der Polizei zur Verfügung gestellt.*"

21. The postwar German investigation (1965) was met with stonewalling by the surviving German murderers. However, the testimony of Dr. Oswald Cornelissen, a German medical student stationed at the Brest hospital, confirms the testimonies quoted above in the details of the murder in the ghetto, on 128 Dluga Street (cf. Zentralstelle Ludwigsburg, 204 AR 334/59).

22. Franz Burat was the mayor (*Kommissar*) of the town and area from September 1942 on. He had been the mayor of a small east Prussian town before the war. The gendarmerie for Volhynia had its seat at Luzk and was commanded by Walter Rohse. The Bezirk Order Police (ORPO) was commanded, also from Luzk, by Willi Dressler. None of these or any other of the murderers, direct or indirect, were brought to justice after the war.

23. I wrote this before the publication of Ulrich Herbert, ed., *Nationalsozialistischer Vernichtungskrieg* (Fischer, Frankfurt, 1998), which proves this thesis thoroughly. I arrived at the same conclusion on the basis of an eclectic and localistic approach drawing mainly on Jewish materials. Christian Gerlach, in his *Kalkulierte Morde* (Calculated Murders), Hamburger Edition, Hamburg, 1999, which also appeared after this chapter was written, argues that the murder of Jews in what is now Belarus occurred as part of the German intent to starve up to 30 million local inhabitants to death. Jews were an obvious target because of the preexisting racist antisemitism.

24. See Gluzman.

25. Bundesarchiv, R94/7, copy at YVA, M. 29/154 (14245). "*Im ganzen sollen bis jetzt etwa 20,000 Juden umgesiedelt worden sein*" (11/8/42).

26. Smolar, pp. 90–105, and elsewhere. Kuryanovich was recognized by Yad Vashem as "Righteous Among the Nations."

27. Leah Ben-Chorin, YVA, 03/6485; and Brachah Bentor, "Bizehut Mush'elet—Eduta shel Leah Ben-Chorin" (With a Borrowed Identity—The Testimony of Leah Ben-Chorin), *Yalkut Moreshet*, no. 46, April 1989, pp. 175–196.

28. The information about Polenia Golovchenko is in a very important documentary film made by Ilya Altman and Elena Yakovich called *Brestskoye Getto* (1995). The film contains testimonies of three survivors.

29. E.g., Marisha Popowska and an unnamed mistress of a Polish engineer by the name of Tadeusz Brzezinski, both mentioned in Gluzman. On the other hand, Gluzman relates the story of the brutal mass murder of elderly Jewish men by German and Polish railway workers at the beginning of the German occupation.

30. Marian Klinowsky, testimony, YVA, 03/3434.

31. Altman and Yakovich's documentary film, *Brestskoye Getto*, says that there were 16,934 people in the ghetto. No exact source is given, but the implication is that the precise figure came from material in the municipal archive of Brest.

32. Asher Zisman, "Blettlech fun Tog-Buch" (Pages from a Diary), in Eliezer Sheinman, ed., *Brisk-DeLitta*, Enzyklopedia shel Galuyot, Jerusalem, 1955, pp. 595–596.

33. Winograd; my translation from the Yiddish.

34. Recently my colleague Dan Michman argued that the Judenrat, a group imposed upon the Jews under the Nazis, cannot be considered a leadership group. I cannot accept this argument, not only because most of the Judenräte of the first instance were a direct continuation of Jewish leadership groups from before the war, but also because in all essentials they fulfilled the functions of leadership and representation in their communities, even though they had been nominated by an enemy.

35. Michael Omlinsky, YVA, 03/3637: *"Mir zennen nachgeloifen di autos, hobn di Yekkes geshrien: Wohin laufen Sie? Zurück, zurück!"*

36. Ibid.: *"Der ganzer getto hot genummen redn un shreien az men soll es nisht ton, men soll nisht stelln kein Widerstand"* (The whole ghetto began to talk and argue that one should not do it, one should not engage in resistance).

37. I am grateful to Dr. Jean Ancel for telling me this story; see his forthcoming major volume on Romanian Jewry during the Holocaust. See also his "Antonescu and the Jews," in Michael Berenbaum and Abraham J. Peck, eds., *The Holocaust and History*, Indiana University Press, Bloomington, 1998, pp. 463–479.

Chapter Eight
The Problem of Gender: The Case of Gisi Fleischmann

1. For details, see Yehuda Slutzky, ed., *Sefer Toldot Hahaganah*, Ministry of Defence, Tel Aviv, 1961–1963, vols. 1–3, passim. Mania Shochat was one of the founders of the armed Jewish underground in Palestine, as was Rachel Yannait-Ben Zvi, who was later the wife of the second president of Israel and an important author and educator in her own right. Rachel Katznelson was a writer and a political leader. Beba Idelson was an outstanding labor leader—as was, of course, Golda Meir.

2. See Sandra F. Kadosh, *Ideology Versus Reality: Youth Aliyah and the Rescue of Jewish Children During the Holocaust Era, 1933–1945*, Columbia University Press, New York, 1995, passim.

3. See Yehuda Bauer, *American Jewry and the Holocaust*, Wayne State University Press, Detroit, Mich., 1981, pp. 273–276.

4. For details regarding Germany, see, e.g., Wolfgang Benz, *Die Juden in Deutschland*, C. H. Beck, Munich, 1988.

5. Livia Rothkirchen, "The Jews of Bohemia and Moravia, 1938–1845," in Avigdor Dagan, ed., *The Jews of Czechoslovakia*, vol. 3, Jewish Publication Society, Philadelphia, 1984.

6. Jeffrey Herf, *Reactionary Modernism*, Cambridge University Press, New York, 1984.

7. See Gisela Bock, "Ordinary Women in Nazi Germany," in Dalia Ofer and Leonore J. Weitzman, eds., *Women in the Holocaust*, Yale University Press, New Haven, 1998.

8. Felicja Karay, *Death Comes in Yellow*, Harwood, Amsterdam, 1996.

9. Joseph Kermish, "Daily Entries of Hersh Wasser," in *Yad Vashem Studies*, vol. 15, Yad Vashem, Jerusalem, 1983, pp. 201–282.

10. Yisrael Gutman, *The Jews of Warsaw, 1939–1943*, Indiana University Press, Bloomington, 1982.

11. Rivka Perlis, *Tnuot Hanoar Hachalutziot bePolin Hakvusha* (Pioneering Youth Movements in Occupied Poland), Kibbutz Meuchad, Ghetto Fighters Kibbutz, 1987, passim; Yael Peled, *Krakow Hayehudit, 1939–1945* (Jewish Cracow, 1939–1945), Kibbutz Meuchad-Massuah, Tel Aviv, 1993.

12. Yitzhak Arad, *Ghetto in Flames*, Yad Vashem, Jerusalem, 1980.

13. Vladka Meed, *On Both Sides of the Wall*, Holocaust Library, New York, 1979.

14. Gisi Fleischmann's life has been the subject of a number of studies. Promi-

nent among them is Joan Campion, *In the Lion's Mouth*, United Press of America, Lanham, Md., 1987; and Hannah Yablonka, "Gisi Fleischmann" (Hebrew), in Akiva Nir, ed., *Prakim Bekorot Shoat Yahadut Slovakia* (Chapters in the History of the Holocaust of Slovak Jewry), Moreshet, Givat Haviva, 1984, pp. 103-108.

15. Bauer, esp. pp. 356-379.

16. Dalia Ofer and Hannah Weiner, *Dead End Journey*, United Press of America, Lanham, Md., 1996; Dalia Ofer, "The Rescue of European Jewry and Illegal Immigration to Palestine," in Michael R. Marrus, ed., *The Nazi Holocaust*, vol. 9, Meckler, London, 1989, pp. 199-222.

17. Bauer, *Jews for Sale?* Yale University Press, New Haven, 1994.

18. Livia Rothkirchen, *Churban Yahadut Slovakia* (The Destruction of Slovak Jewry), Yad Vashem, Jerusalem, 1961.

19. Oskar Neumann, *Im Schatten des Todes*, Olamenu, Tel Aviv, 1956; Yaakov Ronen, "Tnuot Hanoar Bamachteret beSlovakia" (Youth Movements in the Underground in Slovakia), in Akiva Nir, ed., *Prakim Bekorot Shoat Yahadut Slovakia*, Moreshet, Givat Haviva, 1984.

20. Gila Fatran, *Ha'im Ma'avak al Hissardut?* (Was It a Struggle for Survival?), Moreshet, Tel Aviv, 1992. Much of the material on Gisi Fleischmann in this chapter comes from Fatran's book.

21. Bauer, *Jews For Sale?* pp. 62-101.

22. John S. Conway, "Frühe Augenzeugenberichte aus Auschwitz: Glaubenswürdigkeit und Wirkungsgeschichte," *Vierteljahresehfte für Zeitgeschichte*, vol. 2, 1979, pp. 260-284; and Conway, "Der Holocaust in Ungarn," *Vierteljahresehfte für Zeitgeschichte*, vol. 2, 1984, pp. 179-212.

23. See Michael Dov-Ber Weissmandel, *Min Hametzar*, Emunah, New York, 1960; and Bauer, *Jews for Sale?* passim.

24. Fatran, pp. 247-261.

Chapter Nine
Theology, or God the Surgeon

1. I am here relying on the brilliant analysis of ultraorthodox thinking about the Holocaust by Eliezer Schweid, *Bein Khurban L'yeshu'ah* (From Ruin to Salvation), Kibbutz Meuchad, Tel Aviv, 1994.

2. I am indebted to Professor Avi Sagi (Bar Ilan University) and his penetrating analysis of the problem at a conference at Yad Vashem, January 9, 1999.

3. See Martin Buber, *Pnei Adam* (The Face of Man), Mosad Bialik, Jerusalem, 1966, pp. 221–321; Eliezer Berkovits, *Faith After the Holocaust*, Ktav, New York, 1973, passim; Emil Fackenheim, *Quest of the Past and Present*, Beacon, Boston, 1970, pp. 229–243; Norman Lamm, "The Face of God," New York, May 1986 (address delivered to students of Yeshiva College and Stern College for Women). See also Pinhas Pel'i, "Be-khippus akhar lashon datit la-Shoah" (In Search of a Religious Language for the Holocaust), *Meassef Yerushalayim*, vol. 11–12, 1977, pp. 105–125. For haredi works, see Schweid.

4. Irving Greenberg, "History, Holocaust and Covenant," *Holocaust and Genocide Studies*, vol. 5, no. 1, 1990, pp. 1–12.

5. Greenberg presented these views at an international conference at Yad Vashem on January 7, 1999.

6. Among the rabbis voicing this view are Yoel Teitelboym, *Vayoel Moshe* (Moshe Acquiesced [a wordplay on the author's name]), S. Deutsch, New York, 1961; Nisson Woltin and Yitzchok Hutner, *A Path Through the Ashes*, Mesorah Publications, Brooklyn, N.Y., 1986; Hayim Ozer Grodzinski, *Shut Ahiezer* (The Responsa of Ahiezer [another wordplay on the author's name]), Sh. P. Garber, Vilna, 1939; Elhanan Wasserman, *Ikveta Di'-Meshikha* (The Footprints of the Messiah), Netzach, Tel Aviv, 1942; Menachem Hartom, "Hirhurim al haShoah" (Reflections on the Holocaust), *Deot* (Jerusalem), no. 18, 1961–1962, pp. 28–31. Pinhas Pel'i remarks that any attempt at theodicy is problematic because by justifying God's actions one implicitly accuses the people of Israel, and "our humility in regard to the victims of the Shoah hinders us from easily accepting such a conclusion" (Pel'i, p. 108). For a detailed analysis of some of these and other texts, see Schweid.

7. Immanuel Jacobovits, "Some Personal, Theological and Religious Responses to the Holocaust," *Holocaust and Genocide Studies*, vol. 3, no. 4, 1990, pp. 373–376.

8. Kalman Klonymus Shapira, *Esh Kodesh* (Holy Fire), Piasecina Hassidim, Jerusalem, 1960. Cf. Schweid, pp. 105–154.

9. Shneersohn's letter is in the possession of Grossman's widower, Meir Orkin, who lives in Kibbutz Evron, near Nahariya. A copy is in my possession.

10. Schweid, pp. 39–64.

11. See Efraim Zuroff, "Attempts to Obtain Shanghai Permits in 1941," in *Yad Vashem Studies*, vol. 13, Yad Vashem, Jerusalem, 1979, pp. 321–352.

Chapter Ten
Rescue Attempts: The Case of the Auschwitz Protocols

1. This chapter is based on, but is not identical with, my article "Anmerkungen zum 'Auschwitz-Bericht' von Rudolf Vrba," *Vierteljahreshefte für Zeitgeschichte*, vol. 45, no. 2, 1997, pp. 297–307.

2. There is a wealth of literature on the subject, e.g., Dalia Ofer, *Escaping the Holocaust*, Oxford University Press, New York, 1990; Ofer, "The Yishuv and the Jews in Europe, 1939–1945," in Jonathan Frankel, ed., *Studies in Contemporary Jewry*, vol. 7, Oxford University Press, New York, 1991, pp. 217–296; Ofer, "The Rescue of European Jewry and Illegal Immigration to Palestine," in Michael R. Marrus, ed., *The Nazi Holocaust*, vol. 9, Meckler, Westport, Conn, 1989, pp. 159–189; Dina Porat, *The Blue and Yellow Star of David*, Harvard University Press, Cambridge, 1990, passim; Martin Gilbert, "British Government Policy Towards Jewish Refugees (November 1937–September 1939)," in *Yad Vashem Studies*, no. 13, Yad Vashem, Jerusalem, 1979, pp. 127–168; Ronald W. Zweig, *Britain and Palestine During the Second World War*, Royal Historical Society, London, 1986, passim; Michael J. Cohen, "The British White Paper on Palestine, May, 1939: Part II, The Testing of a Policy, 1942–1945," *Historical Journal*, vol. 19, no. 3, 1976, pp. 727–758; and Yehuda Bauer, *From Diplomacy to Resistance*, Jewish Publication Society, Philadelphia, 1970.

3. Dina Porat, "The Story of 29,000 Immigration Certificates for Children," *Jerusalem Quarterly*, no. 47, 1988, pp. 108–130; Tuvia Friling, *Chetz Ba'arafel* (An Arrow in the Mist), Center for Ben Gurion's Legacy, Sdeh Boker, 1998, pp. 211–234.

4. Bernard Wasserstein, *Britain and the Jews of Europe*, Clarendon, Oxford, 1970, p. 17; Michael J. Cohen, *Retreat from the Mandate*, Paul Elek, London, 1978, pp. 151–175.

5. Lukasz Hirszowicz, *The Third Reich and the Middle East*, Routledge and Kegan Paul, London, 1966, passim.

6. Hirszowicz, pp. 112–172.

7. Hirszowicz, pp. 204, 218–221, 312.

8. David A. Charters, *The British Army and Jewish Insurgency in Palestine, 1945–1947*, St. Martin's Press, London, 1989; Bruce Hoffman, *The Failure of British Military Strategy Within Palestine*, Bar Ilan University Press, Tel Aviv, 1983.

9. Friling, passim; and Porat, *Blue and Yellow Star of David*, passim.

10. Ofer, *Escaping the Holocaust*, pp. 319–320. Between the outbreak of war and the end of 1944, the number of Jews who reached Palestine was 49,410 (out of the 75,000 permitted by the 1939 White Paper). Between January and May 1945 another 3,000 immigration certificates were issued by the British, but many of the recipients may have come after the war ended.

11. Richard Breitman, *Official Secrets*, Hill and Wang, New York, 1998, p. 96.

12. Michael Wildt et al., eds., *Himmler's Terminkalender für 1941 / 1942*, Christians, Hamburg, 1999, esp. the introduction; see also Ulrich Herbert, ed., *Nationalsozialistische Vernichtungspolitik*, Fischer, Frankfurt, 1998, passim.

13. Breitman, p. 93.

14. Breitman, pp. 100–101.

15. Alfred A. Häsler, *Das Boot ist Voll*, Ex Libris, Zurich, 1967, pp. 84–87; Jacques Picard, *Die Schweiz und die Juden*, Chronos, Zurich, 1994, pp. 407–408, quoting Peter Hufschmid, "Schweizer Ärzte unter dem Hakenkreuz," *Das Magazin* (Zurich) 13, 1990; Franz Bucher, *Zwischen Verrat und Menschlichkeit*, Huber, Frauenfeld, 1967; and an unpublished thesis by Gaston Haas, "Wenn man gewusst hätte . . . ," University of Zurich, 1988.

16. Yehuda Bauer, *When Did They Know?* Midstream, New York, April 1968.

17. The text is in Arthur D. Morse, *While Six Million Died*, Random House, New York, 1967, p. 8.

18. Breitman, pp. 180–181.

19. Breitman, p. 157.

20. Breitman, p. 116.

21. Breitman, pp. 116–117, quoting David Engel, *Facing the Holocaust*, University of North Carolina Press, Chapel Hill, 1993, p. 23. Engel's other important book on the subject, *In the Shadow of Auschwitz*, University of North Carolina Press, Chapel Hill, 1987, is also mentioned in this connection.

22. Breitman, p. 120.

23. Breitman, p. 119.

24. Deborah E. Lipstadt, *Beyond Belief*, Free Press, New York, 1986.

25. Yehuda Bauer, *Jews for Sale?* Yale University Press, New Haven, 1994.

26. U.S. Military History Institute, Carlisle Barracks, Md., Box 90C: There were 822,000 licensed radios in Hungary in March 1943, of which 88 percent were capable of picking up foreign programs; 43.7 percent of the listeners did tune in to foreign programs.

27. Avihu Ronen, "Moetzet Hashomer Hatzair beNové Mesto" (The Meeting of Hashomer Hatzair at Nové Mesto), *Yalkut Moreshet*, no. 50, 1991, pp.

137–158; Ronen, *Hakrav al Hachayim* (The Battle for Life), Yad Yaari, Giv'at Haviva, 1994, passim.

28. Vrba thought that 1.75 million people had been killed (it is not clear whether he was talking only of Jews, or of the overall death toll); see Rudolf Vrba, "Die missachtete Warnung. Betrachtungen über den Auschwitz-Bericht, 1944," *Vierteljahreshefte fur Zeitgeschichte*, vol. 44, no. 1, January 1996, pp. 1–24. We now know that the figure was somewhere between 1 million and 1.25 million, of whom over 90 percent were Jews.

29. Vrba. For my response, see above, note 1.

30. Vrba, p. 17.

31. Vrba, p. 13.

32. Fatran, pp. 230–238. Gila Fatran quotes from three depositions by Krasniansky: one in the Oral History Department of the Institute of Contemporary Jewry, Hebrew University, (65) 1; a second at the Yad Vashem Archive, 03/3366; and a third in Randolph L. Braham, *The Politics of Genocide*, Columbia University Press, New York, 1981, p. 711.

33. Hansi Brand, in a deposition on April 27, 1996, to Mrs. Sari Reuveni, of Yad Vashem.

34. Martin Gilbert, *Auschwitz and the Allies*, Henry Holt, New York, 1981, p. 204. Gilbert ties a visit by Kastner to Bratislava to a meeting between Brand and Eichmann in Budapest on April 25, but it is hard to see a necessary connection.

35. Hava Baruch, "Haprotokolim shel Auschwitz be'Hungaria" (The Auschwitz protocols in Hungary), seminar paper at the Institute of Contemporary Jewry, Hebrew University, 1996; Rudolf Kastner, *Der Kastner-Bericht über Eichmanns Menschenhandel in Ungarn*, ed. Ernest Landau, Munich, 1961, pp. 57, 88; Braham, p. 711.

36. Braham, p. 711.

37. Baruch, passim.

38. Sandor Szenes, *Befejezetlen Mult*, Pecsi Szirka Nyomda, Budapest, 1986, pp. 53–58.

39. Vrba erroneously dates it May 22. See Weissmandel's *Min Hametzar*, Emunah, New York, 1960, p. 103, which Vrba apparently did not read, possibly because of language difficulties.

40. Yehuda Bauer, *American Jewry and the Holocaust*, Wayne State University Press, Detroit, Mich., 1981, p. 397; and Gilbert, *Auschwitz and the Allies*, p. 209.

41. Henryk Swiebocki, "Osvětímská Zpráva Alfreda Wetzlera a Rudolfa Vrby," in Miroslav Kárný, ed., *Terezínský Rodinný Tábor v Osvětími-Birke-*

nau-Sborník z mezinárodní konference, Praha, 7–8 března 1994, Terezínská Iniciativa, Prague, 1994, p. 109.

42. Jenö Levai, *Abscheu und Grauen vor dem Genocid in aller Welt,* Living Books, Toronto, 1968, pp. 31 ff.

43. Braham, p. 711; Levai, passim.

44. Vrba, passim. See also a book written on the basis of his testimony: Rudolf Vrba and Alan Bestic, *I Cannot Forgive,* Sidgwick and Jackson, London, 1963, passim.

45. Asher Cohen, *Hamachteret Hachalutzit be'Hungaria* (The Pioneering Underground in Hungary), Hakkibutz Hameuchad, Tel Aviv, 1984, pp. 102 ff.

46. Weissmandel, p. 117. He quotes from the letter from memory: "They should hide, rebel, flee, but refuse to go into the ghetto—and if they are already there, they should break down the fences—and if they murder them, the number killed will most certainly be smaller than if they do not [do what Weissmandel recommended]." Weissmandel died in 1960, before his book was published. He recollected that he had sent a man, whose name he could no longer remember, to Ungvar with the letter. The man survived, and he surfaced in the 1960s after the story appeared in Weissmandel's book. His name was Menachem Feldman, and he testified that he took one hundred copies of the letter, written in rabbinical Hebrew, from the Bratislava Judenrat (i.e., the Working Group) so he could distribute it among as many communities as possible. When he went to Ungvar, the Judenrat members said, "It is better that they die without prior knowledge than that they should know. It is in any case impossible to help them. Why should we make them crazy by telling them where they were being led?" This stands in apparent contradiction to the documented story about Laszlo, but there may be no contradiction: Laszlo was naive enough to go to the Gestapo, whereas others took the same view as Rabbi Leo Baeck did in Theresienstadt when he refused to spread the knowledge in the ghetto about where the transports to the East were going. However, some families who did hear the news took the warning to heart and escaped into neighboring Slovakia or into the Carpathian Mountains. The details about Feldman and the reconstruction of the letter can be found in Dov Dinur, "Kehillat Uzhorod," M.A. thesis, Institute of Contemporary Jewry, Hebrew University, 1985, pp. 250 ff. It is worth adding that Jews in Ungvar were also warned by students of the Hebrew High School in town. The students did not know anything about Auschwitz but were fully aware of the mass murders in Poland. If they were, weren't others?

47. Braham, p. 714. The intervention of the Pope came on June 25, Roosevelt's warning on the 26th, King Gustav's letter on the 30th.

48. Randolph L. Braham, *The Destruction of Hungarian Jewry: A Documentary Record*, World Federation of Hungarian Jews, New York, 1963, pp. 419, 430, for two messages by Veesenmayer to the *Auswärtiges Amt*, July 6 and 7, 1944, reporting on his conversations with Horthy.

49. Gilbert, *Auschwitz and the Allies*, pp. 204 f.; Tom Segev, *The Seventh Million*, Wang and Hill, New York, 1993, passim.

50. Bauer, *Jews for Sale*, pp. 145–171.

51. Amos Elon, *Timetable*, Doubleday, New York, 1980.

52. In late January 1999, the Chief Sephardi Rabbi of Israel, Eliyahu Bakshi-Doron, stated publicly that what the Reform Jews had done to the Jewish people was worse than what had happened to the Jews during the Holocaust. In most other countries such a spokesman would have been put on trial for antisemitism and racial incitement. In Israel he continues to hold a position of moral authority.

Chapter Eleven
From the Holocaust to the State of Israel

1. This chapter is based on, but is not identical with, a lecture given at the Washington Holocaust Memorial Museum in November 1998. In it I summarize secondary literature based on primary sources, including works written by myself.

2. The literature on the period 1945–1948 is immense. I can mention only a few secondary sources used for this particular overview, including some of my own writings, which were based on primary sources: Yisrael Gutman and Avital Saf, eds., *She'erit Hapletah*, Proceedings of a conference held at Yad Vashem in October 1985, Yad Vashem, Jerusalem, 1990; Michael J. Cohen, *From Mandate to Independence*, Frank Cass, London, 1988; Arieh J. Kochavi, *Akurim uFolitika Beinleumit* (D.P.s and International Politics), Am Oved, Tel Aviv, 1992; Kochavi, "Britain and the Illegal Immigration to Palestine from France Following World War II," *Holocaust and Genocide Studies*, vol. 6, no. 4, 1991, pp. 383–396; Leonard Dinnerstein, *America and the Survivors of the Holocaust*, Columbia University Press, New York, 1982; Dinnerstein, *The United States and the DPs*, Yad Vashem, Jerusalem 1990; Irit Keinan, *Lo Nirga Hara'av* (The Hunger Was Not Stilled), Am Oved, Tel Aviv, 1996; Idit Zertal, *Zehavam shel Hayehudim* (The Gold of the

Jews), Am Oved, Tel Aviv, 1996; Gavriel Shefer, "Shikulim Politiim bi-Kviat Mediniut Britania biShe'elat Hagirat Yehudim leEretz Yisrael" (Political Considerations in the Determination of British Policies Toward Illegal Immigrants to Palestine), *Hatzionut*, no. 5, 1989, pp. 221–226.

3. For my own interpretation, see Yehuda Bauer, *Flight and Rescue*, Random House, New York, 1970.

4. Ilan Pappe, *The Making of the Arab-Israeli Conflict, 1947–1951*, I. B. Tauris, London, 1992; Ilan Pappe et al., "She'erit Hapletah Vehakamat Ham'dinah" (The She'erith Hapletah and the Establishment of the State), proceedings of a symposium, *Yalkut Moreshet*, no. 65, 1998, pp. 11–45; Rochelle Fuerstenberg, *Post-Zionism, the Challenge to Israel*, American Jewish Committee and Bar Ilan University, Tel Aviv, 1997.

5. See Cohen; and Bauer.

6. Yehuda Bauer, *Out of the Ashes*, Pergamon, Oxford, 1989; Abraham S. Hyman, *The Undefeated*, Gefen, Jerusalem, 1993. On the chaplains mentioned above, see Alex Grobman, *Rekindling the Flame*, Wayne State University Press, Detroit, Mich., 1993; on the death marches, see Yehuda Bauer, "The Death Marches," in Michael R. Marrus, ed., *The Nazi Holocaust*, Meckler, Westport, Conn., 1989, pp. 497–511; and Shmuel Krakowski, "Bemitz'ad Hamavet" (In the Death March), *Yalkut Moreshet*, no. 31, 1994, pp. 133–176; on the Palestine mission to the D.P. camps, see Hayim Yahil, "Hamishlachat Ha'eretzyisraelit Leshe'erit Hapletah" (The Palestinian Mission to the She'erit Hapletah), *Yalkut Moreshet*, no. 31, 1981, pp. 133–176.

7. Yosef Grudzinski, *Chomer Enoshi Tov* (Good Human Material), Hed Artzi, Tel Aviv, 1998. The facts, pace Grudzinski, are presented, e.g., by Yakov Markovitsky, *Gachelet Lochemet* (The Fighting Ember), Ministry of Defence, Tel Aviv, 1995.

8. Bauer, *Flight and Rescue*; and Bauer, *Out of the Ashes*.

9. Bauer, *Flight and Rescue*; and Bauer, *Out of the Ashes*; Dinnerstein, *America and the Survivors*; Grobman; Hyman.

10. Dinnerstein, *America and the Survivors*; Dinnerstein, *The United States and the DPs*.

11. Kochavi, "Britain and the Illegal Immigration to Palestine."

12. On the Brichah, see Bauer, *Flight and Rescue*. On the Brichah and the attitude of the Polish government, see Yitzhak Zuckerman, *A Surplus of Memory*, University of California Press, Berkeley, 1993. On the Jews in Poland after the war, see Yisrael Gutman, *Hayehudim BePolin Acharei Milchemet Ha'olam Hashniyah* (The Jews in Poland After World War II),

Shazar, Jerusalem, 1985; and David J. Engel, *Patterns of Anti-Jewish Violence in Poland, 1944–1946,* Yad Vashem, Jerusalem, 1998; see also Engel, *The Reconstruction of Jewish Communal Institutions in Postwar Poland,* American Council of Learned Societies, New York, 1996. On the Czechs, see Marie Bulinová, Jiří Dufek, and Karel Kaplan, eds., *Československo a Izrael 1945–1956, Ústav pro soudobé dějiny,* Doplňek, Prague, 1993.
13. Anita Shapira, "Historiografia Vezikaron: Mikre Latrun," *Alpayim* (University of Tel Aviv), no. 10, 1994, pp. 3–41.

bibliography

Adam, Dietrich Uwe. *Die Judenpolitik im Dritten Reich.* Droste, Düsseldorf, 1972.

Alexander, Edward. *The Resonance of Dust.* Ohio State University Press, Columbus, 1979.

Allen, William Sheridan. *The Nazi Seizure of Power.* Franklin Watts, New York, 1965.

Aly, Goetz. *Endlösung.* Fischer, Frankfurt, 1995.

Aly, Goetz, and Heim, Suzanne. *Vordenker der Vernichtung.* Hoffmann und Campe, Hamburg, 1991.

Aly, Goetz, and Roth, Heinz. *Die Restlose Erfassung.* Berlin, 1984.

Arad, Yitzhak. *Ghetto in Flames.* Yad Vashem, Jerusalem, 1980.

Balinová, Marie, et al. *Československo a Izrael, 1945–1956.* Doplňek, Prague, 1993.

Bankier, David. *The Germans and the Final Solution.* Blackwell, Oxford, 1992.

Bardakjian, Kevork B. *Hitler and the Armenian Genocide.* Zoryan Institute, Cambridge, Mass., 1985.

Bar-On, Zvi, and Levin, Dov. *Toldoteha shel Machteret.* Yad Vashem, Jerusalem, 1962.

Bartov, Omer. *The Eastern Front, 1941–1945.* Macmillan, London, 1985.

———. *Hitler's Army.* Oxford University Press, New York, 1992.

Bauer, Yehuda. *Diplomacy and Resistance*. Jewish Publication Society, Philadelphia, 1970.

——. *Flight and Rescue*. Random House, New York, 1970.

——. *The Holocaust in Historical Perspective*. University of Washington, Seattle, 1978.

——. *The Jewish Emergence from Powerlessness*. University of Toronto Press, Toronto, 1979.

——. *American Jewry and the Holocaust*. Wayne State University Press, Detroit, 1981.

——. *Jewish Reactions to the Holocaust*. Ministry of Defence Books, Tel Aviv, 1989.

——. *Out of the Ashes*. Pergamon, Oxford, 1989.

——. *Jews for Sale?* Yale University Press, New Haven, 1994.

Bauer, Yehuda, and Rotenstreich, Nathan, eds. *The Holocaust as Historical Experience*. Holmes and Meier, New York, 1981.

Bauman, Zygmunt. *Modernity and the Holocaust*. Polity Press, Cambridge, U.K., 1989.

Beloff, Max, ed. *On the Tracks of Tyranny*. Valentine Mitchell, London, 1960.

Bender, Sara. *Mul Mavet Orev*. Am Oved, Tel Aviv, 1997.

Benshalom, Raffi. *Ne'evaknu Lema'an Hachayim*. Moreshet, Tel Aviv, 1977.

Benz, Wolfgang. *Die Juden in Deutschland, 1933–1945*. C. H. Beck, Munich, 1988.

Berenbaum, Michael, and Peck, Abraham J. *The Holocaust in History*. Indiana University Press, Bloomington, 1998.

Berkovitz, Eliezer. *Faith After the Holocaust*. Ktav, New York, 1973.

Bondy, Ruth. *Chayim Keilu—Yoman Egon Redlich*. Kibbutz Meuchad, Tel Aviv, 1993.

——. *Kar'u Lo Chaver*. Yad Vashem, Jerusalem, 1998.

Bor, Josef. *Requiem Theresienstadt*. Moreshet, Tel Aviv, 1965.

Braham, Randolph L. *The Destruction of Hungarian Jewry, a Documentary Record*. World Federation of Hungarian Jews, New York, 1963.

Breitman, Richard. *Official Secrets*. Hill and Wang, New York, 1998.

Brenner, Lieber. *Widerstand un Umkum in Czenstochower Getto*. Jewish Historical Institute, Warsaw, 1984.

Browning, Christopher R. *Ordinary Men*. HarperCollins, New York, 1992.

——. *The Path to Genocide*. Cambridge University Press, Cambridge, 1992.

Buber, Martin. *Pnei Adam*. Bialik, Jerusalem, 1966.

Bucher, Franz. *Zwischen Verrat und Menschlichkeit*. Huber, Frauenfeld, 1967.

Campion, Joan. *In the Lion's Mouth*. University Press of America, Lanham, Md., 1987.

Chalk, Frank, and Jonassohn, Kurt. *The History and Sociology of Genocide.* Yale University Press, New Haven, 1983.

Charters, David. *The British Army and Jewish Insurgency in Palestine.* St. Martin's Press, London, 1989.

Childers, Thomas. *The Nazi Voter.* University of North Carolina Press, Chapel Hill, 1983.

Cholavsky, Shalom. *Al Naharot Haniemen Vehadniepr.* Moreshet, Tel Aviv, 1982.

——. *Besufat Hakilayon.* Moreshet, Tel Aviv, 1988.

Chorbajian, Levon, and Chirinian, George, eds. *Problems of Genocide.* Zoryan Institute, Toronto, 1997.

Cohen, Arthur A. *Thinking the Tremendum.* Leo Baeck, New York, 1974.

Cohen, Asher. *Hamachteret Hachalutzit be'Hungaria.* Kibbutz Meuchad, Tel Aviv, 1984.

Cohen, Michael J. *Retreat from the Mandate.* Paul Elek, London, 1978.

——. *From Mandate to Independence.* Frank Cass, London, 1988.

Craig, Gordon A. *The Politics of the Prussian Army.* Oxford University Press, New York, 1964.

Dagan, Avigdor, ed. *The Jews of Czechoslovakia.* Jewish Publication Society, Philadelphia, 1984.

Dawidowicz, Lucy. *The War Against the Jews.* Weidenfeld and Nicholson, London, 1975.

Dinnerstein, Leonard. *America and the Survivors of the Holocaust.* Columbia University Press, New York, 1982.

Dobroszycki, Lucjan. *The Chronicle of the Łódź Ghetto.* Yale University Press, New Haven, 1984.

Dwórk, Debórah. *Children with a Star.* Yale University Press, New Haven, 1991.

Eck, Natan. *Hato'im Bedarkei Hamavet.* Yad Vashem, Jerusalem, 1960.

Elon, Amos. *Timetable.* Doubleday, New York, 1980.

Engel, David J. *In the Shadow of Auschwitz.* University of North Carolina Press, Chapel Hill, 1987.

——. *Facing the Holocaust.* University of North Carolina Press, Chapel Hill, 1993.

——. *A Reconstruction of Jewish Communal Institutions in Postwar Poland.* Council of Learned Societies, New York, 1996.

——. *Patterns of Anti-Jewish Violence in Poland, 1944–1946.* Yad Vashem, Jerusalem, 1998.

Fackenheim, Emil. *Questions of the Past and Present.* Beacon Press, Boston, 1970.

Fatran, Gila. *Ha'im Ma'avak al Hissardut.* Moreshet, Tel Aviv, 1992.

Fein, Helen. *Accounting for Genocide.* Free Press, New York, 1979.

Frankel, Jonathan, ed. *The Fate of the European Jews.* Studies in Contemporary Jewry, vol. 13. Oxford University Press, New York, 1997.

Frankl, Viktor. *Man's Search for Meaning.* Pocket Books, New York, 1973.

Fried, Hedi. *Ressisei Chayim.* Eked, Tel Aviv, 1995.

Friedlander, Henry. *The Origins of Nazi Genocide.* University of North Carolina Press, Chapel Hill, 1995.

Friedländer, Saul. *Nazi Germany and the Jews.* HarperCollins, New York, 1997.

Friedman, Philip. *Their Brother's Keepers.* Holocaust Library, New York, 1978.

Friling, Tuvia. *Chetz Ba'arafel.* Center for Ben-Gurion's Legacy, Sdeh Boker, 1998.

Fromm, Erich. *The Sane Society.* Fawcett, Greenwich, Conn., 1955.

———. *The Anatomy of Human Destructiveness.* J. Cape, London, 1974.

Fuerstenberg, Rochelle. *Post-Zionism, the Challenge to Israel.* American Jewish Committee and Bar Ilan University, Tel Aviv, 1997.

Garlinsky, Jozef. *Fighting Auschwitz.* Friedman, Fontana, 1975.

Gerlach, Christian. *Krieg, Ernährung, Völkermord.* Hamburger Edition, Hamburg, 1998.

———. *Kalkulierte Morde.* Hamburger Edition, Hamburg, 1999.

Gerlach, Wolfgang. *Als die Zeugen Schwiegen.* Institut Kirche und Judentum, Berlin, 1987.

Gertner, Yehoshua, and Gertner, Danek. *Der Untergang von Kosow und Zabie.* Wiener Verlag, Vienna, 1998.

Gilbert, Martin. *Auschwitz and the Allies.* Henry Holt, New York, 1981.

Gieselbusch, Hermann, ed. *Über Karlheinz Denscher.* Rowohlt, Reinsbek, 1986.

Goldhagen, Daniel J. *Hitler's Willing Executioners.* Knopf, New York, 1996.

Grobman, Alex. *Rekindling the Flame.* Wayne State University Press, Detroit, 1993.

Grodzinski, Hayim Ozer. *Shut Ahiezer.* Garber, Vilna, 1939.

Grudzinski, Yosef. *Chomer Enoshi Tov.* Hed Artzi, Tel Aviv, 1998.

Gutman, Yisrael. *Ha'amidah Hayehudit Bitkufat Hasho'ah.* Yad Vashem, Jerusalem, 1970.

———. *The Jews of Warsaw.* Indiana University Press, Bloomington, 1982.

———. *Ba'alatah Uvema'avak.* Moreshet, Tel Aviv, 1985.

———. *Hayehudim bePolin Acharei Milchemet Ha'olam Hashniyah.* Shazar, Jerusalem, 1985.

———, ed. *Sho'at Yehudei Eropa.* Yad Vashem, Jerusalem, 1973.

——, ed. *Patterns of Jewish Leadership in Nazi Europe.* Yad Vashem, Jerusalem, 1979.

——, ed. *The Concentration Camps.* Yad Vashem, Jerusalem, 1980.

——, ed. *Emmanuel Ringelblum: Yoman Urshimot Mitkufat Hamilchama.* Lohamei Getaot and Yad Vashem, Jerusalem, 1993.

Gutman, Yisreal, Arad, Yitzhak, and Margaliot, Avraham. *Documents on the Holocaust.* Yad Vashem, Jerusalem, 1981.

Gutman, Yisreal, and Berenbaum, Michael, eds. *Anatomy of the Auschwitz Death Camp.* Indiana University Press, Bloomington, 1994.

Gutman, Yisreal, and Saf, Avital, eds. *She'erith Hapletah.* Yad Vashem, Jerusalem, 1985.

Gutman, Yisreal, and Zuroff, Efraim, eds. *Rescue Attempts During the Holocaust.* Yad Vashem, Jerusalem, 1977.

Häsler, Alfred A. *Das Boot ist Voll.* Ex Libris, Zurich, 1967.

Hayes, Peter, ed. *Lessons and Legacies.* Northwestern University Press, Evanston, Ill., 1991.

Heer, Hannes, and Naumann, Klaus, eds. *Verbrechen der Wehrmacht.* Hamburger Edition, Hamburg, 1995.

Hentig, Otto von. *Mein Leben, eine Dienstreise.* Vendenhoek und Ruprecht, Göttingen, 1962.

Herbert, Ulrich, ed. *Nationalsozialistische Vernichtungspolitik.* Fischer, Frankfurt, 1998.

Herf, Jeffrey. *Reactionary Modernism.* Cambridge University Press, New York, 1984.

Hilberg, Raul. *The Destruction of the European Jews.* Quadrangle, Chicago, 1961.

Hindls, Arnold. *Einer Kehrte Zurück.* Deutsche Verlagsanstalt, Stuttgart, 1965.

Hirschfeld, Gerhard, ed. *The Politics of Genocide.* Allen and Unwin, London, 1986.

Hirszowicz, Lukasz. *The Third Reich and the Middle East.* Routledge and Kegan Paul, London, 1966.

Hitler, Adolf. *Hitler's Second Book.* Grove Press, New York, 1961.

Hoffman, Bruce. *The Failure of British Military Strategy Within Palestine.* Bar Ilan University, Tel Aviv, 1983.

Hovanissian, Richard, ed. *The Armenian Genocide.* St. Martin's, New York, 1992.

Hyman, Abraham S. *The Undefeated.* Gefen, Jerusalem, 1993.

Jäckel, Eberhard. *Hitlers Herrschaft.* Deutsche Verlagsanstalt, Stuttgart, 1986.

Jong, Louis de. *Het Koningrijk der Nederlande in de Tweede Wereldorlog.* RIOD, Nijhoff, The Hague, 1969–1991.

Kadosh, Sandra F. *Ideology Versus Reality: Youth Aliyah and the Rescue of Jewish Children During the Holocaust Era, 1933–1945.* Columbia University Press, New York, 1995.

Karay, Felicja. *Death Comes in Yellow.* Harwood Press, Amsterdam, 1996.

——. *Pagazim Vecharuzim.* Moreshet, Tel Aviv, 1997.

Kárný, Miroslav, ed. *Terezínský Rodinný Tábor v Osvětími-Birkenau-Sborník z mezinárodní konference, Praha, 7–8 března 1994.* Terezínská Iniciativa, Prague, 1994.

Kastner, Rudolf. *Der Kastner-Bericht über Eichmanns Menschenhandel in Ungarn.* Kindler, Munich, 1961.

Kater, Michael H. *The Nazi Party.* Harvard University Press, Cambridge, 1983.

Katsh, Abraham I. *The Warsaw Diary of Chaim A. Kaplan.* Colliers, New York, 1973.

Katz, Steven T. *The Holocaust in Historical Context.* Oxford University Press, New York, 1994.

Katznelson, Yitzhak. *Ktavim Achronim.* Kibbutz Meuchad, Tel Aviv, 1956.

Keinan, Irit. *Lo Nirga Hara'av.* Am Oved, Tel Aviv, 1996.

Kenrick, Donald, and Puxon, Grattan. *The Destiny of Europe's Gypsies.* Chatto-Heinemann, London, 1972.

Keren, Nili. *Ressisei Yaldut.* Kibbutz Meuchad, Tel Aviv, 1993.

Kershaw, Ian. *Der Hitler-Mythos, Volksmeinung und Propaganda im Dritten Reich.* Deutsche Verlagsanstalt, Stuttgart, 1980.

——. *The Nazi Dictatorship.* Edward Arnold, London, 1985.

Kiernan, Ben. *The Pol Pot Regime.* Yale University Press, New Haven, 1996.

Klemperer, Victor. *Ich Will Zeugnis Ablegen bis zum Letzten.* Aufbau, Munich, 1995.

Kochavi, Arieh J. *Akurim uFolitika Beinleumit.* Am Oved, Tel Aviv, 1992.

Kochavi, Yehoyakim. *Chimush Lekiyum Ruchani.* Lohamei Getaot, Haifa, 1988.

Krakowski, Shmuel. *The War of the Doomed.* Holmes and Meier, New York, 1984.

Kruk, Herman. *Togbuch fun Vilner Getto.* YIVO, New York, 1961.

Kwiet, Konrad, and Eschwege, Helmut. *Selbstbehauptung und Widerstand.* Hans Christians, Hamburg, 1984.

Langer, Lawrence. *The Holocaust and the Literary Imagination.* Yale University Press, New Haven, 1975.

Lavie, Theodor. *Yahadut Romania Bema'avak al Hatzalata.* Yad Vashem, Jerusalem, 1965.

Lazare, Lucien. *Rescue as Resistance.* Columbia University Press, New York, 1996.

Lemkin, Raphael. *Axis Rule in Occupied Europe.* Howard Fertig, New York, 1973.

Levai, Jenö. *Abscheu und Grauen vor dem Genocid in aller Welt.* Living Books, Toronto, 1968.

Lipstadt, Deborah E. *Beyond Belief.* Free Press, New York, 1986.

Littell, Franklin H. *The Crucifixion of the Jews.* Harper and Row, New York, 1979.

Madajczyk, Czeslaw. *Generalni Plan Wschodni—Zbor Dokumentow.* Institut Historii Polskiej Akademii Nauk, Warsaw, 1990.

Mais, Yitzhak, ed. *Judaism and Christianity Under the Impact of National Socialism.* Historical Society of Israel, Jerusalem, 1982.

Margaliot, Abraham, and Kochavi, Yehoyakim, eds. *Germania.* Yad Vashem, Jerusalem, 1998.

Markovitsky, Yakov. *Gachelet Lochemet.* Ministry of Defence, Tel Aviv, 1995.

Marrus, Michael R. *The Nazi Holocaust.* Meckler, London, 1989.

Marrus, Michael R., and Paxton, Robert O. *Vichy France and the Jews.* Basic Books, New York, 1981.

Meed, Vladka. *On Both Sides of the Wall.* Holocaust Library, New York, 1979.

Merkl, Peter H. *Political Violence Under the Swastika.* Princeton University Press, Princeton, 1975.

Morse, Arthur D. *While Six Million Died.* Random House, New York, 1967.

Mosse, George. *The Crisis of German Ideology.* Grosset and Dunlap, New York, 1964.

——. *The Nationalization of the Masses.* Howard Fertig, New York, 1973.

Mueller, Filip. *Auschwitz Inferno.* Routledge and Kegan Paul, London, 1979.

Neumann, Oskar. *Im Schatten des Todes.* Olamenu, Tel Aviv, 1956.

Nicholls, William. *Christian Antisemitism.* Aronson, Northvale, N.J., 1993.

Nir, Akiva, ed. *Prakim Bekorot Sho' at Yahadut Slovakia.* Moreshet, Giv'at Haviva, 1988.

Nolte, Ernst. *Three Faces of Fascism.* Reinhart and Winston, New York, 1966.

Ofer, Dalia. *Escaping the Holocaust.* Oxford University Press, New York, 1996.

Ofer, Dalia, and Weiner, Hannah. *Dead End Journey.* University Press of America, Lanham, Md., 1996.

Ofer, Dalia, and Weitzman, Lenore J., eds. *Women in the Holocaust.* Yale University Press, New Haven, 1998.

Pacy, James S., and Wertheimer, Alan P., eds. *Perspectives on the Holocaust.* Westview Press, Boulder, Colo., 1995.

Pappe, Ilan. *The Making of the Arab-Israeli Conflict, 1947–1951*. Tauris, London, 1992.

Paucker, Arnold, ed. *Die Juden im Nationalsozialistischen Deutschland*. Mohr, Tübingen, 1986.

Peck, Abraham J., ed. *Jews and Christians After the Holocaust*. Fortress, Philadelphia, 1982.

Peled, Yael. *Krakow Hayehudit, 1939–1945*. Kibbutz Meuchad, Tel Aviv, 1993.

Perechodnik, Calek. *Am I a Murderer?* Westview Press, Boulder, Colo., 1991.

Perlis, Rivka. *Tnuot Hanoar Hachalutziot bePolin Hakvusha*. Kibbutz Meuchad, Tel Aviv, 1987.

Petrasová, Marketa. *Theresienstadt in den Zeichnungen der Häftlinge, 1941–1945*. Staatliches Jüdisches Museum, Prague, 1983.

Picard, Jacques. *Die Schweiz und die Juden*. Chronos, Zurich, 1994.

Polak, Josef, and Lagus, Karel. *Město za Mřižemi*. Naše Vojsko, Prague, 1964.

Porat, Dina. *The Blue and Yellow Star of David*. Harvard University Press, Cambridge, 1990.

Poznansky, Renée. *Les Juifs en France Pendant la Seconde Guerre Mondiale*. Hachette, Paris, 1997.

Presser, Jacob. *The Destruction of the Dutch Jews*. Dutton, New York, 1969.

Rauschning, Hermann. *Hitler Speaks*. Butterworth, London, 1939.

Rayski, Adam. *Zwischen Thora und Partei*. Herder, Freiburg, 1987.

Reitlinger, Gerald. *The Final Solution*. Valentine Mitchell, London, 1953.

Ronen, Avihu. *Hakrav al Hachayim*. Yad Ya'ari, Giv'at Haviva, 1994.

Rothkirchen, Livia. *Churban Yahadut Slovakia*. Yad Vashem, Jerusalem, 1961.

Rummel, Rudolph J. *Democide*. Transaction Press, New Brunswick, N.J., 1992.

———. *Death by Government*. Transaction Press, New Brunswick, N.J., 1995.

Schleunes, Karl A. *The Twisted Road to Auschwitz*. Illinois University Press, Chicago, 1990.

Schweid, Eliezer. *Bein Khurban L'yeshu'ah*. Kibbutz Meuchad, Tel Aviv, 1992.

Segev, Tom. *The Seventh Million*. Wang and Hill, New York, 1993.

Shachan, Avigdor. *Hakfor Halohet*. Kibbutz Meuchad, Tel Aviv, 1988.

Shapira, Kalman Klonymus. *Esh Kodesh*. Va'ad Chassidei Piaseczna, Jerusalem, 1960.

Shelley, Lore. *The Union Kommando in Auschwitz*. Studies in the Sho'ah, vol. 12, University Press of America, Lanham, Md., 1996.

Sherman, Joshua A. *Island Refuge*. Paul Elek, London, 1973.

Sloan, Jacob, ed. *Notes from the Warsaw Ghetto*. McGraw-Hill, New York, 1958.

Slutzky, Yehuda, ed. *Sefer Toldot Hahaganah*. Ministry of Defence, Tel Aviv, 1961–1963.

Smolar, Moshe. *Ne'evakti Al Chayay.* Moreshet, Tel Aviv, 1978.

Smoliar, Moshe. *Yehudim Sovietiyim Me'achorei Gderot Hagetto.* Sifriat Poalim, Tel Aviv, 1984.

Sorkin, David. *The Transformation of German Jewry.* Oxford University Press, New York, 1987.

Spitzer, Juraj. *Patřím k Vám.* Ceskoslovenský Spisovatel, Prague, 1964.

Stroop, Jürgen. *The Stroop Report.* Pantheon, New York, 1979.

Szenes, Sandor. *Befejezetlen Mult.* Pecsi Szirka Nyomda, Budapest, 1986.

Tal, Uriel. *Christians and Jews in Germany, 1870–1914.* Cornell University Press, Ithaca, N.Y., 1975.

Teichthal, Issachar. *Em Habanim Samecha.* Meshulam Katzburg, Budapest, 1943.

Teitelboym, Yoel. *Vayoel Moshe.* S. Deutsch, New York, 1961.

Tennenbaum, Joseph. *Race and Reich.* Twayne, New York, 1956.

Trunk, Isaiah. *Judenrat.* Macmillan, New York, 1973.

Unesco Yearbook on Peace and Conflict Studies. UNESCO, Paris, 1985.

Walk, Joseph, ed. *Iyunim Be'Heker Yahadut Zmanenu.* Yad Vashem, Jerusalem, 1973.

Wasserman, Elhanan. *Ikveta DiMeshikha.* Netzach, Tel Aviv, 1942.

Wasserstein, Bernard. *Britain and the Jews of Europe.* Clarendon, Oxford, 1979.

Weiss, John. *Ideology of Death.* Ivan R. Dee, Chicago, 1996.

Weissmandel, Michael Dov-Ber. *Min Hametzar.* Emunah, New York, 1960.

Wildt, Michael, ed. *Himmlers Terminkalender, 1941–1942.* Christians, Hamburg, 1999.

Woltin, Nisson, and Hutner, Yitzchok. *A Path Through the Ashes.* Mesorah, New York, 1986.

Wyman, David S. *Paper Walls.* University of Massachusetts Press, Amherst, 1968.

——. *The Abandonment of the Jews.* Pantheon, New York, 1984.

Yahil, Leni. *The Holocaust.* Oxford University Press, New York, 1990.

Zertal, Idit. *Zehavam shel Hayehudim.* Am Oved, Tel Aviv, 1996.

Zimmermann, Michael. *Rassenutopie und Genozid.* Christians, Hamburg, 1996.

Zuckerman, Yitzhak. *A Surplus of Memory.* University of California Press, Berkeley, 1993.

Zulch, Tilman, ed. *In Auschwitz vergast, bis heute verfolgt.* Rowohlt, Reinbek, 1979.

Zweig, Ronald W. *Britain and Palestine During the Second World War.* Royal Historical Society, London, 1986.

index

Abel, Wolfgang, 57

Abeles, Ernst, 176

Accusations among Jews that Jews did not attempt to save other Jews during Holocaust, 240–41

Adam, Dietrich Uwe, 68

Aid and Rescue Committee (Hungary), 228

Akiva, Rabbi, 205

Allies' assistance: to Jewish resistance, 141; to rescue of Jews, 216

Altmann, Tosia, 171–72

Aly, Goetz, 4, 34, 86–90, 92, 95–96, 111

American Indians, 20, 48, 49, 51, 59

Amidah. *See* Resistance, Jewish

Antisemitism: Anglo-American, 221; in Austria, 99; Brest murder of Jews, 159; as cause of Holo-

caust or not, 71–74, 86, 95–111; Christian, 28, 42, 71–72, 105; in France, 106; of German intelligentsia, 91, 269; of German people, 94–110, 269; in Hungary, 224–25, 235; modernity and, 73; in Nazi Party, 30–32, 42, 44, 48, 53–55; in Poland, 152, 248; racist, 115, 269; redemptive, 114–17; in Romania, 106–7; socioeconomic analysis and, 72–73; in Soviet partisan groups, 138, 141; in United States, 220–21; utopian view of racial purity, 45

Arab relationship with British, 214–15, 245

Arab-Jewish conflict, 244, 256, 259–60

Arendt, Hannah, 77, 129

321

Grossman, Chaika, 171, 198–99, 201, 203

Guggenheim, Paul, 220

Günther, Willi, 158

Gutman, Hugo, 100

Gutman, Yisrael, 68, 93, 96, 103, 104, 144, 145

Gypsies. *See* Roma (Gypsies)

Habad, 195–212; founding, 195–96; Holocaust views of, published in responsum, 198–212; messianic views, 197–98; missionary ideology, 196–97

Hadassah Organization, 169

Hagana, 243, 244, 251, 256, 258

"Half-Jews," 62, 265

Halperin, Israel, 72

Handicapped people and "euthanasia," 36, 60, 88, 269

Haredi. *See* Orthodox Jews

Harrison, Earl, 249

Hashomer Hatzair, 228–29

Hasse, Ernst, 116

Hechalutz, 179–80

Heer, Hannes, 108

Heise, Hermann, 160

Hentig, Otto von, 148

Herbert, Ulrich, 6, 30, 91

Herf, Jeffrey, 68–69, 84–86, 111, 170

Herzog, Rabbi Yitzhak Halevi, 193, 200

Heydrich, Rienhard, 5, 31, 158

Hielscher, Friedrich, 80–82, 121

Hilberg, Raul: analysis of Holocaust, 96; on armed Jewish resistance, 142, 165–66; on bureaucracy as cause of Holocaust, 29, 55, 70, 71; on Judenräte role,

77–79, 128–29; pioneer of Holocaust research, 68, 69; on value of testimonies, 23

Himmler, Heinrich: antisemitism of, 31; appointment book of, 4–5; attempts of Jews to bribe, 181; and decision to murder Brest Jews, 154; and decision to murder Łódź ghetto Jews, 131; desire for contacts with Americans, 181; judicial system agreement with Thierack, 83; Poznań speech on murder of the Jews, 21–22; reaction to proposed mass murder of Russians, 57–58; views on Roma, 60–62, 64–66

Hitler, Adolf: antisemitism of, 31, 117; awareness of attempt to change world, 53; and decision to mass-murder Jews, 4–7, 29–32, 49, 133; in Habad view, 203–4, 211; internal politics of Nazi Party and, 87; rise to power, 32; views on Poles, 58; views on Roma, 61–62; wish of, taken as law, 84

Hochberg, Karel, 179–80

Holland, 169, 194

Holocaust. *See* Comparison of Holocaust to other genocides; Definition of Holocaust; Determinism and the Holocaust; Documentation of the Holocaust; Explicability of the Holocaust; Genocides; Knowledge of the Holocaust; Mystification of the Holocaust; Unprecedentedness of the Holocaust; Women's fate and role; *and other specific topics*

Smolar, Hersh, 79

Smolar, Moshe, 160

Smoliar, Hersh, 134

Sobibor, 139

Sobieski, Jan, 150

Sobol, Yehoshua, 121–22

Social Darwinism, 43, 115, 116

Social Democrats, 98–101

Soloveitchik, Rabbi Chayim, 151

Soloveitchik, Rabbi Yitzhak Ze'ev, 152

Sonderweg, 103–4

Soos, Geza, 233

Soviets: advance into Poland during World War II, 131–33; Brest under, 153, 163; destruction of Jewish life in occupied areas, 163; and establishment of Israel, 254, 255, 258; Jewish resistance fighters and Jewish soldiers, 138; Nazi mass murder of Russians, 57–58; post–World War II treatment of Jews, 255–56; Stalinist compared to Hitlerite regime, 76, 105

Spaniards in New World, 20, 47, 49, 51, 59, 76–77

Spanish explusion of Jews, 41

S.S.: at Auschwitz, 261; and deportation of Slovak Jews, 183; role in murder of Brest Jews, 158–60

Stahlecker, Walther, 35

Stanski, Zalman, 153

Starvation of the Jews, 137, 144, 155, 163–65

Steinberg, Xavery, 151

Steiner, Andrej, 178–79

Steiner, Chaim Zwi, 135

Steiner, Hannah, 169

Stern, Avraham, 147

Stern Group. *See* Lohamey Herut Yisrael (LHY)

Sternbuch, Recha and Isaac, 234–35

Storfer, Bernhard, 175

Streicher, Julius, 31

Stroop, Jürgen, 24

Survivors, Jewish: Brest survivors, 158; number of, 246; Orthodox Jews, 194; participation in Israeli War of Independence, 257; testimonies of, 23–24. *See also* Displaced persons (D.P.) camps

Swiss knowledge of the Holocaust, 180, 219, 234

Szekely, Maria, 233–34

Szold, Henrietta, 169

Tal, Uriel, 94, 98

Teichthal, Rabbi Issachar, 124

Teitelboym, Reb Yoel "Yoelish", 193, 195

Tennenbaum, Joseph, 68

Testimonies of survivors, 23–24

Theological explanations and justifications, 41–42, 186–212; brokenness of religious world, 192; difference of Holocaust from previous calamities, 27–28; evil as part of God's plan, 188; God's choice to be absent, 189–91; Habad explanation, 197–212; human choice of evil, 186–87; inability of human beings to understand God, 186–88; magical interpretation of the universe, 192–93; mystical approach, 189–91; punishment of Jews by